Life of St. Francis of Assisi

Paul Sabatier

Translated by Louise Seymour Houghton

LIFE OF

ST. FRANCIS OF ASSISI

BY

PAUL SABATIER

*Quivere monachus est nihil
reputat esse suum nisi citharam*

GIOACCHINO DI FIORE *in Apoc. 182 a 2*

TRANSLATED BY

LOUISE SEYMOUR HOUGHTON

LONDON
HODDER & STOUGHTON

1919

TO THE STRASBURGHERS

Friends!

At last here is this book which I told you about so long ago. The result is small indeed in relation to the endeavor, as I, alas! see better than anyone. The widow of the Gospel put only one mite into the alms-box of the temple, but this mite, they tell us, won her Paradise. Accept the mite that I offer you to-day as God accepted that of the poor woman, looking not at her offering, but at her love, Feci quod potui, omnia dedi.

Do not chide me too severely for this long delay, for you are somewhat its cause. Many times a day at Florence, at Assisi, at Rome, I have forgotten the document I had to study. Something in me seemed to have gone to flutter at your windows, and sometimes they opened.... One evening at St. Damian I forgot myself and remained long after sunset. An old monk came to warn me that the sanctuary was closed. "Per Bacco! " *he gently murmured as he led me away, all ready to receive my confidence,* "sognava d'amore o di tristitia? " *Well, yes. I was dreaming of love and of sadness, for I was dreaming of Strasbourg.*

CONTENTS

INTRODUCTION

CHAPTER I.
YOUTH

CHAPTER II.
STAGES OF CONVERSION

CHAPTER III.
THE CHURCH ABOUT 1209

CHAPTER IV.
STRUGGLES AND TRIUMPHS

CHAPTER V.
FIRST YEAR OF APOSTOLATE

CHAPTER VI.
ST. FRANCIS AND INNOCENT III

CHAPTER VII.
RIVO-TORTO

CHAPTER VIII.
PORTIUNCULA

CHAPTER IX.
SANTA CLARA

CHAPTER X.
FIRST ATTEMPTS TO REACH THE INFIDELS

CHAPTER XI.
THE INNER MAN AND WONDER-WORKING

CHAPTER XII.
THE CHAPTER-GENERAL OF 1217

CHAPTER XIII.
ST. DOMINIC AND ST. FRANCIS

CHAPTER XIV.
THE CRISIS OF THE ORDER

CHAPTER XV.
THE RULE OF 1221

CHAPTER XVI.
THE BROTHERS MINOR AND LEARNING

CHAPTER XVII.
THE STIGMATA

CHAPTER XVIII.
THE CANTICLE OF THE SUN

CHAPTER XIX.
THE LAST YEAR

CHAPTER XX.
FRANCIS'S WILL AND DEATH

CRITICAL STUDY OF THE SOURCES

APPENDIX.
CRITICAL STUDY OF THE STIGMATA AND OF THE INDULGENCE OF AUGUST 2

INTRODUCTION

In the renascence of history which is in a manner the characteristic of our time, the Middle Ages have been the object of peculiar fondness with both criticism and erudition. We rummage all the dark corners of the libraries, we bring old parchments to light, and in the zeal and ardor we put into our search there is an indefinable touch of piety.

These efforts to make the past live again reveal not merely our curiosity, or the lack of power to grapple with great philosophic problems, they are a token of wisdom and modesty; we are beginning to feel that the present has its roots in the past, and that in the fields of politics and religion, as in others, slow, modest, persevering toil is that which has the best results.

There is also a token of love in this. We love our ancestors of five or six centuries ago, and we mingle not a little emotion and gratitude with this love. So, if one may hope everything of a son who loves his parents, we must not despair of an age that loves history.

The Middle Ages form an organic period in the life of humanity. Like all powerful organisms the period began with a long and mysterious gestation; it had its youth, its manhood, its decrepitude. The end of the twelfth century and the beginning of the thirteenth mark its full expansion; it is the twentieth year of life, with its poetry, its dreams, its enthusiasm, its generosity, its daring. Love overflowed with vigor; men everywhere had but one desire—to devote themselves to some great and holy cause.

Curiously enough, though Europe was more parcelled out than ever, it felt a new thrill run through its entire extent. There was what we might call a state of European consciousness.

In ordinary periods each people has its own interests, its tendencies, its tears, and its joys; but let a time of crisis come, and the true unity of the human family will suddenly make itself felt with a strength never before suspected. Each body of water has its own currents, but when the hurricane is abroad they mysteriously intermingle, and from the ocean to the remotest mountain lake the same tremor will upheave them all.

It was thus in '89, it was thus also in the thirteenth century.

Never was there less of frontier, never, either before or since, such a mingling of nationalities; and at the present day, with all our highways and railroads, the people live more apart. [1]

The great movement of thought of the thirteenth century is above all a religious movement, presenting a double character—it is popular and it is laic. It comes out from the heart of the people, and it looks athwart many uncertainties at nothing less than wresting the sacred things from the hands of the clergy.

The conservatives of our time who turn to the thirteenth century as to the golden age of authoritative faith make a strange mistake. If it is especially the century of saints, it is also that of heretics. We shall soon see that the two words are not so contradictory as might appear; it is enough for the moment to point out that the Church had never been more powerful nor more threatened.

There was a genuine attempt at a religious revolution, which, if it had succeeded, would have ended in a universal priesthood, in the proclamation of the rights of the individual conscience.

The effort failed, and though later on the Revolution made us all kings, neither the thirteenth century nor the Reformation was able to make us all priests. Herein, no doubt, lies the essential contradiction of our lives and that which periodically puts our national institutions in peril. Politically emancipated, we are not morally or religiously free. [2]

The thirteenth century with juvenile ardor undertook this revolution, which has not yet reached its end. In the north of Europe it became incarnate in cathedrals, in the south, in saints.

The cathedrals were the lay churches of the thirteenth century. Built by the people for the people, they were originally the true common house of our old cities. Museums, granaries, chambers of commerce, halls of justice, depositories of archives, and even labor exchanges, they were all these at once.

That art of the Middle Ages which Victor Hugo and Viollet-le-Duc have taught us to understand and love was the visible expression of the enthusiasm of a people who were achieving communal liberty. Very far from being the gift of the Church, it was in its beginning an unconscious protest against the hieratic, impassive, esoteric art of the religious orders. We find only laymen in the long list of master-workmen and painters who have left us the innumerable Gothic monuments which stud the soil of Europe. Those artists of genius who, like those of Greece, knew how to speak to the populace without being common, were for the most part humble workmen; they found their inspiration not in the formulas of the masters of monastic art, but in constant communion with the very soul of the nation. Therefore this renascence, in its most profound features, concerns less the archæology or the architecture than the history of a country.

While in the northern countries the people were building their own churches, and finding in their enthusiasm an art which was new, original, complete, in the south, above the official, clerical priesthood of divine right they were greeting and consecrating a new priesthood, that of the saints.

The priest of the thirteenth century is the antithesis of the saint, he is almost always his enemy. Separated by the holy unction from the rest of mankind, inspiring awe as the representative of an all-powerful God, able by a few signs to perform unheard-of mysteries, with a word to change bread into flesh and wine into blood, he appeared as a sort of idol which can do all things for or against you and before which you have only to adore and tremble.

The saint, on the contrary, was one whose mission was proclaimed by nothing in his apparel, but whose life and words made themselves felt in all hearts and consciences; he was one who, with no cure of souls in the Church, felt himself suddenly impelled to lift up his voice. The child of the people, he knew all their material and moral woes, and their mysterious echo sounded in his own heart. Like the ancient prophet of Israel, he heard an imperious voice saying to him: "Go and speak to the children of my people. " "Ah, Lord God, I am but a child, I know not how to speak. " "Say not, I am but a child, for thou shalt go to all those to whom I shall send thee. Behold I have set thee to-day as a strong city, a pillar of iron and a wall of brass against the kings of Judah, against its princes and against its priests. "

These thirteenth-century saints were in fact true prophets. Apostles like St. Paul, not as the result of a canonical consecration, but by the interior order of the Spirit, they were the witnesses of liberty against authority.

The Calabrian seer, Gioacchino di Fiore, hailed the new-born revolution; he believed in its success and proclaimed to the wondering world the advent of a new ministry. He was mistaken.

When the priest sees himself vanquished by the prophet he suddenly changes his method. He takes him under his protection, he introduces his harangues into the sacred canon, he throws over his shoulders the priestly chasuble. The days pass on, the years roll by, and the moment comes when the heedless crowd no longer distinguishes between them, and it ends by believing the prophet to be an emanation of the clergy.

This is one of the bitterest ironies of history.

Francis of Assisi is pre-eminently the saint of the Middle Ages. Owing nothing to church or school he was truly *theodidact*, [3] and if he perhaps did not perceive the revolutionary bearing of his preaching, he at least always refused to be ordained priest. He divined the superiority of the spiritual priesthood.

The charm of his life is that, thanks to reliable documents, we find the man behind the wonder worker. We find in him not merely noble actions, we find in him a life in the true meaning of the word; I mean, we feel in him both development and struggle.

How mistaken are the annals of the Saints in representing him as from the very cradle surrounded with aureole and nimbus! As if the finest and most manly of spectacles were not that of the man who conquers his soul hour after hour, fighting first against himself, against the suggestions of egoism, idleness, discouragement, then at the moment when he might believe himself victorious, finding in the champions attracted by his ideal those who are destined if not to bring about its complete ruin, at least to give it its most terrible blows. Poor Francis! The last years of his life were indeed a *via dolorosa* as painful as that where his master sank down under the weight of the cross; for it is still a joy to die for one's ideal, but what bitter pain to look on in advance at the apotheosis of one's body, while seeing one's soul—I would say his thought—misunderstood and frustrated.

If we ask for the origins of his idea we find them exclusively among the common people of his time; he is the incarnation of the Italian soul at the beginning of the thirteenth century, as Dante was to be its incarnation a hundred years later.

He was of the people and the people recognized themselves in him. He had their poetry and their aspirations, he espoused their claims, and the very name of his institute had at first a political signification: in Assisi as in most other Italian towns there were *majores* and *minores*, the *popolo grasso* and the *popolo minuto*; he resolutely placed himself among the latter. This political side of his apostolate needs to be clearly apprehended if we would understand its amazing success and the wholly unique character of the Franciscan movement in its beginning.

As to its attitude toward the Church, it was that of filial obedience. This may perhaps appear strange at first as regards an unauthorized preacher who comes speaking to the world in the name of his own immediate personal inspiration. But did not most of the men of '89 believe themselves good and loyal subjects of Louis XVI.?

The Church was to our ancestors what the fatherland is to us; we may wish to remodel its government, overturn its administration, change its constitution, but we do not think ourselves less good patriots for that.

In the same way, in an age of simple faith when religious beliefs seemed to be in the very fibre and flesh of humanity, Dante, without ceasing to be a good Catholic, could attack the clergy and the court of Rome with a violence that has never been surpassed. St. Francis so surely believed that the Church had become unfaithful to her mission that he could speak in his symbolic language of the widowhood of his Lady Poverty, who from Christ's time to his own had found no husband. How could he better have declared his purposes or revealed his dreams?

What he purposed was far more than the foundation of an order, and it is to do him great wrong thus to restrict his endeavor. He longed for a true awakening of the Church in the name of the evangelical ideal which he had regained. All Europe awoke with a start when it heard of these penitents from a little Umbrian town. It was reported that they had craved a strange privilege from the court of Rome: that of possessing nothing. Men saw them pass by, earning their bread by the labor of their hands, accepting only the bare necessities of bodily sustenance from them to whom they had given with lavish hands the bread of life. The people lifted up their heads, breathing in with deep inspirations the airs of a springtime upon which was already floating the perfume of new flowers.

Here and there in the world there are many souls capable of all heroism, if only they can see before them a true leader. St. Francis became for these the guide they had longed for, and whatever was best in humanity at that time leaped to follow in his footsteps.

This movement, which was destined to result in the constitution of a new family of monks, was in the beginning anti-monastic. It is not rare for history to have similar contradictions to record. The meek Galilean who preached the religion of a personal revelation, without ceremonial or dogmatic law, triumphed only on condition of being conquered, and of permitting his words of spirit and life to be confiscated by a church essentially dogmatic and sacerdotal.

In the same way the Franciscan movement was originally, if not the protest of the Christian consciousness against monachism, at least the recognition of an ideal singularly higher than that of the clergy of that time. Let us picture to ourselves the Italy of the beginning of the thirteenth century with its divisions, its perpetual warfare, its depopulated country districts, the impossibility of tilling the fields except in the narrow circle which the garrisons of the towns might protect; all these cities from the greatest to the least occupied in watching for the most favorable moment for falling upon and pillaging their neighbors; sieges terminated by unspeakable atrocities, and after all this, famine, speedily followed by pestilence to complete the devastation. Then let us picture to ourselves the rich Benedictine abbeys, veritable fortresses set upon the hill-tops, whence they seemed to command all the surrounding plains. There was nothing surprising in their prosperity. Shielded by their inviolability, they were in these disordered times the only refuge of peaceful souls and timid hearts. [4] The monks were in great majority deserters from life, who for motives entirely aside from religion had taken refuge behind the only walls which at this period were secure.

Overlook this as we may, forget as we may the demoralization and ignorance of the inferior clergy, the simony and the vices of the prelates, the coarseness and avarice of the monks, judging the Church of the thirteenth century only by those of her sons who do her the most honor; none the less are these the anchorites who flee into the desert to escape from wars and vices, pausing only when they are very sure that none of the world's noises will interrupt their meditations. Sometimes they will draw away with them hundreds of imitators, to the solitudes of Clairvaux, of the Chartreuse, of Vallombrosa, of the Camaldoli; but even when they are a multitude they are alone; for they are dead to the world and to their brethren. Each cell is a desert, on whose threshold they cry

> O beata solitudo.
> O sola beatitudo.

The book of the Imitation is the picture of all that is purest in this cloistered life.

But is this abstinence from action truly Christian?

No, replied St. Francis. He for his part would do like Jesus, and we may say that his life is an imitation of Christ singularly more real than that of Thomas à Kempis.

Jesus went indeed into the desert, but only that he might find in prayer and communion with the heavenly Father the inspiration and strength necessary for keeping up the struggle against evil. Far from avoiding the multitude, he sought them out to enlighten, console, and convert them.

This is what St. Francis desired to imitate. More than once he felt the seduction of the purely contemplative life, but each time his own spirit warned him that this was only a disguised selfishness; that one saves oneself only in saving others.

When he saw suffering, wretchedness, corruption, instead of fleeing he stopped to bind up, to heal, feeling in his heart the surging of waves of compassion. He not only preached love to others; he himself was ravished with it; he sang it, and what was of greater value, he lived it.

There had indeed been preachers of love before his day, but most generally they had appealed to the lowest selfishness. They had thought to triumph by proving that in fact to give to others is to put one's money out at a usurious interest. "Give to the poor, " said St. Peter Chrysologus, [5] "that you may give to yourself; give him a crumb in order to receive a loaf; give him a shelter to receive heaven. "

There was nothing like this in Francis; his charity is not selfishness, it is love. He went, not to the whole, who need no physician, but to the sick, the forgotten, the disdained. He dispensed the treasures of his heart according to the need and reserved the best of himself for the poorest and the most lost, for lepers and thieves.

The gaps in his education were of marvellous service to him. More learned, the formal logic of the schools would have robbed him of that flower of simplicity which is the great charm of his life; he would have seen the whole extent of the sore of the Church, and would no doubt have despaired of healing it. If he had known the ecclesiastical discipline he would have felt obliged to observe it; but thanks to his ignorance he could often violate it without knowing it, [6] and be a heretic quite unawares.

We can now determine to what religious family St. Francis belongs.

Looking at the question from a somewhat high standpoint we see that in the last analysis minds, like religious systems, are to be found in two great families, standing, so to say, at the two poles of thought. These two poles are only mathematical points, they do not exist in concrete reality; but for all that we can set them down on the chart of philosophic and moral ideas.

There are religions which look toward divinity and religions which look toward man. Here again the line of demarcation between the two families is purely ideal and artificial; they often so mingle and blend with one another that we have much difficulty in distinguishing them, especially in the intermediate zone in which our civilization finds its place; but if we go toward the poles we shall find their characteristics growing gradually distinct.

In the religions which look toward divinity all effort is concentrated on worship, and especially on sacrifice. The end aimed at is a change in the disposition of the gods. They are mighty kings whose support or favor one must purchase by gifts.

Most pagan religions belong to this category and pharisaic Judaism as well. This is also the tendency of certain Catholics of the old school for whom the great thing is to appease God or to buy the protection of the Virgin and the saints by means of prayers, candles, and masses.

The other religions look toward man; their effort is directed to the heart and conscience with the purpose of transforming them. Sacrifice disappears, or rather it changes from the exterior to the interior. God is conceived of as a father, always ready to welcome him who comes to him. Conversion, perfection, sanctification become the pre-eminent religious acts. Worship and prayer cease to be incantations and become reflection, meditation, virile effort; while in religions of the first class the clergy have an essential part, as intermediaries between heaven and earth, in those of the second they have none, each conscience entering into direct relations with God.

It was reserved to the prophets of Israel to formulate, with a precision before unknown, the starting-point of spiritual worship.

> Bring no more vain offerings;
> I have a horror of incense,
> Your new moons, your Sabbaths, and your assemblies;
> When you multiply prayers I will not hearken.
> Your hands are full of blood,
> Wash you, make you clean,
> Put away from before my eyes the evil of your ways,
> Cease to do evil,
> Learn to do well. [7]

With Isaiah these vehement apostrophes are but flashes of genius, but with Jesus the interior change becomes at once the principle and the end of the religious life. His promises were not for those who were right with the ceremonial law, or who offered the greatest number of sacrifices, but for the pure in heart, for men of good will.

These considerations are not perhaps without their use in showing the spiritual ancestry of the Saint of Assisi.

For him, as for St. Paul and St. Augustine, conversion was a radical and complete change, the act of will by which man wrests himself from the slavery of sin and places himself under the yoke of divine authority. Thenceforth prayer, become a necessary act of life, ceases to be a magic formula; it is an impulse of the heart, it is reflection and meditation rising above the commonplaces of this mortal life, to enter into the mystery of the divine will and conform itself to it; it is the act of the atom which understands its littleness, but which desires, though only by a single note, to be in harmony with the divine symphony.

Ecce adsum Domine, ut faciam voluntatem tuam.

When we reach these heights we belong not to a sect, but to humanity; we are like those wonders of nature which the accident of circumstances has placed upon the territory of this or that people, but which belong to all the world, because in fact they belong to no one, or rather they are the common and inalienable property of the entire human race. Homer, Shakespeare, Dante, Goethe, Michael Angelo, Rembrandt belong to us all as much as the ruins of Athens or Rome, or, rather, they belong to those who love them most and understand them best.

But that which is a truism, so far as men of genius in the domain of imagination or thought are concerned, still appears like a paradox when we speak of men of religious genius. The Church has laid such absolute claim to them that she has created in her own favor a sort of right. It cannot be that this arbitrary confiscation shall endure forever. To prevent it we have not to perform an act of negation or demolition: let us leave to the chapels their statues and their relics, and far from belittling the saints, let us make their true grandeur shine forth.

* * * * *

It is time to say a few words concerning the difficulties of the work here presented to the public. History always embraces but a very feeble part of the reality: ignorant, she is like the stories children tell of the events that have occurred before their eyes; learned, she reminds us of a museum organized with all the modern improvements. Instead of making you see nature with its external covering, its diffuse life, its mysterious echoes in your own heart, they offer you a herbarium.

If it is difficult to narrate an ordinary event of our own time, it is far more so to describe the great crises where restless humanity is seeking its true path.

The first duty of the historian is to forget his own time and country and become the sympathetic and interested contemporary of what he relates; but if it is difficult to give oneself the heart of a Greek or a Roman, it is infinitely more so to give oneself a heart of the thirteenth century. I have said that at that period the Middle Age was twenty years old, and the feelings of the twentieth year are, if not the most fugitive, at least the most difficult to note down. Everyone knows that it is impossible to recall the feelings of youth with the same clearness as those of childhood or mature age. Doubtless we may have external facts in the memory, but we cannot recall the sensations and the sentiments; the confused forces which seek to move us are then all at work at once, and to speak the language of beyond the Rhine, it is *the essentially phenomenal hour of the phenomena that we are;* everything in us crosses, intermingles, collides, in desperate conflict: it is a time of diabolic or divine excitement. Let a few years pass, and nothing in the world can make us live those hours over again. Where was once a volcano, we perceive only a heap of blackened ashes, and scarcely, at long intervals, will a chance meeting, a sound, a word, awaken memory and unseal the fountain of recollection; and even then it is only a flash; we have had but a glimpse and all has sunk back into shadow and silence.

We find the same difficulty when we try to take note of the fiery enthusiasms of the thirteenth century, its poetic inspirations, its amorous and chaste visions—all this is thrown up against a background of coarseness, wretchedness, corruption, and folly.

The men of that time had all the vices except triviality, all the virtues except moderation; they were either ruffians or saints. Life was rude enough to kill feeble organisms; and thus characters had an energy unknown to-day. It was forever necessary to provide beforehand against a thousand dangers, to take those sudden resolutions in which one risks his life. Open the chronicle of Fra Salimbeni and you will be shocked to find that the largest place is taken up with the account of the annual expeditions of Parma against the neighboring cities, or of the neighboring cities against Parma. What would it have been if this chronicle, instead of being written by a monk of uncommonly open mind, a lover of music, at certain times an ardent Joachimite, an indefatigable traveller, had been written by a warrior? And this is not all; these wars between city and city were complicated with civil dissensions, plots were hatched periodically, conspirators were massacred if they were discovered, or massacred and exiled others in their turn if they were triumphant. [8] When we picture to ourselves this state of things dominated by the grand struggles of the papacy against the empire, heretics, and infidels, we may understand how difficult it is to describe such a time.

The imagination being haunted by horrible or entrancing pictures like those of the frescos in the *Campo Santo* of Pisa, men were always thinking of heaven and hell; they informed themselves about them with the feverish curiosity of emigrants, who pass their days on shipboard in trying to picture that spot in America where in a few days they will pitch their tent.

Every monk of any notoriety must have gone through this. Dante's poem is not an isolated work; it is the noblest result of a condition which had given birth to hundreds of compositions, and Alighieri had little more to do than to co-ordinate the works of his predecessors and vivify them with the breath of his own genius.

The unsettled state of men's minds was unimaginable. That unhealthy curiosity which lies at the bottom of the human heart, and which at the present day impels men to seek for refined and even perverse enjoyments, impelled men of that time to devotions which seem like a defiance to common sense.

Never had hearts been shaken with such terrors, nor ever thrilled with such radiant hopes. The noblest hymns of the liturgy, the *Stabat* and the *Dies Iræ*, come to us from the thirteenth century, and we may well say that never has the human plaint been more agonized.

When we look through history, not to find accounts of battles or of the succession of dynasties, but to try to grasp the evolution of ideas and feelings, when we seek above all to discover the heart of man and of epochs, we perceive, on arriving at the thirteenth century, that a fresh wind has blown over the world, the human lyre has a new string, the lowest, the most profound; one which sings of woes and hopes to which the ancient world had not vibrated.

In the breast of the men of that time we think sometimes we feel the beating of a woman's heart; they have exquisite sentiments, delightful inspirations, with absurd terrors, fantastic angers, infernal cruelties. Weakness and fear often make them insincere; they have the idea of the grand, the beautiful, the ugly, but that of order is wanting; they fast or feast; the notion of the laws of nature, so deeply graven in our own minds, is to them entirely a stranger; the words possible and impossible have for them no meaning. Some give themselves to God, others sell themselves to the devil, but not one feels himself strong enough to walk alone, strong enough to have no need to hold on by some one's skirt.

Peopled with spirits and demons nature appeared to them singularly animated; in her presence they have all the emotions which a child experiences at night before the trees on the roadside and the vague forms of the rocks.

Unfortunately, our language is a very imperfect instrument for rendering all this; it is neither musical nor flexible; since the seventeenth century it has been deemed seemly to keep one's emotions to oneself, and the old words which served to note states of the soul have fallen into neglect; the Imitation and the Fioretti have become untranslatable.

More than this, in a history like the present one, we must give a large place to the Italian spirit; it is evident that in a country where they call a chapel *basilica* and a tiny house *palazzo*, or in speaking to a seminarist say "Your Reverence, " words have not the same value as on this side of the Alps.

The Italians have an imagination which enlarges and simplifies. They see the forms and outlines of men and things more than they grasp their spirit. What they most admire in Michael Angelo is gigantic forms, noble and proud attitudes, while we better understand his secret thoughts, hidden sorrows, groans, and sighs.

Place before their eyes a picture by Rembrandt, and more often than not it will appear to them ugly; its charm cannot be caught at a glance as in those of their artists; to see it you must examine it, make an effort, and with them effort is the beginning of pain.

Do not ask them, then, to understand the pathos of things, to be touched by the mysterious and almost fanciful emotion which northern hearts discover and enjoy in the works of the Amsterdam master. No, instead of a forest they want a few trees, standing out clearly against the horizon; instead of a multitude swarming in the penumbra of reality, a few personages, larger than nature, forming harmonious groups in an ideal temple.

The genius of a people[9] is all of a piece: they apply to history the same processes that they apply to the arts. While the Germanic spirit considers events rather in their evolution, in their complex becoming, the Italian spirit takes them at a given moment, overlooks the shadows, the clouds, the mists, everything that makes the line indistinct, brings out the contour sharply, and thus constructs a very lucid story, which is a delight to the eyes, but which is little more than a symbol of the reality.

At other times it takes a man, separates him from the unnamed crowd, and by a labor often unconscious, makes him the ideal type of a whole epoch. [10]

Certainly there is in every people a tendency to give themselves a circle of divinities and heroes who are, so to say, the incarnation of its instincts; but generally that requires the long labor of centuries. The Italian character will not suffer this slow action; as soon as it recognizes a man it says so, it even shouts it aloud if that is necessary, and makes him enter upon immortality while still alive. Thus legend almost confounds itself with history, and it becomes very difficult to reduce men to their true proportions.

We must not, then, ask too much of history. The more beautiful is the dawn, the less one can describe it. The most beautiful things in nature, the flower and the butterfly, should be touched only by delicate hands.

The effort here made to indicate the variegated, wavering tints which form the atmosphere in which St. Francis lived is therefore of very uncertain success. It was perhaps presumptuous to undertake it.

Happily we are no longer in the time when historians thought they had done the right thing when they had reduced everything to its proper size, contenting themselves with denying or omitting everything in the life of the heroes of humanity which rises above the level of our every-day experience.

No doubt Francis did not meet on the road to Sienna three pure and gentle virgins come from heaven to greet him; the devil did not overturn rocks for the sake of terrifying him; but when we deny these visions and apparitions, we are victims of an error graver, perhaps, than that of those who affirm them.

The first time that I was at Assisi I arrived in the middle of the night. When the sun rose, flooding everything with warmth and light, the old basilica[11] seemed suddenly to quiver; one might have said that it wished to speak and sing. Giotto's frescos, but now invisible, awoke to a strange life, you might have thought them painted the evening before so much alive they were; everything was moving without awkwardness or jar.

I returned six months later. A scaffold had been put up in the middle of the nave; upon it an art critic was examining the paintings, and as the day was overcast he threw upon the walls the beams of a lamp with a reflector. Then you saw arms thrown out, faces grimacing, without unity, without harmony; the most exquisite figures took on something fantastic and grotesque.

He came down triumphant, with a portfolio stuffed with sketches; here a foot, there a muscle, farther on a bit of face, and I could not refrain from musing on the frescos as I had seen them bathed in sunlight.

The sun and the lamp are both deceivers; they transform what they show; but if the truth must be told I own to my preference for the falsehoods of the sun.

History is a landscape, and like those of nature it is continually changing. Two persons who look at it at the same time do not find in it the same charm, and you yourself, if you had it continually before your eyes, would never see it twice alike. The general lines are permanent, but it needs only a cloud to hide the most important ones, as it needs only a jet of light to bring out such or such a detail and give it a false value.

When I began this page the sun was disappearing behind the rains of the Castle of Crussol and the splendors of the sunset gave it a shining aureola; the light flooded everything, and you no longer saw anywhere the damage which wars have inflicted upon the old feudal manor. I looked, almost thinking I could perceive at the window the figure of the chatelaine... Twilight has come, and now there is nothing up there but crumbling walls, a discrowned tower, nothing but ruins and rubbish, which seem to beg for pity.

It is the same with the landscapes of history. Narrow minds cannot accommodate themselves to these perpetual transformations: they want an objective history in which the author will study the people as a chemist studies a body. It is very possible that there may be laws for historic evolution and social transformations as exact as those of chemical combinations, and we must hope that in the end they will be discovered; but for the present there is no purely objective truth of history.

To write history we must think it, and to think it is to transform it. Within a few years, it is true, men have believed they had found the secret of objectivity, in the publication of original documents. This is a true progress which renders inestimable service, but here again we must not deceive ourselves as to its significance. All the documents on an epoch or an event cannot usually be published, a selection must be made, and in it will necessarily appear the turn of mind of him who makes it. Let us admit that all that can be found is published; but alas, the most unusual movements have generally the fewest documents. Take, for instance, the religious history of the Middle Ages: it is already a pretty delicate task to collect official documents, such as bulls, briefs, conciliary canons, monastic constitutions, etc., but do these documents contain all the life of the Church? Much is still wanting, and to my mind the movements which secretly agitated the masses are much more important, although to testify to them we have only a few fragments.

Poor heretics, they were not only imprisoned and burned, but their books were destroyed and everything that spoke of them; and more than one historian, finding scarcely a trace of them in his heaps of documents, forgets these prophets with their strange visions, these poet-monks who from the depths of their cells made the world to thrill and the papacy to tremble.

Objective history is then a utopia. We create God in our own image, and we impress the mark of our personality in places where we least expect to find it again.

But by dint of talking about the tribunal of history we have made most authors think that they owe to themselves and their readers definitive and irrevocable judgments.

It is always easier to pronounce a sentence than to wait, to reserve one's opinion, to re-examine. The crowd which has put itself out to be present at a trial is almost always furious with the judges when they reserve the case for further information; its mind is so made that it requires precision in things which will bear it the least; it puts questions right and left, as children do; if you appear to hesitate or to be embarrassed you are lost in its estimation, you are evidently only an ignoramus.

But perhaps below the Areopagites, obliged by their functions to pronounce sentence, there is place at the famous tribunal for a simple spectator who has come in by accident. He has made out a brief and would like very simply to tell his neighbors his opinion.

This, then, is not a history *ad probandum*, to use the ancient formula. Is this to say that I have only desired to give the reader a moment of diversion? That would be to understand my thought very ill. In the grand spectacles of history as in those of nature there is something divine; from it our minds and hearts gain a virtue at once pacifying and encouraging, we experience the salutary sensation of littleness, and seeing the beauties and the sadnesses of the past we learn better how to judge the present hour.

In one of the frescos of the Upper Church of Assisi, Giotto has represented St. Clara and her companions coming out from St. Damian all in tears, to kiss their spiritual father's corpse as it is being carried to its last home. With an artist's liberty he has made the chapel a rich church built of precious marbles.

Happily the real St. Damian is still there, nestled under some olive-trees like a lark under the heather; it still has its ill-made walls of irregular stones, like those which bound the neighboring fields. Which is the more beautiful, the ideal temple of the artist's fancy, or the poor chapel of reality? No heart will be in doubt.

Francis's official historians have done for his biography what Giotto did for his little sanctuary. In general they have done him ill-service. Their embellishments have hidden the real St. Francis, who was, in fact, infinitely nobler than they have made him to be. Ecclesiastical writers appear to make a great mistake in thus adorning the lives of their heroes, and only mentioning their edifying features. They thus give occasion, even to the most devout, to suspect their testimony. Besides, by thus surrounding their saints with light they make them superhuman creatures, having nothing in common with us; they are privileged characters, marked with the divine seal; they are, as the litanies say, vials of election, into which God has poured the sweetest perfumes; their sanctity is revealed almost in spite of themselves; they are born saints as others are born kings or slaves, their life is set out against the golden background of a tryptich, and not against the sombre background of reality.

By such means the saints, perhaps, gain something in the respect of the superstitious; but their lives lose something of virtue and of communicable strength. Forgetting that they were men like ourselves, we no longer hear in our conscience the command, "Go and do likewise. "

It is, then, a work of piety to seek behind the legend for the history. Is it presumptuous to ask our readers to try to understand the thirteenth century and love St. Francis? They will be amply rewarded for the effort, and will soon find an unexpected charm in these too meagre landscapes, these incorporate souls, these sickly imaginations which will pass before their eyes. Love is the true key of history.

A book has always a great number of authors, and the following pages owe much to the researches of others; I have tried in the notes to show the whole value of these debts.

I have also had colaborers to whom it will be more difficult for me to express my gratitude. I refer to the librarians of the libraries of Italy and their assistants; it is impossible to name them all, their faces are better known to me than their names, but I would here say that during long months passed in the various collections of the Peninsula, all, even to the most humble employees, have shown a tireless helpfulness even at those periods of the year when the number of attendants was the smallest.

Professor Alessandro Leto, who, barely recovered from a grave attack of influenza, kindly served as my guide among the archives of Assisi, deserves a very particular mention. To the Syndic and municipality of that city I desire also to express my gratitude.

I cannot close without a warm remembrance to the spiritual sons of St. Francis dispersed in the mountains of Umbria and Tuscany.

Dear dwellers in St. Damian, Portiuncula, the Carceri, the Verna, Monte Colombo, you perhaps remember the strange pilgrim who, though he wore neither the frock nor the cord, used to talk with you of the Seraphic Father with as much love as the most pious Franciscan; you used to be surprised at his eagerness to see everything, to look at everything, to thread all the unexplored paths. You often tried to restrain him by telling him that there was not the smallest relic, the most meagre indulgence in the far-away grottos to which he was dragging you, but you always ended by going with him, thinking that none but a Frenchman could be possessed by a devotion so fervent and so imprudent.

Thank you, pious anchorites of Greccio, thank you for the bread that you went out and begged when I arrived at your hermitage benumbed with cold and hunger. If you read these lines, read here my gratitude and also a little admiration. You are not all saints, but nearly all of you have hours of saintliness, flights of pure love.

If some pages of this book give you pain, turn them over quickly; let me think that others of them will give you pleasure, and will make the name you bear, if possible, still more precious to you than it now is.

FOOTNOTES:

[1]   The mendicant orders were in their origin a true *International*. When in the spring of 1216 St. Dominic assembled his friars at Notre Dame de la Prouille, they were found to be sixteen in number, and among them Castilians, Navarese, Normans, French, Languedocians, and even English and Germans.

Heretics travelled all over Europe, and nowhere do we find them checked by the diversity of languages. Arnold of Brescia, for example, the famous Tribune of Rome, appeared in France and Switzerland and in the heart of Germany.

[2]   The Reformation only substituted the authority of the book for that of the priest; it is a change of dynasty and nothing more. As to the majority of those who to-day call themselves free-thinkers, they confuse religious freedom with irreligion; they choose not to see that in religion as in politics, between a royalty based on divine right and anarchy there is room for a government which may be as strong as the first and a better guarantee of freedom than the second. The spirit of the older time put God outside of the world; the sovereignty outside of the people; authority outside of the conscience. The spirit of the new times has the contrary tendency: it denies neither God nor sovereignty nor authority, but it sees them where they really are.

[3] *Nemo ostendebat mihi quod deberem facere, sed ipse Altissimus revelavit mihi quod deberem vivere secundem formam sancti Evangelii.* Testamentum Fr.

[4] The wealthiest monasteries of France are of the twelfth century or were enlarged at that time: Arles, S. Gilles, S. Sernin, Cluny, Vézelay, Brioude, Issoire, Paray-le-Monial. The same was the case in Italy.

Down to the year 1000, 1,108 monasteries had been founded in France. The eleventh century saw the birth of 326 and the twelfth of 702. The convents of Mount Athos in their present state give us a very accurate notion of the great monasteries of Europe at the close of the twelfth century.

[5] St. Petrus Chrysologus, sermo viii., de jejunio et eleemosyna. *Da pauperi ut des tibi: da micam ut accipias totum panem; da tectum, accipe coelum.*

[6] By what right did he begin to preach? By what right did he, a mere deacon, admit to profession and cut off the hair of a young girl of eighteen? That is an episcopal function, one which can only devolve even upon priests by an express commission.

[7] Isaiah i. 10-17. Cf. Joel 2, Psalm 50.

[8] The chronicles of Orvieto (*Archivio, storico italiano,* t. i., of 1889, pp. 7 and following) are nothing more than a list, as melancholy as they are tedious of wars, which, during the thirteenth and fourteenth centuries, all the places of that region carried on, from the greatest to the smallest.

[9] Do not forget that in the thirteenth century Italy was not a mere geographical expression. It was of all the countries of Europe the one which, notwithstanding its partitions, had the clearest consciousness of its unity. The expression *profectus et honor Italiæ* often appeared from the pen of Innocent III. See, for instance, the bull of April 16, 1198, *Mirari cogimur,* addressed particularly to the Assisans.

[10] Note what the Fioretti say of Brother Bernard: "*Stava solo sulle cime dei monti altissimi contemplando le cose celesti.* " Fior., 28.

The learned historian of Assisi, Mr. Cristofani, has used similar expressions; speaking of St. Francis, he says: "*Nuovo Christo in somma e pero degno d'essere riguardoto come la piu gigantesca, la piu splendida, la piu cara tra le grandi figure campeggianti nell' aere del medio evo*" (*Storia d'Assisi*, t. i., p. 70, ed. of 1885).

[11]   It remains open all night.

CHAPTER I

YOUTH

Assisi is to-day very much what it was six or seven hundred years ago. The feudal castle is in ruins, but the aspect of the city is just the same. Its long-deserted streets, bordered by ancient houses, lie in terraces half-way up the steep hill-side. Above it Mount Subasio[1] proudly towers, at its feet lies outspread all the Umbrian plain from Perugia to Spoleto. The crowded houses clamber up the rocks like children a-tiptoe to see all that is to be seen; they succeed so well that every window gives the whole panorama set in its frame of rounded hills, from whose summits castles and villages stand sharply out against a sky of incomparable purity.

These simple dwellings contain no more than five or six little rooms, [2] but the rosy hues of the stone of which they are built give them a wonderfully cheerful air. The one in which, according to the story, St. Francis was born has almost entirely disappeared, to make room for a church; but the street is so modest, and all that remains of the *palazzo dei genitori di San Francesco* is so precisely like the neighboring houses that the tradition must be correct. Francis entered into glory in his lifetime; it would be surprising if a sort of worship had not from the first been centred around the house in which he saw the light and where he passed the first twenty-five years of his life.

He was born about 1182. [3] The biographies have preserved to us few details about his parents. [4] His father, Pietro Bernardone, was a wealthy cloth-merchant. We know how different was the life of the merchants of that period from what it is to-day. A great portion of their time was spent in extensive journeys for the purchase of goods. Such tours were little short of expeditions. The roads being insecure, a strong escort was needed for the journey to those famous fairs where, for long weeks at a time, merchants from the most remote parts of Europe were gathered together. In certain cities, Montpellier for example, the fair was perpetual. Benjamin of Tudela shows us that city frequented by all nations, Christian and Mohammedan. "One meets there merchants from Africa, from Italy, Egypt, Palestine, Greece, Gaul, Spain, and England, so that one sees men of all languages, with the Genoese and the Pisans. "

1

Among all these merchants the richest were those who dealt in textile stuffs. They were literally the bankers of the time, and their heavy wagons were often laden with the sums levied by the popes in England or France.

Their arrival at a castle was one of the great events. They were kept as long as possible, everyone being eager for the news they brought. It is easy to understand how close must have been their relations with the nobility; in certain countries, Provence for example, the merchants were considered as nobles of a second order. [5]

Bernardone often made these long journeys; he went even as far as France, and by this we must surely understand Northern France, and particularly Champagne, which was the seat of commercial exchange between Northern and Southern Europe.

He was there at the very time of his son's birth. The mother, presenting the child at the font of San Rufino, [6] had him baptized by the name of John, but the father on his return chose to call him Francis. [7] Had he already determined on the education he was to give the child; did he name him thus because he even then intended to bring him up after the French fashion, to make a little Frenchman of him? It is by no means improbable. Perhaps, indeed, the name was only a sort of grateful homage tendered by the Assisan burgher to his noble clients beyond the Alps. However this may be, the child was taught to speak French, and always had a special fondness for both the language and the country. [8]

These facts about Bernardone are of real importance; they reveal the influences in the midst of which Francis grew up. Merchants, indeed, play a considerable part in the religious movements of the thirteenth century. Their calling in some sense forced them to become colporters of ideas. What else could they do, on arriving in a country, but answer those who asked for news? And the news most eagerly looked for was religious news, for men's minds were turned upon very different subjects then from now. They accommodated themselves to the popular wish, observing, hearkening everywhere, keeping eyes and ears open, glad to find anything to tell; and little by little many of them became active propagandists of ideas concerning which at first they had been simply curious.

The importance of the part thus played by the merchants as they came and went, everywhere sowing the new ideas which they had gathered up in their travels, has not been put in a clear enough light; they were often, unconsciously and quite involuntarily, the carriers of ideas of all kinds, especially of heresy and rebellion. It was they who made the success of the Waldenses, the Albigenses, the Humiliati, and many other sects.

Thus Bernardone, without dreaming of such a thing, became the artisan of his son's religious vocation. The tales which he brought home from his travels seemed at first, perhaps, not to have aroused the child's attention, but they were like germs a long time buried, which suddenly, under a warm ray of sunlight, bring forth unlooked-for fruit.

The boy's education was not carried very far; [9] the school was in those days overshadowed by the church. The priests of San Giorgio were his teachers, [10] and taught him a little Latin. This language was spoken in Umbria until toward the middle of the thirteenth century; every one understood it and spoke it a little; it was still the language of sermons and of political deliberations. [11]

He learned also to write, but with less success; all through his life we see him take up the pen only on rare occasions, and for but a few words. [12] The autograph of Sacro-Convento, which appears to be entirely authentic, shows extreme awkwardness; in general he dictated, signing his letters by a simple [Greek: tau], the symbol of the cross of Jesus. [13]

That part of his education which was destined to have most influence upon his life was the French language, [14] which he perhaps spoke in his own family. It has been rightly said that to know two languages is to have two souls; in learning that of France the boy felt his heart thrill to the melody of its youthful poetry, and his imagination was mysteriously stirred with dreams of imitating the exploits of the French cavaliers.

But let us not anticipate. His early life was that of other children of his age. In the quarter of the town where his house is still shown no vehicles are ever seen; from morning till night the narrow streets are given over to the children. They play there in many groups, frolicking with an exquisite charm, very different from the little Romans, who, from the time they are six or seven years old, spend hours at a time squatting behind a pillar, or in a corner of a wall or a ruin, to play dice or "morra, " putting a passionate ferocity even into their play.

In Umbria, as in Tuscany, children love above all things games in which they can make a parade; to play at soldiers or procession is the supreme delight of Assisan children. Through the day they keep to the narrow streets, but toward evening they go, singing and dancing, to one of the open squares of the city. These squares are one of the charms of Assisi. Every few paces an interval occurs between the houses looking toward the plain, and you find a delightful terrace, shaded by a few trees, the very place for enjoying the sunset without losing one of its splendors. Hither no doubt came often the son of Bernardone, leading one of those *farandoles* which you may see there to this day: from his very babyhood he was a prince among the children.

Thomas of Celano draws an appalling picture of the education of that day. He describes parents inciting their children to vice, and driving them by main force to wrong-doing. Francis responded only too quickly to these unhappy lessons. [15]

His father's profession and the possibly noble origin of his mother raised him almost to the level of the titled families of the country; money, which he spent with both hands, made him welcome among them. Well pleased to enjoy themselves at his expense, the young nobles paid him a sort of court. As to Bernardone, he was too happy to see his son associating with them to be niggardly as to the means. He was miserly, as the course of this history will show, but his pride and self-conceit exceeded his avarice.

Pica, his wife, gentle and modest creature, [16] concerning whom the biographers have been only too laconic, saw all this, and mourned over it in silence, but though weak as mothers are, she would not despair of her son, and when the neighbors told her of Francis's escapades, she would calmly reply, "What are you thinking about? I am very sure that, if it pleases God, he will become a good Christian. "[17] The words were natural enough from a mother's lips, but later on they were held to have been truly prophetic.

How far did the young man permit himself to be led on? It would be difficult to say. The question which, as we are told, tormented Brother Leo, could only have suggested itself to a diseased imagination. [18] Thomas of Celano and the Three Companions agree in picturing him as going to the worst excesses. Later biographers speak with more circumspection of his worldly career. A too widely credited story gathered from Celano's narrative was modified by the chapter-general of 1260, [19] and the frankness of the early biographers was, no doubt, one of the causes which most effectively contributed to their definitive condemnation three years later. [20]

Their statements are in no sense obscure; according to them the son of Bernardone not only patterned himself after the young men of his age, he made it a point of honor to exceed them. What with eccentricities, buffooneries, pranks, prodigalities, he ended by achieving a sort of celebrity. He was forever in the streets with his companions, compelling attention by his extravagant or fantastic attire. Even at night the joyous company kept up their merrymakings, causing the town to ring with their noisy songs. [21]

At this very time the troubadours were roaming over the towns of Northern Italy[22] and bringing brilliant festivities and especially Courts of Love into vogue. If they worked upon the passions, they also made appeal to feelings of courtesy and delicacy; it was this that saved Francis. In the midst of his excesses he was always refined and considerate, carefully abstaining from every base or indecent utterance. [23] Already his chief aspiration was to rise above the commonplace. Tortured with the desire for that which is far off and high, [24] he had conceived a sort of passion for chivalry, and fancying that dissipation was one of the distinguishing features of nobility, he had thrown himself into it with all his soul.

But he who, at twenty, goes from pleasure to pleasure with the heart not absolutely closed to good, must now and then, at some turning of the road, become aware that there are hungry folk, who could live a month on what he spends in a few hours on frivolity. Francis saw them, and with his impressionable nature for the moment forgot everything else. In thought he put himself in their place, and it sometimes happened that he gave them all the money he had about him and even his clothes.

One day he was busy with some customers in his father's shop, when a man came in, begging for charity in the name of God. Losing his patience Francis sharply turned him away; but quickly reproaching himself for his harshness he thought, "What would I not have done if this man had asked something of me in the name of a count or a baron? What ought I not to have done when he came in the name of God? I am no better than a clown! " Leaving his customers he ran after the beggar. [25]

Bernardone had been well pleased with his son's commercial aptitude in the early days when the young man was first in his father's employ. Francis was only too proficient in spending money; he at least knew well how to make it. [26] But this satisfaction did not last long. Francis's bad companions were exercising over him a most pernicious influence. The time came when he could no longer endure to be separated from them; if he heard their call, nothing could keep him, he would leave everything and go after them. [27]

All this time political events were hurrying on in Umbria and Italy; after a formidable struggle the allied republics had forced the empire to recognize them. By the immortal victory of Legnano (May 29, 1176) and the Peace of Constance (June 25, 1183) the Lombard League had wrested from Frederick Barbarossa almost all the prerogatives of power; little was left to the emperor but insignia and outward show.

From one end of the Peninsula to the other visions of liberty were making hearts beat high. For an instant it seemed as if all Italy was about to regain consciousness of its unity, was about to rise up as one man and hurl the foreigner from its borders; but the rivalries of the cities were too strong for them to see that local liberty without a common independence is precarious and illusory. Henry VI., the successor of Barbarossa (1183-1196), laid Italy under a yoke of iron; he might perhaps in the end have assured the domination of the empire, if his career had not been suddenly cut short by a premature death.

Yet he had not been able to put fetters upon ideas. The communal movement which was shaking the north of France reverberated beyond the Alps.

Although a city of second rank, Assisi had not been behind in the great struggles for independence. [28] She had been severely chastised, had lost her franchise, and was obliged to submit to Conrad of Suabia, Duke of Spoleto, who from the heights of his fortress kept her in subjection.

But when Innocent III. ascended the pontifical throne (January 8, 1199) the old duke knew himself to be lost. He made a tender to him of money, men, his faith even, but the pontiff refused them all. He had no desire to appear to favor the Tedeschi, who had so odiously oppressed the country. Conrad of Suabia was forced to yield at mercy, and to go to Narni to put his submission into the hands of two cardinals.

Like the practical folk that they were, the Assisans did not hesitate an instant. No sooner was the count on the road to Narni than they rushed to the assault of the castle. The arrival of envoys charged to take possession of it as a pontifical domain by no means gave them pause. Not one stone of it was left upon another. [29] Then, with incredible rapidity they enclosed their city with walls, parts of which are still standing, their formidable ruins a witness to the zeal with which the whole population labored on them.

It is natural to think that Francis, then seventeen years old, was one of the most gallant laborers of those glorious days, and it was perhaps there that he gained the habit of carrying stones and wielding the trowel which was destined to serve him so well a few years later.

Unhappily his fellow-citizens had not the sense to profit by their hard-won liberty. The lower classes, who in this revolution had become aware of their strength, determined to follow out the victory by taking possession of the property of the nobles. The latter took refuge in their fortified houses in the interior of the city, or in their castles in the suburbs. The townspeople burned down several of the latter, whereupon counts and barons made request of aid and succor from the neighboring cities.

Perugia was at this time at the apogee of its power, [30] and had already made many efforts to reduce Assisi to submission. It therefore received the fugitives with alacrity, and making their cause its own, declared war upon Assisi. This was in 1202. An encounter took place in the plain about half way between the two cities, not far from *Ponte San Giovanni*. Assisi was defeated, and Francis, who was in the ranks, was made prisoner. [31]

The treachery of the nobles had not been universal; a few had fought with the people. It was with them and not with the *popolani* that Francis, in consideration of the nobility of his manners, [32] passed

7

the time of his captivity, which lasted an entire year. He greatly astonished his companions by his lightness of heart. Very often they thought him almost crazy. Instead of passing his time in wailing and cursing he made plans for the future, about which he was glad to talk to any one who came along. To his fancy life was what the songs of the troubadours had painted it; he dreamed of glorious adventures, and always ended by saying: "You will see that one day I shall be adored by the whole world. "[33]

During these long months Francis must have been pretty rudely undeceived with respect to those nobles whom from afar he had so heartily admired. However that may be, he retained with them not only his frankness of speech, but also his full freedom of action. One of them, a knight, had always held aloof from the others, out of vanity and bad temper. Francis, far from leaving him to himself, always showed him affection, and finally had the joy of reconciling him with his fellow-captives.

A compromise was finally arrived at between the counts and the people of Assisi. In November, 1203, the arbitrators designated by the two parties announced their decision. The commons of Assisi were to repair in a certain measure the damage done to the lords, and the latter agreed, on their part, to make no further alliances without authorization of the commons. [34] Rural serfage was maintained, which proves that the revolution had been directed by the burghers, and for their own profit. Ten years more were not, however, to elapse before the common people also would succeed in achieving liberty. In this cause we shall again see Francis fighting on the side of the oppressed, earning the title of *Patriarch of religious democracy* which has been accorded him by one of his compatriots. [35]

The agreement being made the prisoners detained at Perugia were released, and Francis returned to Assisi. He was twenty-two years old.

FOOTNOTES:

[1]   Eleven hundred and one metres above the level of the sea; the plain around Assisi has an average of two hundred, and the town of two hundred and fifty, metres above.

[2]   As in the majority of Tuscan cities the dimensions of the houses were formerly fixed by law.

[3]   The biographies say that he died (October 3, 1226) in his forty-fifth year. But the terms are not precise enough to make the date 1181 improbable. For that matter the question is of small importance. A Franciscan of Erfurt, about the middle of the thirteenth century, fixes the date at 1182. Pertz, vol. xxiv., p. 193.

[4]   A number of different genealogies have been fabricated for Francis; they prove only one thing, the wreck of the Franciscan idea. How little they understood their hero, who thought to magnify and glorify him by making him spring from a noble family! "*Quæ rero,*" says Father Suysken, S. J., "*de ejus gentilitio insigni disserit Waddingus, non lubet mihi attingere. Factis et virtutibus eluxit S. Franciscus non proavorum insignibus aut titulis, quos nec desideravit.*" (A. SS. p. 557a.) It could not be better said.

In the fourteenth century a whole cycle of legends had gathered about his birth. It could not have been otherwise. They all grow out of the story that tells of an old man who comes knocking at the parents' door, begging them to let him take the infant in his arms, when he announces that it will do great things. Under this form the episode certainly presents nothing impossible, but very soon marvellous incidents begin to gather around this nucleus until it becomes unrecognizable. Bartholomew of Pisa has preserved it in almost its primitive form. *Conform.,* 28a 2. Francis certainly had several brothers [3 Soc., 9. *Mater... quæ cum præ ceteris filiis diligebat*], but they have left no trace in history except the incident related farther on. Vide p. 44. Christofani publishes several official pieces concerning *Angelo,* St. Francis's brother, and his descendants: *Storie d'Assisi,* vol. i., p. 78 ff. In these documents Angelo is called *Angelus Pice,* and his son *Johannectus olim Angeli domine Pice,* appellations which might be cited in favor of the noble origin of Pica.

[5]   Documentary History of Languedoc, iii., p. 607.

[6]   The Cathedral of Assisi. To this day all the children of the town are baptized there; the other churches are without fonts.

[7]   3 Soc., 1; 2 Cel., 1, 1. Vide also 3 Soc., edition of Pesaro, 1831.

[8]   The *langue d'oïl* was at this epoch the international language of Europe; in Italy it was the language of games and tourneys, and was spoken in the petty princely courts of Northern Italy. Vide Dante, *De vulgari eloquio*, lib. I., cap. x. Brunetto Latini wrote in French because "the speech of France is more delectable and more common to all people. " At the other end of Europe the Abbot of Stade, in Westphalia, spoke of the *nobility of the Gallic dialect. Ann.* 1224 *apud* Pertz, Script. xvi. We shall find St. Francis often making allusions to the tales of the Round Table and the *Chanson de Roland.*

[9]   We must not be led astray by certain remarks upon his ignorance, from which one might at first conclude that he knew absolutely nothing; for example, 2 Cel., 3, 45: *Quamvis homo iste beatus nullis fuerit scientiæ studiis innutritus.* This evidently refers to science such as the Franciscans soon came to apprehend it, and to theology in particular.

        The close of the passage in Celano is itself an evident proof of this.

[10]   Bon., 219; Cf. A. SS., p. 560a. 1 Cel., 23.

[11]   Ozanam, *Documents inédits pour servir à l'histoire littéraire d'Italie du VIIIe au XIIIe siècle.* Paris, 1851, 8vo, pp. 65, 68, 71, 73. Fauriel, *Dante et les origines de la littérature italienne.* Paris, 1854, 2 vols., 8vo, ii., p. 332, 379, 429.

[12]   V. 3 Soc., 51 and 67; 2 Cel., 3, 110; Bon., 55; 2 Cel., 3, 99; Eccl., 6. Bernard de Besse, Turin MS., fo. 96a, calls Brother Leo the secretary of St. Francis.

[13]   See page 357, n. 8. Bon., 51 and 308.

[14]   1 Cel., 16; 3 Soc., 10; 23; 24; 33; 2 Cel., 1, 8; 3, 67. See also the Testament of St. Clara and the Speculum, 119a.

[15]   *Primum namque cum fari vel balbutire incipiunt, turpia quædam
         et execrabilia valde signis et vocibus edocentur pueri ii nondum
         nati: et cum tempus ablactationis advenerit quædam luxu et
         lascivia plena non solum fari sed et operari coguntur.... Sed et cum
         paulo plusculum ætate profecerint, se ipsis impellentibus, semper
         ad deteriora opera dilabuntur.* 1 Cel., 1.

[16]   2 Cel., 1. Cf. *Conform.* , 14a, 1. There is nothing impossible in
         her having been of Provençal origin, but there is nothing to
         indicate it in any document worthy of credence. She was no
         doubt of noble stock, for official documents always give her
         the title *Domina.* Cristofani I., p. 78 ff. Cf. *Matrem
         honestissimam habuit.* 3 Soc., Edition of Pesaro, 1831, p. 17.

[17]   The reading given by the *Conform.*, 14a, 1, *Meritorum gratia
         dei filium ipsum noveritis affuturum,* seems better than that of 2
         Cel., 1, 1, *Multorum gratia Dei filiorum patrem ipsum noveritis
         affuturum.* Cf. 3 Soc., 2.

[18]   Bernardo of Besse, Turin MS., 102 b. : *An integer carne
         desiderans... quod non extorsisset a Sancto... meruit obtinere a Deo
         quod virgo esset.* Cf. *Conform.*, 211a, 1, and A. SS., p. 560f.

[19]   *"In illa antiphona quæ incipit: Hic vir in vanitatibus nutritus
         insolenter, fiat talis mutatis: Divinis karismatibus preventus est
         clementer. " Archiv.* , vi., p. 35.

[20]   Vide p. 395, the decision of the chapter of 1263 ordaining the
         destruction of legends earlier than that of Bonaventura.

[21]   1 Cel., 1 and 2; 89; 3 Soc., 2. Cf. A. SS., 560c. Vincent of
         Beauvais, *Spec. hist. lib.* , 29, cap. 97.

[22]   Pierre Vidal was at the court of Boniface, Marquis of
         Montferrat, about 1195, and liked his surroundings so well
         that he desired to establish himself there. K. Bartsch, *Piere
         Vidal's Lieder*, Berlin, 1857, n. 41. Ern. Monaci, *Testi antichi
         provenzali*, Rome, 1889, col. 67. One should read this piece to
         have an idea of the fervor with which this poet shared the
         hopes of Italy and desired its independence. This political
         note is found again in a *tenzon* of Manfred II. Lancia,
         addressed to Pierre Vidal. (V. Monaci, *loc. cit.* , col. 68.) —
         Gaucelme Faidit was also at this court as well as Raimbaud

of Vacqueyras (1180-1207). —Folquet de Romans passed nearly all his life in Italy. Bernard of Ventadour (1145-1195), Peirol of Auvergne (1180-1220), and many others abode there a longer or shorter time. Very soon the Italians began to sing in Provençal, among others this Manfred Lancia, and Albert Marquis of Malaspina (1162-1210), Pietro della Caravana, who in 1196 stirred up the Lombard towns against Henry VI., Pietro della Mula, who about 1200 was at the court of Cortemiglia. Fragments from these poets may be found in Monaci, *op. cit.* , col. 69 ff.

[23]   Soc., 3; 2 Cel., 1, 1.

[24]   *Cum esset gloriosus animo et nollet aliquem se præcellere*, Giord. 20.

[25]   1 Cel., 17; 3 Soc., 3; Bon., 7. Cf. A. SS., p. 562.

[26]   1 Cel., 2; Bon., 6; *Vit. sec. apud*, A. SS., p. 560.

[27]   3 Soc., 9.

[28]   In 1174 Assisi was taken by the chancellor of the empire, Christian, Archbishop of Mayence. A. Cristofani, i., p. 69.

[29]   All these events are related in the *Gesta Innocentii III. ab auctore coætaneo*, edited by Baluze: Migne, *Inn. op.* , vol. i., col. xxiv. See especially the letter of Innocent, *Rectoribus Tusciæ: Mirari cogimur*, of April 16, 1198. Migne, vol. i., col. 75-77. Potthast, No. 82.

[30]   See Luigi Bonazzi, *Storia di Perugia*, 2 vols., 8vo. Perugia, 1875-1879 vol. i., cap. v., pp. 257-322.

[31]   3 Soc., 4; 2 Cel., 1, 1. Cristofani, *op. cit.* , i., p. 88 ff. ; Bonazzi, *op. cit.* , p. 257.

[32]   3 Soc., 4.

[33]   3 Soc., 4; 2 Cel., 1, 1.

[34]   See this arbitration in Cristofani, *op. cit.* , p. 93 ff.

[35]   Cristofani, *loc. cit.* , p. 70.

CHAPTER II

STAGES OF CONVERSION

Spring 1204-Spring 1206

On his return to Assisi Francis at once resumed his former mode of life; perhaps he even tried in some degree to make up for lost time. Fêtes, games, festivals, and dissipations began again. He did his part in them so well that he soon fell gravely ill. [1] For long weeks he looked death so closely in the face that the physical crisis brought about a moral one. Thomas of Celano has preserved for us an incident of Francis's convalescence. He was regaining strength little by little and had begun to go about the house, when one day he felt a desire to walk abroad, to contemplate nature quietly, and so take hold again of life. Leaning on a stick he bent his steps toward the city gate.

The nearest one, called *Porta Nuova*, is the very one which opens upon the finest scenery. Immediately on passing through it one finds one's self in the open country; a fold of the hill hides the city, and cuts off every sound that might come from it. Before you lies the winding road to Foligno; at the left the imposing mass of Mount Subasio; at the right the Umbrian plain with its farms, its villages, its cloud-like hills, on whose slopes pines, cedars, oaks, the vine, and the olive-tree shed abroad an incomparable brightness and animation. The whole country sparkles with beauty, a beauty harmonious and thoroughly human, that is, made to the measure of man.

Francis had hoped by this sight to recover the delicious sensations of his youth. With the sharpened sensibility of the convalescent he breathed in the odors of the spring-time, but spring-time did not come, as he had expected, to his heart. This smiling nature had for him only a message of sadness. He had believed that the breezes of this beloved country-side would carry away the last shudders of the fever, and instead he felt in his heart a discouragement a thousand-fold more painful than any physical ill. The miserable emptiness of his life suddenly appeared before him; he was terrified at his solitude, the solitude of a great soul in which there is no altar.

Memories of the past assailed him with intolerable bitterness; he was seized with a disgust of himself, his former ambitions seemed to him ridiculous or despicable. He went home overwhelmed with the weight of a new suffering.

In such hours of moral anguish man seeks a refuge either in love or in faith. Unhappily the family and friends of Francis were incapable of understanding him. As to religion, it was for him, as for the greater number of his contemporaries, that crass fetichism with Christian terminology which is far from having entirely disappeared. With certain men, in fact, piety consists in making one's self right with a king more powerful than any other, but also more severe and capricious, who is called God. One proves one's loyalty to him as to other sovereigns, by putting his image more or less everywhere, and punctually paying the imposts levied by his ministers. If you are stingy, if you cheat, you run the risk of being severely chastised, but there are courtiers around the king who willingly render services. For a reasonable recompense they will seize a favorable moment to adroitly make away with the sentence of your condemnation or to slip before the prince a form of plenary absolution which in a moment of good humor he will sign without looking at it. [2]

Such was the religious basis upon which Francis had lived up to this time. He did not so much as dream of seeking the spiritual balm which he needed for the healing of his wounds. By a holy violence he was to arrive at last at a pure and virile faith; but the road to this point is long, and sown thick with obstacles, and at the moment at which we have arrived he had not yet entered upon it, he did not even suspect its existence; all he knew was that pleasure leads to nothingness, to satiety and self-contempt.

He knew this, and yet he was about to throw himself once more into a life of pleasure. The body is so weak, so prone to return to the old paths, that it seeks them of itself, the moment an energetic will does not stop it. Though no longer under any illusion with respect to it, Francis returned to his former life. Was he trying to divert his mind, to forget that day of bitter thought? We might suppose so, seeing the ardor with which he threw himself into his new projects. [3]

An opportunity offered itself for him to realize his dreams of glory. A knight of Assisi, perhaps one of those who had been in captivity with him at Perugia, was preparing to go to Apulia under orders from Count Gentile. [4] The latter was to join Gaultier de Brienne, who was in the south of Italy fighting on the side of Innocent III. Gaultier's renown was immense all through the Peninsula; he was held to be one of the most gallant knights of the time. Francis's heart bounded with joy; it seemed to him that at the side of such a hero he should soon cover himself with glory. His departure was decided upon, and he gave himself up, without reserve, to his joy.

He made his preparations with ostentatious prodigality. His equipment, of a princely luxury, soon became the universal subject of conversation. It was all the more talked about because the chief of the expedition, ruined perhaps by the revolution of 1202 or by the expenses of a long captivity, was constrained to order things much more modestly. [5] But with Francis kindliness was much stronger than love of display. He gave his sumptuous clothing to a poor knight. The biographies do not say whether or not it was to the very one whom he was to accompany. [6] To see him running hither and thither in all the bustle of preparation one would have thought him the son of a great lord. His companions were doubtless not slow to feel chafed by his ways and to promise themselves to make him cruelly expiate them. As for him, he perceived nothing of the jealousies which he was exciting, and night and day he thought only of his future glory. In his dreams he seemed to see his parents' house completely transformed. Instead of bales of cloth he saw there only gleaming bucklers hanging on the walls, and arms of all kinds as in a seignorial castle. He saw himself there, beside a noble and beautiful bride, and he never suspected that in this vision there was any presage of the future which was reserved for him. Never had any one seen him so communicative, so radiant; and when he was asked for the hundredth time whence came all this joy, he would reply with surprising assurance: "I know that I shall become a great prince. "[7]

The day of departure arrived at last. Francis on horseback, the little buckler of a page on his arm, bade adieu to his natal city with joy, and with the little troop took the road to Spoleto which winds around the base of Mount Subasio.

What happened next? The documents do not say. They confine themselves to reporting that that very evening Francis had a vision which decided him to return to Assisi. [8] Perhaps it would not be far from the truth to conjecture that once fairly on the way the young nobles took their revenge on the son of Bernardone for his airs as of a future prince. At twenty years one hardly pardons things like these.

If, as we are often assured, there is a pleasure unsuspected by the profane in getting even with a stranger, it must be an almost divine delight to get even with a young coxcomb upon whom one has to exercise so righteous a vengeance.

Arriving at Spoleto, Francis took to his bed. A fever was consuming him; in a few hours he had seen all his dreams crumble away. The very next day he took the road back to Assisi. [9]

So unexpected a return made a great stir in the little city, and was a cruel blow to his parents. As for him, he doubled his charities to the poor, and sought to keep aloof from society, but his old companions came flocking about him from all quarters, hoping to find in him once more the tireless purveyor of their idle wants. He let them have their way.

Nevertheless a great change had taken place in him. Neither pleasures nor work could long hold him; he spent a portion of his days in long country rambles, often accompanied by a friend most different from those whom until now we have seen about him. The name of this friend is not known, but from certain indications one is inclined to believe that he was Bombarone da Beviglia, the future Brother Elias. [10]

Francis now went back to his reflections at the time of his recovery, but with less of bitterness. His own heart and his friend agreed in saying to him that it is possible no longer to trust either in pleasure or in glory and yet to find worthy causes to which to consecrate one's life. It is at this moment that religious thought seems to have awaked in him. From the moment that he saw this new way of life his desire to run in it had all the fiery impetuosity which he put into all his actions. He was continually calling upon his friend and leading him apart into the most sequestered paths.

But intense conflicts are indescribable. We struggle, we suffer alone. It is the nocturnal wrestling of Bethel, mysterious and solitary. The soul of Francis was great enough to endure this tragic duel. His friend had marvellously understood his part in this contest. He gave a few rare counsels, but much of the time he contented himself with manifesting his solicitude by following Francis everywhere and never asking to know more than he could tell him.

Often Francis directed his steps to a grotto in the country near Assisi, which he entered alone. This rocky cave concealed in the midst of the olive trees became for faithful Franciscans that which Gethsemane is for Christians. Here Francis relieved his overcharged heart by heavy groans. Sometimes, seized with a real horror for the disorders of his youth, he would implore mercy, but the greater part of the time his face was turned toward the future; feverishly he sought for that higher truth to which he longed to dedicate himself, that pearl of great price of which the gospel speaks: "Whosoever seeks, finds; he who asks, receives; and to him who knocks, it shall be opened. "

When he came out after long hours of seclusion the pallor of his countenance, the painful tension of his features told plainly enough of the intensity of his asking and the violence of his knocks. [11]

The inward man, to borrow the language of the mystics, was not yet formed in him, but it needed only the occasion to bring about the final break with the past. The occasion soon presented itself.

His friends were making continual efforts to induce him to take up his old habits again. One day he invited them all to a sumptuous banquet. They thought they had conquered, and as in old times they proclaimed him king of the revels. The feast was prolonged far into the night, and at its close the guests rushed out into the streets, which they filled with song and uproar. Suddenly they perceived that Francis was no longer with them. After long searching they at last discovered him far behind them, still holding in his hand his sceptre of king of misrule, but plunged in so profound a revery that he seemed to be riveted to the ground and unconscious of all that was going on.

"What is the matter with you? " they cried, bustling about him as if to awaken him.

"Don't you see that he is thinking of taking a wife? " said one.

"Yes, " answered Francis, arousing himself and looking at them with a smile which they did not recognize. "I am thinking of taking a wife more beautiful, more rich, more pure than you could ever imagine. "[12]

This reply marks a decisive stage in his inner life. By it he cut the last links which bound him to trivial pleasures. It remains for us to see through what struggles he was to give himself to God, after having torn himself free from the world. His friends probably understood nothing of all that had taken place, but he had become aware of the abyss that was opening between them and him. They soon accepted the situation.

As for himself, no longer having any reason for caution, he gave himself up more than ever to his passion for solitude. If he often wept over his past dissipations and wondered how he could have lived so long without tasting the bitterness of the dregs of the enchanted cup, he never allowed himself to be overwhelmed with vain regrets.

The poor had remained faithful to him. They gave him an admiration of which he knew himself to be unworthy, yet which had for him an infinite sweetness. The future grew bright to him in the light of their gratitude, of the timid, trembling affection which they dared not utter but which his heart revealed to him; this worship which he does not deserve to-day he will deserve to-morrow, at least he promises himself to do all he can to deserve it.

To understand these feelings one must understand the condition of the poor of a place like Assisi. In an agricultural country poverty does not, as elsewhere, almost inevitably involve moral destitution, that degeneration of the entire human being which renders charity so difficult. Most of the poor persons whom Francis knew were in straits because of war, of bad harvests, or of illness. In such cases material succor is but a small part. Sympathy is the thing needed above all. Francis had treasures of it to lavish upon them.

He was well requited. All sorrows are sisters; a secret intelligence establishes itself between troubled hearts, however diverse their griefs. The poor people felt that their friend also suffered; they did not precisely know with what, but they forgot their own sorrows in pitying their benefactor. Suffering is the true cement of love. For men to love each other truly, they must have shed tears together.

As yet no influence strictly ecclesiastic had been felt by Francis. Doubtless there was in his heart that leaven of Christian faith which enters one's being without his being aware; but the interior transformation which was going on in him was as yet the fruit of his own intuition. This period was drawing to a close. His thought was soon to find expression, and by that very act to receive the stamp of external circumstances. Christian instruction will give a precise form to ideas of which as yet he has but vague glimpses, but he will find in this form a frame in which his thought will perhaps lose something of its originality and vigor; the new wine will be put into old wine-skins.

By degrees he was becoming calm, was finding in the contemplation of nature joys which up to this time he had sipped but hastily, almost unconsciously, and of which he was now learning to relish the flavor. He drew from them not simply soothing; in his heart he felt new compassions springing into life, and with these the desire to act, to give himself, to cry aloud to these cities perched upon the hill-tops, threatening as warriors who eye one another before the fray, that they should be reconciled and love one another.

Certainly, at this time Francis had no glimpse of what he was some time to become; but these hours are perhaps the most important in the evolution of his thought; it is to them that his life owes that air of liberty, that perfume of the fields which make it as different from the piety of the sacristy as from that of the drawing-room.

About this time he made a pilgrimage to Rome, whether to ask counsel of his friends, whether as a penance imposed by his confessor, or from a mere impulse, no one knows. Perhaps he thought that in a visit to the *Holy Apostles*, as people said then, he should find the answers to all the questions which he was asking himself.

At any rate he went. It is hardly probable that he received from the visit any religious influence, for his biographers relate the pained surprise which he experienced when he saw in Saint Peter's how meagre were the offerings of pilgrims. He wanted to give everything to the prince of the apostles, and emptying his purse he threw its entire contents upon the tomb.

This journey was marked by a more important incident. Many a time when succoring the poor he had asked himself if he himself was able to endure poverty; no one knows the weight of a burden until he has carried it, at least for a moment, upon his own shoulders. He desired to know what it is like to have nothing, and to depend for bread upon the charity or the caprice of the passer by. [13]

There were swarms of beggars crowding the Piazza before the great basilica. He borrowed the rags of one of them, lending him his garment in exchange, and a whole day he stood there, fasting, with outstretched hand. The act was a great victory, the triumph of compassion over natural pride. Returning to Assisi, he doubled his kindnesses to those of whom he had truly the right to call himself the brother. With such sentiments he could not long escape the influence of the Church.

On all the roadsides in the environs of the city there were then, as now, numerous chapels. Very often he must have heard mass in these rustic sanctuaries, alone with the celebrant. Recognizing the tendency of simple natures to bring home to themselves everything that they hear, it is easy to understand his emotion and agitation when the priest, turning toward him, would read the gospel for the day. The Christian ideal was revealed to him, bringing an answer to his secret anxieties. And when, a few moments later, he would plunge into the forest, all his thoughts would be with the poor carpenter of Nazareth, who placed himself in his path, saying to him, even to him, "Follow thou me. "

Nearly two years had passed since the day when he felt the first shock; a life of renunciation appeared to him as the goal of his efforts, but he felt that his spiritual novitiate was not yet ended. He suddenly experienced a bitter assurance of the fact.

He was riding on horseback one day, his mind more than ever possessed with the desire to lead a life of absolute devotion, when at a turn of the road he found himself face to face with a leper. The frightful malady had always inspired in him an invincible repulsion. He could not control a movement of horror, and by instinct he turned his horse in another direction.

If the shock had been severe, the defeat was complete. He reproached himself bitterly. To cherish such fine projects and show himself so cowardly! Was the knight of Christ then going to give up his arms? He retraced his steps and springing from his horse he gave to the astounded sufferer all the money that he had; then kissed his hand as he would have done to a priest. [14] This new victory, as he himself saw, marked an era in his spiritual life. [15]

It is far indeed from hatred of evil to love of good. Those are more numerous than we think who, after severe experience, have renounced what the ancient liturgies call the world, with its pomps and lusts; but the greater number of them have not at the bottom of their hearts the smallest grain of pure love. In vulgar souls disillusion leaves only a frightful egoism.

This victory of Francis had been so sudden that he desired to complete it; a few days later he went to the lazaretto. [16] One can imagine the stupefaction of these wretches at the entrance of the brilliant cavalier. If in our days a visit to the sick in our hospitals is a real event awaited with feverish impatience, what must not have been the appearance of Francis among these poor recluses? One must have seen sufferers thus abandoned, to understand what joy may be given by an affectionate word, sometimes even a simple glance.

Moved and transported, Francis felt his whole being vibrate with unfamiliar sensations. For the first time he heard the unspeakable accents of a gratitude which cannot find words burning enough to express itself, which admires and adores the benefactor almost like an angel from heaven.

FOOTNOTES:

[1]   1 Cel., 3; cf. Bon., 8, and A. SS., p. 563c.

[2]   It is enough to have lived in the country of Naples to know that there is nothing exaggerated in this picture. I am much surprised that intelligent and good men fancy that to change the religious formula of these people would suffice to transform them. What a mistake! To-day, as in the time of Jesus, the important matter is not to adore on Mount Moriah or Mount Zion, but to adore in spirit and in truth.

[3]   1 Cel., 3 and 4.

[4]   3 Soc., 5. In the existing state of the documents it is impossible to know whom this name designates, for at that time it was borne by a number of counts who are only to be distinguished by the names of their castles. The three following are possible: 1. *Gentile comes de Campilio*, who in 1215 paid homage for his property to the commune of Orvieto: *Le antiche cronache di Orvieto, Arch. stor. ital.* , 5th series., 1889, iii., p. 47. 2. *Gentilis comes filius Alberici*, who

with others had made donation of a monastery to the Bishop of Foligno: Confirmatory Bull *In eminenti* of April 10, 1210: Ughelli, *Italia Sacra*, 1, p. 697; Potthast, 3974. 3. *Gentilis comes Manupelli*; whom we find in July, 1200, assuring to Palermo the victory over the troops sent by Innocent III. against Marckwald; Huillard-Bréholles, *Hist. dipl.* , i. p., 46 ff. Cf. Potthast, 1126. *Gesta Innocenti*, Migne, vol. i., xxxii, ff. Cf. Huillard-Bréholles, *loc. cit.* , pages 60, 84, 89, 101. It is wrong to consider that Gentile could here be a mere adjective; the 3 Soc. say *Gentile nomine.*

[5]   1 Cel., 4; 3 Soc., 5.

[6]   3 Soc., 6; 2 Cel., 1, 2; Bon., 8.

[7]   1 Cel., 5; 3 Soc., 5; 2 Cel., 1, 2; Bon., 9.

[8]   3 Soc., 6; Bon., 9; 2 Cel., 1, 2.

[9]   3 Soc., 6; 2 Cel., 1, 2.

[10]   These days are recalled by Celano with a very particular precision. It is very improbable that Francis, usually so reserved as to his personal experience, should have told him about them (2 Cel., 3, 68 and 42, cf. Bon., 144). On the other hand, nothing forbids his having been informed on this matter by Brother Elias. (I strongly suspect the legend which tells of an old man appearing on the day Francis was born and begging permission to take the child in his arms, saying, "To-day, two infants were born—this one, who will be among the best of men, and another, who will be among the worst"—of having been invented by the *zelanti* against Brother Elias. It is evident that such a story is aimed at some one. Whom, if not him who was afterward to appear as the Anti-Francis?) We have sufficient details about the eleven first disciples to know that none of them is here in question. There is nothing surprising in the fact that Elias does not appear in the earliest years of the Order (1209-1212), because after having practised at Assisi his double calling of schoolmaster and carriage-trimmer (*suebat cultras et docebat puerulos psalterium legere*, Salimbene, p. 402) he was *scriptor* at Bologna (Eccl., 13). And from the psychological point of view this hypothesis would admirably explain the

ascendency which Elias was destined always to exercise over his master. Still it remains difficult to understand why Celano did not name Elias here, but the passage, 1 Cel., 6, differs in the different manuscripts (cf. A. SS. and Amoni's edition, p. 14) and may have been retouched after the latter's fall.

Beviglia is a simple farm three-quarters of an hour northwest of Assisi, almost half way to Petrignano. Half an hour from Assisi in the direction of Beviglia is a grotto, which may very well be that of which we are about to speak.

[11]   1 Cel., 6; 2 Cel., 1, 5; 3 Soc., 8, 12; Bon., 10, 11, 12.

[12]   3 Soc., 7; 1 Cel., 7; 2 Cel., 1, 3; 3 Soc., 13.

[13]   3 Soc., 8-10; Bon., 13, 14; 2 Cel., 1, 4.

[14]   To this day in the centre and south of Italy they kiss the hand of priests and monks.

[15]   See the Will. Cf. 3 Soc., 11; 1 Cel., 17; Bon., 11; A. SS., p. 566.

[16]   3 Soc., 11; Bon., 13.

CHAPTER III

THE CHURCH ABOUT 1209

St. Francis was inspired as much as any man may be, but it would be a palpable error to study him apart from his age and from the conditions in which he lived.

We know that he desired and believed his life to be an imitation of Jesus, but what we know about the Christ is in fact so little, that St. Francis's life loses none of its strangeness for that. His conviction that he was but an imitator preserved him from all temptation to pride, and enabled him to proclaim his views with incomparable vigor, without seeming in the least to be preaching himself.

We must therefore neither isolate him from external influences nor show him too dependent on them. During the period of his life at which we are now arrived, 1205-1206, the religious situation of Italy must more than at any other time have influenced his thought and urged him into the path which he finally entered.

The morals of the clergy were as corrupt as ever, rendering any serious reform impossible. If some among the heresies of the time were pure and without reproach, many were trivial and impure. Here and there a few voices were raised in protest, but the prophesyings of Gioacchino di Fiore had no more power than those of St. Hildegarde to put a stop to wickedness. Luke Wadding, the pious Franciscan annalist, begins his chronicle with this appalling picture. The advance in historic research permits us to retouch it somewhat more in detail, but the conclusion remains the same; without Francis of Assisi the Church would perhaps have foundered and the Cathari would have won the day. The *little poor man*, driven away, cast out of doors by the creatures of Innocent III., saved Christianity.

We cannot here make a thorough study of the state of the Church at the beginning of the thirteenth century; it will suffice to trace some of its most prominent features.

The first glance at the secular clergy brings out into startling prominence the ravages of simony; the traffic in ecclesiastical places was carried on with boundless audacity; benefices were put up to the highest bidder, and Innocent III. admitted that fire and sword alone could heal this plague. [1] Prelates who declined to be bought by *propinæ*, fees, were held up as astounding exceptions! [2]

"They are stones for understanding, " it was said of the officers of the Roman *curia*, "wood for justice, fire for wrath, iron for forgiveness; deceitful as foxes, proud as bulls, greedy and insatiate as the minotaur. "[3] The praises showered upon Pope Eugenius III. for rebuffing a priest who, at the beginning of a lawsuit, offered him a golden mark, speak only too plainly as to the morals of Rome in this respect. [4]

The bishops, on their part, found a thousand methods, often most out of keeping with their calling, for extorting money from the simple priests. [5] Violent, quarrelsome, contentious, they were held up to ridicule in popular ballads from one end of Europe to the other. [6] As to the priests, they bent all their powers to accumulate benefices, and secure inheritances from the dying, stooping to the most despicable measures for providing for their bastards. [7]

The monastic orders were hardly more reputable. A great number of these had sprung up in the eleventh and twelfth centuries; their reputation for sanctity soon stimulated the liberality of the faithful, and thus fatally brought about their own decadence. Few communities had shown the discretion of the first monks of the Order of Grammont in the diocese of Limoges. When Stephen de Muret, its founder, began to manifest his sanctity by giving sight to a blind man, his disciples took alarm at the thought of the wealth and notoriety which was likely to come to them from this cause. Pierre of Limoges, who had succeeded Stephen as prior, went at once to his tomb, praying:

> "O servant of God, thou hast shown us the way of poverty, and behold, thou wouldst make us leave the strait and difficult path of salvation, and wouldst set us in the broad road of eternal death. Thou hast preached to us (the virtues of) solitude, and thou art about to change this place into a fair and a market-place. We know well that thou art a saint! Thou hast no need to prove it to us by performing miracles which will destroy our humility. Be not so zealous for thy reputation as to augment it to the injury of our salvation. This is what we ask of thee, expecting it of thy love. If not, we declare unto thee by the obedience which we once owed

to thee, we will unearth thy bones and throw them into the river. "

Stephen obeyed up to the time of his canonization (1189), but from that time forward ambition, avarice, and luxury made such inroads upon the solitude of Grammont that its monks became the byword and scoff of the Christian world. [8]

Pierre of Limoges was not entirely without reason in fearing that his monastery would be transformed into a fair-ground; members of the chapters of most of the cathedrals kept wine-shops literally under their shadows, and certain monasteries did not hesitate to attract custom by jugglers of all kinds and even by courtesans. [9]

To form an idea of the degradation of the greater number of the monks it is not enough to read the oratorical and often exaggerated reproofs of preachers obliged to strike hard in order to produce an effect. We must run through the collection of bulls, where appeals to the court of Rome against assassinations, violations, incests, adulteries, recur on almost every page. It is easy to see that even an Innocent III. might feel himself helpless and tempted to yield to discouragement, in the face of so many ills. [10]

The best spirits were turning toward the Orient, asking themselves if perchance the Greek Church might not suddenly come forward to purify all these abuses, and receive for herself the inheritance of her sister. [11]

The clergy, though no longer respected, still overawed the people through their superstitious terror of their power. Here and there might have been perceived many a forewarning of direful revolts; the roads to Rome were crowded with monks hastening to claim the protection of the Holy See against the people among whom they lived. The Pope would promptly declare an interdict, but it was not to be expected that such a resource would avail forever. [12]

To maintain the privileges of the Church the papacy was often obliged to spread the mantle of its protection over those who deserved it least. Its clients were not always as interesting as the unfortunate Ingelburge. It would be easier to give unreserved admiration to the conduct of Innocent III. if in this matter one could feel certain that his only interest was to maintain the cause of a poor abandoned woman. But it is only too evident that he desired above all to keep up the ecclesiastical immunities. This is very evident in his intervention in favor of Waldemar, Bishop of Schleswig.

Yet we must not assume that all was corrupt in the bosom of the Church; then, as always, the evil made more noise than the good, and the voices of those who desired a reformation aroused only passing interest.

Among the populace there was superstition unimaginable; the pulpit, which ought to have shed abroad some little light, was as yet open only to the bishops, and the few pastors who did not neglect their duty in this regard accomplished very little, being too much absorbed in other duties. It was the birth of the mendicant orders which obliged the entire body of secular clergy to take up the practice of preaching.

Public worship, reduced to liturgical ceremonies, no longer preserved anything which appealed to the intelligence; it was more and more becoming a sort of self-acting magic formula. Once upon this road, the absurd was not far distant. Those who deemed themselves pious told of miracles performed by relics with no need of aid from the moral act of faith.

In one case a parrot, being carried away by a kite, uttered the invocation dear to his mistress, *"Sancte Thoma adjuva me,"* and was miraculously rescued. In another, a merchant of Groningen, having purloined an arm of St. John the Baptist, grew rich as if by enchantment so long as he kept it concealed in his house, but was reduced to beggary so soon as, his secret being discovered, the relic was taken away from him and placed in a church. [13]

These stories, we must observe, do not come from ignorant enthusiasts, hidden away in obscure country places; they are given us by one of the most learned monks of his time, who relates them to a novice by way of forming his mind!

Relics, then, were held to be neither more nor less than talismans. Not alone did they perform miracles upon those who were in no special state of faith or devotion, the more potent among them healed the sick in spite of themselves. A chronicler relates that the body of Saint Martin of Tours had in 887 been secretly transported to some remote hiding place for fear of the Danish invasion. When the time came for bringing it home again, there were in Touraine two impotent men who, thanks to their infirmity, gained large sums by begging. They were thrown into great terror by the tidings that the relics were being brought back: Saint Martin would certainly heal them and take away their means of livelihood. Their fears were only too well founded. They had taken to flight, but being too lame to walk fast they had not yet crossed the frontier of Touraine when the saint arrived and healed them!

Hundreds of similar stories might be collected, statistics might be made up to show, at the accession of Innocent III., the greater number of episcopal thrones occupied by unworthy bishops, the religious houses peopled with idle and debauched monks; but would this give a truly accurate picture of the Church at this epoch? I do not think so. In the first place, we must reckon with the choice spirits, who were without doubt more numerous than is generally supposed. Five righteous men would have saved Sodom; the Almighty did not find them there, but he perhaps might have found them had He Himself made search for them instead of trusting to Lot. The Church of the thirteenth century had them, and it was for their sakes that the whirlwind of heresy did not sweep it away.

But this is not all: the Church of that time offered a noble spectacle of moral grandeur. We must learn to lift our eyes from the wretched state of things which has just been pointed out and fix them on the pontifical throne and recognize the beauty of the struggle there going on: a power wholly spiritual undertaking to command the rulers of the world, as the soul masters the body, and triumphing in the end. It is true that both soldiers and generals of this army were often little better than ruffians, but here again, in order to be just, we must understand the end they aimed at.

In that iron age, when brute force was the only force, the Church, notwithstanding its wounds, offered to the world the spectacle of peasants and laboring men receiving the humble homage of the highest potentates of earth, simply because, seated on the throne of Saint Peter, they represented the moral law. This is why Alighieri and many others before and after him, though they might heap curses on wicked ministers, yet in the depths of their heart were never without an immense compassion and an ardent love for the Church which they never ceased to call their mother.

Still, everybody was not like them, and the vices of the clergy explain the innumerable heresies of that day. All of them had a certain success, from those which were simply the outcry of an outraged conscience, like that of the Waldenses, to the most absurd of them all, like that of Eon de l'Étoile. Some of these movements were for great and sacred causes; but we must not let our sympathies be so moved by the persecutions suffered by heretics as to cloud our judgment. It would have been better had Rome triumphed by gentleness, by education and holiness, but unhappily a soldier may not always choose his weapons, and when life is at stake he seizes the first he finds within his reach. The papacy has not always been reactionary and obscurantist; when it overthrew the Cathari, for example, its victory was that of reason and good sense.

The list of the heresies of the thirteenth century is already long, but it is increasing every day, to the great joy of those erudite ones who are making strenuous efforts to classify everything in that tohu-bohu of mysticism and folly. In that day heresy was very much alive; it was consequently very complex and its powers of transformation infinite. One may indicate its currents, mark its direction, but to go farther is to condemn oneself to utter confusion in this medley of impulsive, passionate, fantastic movements which were born, shot upward, and fell to earth again, at the caprice of a thousand incomprehensible circumstances. In certain counties of England there are at the present day villages having as many as eight and ten places of worship for a few hundreds of inhabitants. Many of these people change their denomination every three or four years, returning to that they first quitted, leaving it again only to enter it anew, and so on as long as they live. Their leaders set the example, throwing themselves enthusiastically into each new movement only to leave it before long. They would all alike find it difficult to give an intelligible reason for these changes. They say that the Spirit guides them, and it would be unfair to disbelieve them, but the historian who should investigate conditions like these would lose his head in the labyrinth unless he made a separate study of each of these Protean movements. They are surely not worth the trouble.

In a somewhat similar condition was a great part of Christendom under Innocent III. ; but while the sects of which I have just spoken move in a very narrow circle of dogmas and ideas, in the thirteenth century every sort of excess followed in rapid succession. Without the slightest pause of transition men passed through the most contradictory systems of belief. Still, a few general characteristics may be observed; in the first place, heresies are no longer metaphysical subtleties as in earlier days; Arius and Priscillian,

Nestorius and Eutychus are dead indeed. In the second place, they no longer arise in the upper and governing class, but proceed especially from the inferior clergy and the common people. The blows which actually threatened the Church of the Middle Ages were struck by obscure laboring men, by the poor and the oppressed, who in their wretchedness and degradation felt that she had failed in her mission.

No sooner was a voice uplifted, preaching austerity and simplicity, than it drew together not the laity only, but members of the clergy as well. Toward the close of the twelfth century we find a certain Pons rousing all Perigord, preaching evangelical poverty before the coming of St. Francis. [14]

Two great currents are apparent: on one side the Cathari, on the other, innumerable sects revolting from the Church by very fidelity to Christianity and the desire to return to the primitive Church.

Among the sects of the second category the close of the twelfth century saw in Italy the rise of the *Poor Men*, who without doubt were a part of the movement of Arnold of Brescia; they denied the efficacy of sacraments administered by unworthy hands. [15]

A true attempt at reform was made by the Waldenses. Their history, although better known, still remains obscure on certain sides; their name, *Poor Men of Lyons*, recalls the former movement, with which they were in close agreement, as also with the Humiliants. All these names involuntarily suggest that by which St. Francis afterward called his Order. The analogy between the inspiration of Peter Waldo and that of St. Francis was so close that one might be tempted to believe the latter a sort of imitation of the former. It would be a mistake: the same causes produced in all quarters the same effects; ideas of reform, of a return to gospel poverty, were in the air, and this helps us to understand how it was that before many years the Franciscan preaching reverberated through the entire world. If at the outset the careers of these two men were alike, their later lives were very different. Waldo, driven into heresy almost in spite of himself, was obliged to accept the consequences of the premises which he himself had laid down; [16] while Francis, remaining the obedient son of the Church, bent all his efforts to develop the inner life in himself and his disciples. It is indeed most likely that through his father Francis had become acquainted with the movement of the *Poor Men of Lyons*. Hence his oft-repeated counsels to his friars of the duty of submission to the clergy. When he went to seek the approbation of Innocent III., it is evident that the prelates with whom he had relations warned him, by the very example of Waldo, of the dangers inherent in his own movement. [17]

The latter had gone to Rome in 1179, accompanied by a few followers, to ask at the same time the approbation of their translation of the Scriptures into the vulgar tongue and the permission to preach. They were granted both requests on condition of gaining for their preaching the authorization of their local clergy. Walter Map ([Cross] 1210), who was charged with their examination, was constrained, while ridiculing their simplicity, to admire their poverty and zeal for the apostolic life. [18] Two or three years later they met a very different reception at Rome, and in 1184 they were anathematized by the Council of Verona. From that day nothing could stop them, even to the forming of a new Church. They multiplied with a rapidity hardly exceeded afterward by the Franciscans. By the end of the twelfth century we find them spread abroad from Hungary to Spain; the first attempts to hunt them down were made in the latter country. Other countries were at first satisfied with treating them as excommunicated persons.

Obliged to hide themselves, reduced to the impossibility of holding their chapters, which ought to have come together once or twice a year, and which, had they done so, might have maintained among them a certain unity of doctrine, the Waldenses rapidly underwent a change according to their environment; some obstinately insisting upon calling themselves good Catholics, others going so far as to preach the overthrow of the hierarchy and the uselessness of sacraments. [19] Hence that multiplicity of differing and even hostile branches which seemed to develop almost hourly.

A common persecution brought them nearer to the Cathari and favored the fusion of their ideas. Their activity was inconceivable. Under pretext of pilgrimages to Rome they were always on the road, simple and insinuating. The methods of travel of that day were peculiarly favorable to the diffusion of ideas. While retailing news to those whose hospitality they received, they would speak of the unhappy state of the Church and the reforms that were needed. Such conversations were a means of apostleship much more efficacious than those of the present day, the book and the newspaper; there is nothing like the *viva vox*[20] for spreading thought.

Many vile stories have been told of the Waldenses; calumny is far too facile a weapon not to tempt an adversary at bay. Thus they have been charged with the same indecent promiscuities of which the early Christians were accused. In reality their true strength was in their virtues, which strongly contrasted with the vices of the clergy.

The most powerful and determined enemies of the Church were the Cathari. Sincere, audacious, often learned and keen in argument, having among them some choice spirits and men of great intellectual powers, they were pre-eminently the heretics of the thirteenth century. Their revolt did not bear upon points of detail and questions of discipline, like that of the early Waldenses; it had a definite doctrinal basis, taking issue with the whole body of Catholic dogma. But, although this heresy flourished in Italy and under the very eyes of St. Francis, there is need only to indicate it briefly. His work may have received many infiltrations from the Waldensian movement, but Catharism was wholly foreign to it.

This is naturally explained by the fact that St. Francis never consented to occupy himself with questions of doctrine. For him faith was not of the intellectual but the moral domain; it is the consecration of the heart. Time spent in dogmatizing appeared to him time lost.

An incident in the life of Brother Egidio well brings out the slight esteem in which theology was held by the early Brothers Minor. One day, in the presence of St. Bonaventura, he cried, perhaps not without a touch of irony, "Alas! what shall we ignorant and simple ones do to merit the favor of God? " "My brother, " replied the famous divine, "you know very well that it suffices to love the Lord. " "Are you very sure of that? " replied Egidio; "do you believe that a simple woman might please Him as well as a master in theology? " Upon the affirmative response of his interlocutor, he ran out into the street and calling to a beggar woman with all his might, "Poor old creature, " he exclaimed, "rejoice, for if you love God, you may have a higher place in the kingdom of heaven than Brother Bonaventura! "[21]

The Cathari, then, had no direct influence upon St. Francis, [22] but nothing could better prove the disturbance of thought at this epoch than that resurrection of Manicheism. To what a depth of lassitude and folly must religious Italy have fallen for this mixture of Buddhism, Mazdeism, and gnosticism to have taken such hold upon it! The Catharist doctrine rested upon the antagonism of two principles, one bad, the other good. The first had created matter; the second, the soul, which, for generation after generation passes from one body to another until it achieves salvation. Matter is the cause and the seat of evil; all contact with it constitutes a blemish, [23] consequently the Cathari renounced marriage and property and advocated suicide. All this was mixed up with most complicated cosmogonical myths.

Their adherents were divided into two classes—the pure or perfect, and the believers, who were proselytes in the second degree, and whose obligations were very simple. The adepts, properly so called, were initiated by the ceremony of the *consolamentum* or imposition of hands, which induced the descent upon them of the Consoling Spirit. Among them were enthusiasts who after this ceremony placed themselves in *endura*—that is to say, they starved themselves to death in order not to descend from this state of grace.

In Languedoc, where this sect went by the name of Albigenses, they had an organization which embraced all Central Europe, and everywhere supported flourishing schools attended by the children of the nobles. In Italy they were hardly less powerful; Concorrezo, near Monza in Lombardy, and Bagnolo, gave their names to two congregations slightly different from those in Languedoc. [24]

But it was especially from Milan[25] that they spread abroad over all the Peninsula, making proselytes even in the most remote districts of Calabria. The state of anarchy prevailing in the country was very favorable to them. The papacy was too much occupied in baffling the spasmodic efforts of the Hohenstaufen, to put the necessary perseverance and system into its struggles against heresy. Thus the new ideas were preached under the very shadow of the Lateran; in 1209, Otho IV., coming to Rome to be crowned, found there a school in which Manicheism was publicly taught. [26]

With all his energy Innocent III. had not been able to check this evil in the States of the Church. The case of Viterbo tells much of the difficulty of repressing it; in March, 1199, the pope wrote to the clergy and people of this town to recall to their minds, and at the same time to increase, the penalties pronounced against heresy. For all that, the Patarini had the majority in 1205, and succeeded in naming one of themselves consul. [27]

The wrath of the pontiff at this event was unbounded; he fulminated a bull menacing the city with fire and sword, and commanding the neighboring towns to throw themselves upon her if within a fortnight she had not given satisfaction. [28] It was all in vain: the Patarini were dealt with only as a matter of form; it needed the presence of the pope himself to assure the execution of his orders and obtain the demolition of the houses of the heretics and their abettors (autumn of 1207). [29]

But stifled at one point the revolt burst out at a hundred others; at this moment it was triumphant on all sides; at Ferrara, Verona, Rimini, Florence, Prato, Faenza, Treviso, Piacenza. The clergy were expelled from this last town, which remained more than three years without a priest. [30]

Viterbo is twenty leagues from Assisi, Orvieto only ten, and disturbances in this town were equally grave. A noble Roman, Pietro Parentio, the deputy of the Holy See in this place, endeavored to exterminate the Patarini. He was assassinated. [31]

But Francis needed not to go even so far as Orvieto to become acquainted with heretics. In Assisi the same things were going on as in the neighboring cities. In 1203 this town had elected for podestà a heretic named Giraldo di Gilberto, and in spite of warnings from Rome had persisted in keeping him at the head of affairs until the expiration of his term of office (1204). Innocent III., who had not yet been obliged to use vigor with Viterbo, resorted to persuasion and despatched to Umbria the Cardinal Leo di Santa Croce, who will appear more than once in this history. [32] The successor of Giraldo and fifty of the principal citizens made the *amende honorable* and swore fidelity to the Church.

It is easy to perceive in what a state of ferment Italy was during these early years of the thirteenth century. The moral discredit of the clergy must have been deep indeed for souls to have turned toward Manicheism with such ardor.

Italy may well be grateful to St. Francis; it was as much infected with Catharism as Languedoc, and it was he who wrought its purification. He did not pause to demonstrate by syllogisms or theological theses the vanity of the Catharist doctrines; but soaring as on wings to the religious life, he suddenly made a new ideal to shine out before the eyes of his contemporaries, an ideal before which all these fantastic sects vanished as birds of the night take flight at the first rays of the sun.

A great part of St. Francis's power came to him thus through his systematic avoidance of polemics. The latter is always more or less a form of spiritual pride; it only deepens the chasm which it undertakes to fill up. Truth needs not to be proved; it is its own witness.

The only weapon which he would use against the wicked was the holiness of a life so full of love as to enlighten and revive those about him, and compel them to love. [33] The disappearance of Catharism in Italy, without an upheaval, and above all without the Inquisition, is thus an indirect result of the Franciscan movement, and not the least important among them. [34]

At the voice of the Umbrian reformer Italy roused herself, recovered her good sense and fine temper; she cast out those doctrines of pessimism and death, as a robust organism casts out morbid substances.

I have already endeavored to show the strong analogy between the initial efforts of Francis and those of the Poor Men of Lyons. His thought ripened in an atmosphere thoroughly saturated with their ideas; unconsciously to himself they entered into his being.

The prophecies of the Calabrian abbot exerted upon him an influence quite as difficult to appreciate, but no less profound.

Standing on the confines of Italy and as it were at the threshold of Greece, Gioacchino di Fiore[35] was the last link in a chain of monastic prophets, who during nearly four hundred years succeeded one another in the monasteries and hermitages of Southern Italy. The most famous among them had been St. Nilo, a sort of untamed John the Baptist, living in desert places, but suddenly emerging from them when his duties of maintaining the right called him elsewhere. We see him on one occasion appearing in Rome itself, to announce to pope and emperor the unloosing of the divine wrath. [36]

Scattered in the Alpine solitudes of Basilicata these Calabrian hermits were continually obliged to retreat higher and higher into the mountain fastnesses to escape the populace, who, pursued by pirates, were taking refuge in these mountains. They thus passed their lives between heaven and earth, with two seas for their horizon. Disquieted by fear of the corsairs, and by the war-cries whose echoes reached even to them, they turned their thoughts toward the future. The ages of great terror are also the ages of great hope; it is to the captivity of Babylon that we owe, with the second part of Isaiah, those pictures of the future which have not yet ceased to charm the soul of man; Nero's persecutions gave us the Apocalypse of St. John, and the paroxysms of the twelfth century the eternal Gospel.

Converted after a life of dissipation, Gioacchino di Fiore travelled extensively in the Holy Land, Greece, and Constantinople. Returning to Italy he began, though a layman, to preach in the outskirts of Rende and Cosenza. Later on he joined the Cistercians of Cortale, near Catanzaro, and there took vows. Shortly after elected abbot of the monastery in spite of refusal and even flight, he was seized after a few years with the nostalgia of solitude, and sought from Pope Lucius III. a discharge from his functions (1181), that he might consecrate all his time to the works which he had in mind. The pope granted his request, and even permitted him to go wherever he might deem best in the interest of his work. Then began for Gioacchino a life of wandering from convent to convent, which carried him even as far as Lombardy, to Verona, where we find him with Pope Urban III.

When he returned to the south, a group of disciples gathered around him to hear his explanations of the most obscure passages of the Bible. Whether he would or no he was obliged to receive them, to talk with them, to give them a rule, and, finally, to instal them in the very heart of the Sila, the Black Forest of Italy, [37] over against the highest peak, in gorges where the silence is interrupted only by the murmurs of the Arvo and the Neto, which have their source not far from there. The new Athos received the name of Fiore (flower), transparent symbol of the hopes of its founder. [38] It was there that he put the finishing touch to writings which, after fifty years of neglect, were to become the starting-point of all heresies, and the aliment of all souls burdened with the salvation of Christendom. The men of the first half of the thirteenth century, too much occupied with other things, did not perceive that the spiritual streams at which they were drinking descended from the snowy mountain-tops of Calabria.

It is always thus with mystical influences. There is in them something vague, tenuous, and penetrating which escapes an exact estimation. Let two choice souls meet, and they will find it a difficult thing to analyze and name the impressions which each has received from the other. It is so with an epoch; it is not always those who speak to her the oftenest and loudest whom she best understands; nor even those at whose feet she sits, a faithful pupil, day after day. Sometimes, while on the way to her accustomed masters, she suddenly meets a stranger; she barely catches a few words of what he says; she knows not whence he comes nor whither he goes; she never sees him again, but those few words of his go on surging in the depths of her soul, agitating and disquieting her.

Thus it was for a long while with Gioacchino di Fiore. His teachings, scattered here and there by enthusiastic disciples, were germinating silently in many hearts. [39] Giving back hope to men, they restored to them strength also. To think is already to act; alone under the shadow of the hoary pines which surrounded his cell, the cenobite of Fiore was laboring for the renovation of the Church with as much vigor as the reformers who came after him.

He was, however, far from attaining the height of the prophets of Israel; instead of soaring like them to the very heavens, he always remained riveted to the text, upon which he commented in the allegorical method, and whence by this method he brought out the most fantastic improbabilities. A few pages of his books would wear out the most patient reader, but in these fields, burnt over by theological arguments more drying than the winds of the desert, fields where one at first perceives only stones and thistles, one comes at last to the charming oasis, with repose and dreams in its shade.

The exegesis of Gioacchino di Fiore in fact led up to a sort of philosophy of history; its grand lines were calculated to make a striking appeal to the imagination. The life of humanity is divided into three periods: in the first, under the reign of the Father, men lived under the rigor of the law; in the second, reigned over by the Son, men live under the rule of grace; in the third, the Spirit shall reign and men shall live in the plenitude of love. The first is the period of servile obedience; the second, that of filial obedience; the third, that of liberty. In the first, men lived in fear; in the second, they rest in faith; in the third, they shall burn with love. The first saw the shining of the stars; the second sees the whitening of the dawn; the third will behold the glory of the day. The first produced nettles, the second gives roses, the third will be the age of lilies.

If now we consider that in the thought of Gioacchino the third period, the Age of the Spirit, was about to open, we shall understand with what enthusiasm men hailed the words which restored joy to hearts still disturbed with millenarian fears.

It is evident that St. Francis knew these radiant hopes. Who knows even that it was not the Calabrian Seer who awoke his heart to its transports of love? If this be so, Gioacchino was not merely his precursor; he was his true spiritual father. However this may be, St. Francis found in Gioacchino's thought many of the elements which, unconsciously to himself, were to become the foundation of his institute.

The noble disdain which he shows for all men of learning, and which he sought to inculcate upon his Order, was for Gioacchino one of the characteristics of the new era. "The truth which remains hidden to the wise, " he says, "is revealed to babes; dialectics closes that which is open, obscures that which is clear; it is the mother of useless talk, of rivalries and blasphemy. Learning does not edify, and it may destroy, as is proved by the scribes of the Church, swollen with pride and arrogance, who by dint of reasoning fall into heresy. "[40]

We have seen that the return to evangelical simplicity had become a necessity; all the heretical sects were on this point in accord with pious Catholics, but no one spoke in a manner so Franciscan as Gioacchino di Fiore. Not only did he make voluntary poverty one of the characteristics of the age of lilies, but he speaks of it in his pages with so profound, so living an emotion, that St. Francis could do little more than repeat his words. The ideal monk whom he describes, [41] whose only property is a lyre, is a true Franciscan before the letter, him of whom the *Poverello* of Assisi always dreamed.

The feeling for nature also bursts forth in him with incomparable vigor. One day he was preaching in a chapel which was plunged in almost total darkness, the sky being quite overcast with clouds. Suddenly the clouds broke away, the sun shone, the church was flooded with light. Gioacchino paused, saluted the sun, intoned the *Veni Creator*, and led his congregation out to gaze upon the landscape.

It would be by no means surprising if toward 1205 Francis should have heard of this prophet, toward whom so many hearts were turning, this anchorite who, gazing up into heaven, spoke with Jesus as a friend talks with his friend, yet knew also how to come down to console men and warm the faces of the dying at his own breast.

At the other end of Europe, in the heart of Germany, the same causes had produced the same effects. From the excess of the people's sufferings and the despair of religious souls was being born a movement of apocalyptic mysticism which seemed to have secret communication with that which was rousing the Peninsula. They had the same views of the future, the same anxious expectation of new cataclysms, joined with a prospect of a reviving of the Church.

"Cry with a loud voice, " said her guardian angel to St. Elizabeth of Schonau ([Cross] 1164), "cry to all nations: Woe! for the whole world has become darkness. The Lord's vine has withered, there is no one to tend it. The Lord has sent laborers, but they have all been found idle. The head of the Church is ill and her members are dead.... Shepherds of my Church, you are sleeping, but I shall awaken you! Kings of the earth, the cry of your iniquity has risen even to me. "[42]

"Divine justice, " said St. Hildegarde ([Cross] 1178), "shall have its hour; the last of the seven epochs symbolized by the seven days of creation has arrived, the judgments of God are about to be accomplished; the empire and the papacy, sunk into impiety, shall crumble away together.... But upon their ruins shall appear a new nation of God, a nation of prophets illuminated from on high, living in poverty and solitude. Then the divine mysteries shall be revealed, and the saying of Joel shall be fulfilled; the Holy Spirit shall shed abroad upon the people the dew of his prophecies, of his wisdom and holiness; the heathen, the Jews, the worldly and the unbelieving shall be converted together, spring-time and peace shall reign over a regenerated world, and the angels will return with confidence to dwell among men. "

These hopes were not wholly confounded. In the evening of his days the prophet of Fiore was able, like a new Simeon, to utter his *Nunc dimittis*, and for a few years Christendom could turn in amazement to Assisi as to a new Bethlehem.

FOOTNOTES:

[1]   Bull of June 8, 1198, *Quamvis*. Migne, i., col. 220; Potthast, 265.

[2]   For example, Pierre, Cardinal of St. Chryzogone and former Bishop of Meaux, who in a single election refused the dazzling offer of five hundred silver marks. Alexander III., Migne's edition, *epist.* 395.

[3]   *Fasciculus rerum expetend. et fugiend.* , t. ii., 7, pp. 254, 255 (Brown, 1690).

[4]   John of Salisbury, *Policrat.* Migne, v. 15.

[5]   Among their sources of revenue we find the right of *collagium*, by payment of which clerics acquired the right to keep a concubine. Pierre le Chantre, *Verb. abbrev.* , 24.

[6]   Vide *Carmina Burana*, Breslau, 8vo, 1883; Political Songs of England, published by Th. Wright, London, 8vo, 1893; *Poésies populaires latines du moyen âge*, du Méril, Paris, 1847. See also Raynouard, *Lexique roman*, i., 446, 451, 464, the fine poems of the troubadour Pierre Cardinal, contemporary of St. Francis, upon the woes of the Church, and Dante, *Inferno*, xix. If one would gain an idea of what the bishop of a small city in those days cost his flock, he has only to read the bull of February 12, 1219, *Justis petentium*, addressed by Honorius III. to the Bishop of Terni, and including the contract by which the inhabitants of that city settled the revenues of the episcopal see. Horoy, t. iii., col. 114, or the *Bullarium romanum*, t. iii., p. 348, Turin.

[7]   *Conosco sacerdoti che fanno gli usura per formare un patrimonio da lasciare ai loro spurii; altri che tengono osteria coll' insegna del collare e vendono vino...* Salimbene, Cantarelli, Parma, 1882, 2 vols., 8vo, ii., p. 307.

[8]   Vide *Brevis historia Prior. Grandimont. — Stephani Tornacensis.* Epist. 115, 152, 153, 156, 162; Honorius III., Horoy's edition, lib. i., 280, 284, 286-288; ii., 12, 130, 136, 383-387.

[9]   Guérard, *Cartulaire de N. D. de Paris*, t. i., p. cxi; t. ii., p. 406. Cf. Honorius III., Bull *Inter statuta* of July 25, 1223, Horoy, t. iv., col. 401. See also canon 23 of the Council of Beziers, 1233; Guibert de Gemblours, *epist.* 5 and 6 (Migne); Honorius III., lib. ix., 32, 81; ii., 193; iv., 10; iii., 253 and 258; iv., 33, 27, 70, 144; v., 56, 291, 420, 430; vi., 214, 132, 139, 204; vii., 127; ix., 51.

[10]   Vide Bull *Postquam vocante Domino* of July 11, 1206. Potthast 2840.

[11]   V. *Annales Stadenses* [*Monumenta Germaniæ historica, Scriptorum*, t. 16], *ad ann. 1237*. Among the comprehensive pictures of the situation of the Church in the thirteenth century, there is none more interesting than that left us by the Cardinal Jacques de Vitry in his *Historia occidentalis: Libri duo quorum prior Orientalis, alter Occidentalis historiæ nomine inscribitur Duaci*, 1597, 16mo. pp. 259-480.

[12]   V. Honorius III., Horoy's edition, lib. i., ep. 109, 125, 135, 206, 273; ii., 128, 164; iv., 120, etc.

[13]   *Dialogus miraculorum* of Cesar of Heisterbach [Strange's edition, Cologne, 1851, 2 vols., 8vo], t. ii., pp. 255 and 125. This book, with the Golden Legend of Giacomo di Varaggio, gives the best idea of the state of religious thought in the thirteenth century.

[14]   *Recueil des historiens de France.* Bouquet, t. xii., pp. 550, 551.

[15]   Bonacorsi: *Vitæ hæreticorum* [d'Achery, *Spicilegium*, t. i., p. 215] Cf. Lucius III., epist. 171, Migne.

[16]   Vide Bernard Gui, *Practica inquisitionis*, Douai edition, 4to, Paris, 1886 p. 244 ff., and especially the Vatican MS., 2548, folio 71.

[17]   A chronicle of St. Francis's time makes this same comparison: Burchard, Abbot of Urspurg ([Cross] 1226) [*Burchardi et Cuonradi chronicon. Monum. Germ. hist. Script.* , t. 23], has left us an account of the approbation of Francis by the Pope, all the more precious for being that of a contemporary. *Loc. cit.* , p. 376.

[18]   *De nugis Curialium*, Dist. 1, cap. 31, p. 64, Wright's edition.
Cf. *Chronique de Laon*, Bouquet xiii., p. 680.

[19]   See, for example, the letter of the Italian branch of the Poor
Men of Lyons [*Pauperos Lombardi*] to their brethren of
Germany, there called Leonistes. In it they show the points
in which they are not in harmony with the French
Waldenses. Published by Preger: *Abhandlungen der K. bayer.
Akademie der Wiss. Hist. Cl.* , t. xiii., 1875, p. 19 ff.

[20]   These continual journeyings sometimes gained for them the
name of *Passagieni*, as in the south of France the preachers of
certain sects are to-day called *Courriers*. The term, however,
specially designates a Judaizing sect who returned to the
literal observation of the Mosaic law: Döllinger, *Beiträge*, t. ii.,
pp. 327 and 375. They should therefore be identified with the
Circonsisi of the constitution of Frederic II. (Huillard-
Bréholles, t. v., p. 280). See especially the fine monograph of
M. C. Molinier: *Mémoires de l'Académie de Toulouse*, 1888.

[21]   A. SS., Aprilis, t. iii., p. 238d.

[22]   I would say that between the inspiration of Francis and the
Catharian doctrines there is an irreconcilable opposition; but
it would not be difficult to find acts and words of his which
recall the contempt for matter of the Cathari; for example,
his way of treating his body. Some of his counsels to the
friars: *Unusquisque habet in potestate sua inimicum suum
videlicit corpus, per quod peccat.* Assisi MS. 338, folio 20b.
Conform. 138, b. 2. —*Cum majorem inimicum corpore non
habeam.* 2 Cel., 3, 63. These are momentary but inevitable
obscurations, moments of forgetfulness, of discouragement,
when a man is not himself, and repeats mechanically what
he hears said around him. The real St. Francis is, on the
contrary, the lover of nature, he who sees in the whole
creation the work of divine goodness, the radiance of the
eternal beauty, he who, in the Canticle of the Creatures, sees
in the body not the Enemy but a brother: *Cæpit hilariter loqui
ad corpus; Gaude, frater corpus.* 2 Cel., 3, 137.

[23]   *Quodam die, dicta fabrissa dixit ipsi testi prægnanti, quod rogaret
Deum, ut liberaret eam a Dæmone, quem habebat in ventre...*

Gulielmus dixit quod ita magnum peccatum erat jacere cum uxore sua quam cum concubina. Döllinger, *loc. cit.* , pp. 24, 35.

[24]   Those of the *Concorrezenses* and *Bajolenses*. In Italy *Cathari* becomes *Gazzari*; for that matter, each country had its special appellatives; one of the most general in the north was that of the *Bulgari*, which marks the oriental origin of the sect, whence the slang term Boulgres and its derivatives (vide Matthew Paris, ann. 1238). Cf. Schmit, *Histoire des Cathares*, 8vo, 2 vols, Paris, 1849.

[25]   The most current name in Italy was that of the *Patarini*, given them no doubt from their inhabiting the quarter of second-hand dealers in Milan: *la contrada dei Patari*, found in many cities. *Patari!* is still the cry of the ragpickers in the small towns of Provence. In the thirteenth century Patarino and Catharo were synonyms. But before that the term Patarini had an entirely different sense. See the very remarkable study of M. Felice Tocco on this subject in his *Eresia net medio evo*, 12mo, Florence, 1884.

[26]   Cesar von Heisterbach, *Dial. mirac.* , t. i., p. 309, Strange's edition.

[27]   *Innocentii opera*, Migne, t. i., col. 537; t. ii., 654.

[28]   *Computruistis in peccatis sicut jumenta in stercore suo ut fumus ac fimus putrefactionis vestræ jam fere circumadjacentes regionis infecerit, ac ipsum Dominum ut credimus ad nauseam provocaverit. Loc. cit.* , col. 654. Cf. 673; Potthast, 2532, 2539.

[29]   *Gesta Innocentii*, Migne, t. i., col. clxii. Cf. *epist.* viii., 85 and 105.

[30]   Campi, *Historia Ecclesiastica di Piacenza*, parte ii., p. 92 ff. Cf. *Innoc., epist.* ix., 131, 166-169; x., 54, 64, 222.

[31]   A. SS., Maii, t. v., p. 87.

[32]   Bull of June 6, 1205, Potthast, 2237; Migne, vii., 83. This Cardinal Leo (of the presbyterial title of Holy Cross of Jerusalem) was one most valued by Innocent III. To him and Ugolini, the future Gregory IX., he at this epoch confided the

most delicate missions (for example, in 1209, they were named legates to Otho IV.). This embassy shows in what importance the pope held the affairs of Assisi, though it was a very small city.

[33] Not once do we find him fighting heretics. The early Dominicans, on the contrary, are incessantly occupied with arguing. See 2 Cel., 3, 46.

[34] It need not be said that I do not assert that no trace of it is to be found after the ministry of St. Francis, but it was no longer a force, and no longer endangered the very existence of the Church.

[35] This strange personality will charm historians and philosophers for a long while to come. I know nothing more learned or more luminous than M. Felice Tocco's fine study in his *Eresia nel medio evo*, Florence, 1884, 1 vol., 12mo, pp. 261-409.

[36] A. SS., Sept., t. vii., p. 283 ff.

[37] A. SS., Maii, vii. ; Vincent de Beauvais, *Speculum historiale, lib.* 29, *cap.* 40. La Sila is a wooded mountain, situated eastward from Cosenza, which the peasants call *Monte Nero*. The summits are nearly 2,000 metres above the sea.

[38] Toward 1195. Gioacchino died there, March 30, 1202.

[39] A whole apochryphal literature has blossomed out around Gioacchino; certain hypercritics have tried to prove that he never wrote anything. These are exaggerations. Three large works are certainly authentic: *The Agreement of the Old and New Testaments*, *The Commentary on the Apocalypse*, and *The Psaltery of Ten Strings*, published in Venice, the first in 1517, the two others in 1527. His prophecies were so well known, even in his lifetime, that an English Cistercian, Rudolph, Abbot of Coggeshall ([Cross] 1228), coming to Rome in 1195, sought a conference with him and has left us an interesting account of it. Martène, *Amplissima Collectio*, t. v., p. 839.

[40] *Comm. in apoc.* , folio 78, b. 2.

[41]   *Qui vere monachus est nihil reputat esse suum nisi citharam:*
        Apoc., ib., folio 183. a. 2.

[42]   E. Roth, *Die Visionen der heiligen Elisabeth von Schönau*: Brünn,
        1884, pp. 115-117.

CHAPTER IV

STRUGGLES AND TRIUMPH

Spring of 1206-February 24, 1209

The biographies of St. Francis have preserved to us an incident which shows how great was the religious ferment even in the little city of Assisi. A stranger was seen to go up and down the streets saying to every one he met, "Peace and welfare! " (*Pax et bonum.*)[1] He thus expressed in his own way the disquietude of those hearts which could neither resign themselves to perpetual warfare nor to the disappearance of faith and love; artless echo, vibrating in response to the hopes and fears that were shaking all Europe!

"Vox clamantis in deserto! " it will be said. No, for every heart-cry leaves its trace even when it seems to be uttered in empty air, and that of the Unknown of Assisi may have contributed in some measure to Francis's definitive call.

Since his abrupt return from Spoleto, life in his father's house had become daily more difficult. Bernardone's self-love had received from his son's discomfiture such a wound as with commonplace men is never healed. He might provide, without counting it, money to be swallowed up in dissipation, that so his son might stand on an equal footing with the young nobles; he could never resign himself to see him giving with lavish hands to every beggar in the streets.

Francis, continually plunged in reverie and spending his days in lonely wanderings in the fields, was no longer of the least use to his father. Months passed, and the distance between the two men grew ever wider; and the gentle and loving Pica could do nothing to prevent a rupture which from this time appeared to be inevitable. Francis soon came to feel only one desire, to flee from the abode where, in the place of love, he found only reproaches, upbraidings, anguish.

The faithful confidant of his earlier struggles had been obliged to leave him, and this absolute solitude weighed heavily upon his warm and loving heart. He did what he could to escape from it, but no one understood him. The ideas which he was beginning timidly to express evoked from those to whom he spoke only mocking smiles or the head-shakings which men sure that they are right bestow upon him who is marching straight to madness. He even went to open his mind to the bishop, but the latter understood no more than others his vague, incoherent plans, filled with ideas impossible to realize and possibly subversive. [2] It was thus that in spite of himself Francis was led to ask nothing of men, but to raise himself by prayer to intuitive knowledge of the divine will. The doors of houses and of hearts were alike closing upon him, but the interior voice was about to speak out with irresistible force and make itself forever obeyed.

Among the numerous chapels in the suburbs of Assisi there was one which he particularly loved, that of St. Damian. It was reached by a few minutes' walk over a stony path, almost trackless, under olive trees, amid odors of lavender and rosemary. Standing on the top of a hillock, the entire plain is visible from it, through a curtain of cypresses and pines which seem to be trying to hide the humble hermitage and set up an ideal barrier between it and the world.

Served by a poor priest who had scarcely the wherewithal for necessary food, the sanctuary was falling into ruin. There was nothing in the interior but a simple altar of masonry, and by way of reredos one of those byzantine crucifixes still so numerous in Italy, where through the work of the artists of the time has come down to us something of the terrors which agitated the twelfth century. In general the Crucified One, frightfully lacerated, with bleeding wounds, appears to seek to inspire only grief and compunction; that of St. Damian, on the contrary, has an expression of inexpressible calm and gentleness; instead of closing the eyelids in eternal surrender to the weight of suffering, it looks down in self-forgetfulness, and its pure, clear gaze says, not "I suffer, " but, "Come unto me. "[3]

One day Francis was praying before the poor altar: "Great and glorious God, and thou, Lord Jesus, I pray ye, shed abroad your light in the darkness of my mind.... Be found of me, Lord, so that in all things I may act only in accordance with thy holy will. "[4]

Thus he prayed in his heart, and behold, little by little it seemed to him that his gaze could not detach itself from that of Jesus; he felt something marvellous taking place in and around him. The sacred victim took on life, and in the outward silence he was aware of a voice which softly stole into the very depths of his heart, speaking to him an ineffable language. Jesus accepted his oblation. Jesus desired his labor, his life, all his being, and the heart of the poor solitary was already bathed in light and strength. [5]

This vision marks the final triumph of Francis. His union with Christ is consummated; from this time he can exclaim with the mystics of every age, "My beloved is mine, and I am his. "

But instead of giving himself up to transports of contemplation he at once asks himself how he may repay to Jesus love for love, in what action he shall employ this life which he has just offered to him. He had not long to seek. We have seen that the chapel where his spiritual espousals had just been celebrated was threatened with ruin. He believed that to repair it was the work assigned to him.

From that day the remembrance of the Crucified One, the thought of the love which had triumphed in immolating itself, became the very centre of his religious life and as it were the soul of his soul. For the first time, no doubt, Francis had been brought into direct, personal, intimate contact with Jesus Christ; from belief he had passed to faith, to that living faith which a distinguished thinker has so well defined: "To believe is to look; it is a serious, attentive, and prolonged look; a look more simple than that of observation, a look which looks, and nothing more; artless, infantine, it has all the soul in it, it is a look of the soul and not the mind, a look which does not seek to analyze its object, but which receives it as a whole into the soul through the eyes. " In these words Vinet unconsciously has marvellously characterized the religious temperament of St. Francis.

This look of love cast upon the crucifix, this mysterious colloquy with the compassionate victim, was never more to cease. At St. Damian, St. Francis's piety took on its outward appearance and its originality. From this time his soul bears the stigmata, and as his biographers have said in words untranslatable, *Ab illa hora vulneratum et liquefactum est cor ejus ed memoriam Dominicæ passionis.* [6]

From that time his way was plain before him. Coming out from the sanctuary, he gave the priest all the money he had about him to keep a lamp always burning, and with ravished heart he returned to Assisi. He had decided to quit his father's house and undertake the restoration of the chapel, after having broken the last ties that bound him to the past. A horse and a few pieces of gayly colored stuffs were all that he possessed. Arrived at home he made a packet of the stuffs, and mounting his horse he set out for Foligno. This city was then as now the most important commercial town of all the region. Its fairs attracted the whole population of Umbria and the Sabines. Bernardone had often taken his son there, [7] and Francis speedily succeeded in selling all he had brought. He even parted with his horse, and full of joy set out upon the road to Assisi. [8]

This act was to him most important; it marked his final rupture with the past; from this day on his life was to be in all points the opposite of what it had been; the Crucified had given himself to him; he on his side had given himself to the Crucified without reserve or return. To uncertainty, disquietude of soul, anguish, longing for an unknown good, bitter regrets, had succeeded a delicious calm, the ecstasy of the lost child who finds his mother, and forgets in a moment the torture of his heart.

From Foligno he returned direct to St. Damian; it was not necessary to pass through the city, and he was in haste to put his projects into execution.

The poor priest was surprised enough when Francis handed over to him the whole product of his sale. He doubtless thought that a passing quarrel had occurred between Bernardone and his son, and for greater prudence refused the gift; but Francis so insisted upon remaining with him that he finally gave him leave to do so. As to the money, now become useless, Francis cast it as a worthless object upon a window-seat in the chapel. [9]

Meanwhile Bernardone, disturbed by his son's failure to return, sought for him in all quarters, and was not long in learning of his presence at St. Damian. In a moment he perceived that Francis was lost to him. Resolved to try every means, he collected a few neighbors, and furious with rage hastened to the hermitage to snatch him away, if need were, by main force.

But Francis knew his father's violence. When he heard the shouts of those who were in pursuit of him he felt his courage fail and hurried to a hiding-place which he had prepared for himself for precisely such an emergency. Bernardone, no doubt ill seconded in the search, ransacked every corner, but was obliged at last to return to Assisi without his son. Francis remained hidden for long days, weeping and groaning, imploring God to show him the path he ought to follow. Notwithstanding his fears he had an infinite joy at heart, and at no price would he have turned back. [10]

This seclusion could not last long. Francis perceived this, and told himself that for a newly made knight of the Christ he was cutting a very pitiful figure. Arming himself, therefore, with courage, he went one day to the city to present himself before his father and make known to him his resolution.

It is easy to imagine the changes wrought in his appearance by these few weeks of seclusion, passed much of them in mental anguish. When he appeared, pale, cadaverous, his clothes in tatters, upon what is now the *Piazza Nuova*, where hundreds of children play all day long, he was greeted with a great shout, *"Pazzo, Pazzo!"* (A madman! a madman!) *"Un pazzo ne fa cento"* (One madman makes a hundred more), says the proverb, but one must have seen the delirious excitement of the street children of Italy at the sight of a madman to gain an idea how true it is. The moment the magic cry resounds they rush into the street with frightful din, and while their parents look on from the windows, they surround the unhappy sufferer with wild dances mingled with songs, shouts, and savage howls. They throw stones at him, fling mud upon him, blindfold him; if he flies into a rage, they double their insults; if he weeps or begs for pity, they repeat his cries and mimic his sobs and supplications without respite and without mercy. [11]

Bernardone soon heard the clamor which filled the narrow streets, and went out to enjoy the show; suddenly he thought he heard his own name and that of his son, and bursting with shame and rage he perceived Francis. Throwing himself upon him, as if to throttle him, he dragged him into the house and cast him, half dead, into a dark closet. Threats, bad usage, everything was brought to bear to change the prisoner's resolves, but all in vain. At last, wearied out and desperate, he left him in peace, though not without having firmly bound him. [12]

A few days after he was obliged to be absent for a short time. Pica, his wife, understood only too well his grievances against Francis, but feeling that violence would be of no avail she resolved to try gentleness. It was all in vain. Then, not being able longer to see him thus tortured, she set him at liberty.

He returned straight to St. Damian. [13]

Bernardone, on his return, went so far as to strike Pica in punishment for her weakness. Then, unable to tolerate the thought of seeing his son the jest of the whole city, he tried to procure his expulsion from the territory of Assisi. Going to St. Damian he summoned him to leave the country. This time Francis did not try to hide. Boldly presenting himself before his father, he declared to him that not only would nothing induce him to abandon his resolutions, but that, moreover, having become the servant of Christ, he had no longer to receive orders from him. [14] As Bernardone launched out into invective, reproaching him with the enormous sums which he had cost him, Francis showed him by a gesture the money which he had brought back from the sale at Foligno lying on the window-ledge. The father greedily seized it and went away, resolving to appeal to the magistrates.

The consuls summoned Francis to appear before them, but he replied simply that as servant of the Church he did not come under their jurisdiction. Glad of this response, which relieved them of a delicate dilemma, they referred the complainant to the diocesan authorities. [15]

The matter took on another aspect before the ecclesiastical tribunal; it was idle to dream of asking the bishop to pronounce a sentence of banishment, since it was his part to preserve the liberty of the clerics. Bernardone could do no more than disinherit his son, or at least induce him of his own accord to renounce all claim upon his inheritance. This was not difficult.

When called upon to appear before the episcopal tribunal[16] Francis experienced a lively joy; his mystical espousals to the Crucified One were now to receive a sort of official consecration. To this Jesus, whom he had so often blasphemed and betrayed by word and conduct, he would now be able with equal publicity to promise obedience and fidelity.

It is easy to imagine the sensation which all this caused in a small town like Assisi, and the crowd that on the appointed day pressed toward the Piazza of Santa Maria Maggiore, where the bishop pronounced sentence. [17] Every one held Francis to be assuredly mad, but they anticipated with relish the shame and rage of Bernardone, whom every one detested, and whose pride was so well punished by all this.

The bishop first set forth the case, and advised Francis to simply give up all his property. To the great surprise of the crowd the latter, instead of replying, retired to a room in the bishop's palace, and immediately reappeared absolutely naked, holding in his hand the packet into which he had rolled his clothes; these he laid down before the bishop with the little money that he still had kept, saying: "Listen, all of you, and understand it well; until this time I have called Pietro Bernardone my father, but now I desire to serve God. This is why I return to him this money, for which he has given himself so much trouble, as well as my clothing, and all that I have had from him, for from henceforth I desire to say nothing else than *'Our Father, who art in heaven.'*"

A long murmur arose from the crowd when Bernardone was seen to gather up and carry off the clothing without the least evidence of compassion, while the bishop was fain to take under his mantle the poor Francis, who was trembling with emotion and cold. [18]

The scene of the judgment hall made an immense impression; the ardor, simplicity, and indignation of Francis had been so profound and sincere that scoffers were disconcerted. On that day he won for himself a secret sympathy in many souls. The populace loves such abrupt conversions, or those which it considers such. Francis once again forced himself upon the attention of his fellow-citizens with a power all the greater for the contrast between his former and his new life.

There are pious folk whose modesty is shocked by the nudity of Francis; but Italy is not Germany nor England, and the thirteenth century would have been astonished indeed at the prudery of the Bollandists. The incident is simply a new manifestation of Francis's character, with its ingenuousness, its exaggerations, its longing to establish a complete harmony, a literal correspondence, between words and actions.

After emotions such as he had just experienced he felt the need of being alone, of realizing his joy, of singing the liberty he had finally achieved along all the lines where once he had so deeply suffered, so ardently struggled. He would not, therefore, return immediately to St. Damian. Leaving the city by the nearest gate, he plunged into the deserted paths which climb the sides of Mount Subasio.

It was the early spring. Here and there were still great drifts of snow, but under the ardor of the March sun winter seemed to own itself vanquished. In the midst of this mysterious and bewildering harmony the heart of Francis felt a delicious thrill, all his being was calmed and uplifted, the soul of things caressed him gently and shed upon him peace. An unwonted happiness swept over him; he made the forest to resound with his hymns of praise.

Men utter in song emotions too sweet or too deep to be expressed in ordinary language, but unworded music is in this respect superior to song, it is above all things the language of the ineffable. Song gains almost the same value when the words are only there as a support for the voice. The great beauty of the psalms and hymns of the Church lies in the fact that being sung in an unknown tongue they make no appeal to the intelligence; they say nothing, but they express everything with marvellous modulations like a celestial accompaniment, which follows the believer's emotions from the most agonizing struggles to the most unspeakable ecstasies.

So Francis went on his way, deeply inhaling the odors of spring, singing at the top of his voice one of those songs of French chivalry which he had learned in days gone by.

The forest in which he was walking was the usual retreat of such people of Assisi and its environs as had any reason for hiding. Some ruffians, aroused by his voice, suddenly fell upon him. "Who are you? " they asked. "I am the herald of the great King, " he answered "but what is that to you? "

His only garment was an old mantle which the bishop's gardener had lent him at his master's request. They stripped it from him, and throwing him into a ditch full of snow, "There is your place, poor herald of God, " they said.

The robbers gone, he shook off the snow which covered him, and after may efforts succeeded in extricating himself from the ditch. Stiff with cold, with no other covering than a worn-out shirt, he none the less resumed his singing, happy to suffer and thus to accustom himself the better to understand the words of the Crucified One. [19]

Not far away was a monastery. He entered and offered his services. In those solitudes, peopled often by such undesirable neighbors, people were suspicious. The monks permitted him to make himself useful in the kitchen, but they gave him nothing to cover himself with and hardly anything to eat. There was nothing for it but to go away; he directed his steps toward Gubbio, where he knew that he should find a friend. Perhaps this was he who had been his confidant on his return from Spoleto. However this may be, he received from him a tunic, and a few days after set out to return to his dear St. Damian. [20]

He did not, however, go directly thither; before beginning to restore the little sanctuary, he desired to see again his friends, the lepers, to promise them that he would love them even better than in the past.

Since his first visit to the leper-house the brilliant cavalier had become a poor beggar; he came with empty hands but with heart overflowing with tenderness and compassion. Taking up his abode in the midst of these afflicted ones he lavished upon them the most touching care, washing and wiping their sores, all the more gentle and radiant as their sores were more repulsive. [21] The neglected sufferer is as much blinded by love of him who comes to visit him as the child by its love for its mother. He believes him to be all powerful; at his approach the most painful sufferings are eased or disappear.

This love inspired by the sympathy of an affectionate heart may become so deep as to appear at times supernatural; the dying have been known to recover consciousness in order to look for the last time into the face, not of some member of the family, but of the friend who has tried to be the sunshine of their last days. The ties of pure love are stronger than the bonds of flesh and blood. Francis had many a time sweet experience of this; from the time of his arrival at the leper-house he felt that if he had lost his life he was about to find it again.

Encouraged by his sojourn among the lepers, he returned to St. Damian and went to work, filled with joy and ardor, his heart as much in the sunshine as the Umbrian plain in this beautiful month of May. After having fashioned for himself a hermit's dress, he began to go into the squares and open places of the city. There having sung a few hymns, he would announce to those who gathered around him his project of restoring the chapel. "Those who will give me one stone, " he would add with a smile, "shall have a reward; those who give me two shall have two rewards, and those who give me three shall have three. "

Many deemed him mad, but others were deeply moved by the remembrance of the past. As for Francis, deaf to mockery, he spared himself no labor, carrying upon his shoulders, so ill-fitted for severe toil, the stones which were given him. [22]

During this time the poor priest of St. Damian felt his heart swelling with love for this companion who had at first caused him such embarrassment, and he strove to prepare for him his favorite dishes. Francis soon perceived it. His delicacy took alarm at the expense which he caused his friend, and, thanking him, he resolved to beg his food from door to door.

It was not an easy task. The first time, when at the end of his round he glanced at the broken food in his wallet, he felt his courage fail him. But the thought of being so soon unfaithful to the spouse to whom he had plighted his faith made his blood run cold with shame and gave him strength to eat ravenously. [23]

Each hour, so to speak, brought to him a new struggle. One day he was going through the town begging for oil for the lamps of St. Damian, when he arrived at a house where a banquet was going on; the greater number of his former companions were there, singing and dancing. At the sound of those well-known voices he felt as if he could not enter; he even turned away, but very soon, filled with confusion by his own cowardice, he returned quickly upon his steps, made his way into the banquet-hall, and after confessing his shame, put so much earnestness and fire into his request that every one desired to co-operate in this pious work. [24]

His bitterest trial however was his father's anger, which remained as violent as ever. Although he had renounced Francis, Bernardone's pride suffered none the less at seeing his mode of life, and whenever he met his son he overwhelmed him with reproaches and maledictions. The tender heart of Francis was so wrung with sorrow that he resorted to a sort of stratagem for charming away the spell of the paternal imprecations. "Come with me, " he said to a beggar; "be to me as a father, and I will give you a part of the alms which I receive. When you see Bernardone curse me, if I say, 'Bless me, my father, ' you must sign me with the cross and bless me in his stead. "[25] His brother was prominent in the front rank of those who harassed him with their mockeries. One winter morning they met in a church; Angelo leaned over to a friend who was with him, saying: "Go, ask

Francis to sell you a farthing's worth of his sweat. " "No, " replied the latter, who overheard. "I shall sell it much dearer to my God. "

In the spring of 1208 he finished the restoration of St. Damian; he had been aided by all people of good will, setting the example of work and above all of joy, cheering everybody by his songs and his projects for the future. He spoke with such enthusiasm and contagious warmth of the transformation of his dear chapel, of the grace which God would accord to those who should come there to pray, that later on it was believed that he had spoken of Clara and her holy maidens who were to retire to this place four years later. [26]

This success soon inspired him with the idea of repairing the other sanctuaries in the suburbs of Assisi. Those which had struck him by their state of decay were St. Peter and Santa Maria, of the *Portiuncula*, called also Santa Maria degli Angeli. The former is not otherwise mentioned in his biographies. [27] As to the second, it was to become the true cradle of the Franciscan movement.

This chapel, still standing at the present day after escaping revolutions and earthquakes, is a true Bethel, one of those rare spots in the world on which rests the mystic ladder which joins heaven to earth; there were dreamed some of the noblest dreams which have soothed the pains of humanity. It is not to Assisi in its marvellous basilica that one must go to divine and comprehend St. Francis; he must turn his steps to Santa Maria degli Angeli at the hours when the stated prayers cease, at the moment when the evening shadows lengthen, when all the fripperies of worship disappear in the obscurity, when all the nation seems to collect itself to listen to the chime of the distant church bells. Doubtless it was Francis's plan to settle there as a hermit. He dreamed of passing his life there in meditation and silence, keeping up the little church and from time to time inviting a priest there to say mass. Nothing as yet suggested to him that he was in the end to become a religious founder. One of the most interesting aspects of his life is in fact the continual development revealing itself in him; he is of the small number to whom to live is to be active, and to be active to make progress. There is hardly anyone, except St. Paul, in whom is found to the same degree the devouring need of being always something more, always something better, and it is so beautiful in both of them only because it is absolutely instinctive.

When he began to restore the Portiuncula his projects hardly went beyond a very narrow horizon; he was preparing himself for a life of penitence rather than a life of activity. But these works once finished it was impossible that this somewhat selfish and passive manner of achieving his own salvation should satisfy him long. At the memory of the appearance of the Crucified One his heart would swell with overpowering emotions, and he would melt into tears without knowing whether they were of admiration, pity, or desire. [28]

When the repairs were finished meditation occupied the greater part of his days. A Benedictine of the Abbey of Mont Subasio[29] came from time to time to say mass at Santa Maria; these were the bright hours of St. Francis's life. One can imagine with what pious care he prepared himself and with what faith he listened to the divine teachings.

One day, it was probably February 24, 1209, the festival of St. Matthias, mass was being celebrated at the Portiuncula. [30] When the priest turned toward him to read the words of Jesus, Francis felt himself overpowered with a profound agitation. He no longer saw the priest; it was Jesus, the Crucified One of St. Damian, who was speaking: "Wherever ye go, preach, saying, 'The kingdom of heaven is at hand. Heal the sick, cleanse the lepers, cast out devils. Freely ye have received, freely give. Provide neither silver nor gold nor brass in your purses, neither scrip nor two coats, nor shoes nor staff, for the laborer is worthy of his meat.'"

These words burst upon him like a revelation, like the answer of Heaven to his sighs and anxieties.

"This is what I want, " he cried, "this is what I was seeking; from this day forth I shall set myself with all my strength to put it in practice. " Immediately throwing aside his stick, his scrip, his purse, his shoes, he determined immediately to obey, observing to the letter the precepts of the apostolic life.

It is quite possible that some allegorizing tendencies have had some influence upon this narrative. [31] The long struggle through which Francis passed before becoming the apostle of the new times assuredly came to a crisis in the scene at Portiuncula; but we have already seen how slow was the interior travail which prepared for it.

The revelation of Francis was in his heart; the sacred fire which he was to communicate to the souls of others came from within his own, but the best causes need a standard. Before the shabby altar of the Portiuncula he had perceived the banner of poverty, sacrifice, and love, he would carry it to the assault of every fortress of sin; under its shadow, a true knight of Christ, he would marshal all the valiant warriors of a spiritual strife.

FOOTNOTES:

[1]   3 Soc., 26.

[2]   3 Soc., 10.

[3]   This crucifix is preserved in the sacristy of Santa Chiara, whither the sisters carried it when they left St. Damian.

[4]   *Opuscula B. Francisci, Oratio I.*

[5]   3 Soc., 13; 2 Cel., 1, 6; Bon., 12; 15; 16.

[6]   3 Soc., 14.

[7]   This incident is found in the narrative of 1 Cel., 8: *Ibi ex more venditis.*

[8]   1 Cel., 8; 3 Soc., 16; Bon. 16. Foligno is a three hours' walk from Assisi.

[9]   1 Cel., 9; 3 Soc., 16; Bon., 6. Cf. A. SS., p. 567.

[10]   1 Cel., 10; 3 Soc., 16; Bon., 17, A. SS. ; p. 568.

[11]   1 Cel., 11.

[12]   1 Cel., 12; 3 Soc., 17; Bon., 18.

[13]   1 Cel., 13; 3 Soc., 18.

[14]   1 Cel., 13. It is possible that at this epoch he had received the lesser order, and that thus he might be subject to the jurisdiction of the Church.

[15]   3 Soc., 18 and 19; 1 Cel., 14; Bon., 19.

[16]   From 1204 until after the death of St. Francis the episcopal throne of Assisi was occupied by Guido II. Vide Cristofano, 1, 169 ff.

[17]   *Piazza di Santa Maria Maggiore o del vescovado.* Everything has remained pretty nearly in the same state as in the thirteenth century.

[18]   1 Cel., 15; 3 Soc., 20; Bon., 20.

[19]   3 Soc., 16; Bon., 21.

[20]   1 Cel., 16; Bon., 21. The curious will read with interest an article by M. Mezzatinti upon the journey to Gubbio entitled *S. Francesco e Frederico Spadalunga da Gubbio.* [Miscellanea, t. v., pp. 76-78.] This Spadalunga da Gubbio was well able to give a garment to Francis, but it is very possible that the gift was made much later and that this solemn date in the saint's life has been fixed by an optical illusion, almost inevitable because of the identity of the fact with the name of the locality.

[21]   1 Cel., 17; Bon., 11; 13; 21; 22; 3 Soc., 11; A. SS., p. 575.

[22]   1 Cel., 18; 3 Soc., 21; Bon., 23.

[23]   3 Soc., 22; 2 Cel., 1, 9.

[24]   3 Soc., 24; 2 Cel., 8; *Spec. ,* 24.

[25]   3 Soc., 23; 2 Cel., 7.

[26]   3 Soc., 24; *Testament de Claire,* Wadding, *ann. 1253* v.

[27]   Cel., 21; Bon., 24.

[28]   3 Soc., 14; 2 Cel., i., 6.

[29]   Portiuncula was a dependence of this abbey.

[30]   This is the date adopted by the Bollandists, because the ancient missals mark the pericope, Matt. x., for the gospel of this day. This entails no difficulty and in any case it cannot be very far distant from the truth. A. SS., p. 574.

[31]   See in particular Bon., 25 and 26. Cf. A. SS., p. 577d.

CHAPTER V

FIRST YEAR OF APOSTOLATE

Spring of 1209-Summer of 1210

The very next morning Francis went up to Assisi and began to preach. His words were simple, but they came so straight from the heart that all who heard him were touched.

It is not easy to hear and apply to one's self the exhortations of preachers who, aloft in the pulpit, seem to be carrying out a mere formality; it is just as difficult to escape from the appeals of a layman who walks at our side. The amazing multitude of Protestant sects is due in a great degree to this superiority of lay preaching over clerical. The most brilliant orators of the Christian pulpit are bad converters; their eloquent appeals may captivate the imagination and lead a few men of the world to the foot of the altar, but these results are not more brilliant than ephemeral. But let a peasant or a workingman speak to those whom he meets a few simple words going directly to the conscience, and the man is always impressed, often won.

Thus the words of Francis seemed to his hearers like a flaming sword penetrating to the very depths of their conscience. His first attempts were the simplest possible; in general they were merely a few words addressed to men whom he knew well enough to recognize their weak points and strike at them with the holy boldness of love. His person, his example, were themselves a sermon, and he spoke only of that which he had himself experienced, proclaiming repentance, the shortness of life, a future retribution, the necessity of arriving at gospel perfection. [1] It is not easy to realize how many waiting souls there are in this world. The greater number of men pass through life with souls asleep. They are like virgins of the sanctuary who sometimes feel a vague agitation; their hearts throb with an infinitely sweet and subtile thrill, but their eyelids droop; again they feel the damp cold of the cloister creeping over them; the delicious but baneful dream vanishes; and this is all they ever know of that love which is stronger than death.

It is thus with many men for all that belongs to the higher life. Sometimes, alone in the wide plain at the hour of twilight, they fix their eyes on the fading lights of the horizon, and on the evening breeze comes to them another breath, more distant, fainter, and almost heavenly, awaking in them a nostalgia for the world beyond and for holiness. But the darkness falls, they must go back to their homes; they shake off their reverie; and it often happens that to the very end of life this is their only glimpse of the Divine; a few sighs, a few thrills, a few inarticulate murmurs—this sums up all our efforts to attain to the sovereign good.

Yet the instinct for love and for the divine is only slumbering. At the sight of beauty love always awakes; at the appeal of holiness the divine witness within us at once responds; and so we see, streaming from all points of the horizon to gather around those who preach in the name of the inward voice, long processions of souls athirst for the ideal. The human heart so naturally yearns to offer itself up, that we have only to meet along our pathway some one who, doubting neither himself nor us, demands it without reserve, and we yield it to him at once. Reason may understand a partial gift, a transient devotion; the heart knows only the entire sacrifice, and like the lover to his beloved, it says to its vanquisher, "Thine alone and forever. "

That which has caused the miserable failure of all the efforts of natural religion is that its founders have not had the courage to lay hold upon the hearts of men, consenting to no partition. They have not understood the imperious desire for immolation which lies in the depths of every soul, and souls have taken their revenge in not heeding these too lukewarm lovers.

Francis had given himself up too completely not to claim from others an absolute self-renunciation. In the two years and more since he had quitted the world, the reality and depth of his conversion had shone out in the sight of all; to the scoffings of the early days had gradually succeeded in the minds of many a feeling closely akin to admiration.

This feeling inevitably provokes imitation. A man of Assisi, hardly mentioned by the biographers, had attached himself to Francis. He was one of those simple-hearted men who find life beautiful enough so long as they can be with him who has kindled the divine spark[2] in their hearts. His arrival at Portiuncula gave Francis a suggestion; from that time he dreamed of the possibility of bringing together a few companions with whom he could carry on his apostolic mission in the neighborhood.

At Assisi he had often enjoyed the hospitality of a rich and prominent man named Bernardo di Quintavalle, [3] who took him to sleep in his own chamber; it is easy to see how such an intimacy would favor confidential outpourings. When in the silence of the early night an ardent and enthusiastic soul pours out to you its disappointments, wounds, dreams, hopes, faith, it is difficult indeed not to be carried along, especially when the apostle has a secret ally in your soul, and unconsciously meets your most secret aspirations.

One day Bernardo begged Francis to pass the following night with him, at the same time giving him to understand that he was about to make a grave resolution upon which he desired to consult him. The joy of Francis was great indeed as he divined his intentions. They passed the night without thinking of sleep; it was a long communion of souls. Bernardo had decided to distribute his goods to the poor and cast in his lot with Francis. The latter desired his friend to pass through a sort of initiation, pointing out to him that what he himself practised, what he preached, was not his own invention, but that Jesus himself had expressly ordained it in his word.

At early dawn they bent their steps to the St. Nicholas Church, accompanied by another neophyte named Pietro, and there, after praying and hearing mass, Francis opened the Gospels that lay on the altar and read to his companions the portion which had decided his own vocation: the words of Jesus sending forth his disciples on their mission.

"Brethren, " he added, "this is our life and our Rule, and that of all who may join us. Go then and do as you have heard. "[4]

The persistence with which the Three Companions relate that Francis consulted the book three times in honor of the Trinity, and that it opened of its own accord at the verses describing the apostolic life, leads to the belief that these passages became the Rule of the new association, if not that very day at least very soon afterward.

> If thou wilt be perfect, go, sell that thou hast, and give to the poor, and thou shalt have treasure in heaven, and come and follow me.

> Jesus having called to him the Twelve, gave them power and authority over all devils and to cure diseases. And he sent them to preach the kingdom of God and to heal the sick.

And he said unto them, Take nothing for your journey, neither staves, nor scrip, neither bread, neither money; neither have two coats apiece. And whatsoever house ye enter into, there abide, and thence depart. And whosoever will not receive you, when ye go out of that city shake off the very dust from your feet for a testimony against them. And they departed and went through the towns, preaching the gospel and healing everywhere.

Then said Jesus unto his disciples, If any man will come after me, let him deny himself, and take up his cross and follow me. For whosoever will save his life shall lose it, and whosoever will lose his life for my sake shall find it. For what is a man profited if he shall gain the whole world and lose his own soul? [5]

At first these verses were hardly more than the official Rule of the Order; the true Rule was Francis himself; but they had the great merit of being short, absolute, of promising perfection, and of being taken from the Gospel.

Bernardo immediately set to work to distribute his fortune among the poor. Full of joy, his friend was looking on at this act, which had drawn together a crowd, when a priest named Sylvester, who had formerly sold him some stones for the repairs of St. Damian, seeing so much money given away to everyone who applied for it, drew near and said:

"Brother, you did not pay me very well for the stones which you bought of me. "

Francis had too thoroughly killed every germ of avarice in himself not to be moved to indignation by hearing a priest speak thus. "Here, " he said, holding out to him a double handful of coins which he took from Bernardo's robe, "here; are you sufficiently paid now? "

"Quite so, " replied Sylvester, somewhat abashed by the murmurs of the bystanders. [6]

This picture, in which the characters stand out so strongly, must have taken strong hold upon the memory of the bystanders: the Italians only thoroughly understand things which they make a picture of. It taught them, better than all Francis's preachings, what manner of men these new friars would be.

The distribution finished, they went at once to Portiuncula, where Bernardo and Pietro built for themselves cabins of boughs, and made themselves tunics like that of Francis. They did not differ much from the garment worn by the peasants, and were of that brown, with its infinite variety of shades, which the Italians call beast color. One finds similar garments to-day among the shepherds of the most remote parts of the Apennines.

A week later, Thursday, April 23, 1209, [7] a new disciple of the name of Egidio presented himself before Francis. Of a gentle and submissive nature, he was of those who need to lean on someone, but who, the needed support having been found and tested, lift themselves sometimes even above it. The pure soul of brother Egidio, supported by that of Francis, came to enjoy the intoxicating delights of contemplation with an unheard-of ardor. [8]

Here we must be on our guard against forcing the authorities, and asking of them more than they can give. Later, when the Order was definitely constituted and its convents organized, men fancied that the past had been like the present, and this error still weighs upon the picture of the origins of the Franciscan movement. The first brothers lived as did the poor people among whom they so willingly moved; Portiuncula was their favorite church, but it would be a mistake to suppose that they sojourned there for any long periods. It was their place of meeting, nothing more. When they set forth they simply knew that they should meet again in the neighborhood of the modest chapel. Their life was that of the Umbrian beggars of the present day, going here and there as fancy dictated, sleeping in hay-lofts, in leper hospitals, or under the porch of some church. So little had they any fixed domicile that Egidio, having decided to join them, was at considerable trouble to learn where to find Francis, and accidentally meeting him in the neighborhood of Rivo-Torto[9] he saw in the fact a providential leading.

They went up and down the country, joyfully sowing their seed. It was the beginning of summer, the time when everybody in Umbria is out of doors mowing or turning the grass. The customs of the country have changed but little. Walking in the end of May in the fields about Florence, Perugia, or Rieti, one still sees, at nightfall, the bagpipers entering the fields as the mowers seat themselves upon the hay-cocks for their evening meal; they play a few pieces, and when the train of haymakers returns to the village, followed by the harvest-laden carts, it is they who lead the procession, rending the air with their sharpest strains.

The joyous Penitents who loved to call themselves *Joculatores Domini*, God's *jongleurs*, no doubt often did the same. [10] They did even better, for not willing to be a charge to anyone, they passed a part of the day in aiding the peasants in their field work. [11] The inhabitants of these districts are for the most part kindly and sedate; the friars soon gained their confidence by relating to them first their history and then their hopes. They worked and ate together; field-hands and friars often slept in the same barn, and when with the morrow's dawn the friars went on their way, the hearts of those they left behind had been touched. They were not yet converted, but they knew that not far away, over toward Assisi, were living men who had renounced all worldly goods, and who, consumed with zeal, were going up and down preaching penitence and peace.

Their reception was very different in the cities. If the peasant of Central Italy is mild and kindly the townsfolk are on a first acquaintance scoffing and ill disposed. We shall shortly see the friars who went to Florence the butt of all sorts of persecutions.

Only a few weeks had passed since Francis began to preach, and already his words and acts were sounding an irresistible appeal in the depths of many a heart. We have arrived at the most unique and interesting period in the history of the Franciscans. These first months are for their institution what the first days of spring are for nature, days when the almond-tree blossoms, bearing witness to the mysterious labor going on in the womb of the earth, and heralding the flowers that will suddenly enamel the fields. At the sight of these men—bare footed, scantily clothed, without money, and yet so happy—men's minds were much divided. Some held them to be mad, others admired them, finding them widely different from the vagrant monks, [12] that plague of Christendom.

Sometimes, however, the friars found success not responding to their efforts, the conversion of souls not taking form with enough rapidity and vigor. To encourage them, Francis would then confide to them his visions and his hopes. "I saw a multitude of men coming toward us, asking that they might receive the habit of our holy religion, and lo, the sound of their footsteps still echoes in my ears. I saw them coming from every direction, filling all the roads. "

Whatever the biographies may say, Francis was far from foreseeing the sorrows that were to follow this rapid increase of his Order. The maiden leaning with trembling rapture on her lover's arm no more dreams of the pangs of motherhood than he thought of the dregs he must drain after quaffing joyfully the generous wine of the chalice. [13]

Every prosperous movement provokes opposition by the very fact of its prosperity. The herbs of the field have their own language for cursing the longer-lived plants that smother them out; one can hardly live without arousing jealousy; in vain the new fraternity showed itself humble, it could not escape this law.

When the brethren went up to Assisi to beg from door to door, many refused to give to them, reproaching them with desiring to live on the goods of others after having squandered their own. Many a time they had barely enough not to starve to death. It would even seem that the clergy were not entirely without part in this opposition. The Bishop of Assisi said to Francis one day: "Your way of living without owning anything seems to me very harsh and difficult. " "My lord, " replied he, "if we possessed property we should have need of arms for its defence, for it is the source of quarrels and lawsuits, and the love of God and of one's neighbor usually finds many obstacles therein; this is why we do not desire temporal goods. "[14]

The argument was unanswerable, but Guido began to rue the encouragement which he had formerly offered the son of Bernardone. He was very nearly in the situation and consequently in the state of mind of the Anglican bishops when they saw the organizing of the Salvation Army. It was not exactly hostility, but a distrust which was all the deeper for hardly daring to show itself. The only counsel which the bishop could give Francis was to come into the ranks of the clergy, or, if asceticism attracted him, to join some already existing monastic order. [15]

If the bishop's perplexities were great, those of Francis were hardly less so. He was too acute not to foresee the conflict that threatened to break out between the friars and the clergy. He saw that the enemies of the priests praised him and his companions beyond measure simply to set off their poverty against the avarice and wealth of the ecclesiastics, yet he felt himself urged on from within to continue his work, and could well have exclaimed with the apostle, *"Woe is me if I preach not the gospel! "* On the other hand, the families of the Penitents could not forgive them for having distributed their goods among the poor, and attacks came from this direction with all the bitter language and the deep hatred natural to disappointed heirs. From this point of view the brotherhood appeared as a menace to families, and many parents trembled lest their sons should join it. Whether the friars would or no, they were an unending subject of interest to the whole city. Evil rumors, plentifully spread abroad against them, simply defeated themselves; flying from mouth to mouth they speedily found contradictors who had no difficulty in showing their absurdity. All this indirectly served their cause and gained to their side those hearts, more numerous than is generally believed, who find the defence of the persecuted a necessity.

As to the clergy, they could not but feel a profound distrust of these lay converters, who, though they aroused the hatred of some interested persons, awakened in more pious souls first astonishment and then admiration. Suddenly to see men without title or diploma succeed brilliantly in the mission which has been officially confided to ourselves, and in which we have made pitiful shipwreck, is cruel torture. Have we not seen generals who preferred to lose a battle rather than gain it with the aid of guerrillas?

This covert opposition has left no characteristic traces in the biographies of St. Francis. It is not to be wondered at; Thomas of Celano, even if he had had information of this matter, would have been wanting in tact to make use of it. The clergy, for that matter, possess a thousand means of working upon public opinion without ceasing to show a religious interest in those whom they detest.

But the more St. Francis shall find himself in contradiction with the clergy of his time, the more he will believe himself the obedient son of the Church. Confounding the gospel with the teaching of the Church, he will for a good while border upon heresy, but without ever falling into it. Happy simplicity, thanks to which he had never to take the attitude of revolt!

It was five years since, a convalescent leaning upon his staff, he had felt himself taken possession of by a loathing of material pleasures. From that time every one of his days had been marked by a step in advance.

It was again the spring-time. Perfectly happy, he felt himself more and more impelled to bring others to share his happiness and to proclaim in the four corners of the world how he had attained it. He resolved, therefore, to undertake a new mission. A few days were spent in preparing for it. The Three Companions have preserved for us the directions which he gave to his disciples:

"Let us consider that God in his goodness has not called us merely for our own salvation, but also for that of many men, that we may go through all the world exhorting men, more by our example than by our words, to repent of their sins and bear the commandments in mind. Be not fearful on the ground that we appear little and ignorant, but simply and without disquietude preach repentance. Have faith in God, who has overcome the world, that his Spirit will speak in you and by you, exhorting men to be converted and keep his commandments.

"You will find men full of faith, gentleness, and goodness, who will receive you and your words with joy; but you will find others, and in greater numbers, faithless, proud, blasphemers, who will speak evil of you, resisting you and your words. Be resolute, then, to endure everything with patience and humility. "

Hearing this, the brethren began to be agitated. St. Francis said to them: "Have no fear, for very soon many nobles and learned men will come to you; they will be with you preaching to kings and princes and to a multitude of peoples. Many will be converted to the Lord, all over the world, who will multiply and increase his family. "

After he had thus spoken he blessed them, saying to each one the word which was in the future to be his supreme consolation:

"My brother, commit yourself to God with all your cares, and he will care for you. "

Then the men of God departed, faithfully observing his instructions, and when they found a church or a cross they bowed in adoration, saying with devotion, "We adore thee, O Christ, and we bless thee here and in all churches in the whole world, for by thy holy cross thou hast ransomed the world. " In fact they believed that they had found a holy place wherever they found a church or a cross.

Some listened willingly, others scoffed, the greater number overwhelmed them with questions. "Whence come you? " "Of what order are you? " And they, though sometimes it was wearisome to answer, said simply, "We are penitents, natives of the city of Assisi. "[16]

This freshness and poetry will not be found in the later missions. Here the river is still itself, and if it knows toward what sea it is hastening, it knows nothing of the streams, more or less turbid, which shall disturb its limpidity, nor the dykes and the straightenings to which it will have to submit.

A long account by the Three Companions gives us a picture from life of these first essays at preaching:

Many men took the friars for knaves or madmen and refused to receive them into their houses for fear of being robbed. So in many places, after having undergone all sorts of bad usage, they could find no other refuge for the night than the porticos of churches or houses. There were at that time two brethren who went to Florence. They begged all through the city but could find no shelter. Coming to a house which had a portico and under the portico a bench, they said to one another, "We shall be very comfortable here for the night. " As the mistress of the house refused to let them enter, they humbly asked her permission to sleep upon the bench.

She was about to grant them permission when her husband appeared. "Why have you permitted these lewd fellows to stay under our portico? " he asked. The woman replied that she had refused to receive them into the house, but had given them permission to sleep under the portico where there was nothing for them to steal but the bench.

The cold was very sharp; but taking them for thieves no one gave them any covering.

As for them, after having enjoyed on their bench no more sleep than was necessary, warmed only by divine warmth, and having for covering only their Lady Poverty, in the early dawn they went to the church to hear mass.

The lady went also on her part, and seeing the friars devoutly praying she said to herself: "If these men were rascals and thieves as my husband said, they would not remain thus in prayer. " And while she was making these reflections behold a man of the name of Guido was giving alms to the poor in the church. Coming to the friars he would have given a piece of money to them as to the others, but they refused his money and would not receive it. "Why, " he asked, "since you are poor, will you not accept like the others? " "It is true that we are poor, " replied Brother Bernardo, "but poverty does not weigh upon us as upon other poor people; for by the grace of God, whose will we are accomplishing, we have voluntarily become poor. "

Much amazed, he asked them if they had ever had anything, and learned that they had possessed much, but that for the love of God they had given everything away.... The lady, seeing that the friars had refused the alms, drew near to them and said that she would gladly receive them into her house if they would be pleased to lodge there. "May the Lord recompense to you your good will, " replied the friars, humbly.

But Guido, learning that they had not been able to find a shelter, took them to his own house, saying, "Here is a refuge prepared for you by the Lord; remain in it as long as you desire. "

As for them, they gave thanks to God and spent several days with him, preaching the fear of the Lord by word and example, so that in the end he made large distributions to the poor.

Well treated by him, they were despised by others. Many men, great and small, attacked and insulted them, sometimes going so far as to tear off their clothing; but though despoiled of their only tunic, they would not ask for its restitution. If, moved to pity, men gave back to them what they had taken away, they accepted it cheerfully.

There were those who threw mud upon them, others who put dice into their hands and invited them to play, and others clutching them by the cowl made them drag them along thus. But seeing that the friars were always full of joy in the midst of their tribulations, that they neither received nor carried money, and that by their love for one another they made themselves known as true disciples of the Lord, many of them felt themselves reproved in their hearts and came asking pardon for the offences which they had committed. They, pardoning them with all their heart, said, "The Lord forgive you, " and gave them pious counsels for the salvation of their souls.

A translation can but imperfectly give all the repressed emotion, the candid simplicity, the modest joy, the fervent love which breathe in the faulty Latin of the Three Companions. Yet these scattered friars sighed after the home-coming and the long conversations with their spiritual father in the tranquil forests of the suburbs of Assisi. Friendship among men, when it overpasses a certain limit, has something deep, high, ideal, infinitely sweet, to which no other friendship attains. There was no woman in the Upper Chamber when, on the last evening of his life, Jesus communed with his disciples and invited the world to the eternal marriage supper.

Francis, above all, was impatient to see his young family once more. They all arrived at Portiuncula almost at the same time, having already, before reaching it, forgotten the torments they had endured, thinking only of the joy of the meeting. [17]

FOOTNOTES:

[1]   1 Cel., 23; 3 Soc., 25 and 26; Bon., 27. Cf. *Auct. Vit. Sec. ap.* , A. SS., p. 579.

[2]   1 Cel., 24. We must correct the Bollandist text: *Inter quos quidam de Assisio puer ac simplicem animum gerens,* by: *quidam de Assisio pium ac simplicem,* etc. The period at which we have arrived is very clear as a whole: the picture which the Three Companions give us is true with a truth which forces conviction at first sight; but neither they nor Celano are giving an official report. Later on men desired to know precisely in what order the early disciples came, and they tortured the texts to find an answer. The same course was

followed with regard to the first missionary journeys. But on both sides they came up against impossibilities and contradictions. What does it matter whether there were two, three, or four missions before the papal approbation? Of what consequence are the names of those early disciples who are entirely secondary in the history of the Franciscan movement? All these things took place with much more simplicity and spontaneity than is generally supposed. There is a wide difference between the plan of a house drawn up by an architect and a view of the same house painted by an artist. The second, though abounding in inexactitudes, gives a more just notion of the reality than the plan. The same is true of the Franciscan biographies.

[3]   1 Cel., 24. Bernard de Besse is the first to call him B. di Quintavalle: *De laudibus,* fo. 95 h. ; cf. upon him Mark of Lisbon, t. i., second part, pp. 68-70; *Conform.* , 47; *Fior.* , 1, 2, 3, 4, 5, 6, 28; 3 Soc., 27, 30, 39; 2 Cel., 1, 10; 2, 19; Bon., 28; 1 Cel., 30; Salimbeni, ann. 1229, and *Tribul. Arch.* , ii., p. 278, etc.

[4]   1 Cel., 24; 3 Soc., 27, 28, 29; 2 Cel., 1, 10; 3, 52; Bon., 28; A. SS., p. 580. It is evident that the tradition has been worked over here: it soon came to be desired to find a miracle in the manner in which Francis found the passage for reading. The St. Nicholas Church is no longer in existence; it stood upon the piece of ground now occupied by the barracks of the *gendarmerie (carabinieri reali).*

[5]   Matt., xix., 21; Luke, ix., 1-6; Matt., xvi., 24-26. The agreement of tradition upon these passages is complete. 3 Soc., 29; 2 Cel., 1, 10; Bon., 28; *Spec.* , 5b. ; *Conform.* , 37b. 2, 47a. 2; *Fior.* , 2; Glassberger and the Chronicle of the xxiv. generals reversing the order (Analecta, fr., t. ii., p. 5) as well as the Conformities in another place, 87b, 2.

[6]   3 Soc., 30. Cf. *Anon. Perus.* , A. SS., p. 581a. This scene is reported neither by Celano nor by St. Bonaventura.

[7]   This date is given in the life of Brother Egidio; A. SS., *Oct.* , t. ii., p. 572; *Aprilis,* t. iii., p. 220. It fits well with the accounts. Through it we obtain the approximate date of the definitive conversion of Francis two full years earlier.

[8]   1 Cel., 25; 3 Soc., 23; Bon. 29. Cf. *Anon. Perus.* , A. SS., p. 582, and A. SS., *Aprilis,* t. iii., p. 220 ff.

[9]   *Spec. ,* 25a: *Qualiter dixit fratri Egidio priusquam esset receptus ut daret mantellum ciudam pauperi. In primordio religionis cum maneret apud Regum Tortum cum duobus fratribus quos tunc tantum habehat.* If we compare this passage with 3 Soc., 44, we shall doubtless arrive at the conclusion that the account in the Speculum is more satisfactory. It is in fact very easy to understand the optical illusion by which later on the Portiuncula was made the scene of the greater number of the events of St. Francis's life, while it would be difficult to see why there should have been any attempt to surround Rivo-Torto with an aureola. The Fioretti say: *Ando inverso lo spedale dei lebbrosi,* which confirms the indication of Rivo-Torto. *Vita d' Egidio,* § 1.

[10]   *An. Perus,* A. SS., p. 582. Cf. *Fior. , Vita di Egidio,* 1; *Spec. ,* 124, 136; 2 Cel., 3, 68; A. SS., *Aprilis,* t. iii., p. 227.

[11]   *Spec. ,* 34a; *Conform. ,* 219b, 1; *Ant. fr. ,* p. 96.

[12]   The Gyrovagi. Tr.

[13]   3 Soc. 32-34; 1 Cel., 27 and 28; Bon., 31.

[14]   3 Soc., 35. Cf. *Anon. Perus.* ; A. SS., p. 584.

[15]   Later on, naturally, it was desired that Francis should have had no better supporter than Guido; some have even made him out to be his spiritual director (St. François, Plon, p. 24)! We have an indirect but unexceptionable proof of the reserve with which these pious traditions must be accepted; Francis did not even tell his bishop (*pater et dominus animarum,* 3 Soc., 29) of his design of having his Rule approved by the pope. This is the more striking because the bishop would have been his natural advocate at the court of Rome, and because in the absence of any other reason the most elementary politeness required that he should have been informed. Add to this that bishops in Italy are not, as elsewhere, *functionaries* approached with difficulty by the common run of mortals. Almost every village in Umbria has its bishop, so that their importance is hardly greater than

that of the curé of a French canton. Furthermore, several pontifical documents throw a sombre light on Guido's character. In a chapter of the decretals of Honorius III. (*Quinta compil.* , lib. ii., tit. iii., cap. i.) is given a complaint against this bishop, brought before the curia by the Crucigeri of the hospital *San Salvatore delle Pareti* (suburbs of Assisi), of having maltreated two of their number, and having stolen a part of the wine belonging to the convent: *pro eo quod Aegidium presbyterum, et fratrem eorem conversum violentas manus injecerat... adjiciens quod idem hospitale quadam vini quantitate fuerat per eumdem episcopum spoliatum. Honorii opera*, Horoy's edition, t. i., col. 200 ff. Cf. Potthast, 7746. The mention of the hospital *de Pariete* proves beyond question that the Bishop of Assisi is here concerned and not the Bishop of Osimo, as some critics have suggested.

Another document shows him at strife with the Benedictines of Mount Subasio (the very ones who afterward gave Portiuncula to Francis), and Honorius III. found the bishop in the wrong: Bull *Conquerente oeconomo monasterii ap*. Richter, *Corpus juris canonici.* Leipzig, 1839, 4to, Horoy, *loc. cit.* , t. i., col. 163; Potthast, 7728.

[16]   3 Soc., 36 and 37. Cf. *Anon. Perus. ap.* , A. SS., p. 585; *Test. B. Francisci.*

[17]   3 Soc., 38-41.

CHAPTER VI

ST. FRANCIS AND INNOCENT III

Summer 1210[1]

Seeing the number of his friars daily increasing, Francis decided to write the Rule of the Order and go to Rome to procure its approval by the Pope.

This resolution was not lightly taken. It would be a mistake in fact to take Francis for one of those inspired ones who rush into action upon the strength of unexpected revelations, and, thanks to their faith in their own infallibility, overawe the multitude. On the contrary, he was filled with a real humility, and if he believed that God reveals himself in prayer, he never for that absolved himself from the duty of reflection nor even from reconsidering his decisions. St. Bonaventura does him great wrong in picturing the greater number of his important resolutions as taken in consequence of dreams; this is to rob his life of its profound originality, his sanctity of its choicest blossom. He was of those who struggle, and, to use one of the noblest expressions of the Bible, of those who *by their perseverance conquer their souls*. Thus we shall see him continually retouching the Rule of his institute, unceasingly revising it down to the last moment, according as the growth of the Order and experience of the human heart suggested to him modifications of it. [2]

The first Rule which he submitted to Rome has not come down to us; we only know that it was extremely simple, and composed especially of passages from the Gospels. It was doubtless only the repetition of those verses which Francis had read to his first companions, with a few precepts about manual labor and the occupations of the new brethren. [3]

It will be well to pause here and consider the brethren who are about to set out for Rome. The biographies are in agreement as to their number; they were twelve, including Francis; but the moment they undertake to give a name to each one of them difficulties begin to arise, and it is only by some exegetical sleight of hand that they can claim to have reconciled the various documents. The table given below[4] briefly shows these difficulties. The question took on some importance when in the fourteenth century men undertook to show an exact conformity between the life of St. Francis and that of Jesus. It is without interest to us. The profiles of two or three of these brethren stand out very clearly in the picture of the origins of the Order; others remind one of the pictures of primitive Umbrian masters, where the figures of the background have a modest and tender grace, but no shadow of personality. The first Franciscans had all the virtues, including the one which is nearly always wanting, willingness to remain unknown.

In the Lower Church of Assisi there is an ancient fresco representing five of the companions of St. Francis. Above them is a Madonna by Cimabue, upon which they are gazing with all their soul. It would be more true if St. Francis were there in the place of the Madonna; one is always changed into the image of what one admires, and they resemble their master and one another. [5] To attempt to give them a name is to make a sort of psychological error and become guilty of infidelity to their memory; the only name they would have desired is that of their father. His love changed their hearts and shed over their whole persons a radiance of light and joy. These are the true personages of the *Fioretti*, the men who brought peace to cities, awakened consciences, changed hearts, conversed with birds, tamed wolves. Of them one may truly say: "Having nothing, yet possessing all things" (*Nihil habentes, omnia possidentes*).

They quitted Portiuncula full of joy and confidence. Francis was too much absorbed in thought not to desire to place in other hands the direction of the little company.

> "Let us choose, " he said, "one from among ourselves to guide us, and let him be to us as the vicar of Jesus Christ. Wherever it may please him to go we will go, and when he may wish to stop anywhere to sleep there we will stop. " They chose Brother Bernardo and did as Francis had said. They went on full of joy, and all their conversations had for their object only the glory of God and the salvation of their souls.
>
> Their journey was happily accomplished. Everywhere they found kindly souls who sheltered them, and they felt beyond a doubt that God was taking care of them. [6]

Francis's thoughts were all fixed upon the purpose of their journey; he thought of it day and night, and naturally interpreted his dreams with reference to it. One time, in his dream, he saw himself walking along a road beside which was a gigantic and wonderfully beautiful tree. And, behold, while he looked upon it, filled with wonder, he felt himself become so tall that he could touch the boughs, and at the same time the tree bent down its branches to him. [7] He awoke full of joy, sure of a gracious reception by the sovereign pontiff.

His hopes were to be somewhat blighted. Innocent III. had now for twelve years occupied the throne of St. Peter. Still young, energetic, resolute, he enjoyed that superfluity of authority given by success. Coming after the feeble Celestine III., he had been able in a few years to reconquer the temporal domain of the Church, and so to improve the papal influence as almost to realize the theocratic dreams of Gregory VII. He had seen King Pedro of Aragon declaring himself his vassal and laying his crown upon the tomb of the apostles, that he might take it back at his hands. At the other end of Europe, John Lackland had been obliged to receive his crown from a legate after having sworn homage, fealty, and an annual tribute to the Holy See. Preaching union to the cities and republics of Italy, causing the cry ITALIA! ITALIA! to resound like the shout of a trumpet, he was the natural representative of the national awakening, and appeared to be in some sort the suzerain of the emperor, as he was already that of other kings. Finally, by his efforts to purify the Church, by his indomitable firmness in defending morality and law in the affair of Ingelburge and in many others, he was gaining a moral strength which in times so disquieted was all the more powerful for being so rare.

But this incomparable power had its hidden dangers. Occupied with defending the prerogatives of the Holy See, Innocent came to forget that the Church does not exist for herself, that her supremacy is only a transitory means; and one part of his pontificate may be likened to wars, legitimate in the beginning, in which the conqueror keeps on with depredations and massacres for no reason, except that he is intoxicated with blood and success.

And so Rome, which canonized the petty Celestine V., refused this supreme consecration to the glorious Innocent III. With exquisite tact she perceived that he was rather king than priest, rather pope than saint.

When he suppressed ecclesiastical disorders it was less for love of good than for hatred of evil; it was the judge who condemns or threatens, himself always supported by the law, not the father who weeps his son's offence. This priest did not comprehend the great movement of his age—the awakening of love, of poetry, of liberty. I have already said that at the opening of the thirteenth century the Middle Age was twenty years old. Innocent III. undertook to treat it as if it were only fifteen. Possessed by his civil and religious dogmas as others are by their educational doctrines, he never suspected the unsatisfied longings, the dreams, unreasoning perhaps, but beneficent and divine, that were dumbly stirring in the depths of men's hearts. He was a believer, although certain sayings of the historians[8] open the door to some doubts on this point, but he drew his religion rather from the Old Testament than from the New, and if he often thought of Moses, the leader of his people, nothing reminded him of Jesus, the shepherd of souls. One cannot be everything; a choice intelligence, an iron will[9] are a sufficient portion even for a *priest-god*; he lacked love. The death of this pontiff, great among the great ones, was destined to be saluted with songs of joy. [10]

His reception of Francis furnished to Giotto, the friend of Dante, one of his most striking frescos; the pope, seated on his throne, turns abruptly toward Francis. He frowns, for he does not understand, and yet he feels a strange power in this mean and despised man, *vilis et despectus*; he makes a real but futile effort to comprehend, and now I see in this pope, who lived upon lemons, [11] something that recalls another choice mind, theocratic like his own, sacrificed like him to his work: Calvin. One might think that the painter had touched his lips to the Calabrian Seer's cup, and that in the attitude of these two men he sought to symbolize a meeting of representatives of the two ages of humanity, that of Law and that of Love. [12]

A surprise awaited the pilgrims on their arrival in Rome: they met the Bishop of Assisi, [13] quite as much to his astonishment as to their own. This detail is precious because it proves that Francis had not confided his plans to Guido. Notwithstanding this the bishop, it is said, offered to make interest for them with the princes of the Church. We may suspect that his commendations were not very warm. At all events they did not avail to save Francis and his company either from a searching inquiry or from the extended fatherly counsels of Cardinal Giovanni di San Paolo[14] upon the difficulties of the Rule, counsels which strongly resemble those of Guido himself. [15]

What Francis asked for was simple enough; he claimed no privilege of any sort, but only that the pope would approve of his undertaking to lead a life of absolute conformity to the precepts of the gospel. There is a delicate point here which it is quite worth while to see clearly. The pope was not called upon to approve the Rule, since that came from Jesus himself; at the very worst all that he could do would be to lay an ecclesiastical censure upon Francis and his companions for having acted without authority, and to enjoin them to leave to the secular and regular clergy the task of reforming the Church.

Cardinal Giovanni di San Paolo, to whom the Bishop of Assisi presented them, had informed himself of the whole history of the Penitents. He lavished upon them the most affectionate tokens of interest, even going so far as to beg for a mention in their prayers. But such assurances, which appear to have been always the small change of the court of Rome, did not prevent his examining them for several successive days, [16] and putting to them an infinite number of questions, of which the conclusion was always the advice to enter some Order already existing.

To this the unlucky Francis would reply as best he could, often not without embarrassment, for he had no wish to appear to think lightly of the cardinal's counsels, and yet he felt in his heart the imperious desire to obey his vocation. The prelate would then return to the charge, insinuating that they would find it very hard to persevere, that the enthusiasm of the early days would pass away, and again pointing out a more easy course. He was obliged in the end to own himself vanquished. The persistence of Francis, who had never weakened for an instant nor doubted his mission, begat in him a sort of awe, while the perfect humility of the Penitents and their simple and striking fidelity to the Roman Church reassured him in the matter of heresy.

He announced to them, therefore, that he would speak of them to the pope, and would act as their advocate with him. According to the Three Companions he said to the pope: "I have found a man of the highest perfection, who desires to live in conformity with the Holy Gospel and observe evangelical perfection in all things. I believe that by him the Lord intends to reform the faith of the Holy Church throughout the whole world. "[17]

On the morrow he presented Francis and his companions to Innocent III. Naturally, the pope was not sparing of expressions of sympathy, but he also repeated to them the remarks and counsels which they had already heard so often. "My dear children, " he said, "your life appears to me too severe; I see indeed that your fervor is too great for any doubt of you to be possible, but I ought to consider those who shall come after you, lest your mode of life should be beyond their strength. "[18]

Adding a few kind words, he dismissed them without coming to any definite conclusion, promising to consult the cardinals, and advising Francis in particular to address himself to God, to the end that he might manifest his will.

Francis's anxiety must have been great; he could not understand these dilatory measures, these expressions of affection which never led to a categorical approbation. It seemed to him that he had said all that he had to say. For new arguments he had only one resource — prayer.

He felt his prayer answered when in his conversation with Jesus the parable of poverty came to him; he returned to lay it before the pope.

> There was in the desert a woman who was very poor, but beautiful. A great king, seeing her beauty, desired to take her for his wife, for he thought that by her he should have beautiful children. The marriage contracted and consummated, many sons were born to him. When they were grown up, their mother spoke to them thus: "My sons, you have no cause to blush, for you are the sons of the king; go, therefore, to his court, and he will give you everything you need. "
>
> When they arrived at the court the king admired their beauty, and finding in them his own likeness he asked, "Whose sons are you? " And when they replied that they were the sons of a poor woman who lived in the desert, the king clasped them to his heart with joy saying, "Have no fear, for you are my sons; if strangers eat at my table, much more shall you who are my lawful sons. " Then the king sent word to the woman to send to his court all the sons which she had borne, that they might be nourished there.

"Very holy father, " added Francis, "I am this poor woman whom God in his love has deigned to make beautiful, and of whom he has been pleased to have lawful sons. The King of Kings has told me that he will provide for all the sons which he may have of me, for if he sustains bastards, how much more his legitimate sons. "[19]

So much simplicity, joined with such pious obstinacy, at last conquered Innocent. In the humble mendicant he perceived an apostle and prophet whose mouth no power could close. Successor of St. Peter and vicar of Jesus Christ that he felt himself, he saw in the mean and despised man before him one who with the authority of absolute faith proclaimed himself the root of a new lineage of most legitimate Christians.

The biographers have held that by this parable Francis sought above all things to tranquillize the pope as to the future of the brethren; they find in it a reply to the anxieties of the pontiff, who feared to see them starve to death. There can be no doubt that its original meaning was totally different. It shows that with all his humility Francis knew how to speak out boldly, and that all his respect for the Church could not hinder his seeing, and, when necessary, saying, that he and his brethren were the lawful sons of the gospel, of which the members of the clergy were only *extranei*. We shall find in the course of his life more than one example of this indomitable boldness, which disarmed Innocent III. as well as the future Gregory IX.

In a consistory which doubtless was held between the two audiences some of the cardinals expressed the opinion that the initiative of the Penitents of Assisi was an innovation, and that their mode of life was entirely beyond human power. "But, " replied Giovanni di San Paolo, "if we hold that to observe gospel perfection and make profession of it is an irrational and impossible innovation, are we not convicted of blasphemy against Christ, the author of the gospel? "[20]

These words struck Innocent III. with great force; he knew better than any one that the possessions of the ecclesiastics were the great obstacles to the reform of the Church, and that the threatened success of the Albigensian heresy was especially due to the fact that it preached the doctrine of poverty.

Two years before he had accorded his approbation to a group of Waldensians, who under the name *Poor Catholics* had desired to remain faithful to the Church; [21] he therefore gave his approval to the Penitents of Assisi, but, as a contemporary chronicler has well observed, it was in the hope that they would wrest the banner from heresy. [22]

Yet his doubts and hesitations were not entirely dissipated. He reserved his definitive approbation, therefore, while lavishing upon the brothers the most affectionate tokens of interest. He authorized them to continue their missions everywhere, after having gained the consent of their ordinaries. He required, however, that they should give themselves a responsible superior to whom the ecclesiastical authorities could always address themselves. Naturally, Francis was chosen. [23] This fact, so humble in appearance, definitively constituted the Franciscan family.

The mystics whom we saw going from village to village transported with love and liberty accepted the yoke almost without thinking about it. This yoke will preserve them from the disintegration of the heretics, but it will make itself sharply felt by those pure souls; they will one day look back to the early days of the Order as the only time when their life was truly conformed to the gospel.

When Francis heard the words of the supreme pontiff he prostrated himself at his feet, promising the most perfect obedience with all his heart. The pope blessed them, saying: "Go, my brethren, and may God be with you. Preach penitence to everyone according as the Lord may deign to inspire you. Then when the All-powerful shall have made you multiply and go forward, you will refer to us; we will concede what you ask, and we may then with greater security accord to you even more than you ask. "[24]

Francis and his companions were too little familiar with Roman phraseology to perceive that after all the Holy See had simply consented to suspend judgment in view of the uprightness of their intentions and the purity of their faith. [25]

The flowers of clerical rhetoric hid from them the shackles which had been laid upon them. The curia, in fact, was not satisfied with Francis's vow of fidelity, it desired in addition to stamp the Penitents with the seal of the Church: the Cardinal of San Paolo was deputed to confer upon them the tonsure. From this time they were all under the spiritual authority of the Roman Church.

The thoroughly lay creation of St. Francis had become, in spite of himself, an ecclesiastical institution: it must soon degenerate into a clerical institution. All unawares, the Franciscan movement had been unfaithful to its origin. The prophet had abdicated in favor of the priest, not indeed without possibility of return, for when a man has once reigned, I would say, thought, in liberty—what other kingdom is there on this earth? —he makes but an indifferent slave; in vain he tries to submit; in spite of himself it happens at times that he lifts his head proudly, he rattles his chains, he remembers the struggles, sadness, anguish of the days of liberty, and weeps their loss. Among the sons of St. Francis many were destined to weep their lost liberty, many to die to conquer it again.

FOOTNOTES:

[1]   The date usually fixed for the approval of the Rule by Innocent III. is the month of August, 1209. The Bollandists had thought themselves able to infer it from the account where Thomas of Celano (1 Cel., 43) refers to the passage through Umbria of the Emperor Otho IV., on his way to be crowned at Rome (October 4, 1209). Upon this journey see Böhmer-Ficker, *Regesta Imperii. Dei Regesten des Kaiserreichs unter Philipp, Otto IV.* , etc., Insbruck, 1879, 4to, pp. 96 and 97. As this account follows that of the approval, they conclude that the latter was earlier. But Thomas of Celano puts this account there because the context led up to it, and not in order to fix its date. Everything leads to the belief that the Brothers retired (*recolligebat*, 1 Cel., 42) to Rivo-Torto before and after their journey to Rome. Besides, the time between April 23d and the middle of August, 1209, is much too short for all that the biographers tell us about the life of the Brothers before their visit to Innocent III. The mission to Florence took place in winter, or at least in a very cold month. But the decisive argument is that Innocent III. quitted Rome toward the end of May, 1209, and went to Viterbo, returning only to crown Otho, October 4th (Potthast, 3727-3803). It is therefore absolutely necessary to postpone to the summer of 1210 the visit of the Penitents to the pope. This is also the date which Wadding arrives at.

[2]   3 Soc., 35.

[3]   1 Cel., 32; 3 Soc., 51; Bon., 34. Cf. *Test. B. Fr.* M. K. Müller of
        Halle, in his *Anfänge,* has made a very remarkable study of
        the Rule of 1221, whence he deduces an earlier Rule, which
        he believes to be that of 1209 (1210). For once I find myself
        entirely in accord with him, except that the Rule thus
        reconstructed (Vide *Anfänge,* pp. 14-25, 184-188) appears to
        me to be not that of 1210, which was very short, but another,
        drawn up between 1210 and 1221. The *plures regulas fecit* of
        the 3 Soc., 35, authorizes us to believe that he made perhaps
        as many as four — 1st, 1210, very short, containing little more
        than the three passages of the vocation; 2d, 1217 (?),
        substantially that proposed by M. Müller; 3d, 1221, that of
        which we shall speak at length farther on; 4th, 1226, the Will,
        which if not a Rule is at least an appendix to the Rule. If
        from 1221-1226 he had time to make two Rules and the Will,
        as is universally admitted, there is nothing surprising in his
        having made two from 1210-1221. Perhaps we have a
        fragment of that of 1217 in the regulation of hermitages.
        Vide below, p. 109.

[4]   Thomas of Celano's list. 1, *Quidam pium gerens animum;* 2,
        Bernardus; 3, *Vir alter;* 4, *Ægidius;* 5, *Unus alius appositus;* 6,
        Philippus; 7, *Alius bonus vir;* 8, 9, 10, 11, *Quatuor boni et idonei
        viri.* 1 Cel., 24, 25, 29, 31. The Rinaldi-Amoni text says
        nothing of the last four. Three Companions: 1, *Bernardus;* 2,
        Petrus; 3, *Ægidius;* 4, *Sabbatinus;* 5, *Moritus; Johannes Capella;*
        7, 8, 9, 10, 11, Disciples received by the brethren in their
        missions. 3 Soc., 33, 35, 41, 46, 52. Bonaventura: 1, *Bernardus;*
        2,... 3, *Ægidius;* 4, 5,... 6, *Silvestro;* 7, *Alius bonus viri;* 8, 9, 10,
        11, *Quatuor viri honesti.* Bon., 28, 29, 30, 31, 33. The Fioretti,
        while insisting on the importance of the twelve Franciscan
        apostles, cite only six in their list: Giovanni di Capella,
        Egidio, Philip, Silvestro, Bernardo, and Rufino. *Fior.* , 1. We
        must go to the Conformities to find the traditional list, f^o
        46b 1: 1, *Bernardus de Quintavalle;* 2, *Petrus Chatanii;* 3,
        Egidius; 4, *Sabatinus;* 5, *Moricus;* 6, *Johannes de Capella;* 7,
        Philippus Longus; 8, *Johannes de Sancto Constantio;* 9, *Barbarus;*
        10, *Bernardus de Cleviridante* (sic); 11, *Angelus Tancredi;* 12,
        Sylvester. As will be seen, in the last two documents twelve
        disciples are in question, while in the preceding ones there
        are only eleven. This is enough to show a dogmatic purpose.
        This list reappears exactly in the *Speculum,* with the sole
        difference that Francis being there included Angelo di

Tancrede is the twelfth brother and Silvestro disappears. *Spec.* , 87a.

[5] According to tradition, the five *compagni del Santo* buried there beside their master are Bernardo, Silvestro, William (an Englishman), Eletto, and Valentino(?)

[6] 3 Soc., 46; 1 Cel., 32; Bon., 34.

[7] 1 Cel., 33; 3 Soc., 53; Bon., 35.

[8] St. Ludgarde (1182-1246) sees him condemned to Purgatory till the Last Judgment. Life of this saint by Thomas of Catimpré in Surius: *Vitæ SS.* (1618), vi., 215-226.

[9] *Vir clari ingenii, magnæ probitatis et sapientiæ, cui nullus secundus tempore suo:* Rigordus, *de gestis Philippi Augusti* in Duchesne. *Historiæ Francorum scriptores coætanei,* t. v., p. 60. —*Nec similem sui scientia, facundia, decretorum et legum perititia, strenuitate, judiciorum nec adhuc visus est habere sequentem.* Cf. Mencken, *Script. rer. Sax.* , Leipzig, 1728, t. iii., p. 252. *Innocentius, qui vere stupor mundi erat et immutator sæculi.* Cotton, *Hist. Anglicana,* Luard, 1859, p. 107.

[10] *Cujus finis lætitiem potius quam tristitiam generavit subjectis.* Alberic delle Tre Fontane. Leibnitz, *Accessiones historicæ,* t. ii., p. 492.

[11] *Decidit in acutam (febrem) quam cum multis diebus fovisset nec a citris quibus in magna quantitatæ et ex consuetudine vescebatur... minime abstineret... ad ultimum in lethargia prolapsus vitam finivit.* Alberic delle Tre Fontane, *loc. cit.*

[12] Fresco in the great nave of the Upper Church of Assisi.

[13] 1 Cel., 32; 3 Soc., 47.

[14] Of the Colonna family; he died in 1216. Cf. 3 Soc., 61. Vide Cardella, *Memorie storiche de' Cardinali,* 9 vols., 8vo, Rome, 1792 ff., t. i., p. 177. He was at Rome in the summer of 1210, for on the 11th of August he countersigned the bull *Religiosem vitam.* Potthast, 4061. Angelo Clareno relates the approbation with more precision in certain respects: *Cum*

vero Summo Pontifici ea quæ postulabat [Franciscus] ardua valde et quasi impossibilia viderentur infirmitate hominum sui temporis, exhortabatur eum, quod aliquem ordinem vel regulam de approbatis assumeret, at ipse se a Christo missum ad talem vitam et non aliam postulandam constanter affirmans, fixus in sua petitione permansit. Tunc dominus Johannes de Sancto Paulo episcopus Sabinensis et dominus Hugo episcopus Hostiensis Dei spiritu moti assisterunt Sancto Francisco et pro his quæ petebat coram summo Pontifice et Cardinalibus plura proposuerunt rationabilia et efficacia valde. Tribul. Laurentinian MS., f° 6a. This intervention of Ugolini is mentioned in no other document. It is, however, by no means impossible. He also was in Rome in the summer of 1210. (Vide Potthast, p. 462.)

[15] 1 Cel., 32 and 33; 3 Soc., 47 and 48. Cf. *An. Per.* , A. SS., p. 590.

[16] 1 Cel., 33.

[17] 3 Soc., 48.

[18] 3 Soc., 49; 1 Cel., 33; Bon., 35 and 36. All this has been much worked over by tradition and gives us only an echo of the reality. It would certainly have needed very little for the Penitents to meet the same fate before Innocent III. as the Waldenses before Lucius III. Traces of this interview are found in two texts which appear to me to be too suspicious to warrant their insertion in the body of the narrative. The first is a fragment of Matthew Paris: *Papa itaque in fratre memorato habitum deformem, vultum despicabilem, barbam prolixam, capillos incultos, supercilia pendentia et nigra diligenter considerans; cum petitionem ejus tam arduam et executione impossibilem recitare fecisset, despexit cum et dixit: Vade frater, et quære porcus, quibus potius debes quam hominibus comparari, et involve te cum eis in volutabro, et regulam illis a te commentatam tradens, officium tuæ prædicationis impende. Quod audiens Franciscus inclinato capite exixit et porcis tandem inventis, in luto se cum eis tamdiu involvit quousque a planta pedis usque ad verticem, corpus suum totum cum ipso habitu polluisset. Sicque ad consistorium revertens Papæ se conspectibus præsentavit dicens: Domine feci sicut præcepisti exaudi nunc obsecro petitionem meam.* Ed. Wats, p. 340. The incident has a real Franciscan color, and should have some historic basis. Curiously, it in some sort meets a passage in the legend of Bonaventura

which is an interpolation of the end of the thirteenth century. See A. SS., p. 591.

[19]   3 Soc., 50 and 51; Bon., 37; 2 Cel., 1, 11; Bernard de Besse, Turin MS., f° 101b. Ubertini di Casali (*Arbor vitæ crucifixæ*, Venice, 1485, lib. v., cap. iii.) tells a curious story in which he depicts the indignation of the prelates against Francis. *Quænam hæc est doctrina nova quam infers auribus nostris? Quis potest vivere sine temporalium possessione? Numquid tu melior es quam patres nostri qui dederunt nobis temporalia et in temporalibus abundantes ecclesias possiderunt?* Then follows the fine prayer inserted by Wadding in Francis's works. The central idea is the same as in the parable of poverty. This story, though not referable to any source, has nevertheless its importance, since it shows how in the year 1300 a man who had all the documents before his eyes, represented to himself Francis's early steps.

[20]   Bon., 36.

[21]   The attempt of Durand of Huesca to create a mendicant order has not yet been studied with sufficient minuteness. Chief of the Waldenses of Aragon, he was present in 1207 at the conference of Pamiers, and decided to return to the Church. Received with kindness by the pope he at first had a great success, and by 1209 had established communities in Aragon, at Carcassonne, Narbonne, Béziers, Nimes, Uzès, Milan. We find in this movement all the lineaments of the institute of St. Dominic; it was an order of priests to whom theological studies were recommended. They disappeared almost completely in the storm of the Albigensian crusade. Innocent III., *epistolæ*, xi., 196, 197, 198; xii., 17, 66; xiii., 63, 77, 78, 94; xv., 82, 83, 90, 91, 92, 93, 94, 96, 137, 146. The first of these bulls contains the very curious Rule of this ephemeral order. Upon its disappearance vide Ripoli, *Bullarium Prædicatorum*, 8 vols., folio, Rome, 1729-1740, t. i., p. 96. Cf. Elie Berger, *Registres d'Innocent IV.* , 2752.

[22]   Burchard, of the order of the Premostrari, who died in 1226. See below, p. 234.

[23]   3 Soc., 52; Bon., 38.

[24]   3 Soc., 52 and 49.

[25]   St. Antonino, Archbishop of Florence, saw very clearly that it
         was *quædam concessio simplex habitus et modi illius vivendi et
         quasi permissio*. A. SS., p. 839. The expression "approbation of
         the Rule" by which the act of Innocent III. is usually
         designated is therefore erroneous.

CHAPTER VII

RIVO-TORTO

1210-1211

The Penitents of Assisi were overflowing with joy. After so many mortally long days spent in that Rome, so different from the other cities that they knew, exposed to the ill-disguised suspicions of the prelates and the jeers of pontifical lackeys, the day of departure seemed to them like a deliverance. At the thought of once more seeing their beloved mountains they were seized by that homesickness of the child for its native village which simple and kindly souls preserve till their latest breath.

Immediately after the ceremony they prayed at the tomb of St. Peter, and then crossing the whole city they quitted Rome by the Porta Salara.

Thomas of Celano, very brief as to all that concerns Francis's sojourn in the Eternal City, recounts at full length the light-heartedness of the little band on quitting it. Already it began to be transfigured in their memory; pains, fatigues, fears, disquietude, hesitations were all forgotten; they thought only of the fatherly assurances of the supreme pontiff—the vicar of Christ, the lord and father of the Christian universe—and promised themselves to make ever new efforts to follow the Rule with fidelity.

Full of these thoughts they had set out, without provisions, to cross the Campagna of Rome, whose few inhabitants never venture out in the heat of the day. The road stretches away northward, keeping at some distance from the Tiber; on the left the jagged crest of Soracte, bathed in mists formed by the exhalations of the earth, looms up disproportionately as it fades in the distance; on the right, the everlasting undulations of the hillocks with their wide pastures separated by thickets so parched and ragged that they seemed to cry for mercy and pardon. Between them the dusty road which goes straight forward, implacable, showing, as far as the eye can reach, nothing but the quivering of the fiery air. Not a house, not a tree, not a passing breeze, nothing to sustain the traveller under the disquietude which creeps over him. Here and there are a few abandoned huts, their ruins looking like the corpses of departed civilizations, and on the edge of the horizon the hills rising up like gigantic and unsurmountable walls.

There are no words to describe the physical and moral sufferings to which he is exposed who undertakes without proper preparation to cross this inhospitable district. To the weakness caused by lack of air soon succeeds an insurmountable lassitude. The feet sink in a soft, tenuous dust which every step sends up in clouds; it covers you, penetrates your skin, and parches your mouth even more than thirst. Little by little all energy ebbs away, a dumb dejection seizes you, sight and thought become alike confused, fever ensues, and you cast yourself down by the roadside, unable to take another step.

In their haste to leave Rome Francis and his companions had forgotten all this, and had imprudently set forth. They would have succumbed if a chance traveller had not brought them succor. He was obliged to leave them before they had shaken off the last hallucinations of fever, leaving them amazed with the unexpected succor which Providence had sent them. [1]

They were so severely shattered that on arriving at Orte they were obliged to stop awhile. In a desert spot not far from this city they found a shelter admirably adapted to serve them for refuge; [2] it was one of those Etruscan tombs so common in that country, whose chambers serve to this day as a shelter for beggars and gypsies. While some of the brethren hastened to the city to beg for food, the others remained in this solitude enjoying the happiness of being together, forming a thousand plans, and more than ever delighting in the charm of freedom from care and renunciation of material goods.

This place had so strong an attraction for them that it required an effort of will to quit it at the end of a fortnight. The seduction of a life purely contemplative assailed Francis, and he asked himself if instead of preaching to the multitudes he would not do better to live in retreat, solely mindful of the inward dialogue between the soul and God. [3]

This aspiration for the selfish repose of the cloister came back to him several times in his life; but love always won the victory. He was too much the child of his time not to be at times tempted by that happiness which the Middle Ages regarded as the supreme bliss of the elect in paradise—peace. *Beati mortui quia quiescunt!* His distinguishing peculiarity is that he never gave way to it.

The reflections of Francis and his companions during their stay at Orte only made their apostolic mission more clear and imperative to them. He, above all, seemed to be filled with a new ardor, and like a valiant knight he burned to throw himself into the thick of the fray.

Their way now led through the valley of the Nera. The contrast between these cool glens, awake with a thousand voices, and the desolation of the Roman Campagna, must have struck them vividly; the stream is only a swollen torrent, but it runs so noisily over pebbles and rocks that it seems to be conversing with them and with the trees of the neighboring forest. In proportion as they had felt themselves alone on the road from Rome to Otricoli, they now felt themselves compassed about with the life, the fecundity, the gayety of the country.

The account of Thomas of Celano becomes so animated as it describes the life of Francis at this epoch that one cannot help thinking that at this time he must have seen him, and that this first meeting remained always in his memory as the radiant dawn of his spiritual life. [4]

The Brothers had taken to preaching in such places as they came upon along their route. Their words were always pretty much the same, they showed the blessedness of peace and exhorted to penitence. Emboldened by the welcome they had received at Rome, which in all innocence they might have taken to be more favorable than it really was, they told the story to everyone they met, and thus set all scruples at rest.

These exhortations, in which Francis spared not his hearers, but in which the sternest reproaches were mingled with so much of love, produced an enormous effect. Man desires above all things to be loved, and when he meets one who loves him sincerely he very seldom refuses him either his love or his admiration.

It is only a low understanding that confounds love with weakness and compliance. We sometimes see sick men feverishly kissing the hand of the surgeon who performs an operation upon them; we sometimes do the same for our spiritual surgeons, for we realize all that there is of vigor, pity, compassion in the tortures which they inflict, and the cries which they force from us are quite as much of gratitude as of pain.

Men hastened from all parts to hear these preachers who were more severe upon themselves than on anyone else. Members of the secular clergy, monks, learned men, rich men even, often mingled in the impromptu audiences gathered in the streets and public places. All were not converted, but it would have been very difficult for any of them to forget this stranger whom they met one day upon their way, and who in a few words had moved them to the very bottom of their hearts with anxiety and fear.

Francis was in truth, as Celano says, the bright morning star. His simple preaching took hold on consciences, snatched his hearers from the mire and blood in which they were painfully trudging, and in spite of themselves carried them to the very heavens, to those serene regions where all is silent save the voice of the heavenly Father. "The whole country trembled, the barren land was already covered with a rich harvest, the withered vine began again to blossom. "[5]

May the supreme grace of the Holy Spi"In the name of God!can understand the transports of joy which overflowed the souls of St. Francis's spiritual sons.

The greatest crime ot our industrial and commercial civilization is that it leaves us a taste only for that which may be bought with money, and makes us overlook the purest and truest joys which are all the time within our reach. The evil has roots far in the past. "Wherefore, " said the God of old Isaiah, "do you weigh money for that which is not meat? why labor for that which satisfieth not? Hearken unto me, and ye shall eat that which is good, and your soul shall delight itself in fatness. "[6]

Joys bought with money—noisy, feverish pleasures—are nothing compared with those sweet, quiet, modest but profound, lasting, and peaceful joys, enlarging, not wearying the heart, which we too often pass by on one side, like those peasants whom we see going into ecstasies over the fireworks of a fair, while they have not so much as a glance for the glorious splendors of a summer night.

In the plain of Assisi, at an hour's walk from the city and near the highway between Perugia and Rome, was a ruinous cottage called

Rivo-Torto. A torrent, almost always dry, but capable of becoming terrible in a storm, descends from Mount Subasio and passes beside it. The ruin had no owner; it had served as a leper hospital before the construction by the Crucigeri[7] of their hospital San Salvatore delle Pareti; but since that time it had been abandoned. Now came Francis and his companions to seek shelter there. [8] It is one of the quietest spots in the suburbs of Assisi, and from thence they could easily go out into the neighborhood in all directions; it being about an equal distance from Portiuncula and St. Damian. But the principal motive for the choice of the place seems to have been the proximity of the *Carceri*, as those shallow natural grottos are called which are found in the forests, half way up the side of Mount Subasio. Following up the bed of the torrent of Rivo-Torto one reaches them in an hour by way of rugged and slippery paths where the very goats do not willingly venture. Once arrived, one might fancy oneself a thousand leagues from any human being, so numerous are the birds of prey which live here quite undisturbed. [9]

Francis loved this solitude and often retired thither with a few companions. The brethren in that case shared between them all care of their material wants, after which, each one retiring into one of these caves, they were able for a few days to listen only to the inner voice.

These little hermitages, sufficiently isolated to secure them from disturbance, but near enough to the cities to permit their going thither to preach, may be found wherever Francis went. They form, as it were, a series of documents about his life quite as important as the written witnesses. Something of his soul may still be found in these caverns in the Apennine forests. He never separated the contemplative from the active life. A precious witness to this fact is found in the regulations for the brethren during their sojourn in hermitage. [10]

The return of the Brothers to Rivo-Torto was marked by a vast increase of popularity. The prejudiced attacks to which they had formerly been subjected were lost in a chorus of praises. Perhaps men suspected the ill-will of the bishop and were happy to see him checked. However this may be, a lively feeling of sympathy and admiration was awakened; the people recalled to mind the indifference manifested by the son of Bernardone a few months before with regard to Otho IV. going to be crowned at Rome. The emperor had made a progress through Italy with a numerous suite and a pomp designed to produce an effect on the minds of the populace; but not only had Francis not interrupted his work to go and see him, he had enjoined upon his friars also to abstain from going, and had merely selected one of them to carry to the monarch a reminder of the ephemeral nature of worldly glory. Later on it was held that he had predicted to the emperor his approaching excommunication.

This spirited attitude made a vivid impression on the popular imagination. [11] Perhaps it was of more service in forming general opinion than anything he had done thus far. The masses, who are not often alive to delicate sentiments, respond quickly to those who, whether rightly or wrongly, do not bow down before power. This time they perceived that where other men would see the poor, the rich, the noble, the common, the learned, Francis saw only souls, which were to him the more precious as they were more neglected or despised.

No biographer informs us how long the Penitents remained at Rivo-Torto. It seems probable, however, that they spent there the latter part of 1210 and the early months of 1211, evangelizing the towns and villages of the neighborhood.

They suffered much; this part of the plain of Assisi is inundated by torrents nearly every autumn, and many times the poor friars, blockaded in the lazaretto, were forced to satisfy their hunger with a few roots from the neighboring fields.

The barrack in which they lived was so narrow that, when they were all there at once, they had much difficulty not to crowd one another. To secure to each one his due quota of space, Francis wrote the name of each brother upon the column which supports the building. But these minor discomforts in no sense disturbed their happiness. No apprehension had as yet come to cloud Francis's hopes; he was overflowing with joy and kindliness; all the memories which Rivo-Torto has left with the Order are fresh and sweet pictures of him. [12]

One night all the brethren seemed to be sleeping, when he heard a moaning. It was one of his sheep, to speak after the manner of the Franciscan biographer, who had denied himself too rigorously and was dying of hunger. Francis immediately rose, called the brother to him, brought forth the meagre reserve of food, and himself began to eat to inspire the other with courage, explaining to him that if penitence is good it is still necessary to temper it with discretion. [13]

Francis had that tact of the heart which divines the secrets of others and anticipates their desires. At another time, still at Rivo-Torto, he took a sick brother by the hand, led him to a grape-vine, and, presenting him with a fine cluster, began himself to eat of it. It was nothing, but the simple act so bound to him the sick man's heart that many years after the brother could not speak of it without emotion. [14]

But Francis was far from neglecting his mission. Ever growing more sure, not of himself but of his duty toward men, he took part in the political and social affairs of his province with the confidence of an upright and pure heart, never able to understand how stupidity, perverseness, pride, and indolence, by leaguing themselves together, may check the finest and most righteous impulses. He had the faith which removes mountains, and was wholly free from that touch of scepticism, so common in our day, which points out that it is of no more use to move mountains than to change the place of difficulties.

When the people of Assisi learned that his Rule had been approved by the pope there was strong excitement; every one desired to hear him preach. The clergy were obliged to give way; they offered him the Church of St. George, but this church was manifestly insufficient for the crowds of hearers; it was necessary to open the cathedral to him.

St. Francis never said anything especially new; to win hearts he had that which is worth more than any arts of oratory—an ardent conviction; he spoke as compelled by the imperious need of kindling others with the flame that burned within himself. When they heard him recall the horrors of war, the crimes of the populace, the laxity of the great, the rapacity which dishonored the Church, the age-long widowhood of Poverty, each one felt himself taken to task in his own conscience.

An attentive or excited crowd is always very impressionable, but this peculiar sensitiveness was perhaps stronger in the Middle Ages than at any other time. Nervous disturbances were in the air, and upon men thus prepared the will of the preacher impressed itself in a manner almost magnetic.

To understand what Francis's preaching must have been like we must forget the manners of to-day, and transport ourselves for a moment to the Cathedral of Assisi in the thirteenth century; it is still standing, but the centuries have given to its stones a fine rust of polished bronze, which recalls Venice and Titian's tones of ruddy gold. It was new then, and all sparkling with whiteness, with the fine rosy tinge of the stones of Mount Subasio. It had been built by the people of Assisi a few years before in one of those outbursts of faith and union which were almost everywhere the prelude of the communal movement. So, when the people thronged into it on their high days, they not merely had none of that vague respect for a holy place which, though it has passed into the customs of other countries, still continues to be unknown in Italy, but they felt themselves at home in a palace which they had built for themselves. More than in any other church they there felt themselves at liberty to criticise the preacher, and they had no hesitation in proving to him, either by murmurs of dissatisfaction or by applause, just what they thought of his words. We must remember also that the churches of Italy have neither pews nor chairs, that one must listen standing or kneeling, while the preacher walks about gesticulating on a platform; add to this the general curiosity, the clamorous sympathies of many, the disguised opposition of some, and we shall have a vague notion of the conditions under which Francis first entered the pulpit of San Rufino.

His success was startling. The poor felt that they had found a friend, a brother, a champion, almost an avenger. The thoughts which they hardly dared murmur beneath their breath Francis proclaimed at the top of his voice, daring to bid all, without distinction, to repent and love one another. His words were a cry of the heart, an appeal to the consciences of all his fellow-citizens, almost recalling the passionate utterances of the prophets of Israel. Like those witnesses for Jehovah the "little poor man" of Assisi had put on sackcloth and ashes to denounce the iniquities of his people, like theirs was his courage and heroism, like theirs the divine tenderness in his heart.

It seemed as if Assisi were about to recover again the feeling of Israel for sin. The effect of these appeals was prodigious; the entire population was thrilled, conquered, desiring in future to live only according to Francis's counsels; his very companions, who had remained behind at Rivo-Torto, hearing of these marvels, felt in themselves an answering thrill, and their vocation took on a new strength; during the night they seemed to see their master in a chariot of fire, soaring to heaven like a new Elijah. [15]

This almost delirious enthusiasm of a whole people was not perhaps so difficult to arouse as might be supposed: the emotional power of the masses was at that time as great all over Europe as it was in Paris during certain days of the Revolution. We all know the tragic and touching story of those companies of children from the north of Europe who appeared in 1212 in troops of several thousands, boys and girls mingled together pell-mell. Nothing could stop them, a mania had overtaken them, in all good faith they believed that they were to deliver the Holy Land, that the sea would be dried up to let them pass. They perished, we hardly know how, perhaps being sold into slavery. [16] They were accounted martyrs, and rightly; popular devotion likened them to the Holy Innocents, dying for a God whom they knew not. Those children of the crusade also perished for an unknown ideal, false no doubt; but is it not better to die for an unknown and even a false ideal than to live for the vain realities of an utterly unpoetic existence? In the end of time we shall be judged neither by philosophers nor by theologians, and if we were, it is to be hoped that even in this case love would cover a multitude of sins and pass by many follies.

Certainly if ever there was a time when religious affections of the nerves were to be dreaded, it was that which produced such movements as these. All Europe seemed to be beside itself; women appeared stark naked in the streets of towns and villages, slowly walking up and down, silent as phantoms. [17] We can understand now the accounts which have come down to us, so fantastic at the first glance, of certain popular orators of this time; of Berthold of Ratisbon, for example, who drew together crowds of sixteen thousand persons, or of that Fra Giovanni Schio di Vicenza, who for a time quieted all Northern Italy and brought Guelphs and Ghibellines into one another's arms. [18]

That popular eloquence which was to accomplish so many marvels in 1233 comes down in a straight line from the Franciscan movement. It was St. Francis who set the example of those open-air sermons given in the vulgar tongue, at street corners, in public squares, in the fields.

To feel the change which he brought about we must read the sermons of his contemporaries; declamatory, scholastic, subtile, they delighted in the minutiæ of exegesis or dogma, serving up refined dissertations on the most obscure texts of the Old Testament, to hearers starving for a simple and wholesome diet.

With Francis, on the contrary, all is incisive, clear, practical. He pays no attention to the precepts of the rhetoricians, he forgets himself completely, thinking only of the end desired, the conversion of souls. And conversion was not in his view something vague and indistinct, which must take place only between God and the hearer. No, he will have immediate and practical proofs of conversion. Men must give up ill-gotten gains, renounce their enmities, be reconciled with their adversaries.

At Assisi he threw himself valiantly into the thick of civil dissensions. The agreement of 1202 between the parties who divided the city had been wholly ephemeral. The common people were continually demanding new liberties, which the nobles and burghers would yield to them only under the pressure of fear. Francis took up the cause of the weak, the *minores*, and succeeded in reconciling them with the rich, the *majores*.

His spiritual family had not as yet, properly speaking, a name, for, unlike those too hasty spirits who baptize their productions before they have come to light, he was waiting for the occasion that should reveal the true name which he ought to give it. [19] One day someone was reading the Rule in his presence. When he came to the passage, "Let the brethren, wherever they may find themselves called to labor or to serve, never take an office which shall put them over others, but on the contrary, let them be always under (*sint minores*) all those who may be in that house, "[20] these words *sint minores* of the Rule, in the circumstances then existing in the city, suddenly appeared to him as a providential indication. His institution should be called the Order of the Brothers Minor.

We may imagine the effect of this determination. The *Saint*, for already this magic word had burst forth where he appeared, [21] the Saint had spoken. It was he who was about to bring peace to the city, acting as arbiter between the two factions which rent it.

We still possess the document of this *pace civile*, exhumed, so to speak, from the communal archives of Assisi by the learned and pious Antonio Cristofani. [22] The opening lines are as follows:

"In the name of God!

"May the supreme grace of the Holy Spirit assist us! To the honor of our Lord Jesus Christ, the blessed Virgin Mary, the Emperor Otho, and Duke Leopold.

"This is the statute and perpetual agreement between the *Majori* and *Minori* of Assisi.

"Without common consent there shall never be any sort of alliance either with the pope and his nuncios or legates, or with the emperor, or with the king, or with their nuncios or legates, or with any city or town, or with any important person, except with a common accord they shall do all which there may be to do for the honor, safety, and advantage of the commune of Assisi. "

What follows is worthy of the beginning. The lords, in consideration of a small periodical payment, should renounce all the feudal rights; the inhabitants of the villages subject to Assisi were put on a par with those of the city, foreigners were protected, the assessment of taxes was fixed. On Wednesday, November 9, 1210, this agreement was signed and sworn to in the public place of Assisi; it was made in such good faith that exiles were able to return in peace, and from this day we find in the city registers the names of those *émigrés* who, in 1202, had betrayed their city and provoked the disastrous war with Perugia. Francis might well be happy. Love had triumphed, and for several years there were at Assisi neither victors nor vanquished.

In the mystic marriages which here and there in history unite a man to a people, something takes place of which the transports of sense, the delirium of love, seem to be the only symbol; a moment comes in which saints, or men of genius, feel unknown powers striving mightily within them; they strive, they seek, they struggle until, triumphing over all obstacles, they have forced trembling, swooning humanity to conceive by them.

This moment had come to St. Francis.

FOOTNOTES:

[1]   1 Cel., 34; 3 Soc., 53; Bon., 39.

[2]   Probably at Otricoli, which lies on the high-road between Rome and Spoleto. Orte is an hour and a half further on. It is the ancient *Otriculum,* where many antiquities have been found.

[3]   1 Cel., 35; Bon., 40 and 41.

[4]   The only road connecting Celano with Rome, as well as with all Central and Northern Italy, passes by Aquila, Rieti, and Terni, where it joins the high-roads leading from the north toward Rome.

[5]   1 Cel., 36 and 37; 3 Soc., 54; Bon., 45-48.

[6]   Isaiah, lv., 2.

[7]   This Order deserves to be better known; it was founded under Alexander III. and rapidly spread all over Central Italy and the East. In Francis's lifetime it had in Italy and the Holy Land about forty houses dedicated to the care of lepers. It is very probable that it was at *San Salvatore delle Pareti* that Francis visited these unhappy sufferers. He there made the particular acquaintance of a Cruciger named *Morico.* The latter afterward falling ill, Francis sent him a remedy which would cure him, informing him at the same time that he was to become his disciple, which shortly afterward took place. The hospital *San Salvatore* has disappeared; it stood in the place now called *Ospedaletto,* where a small chapel now stands half way between Assisi and Santa Maria degli Angeli. It was from there that the dying Francis blessed Assisi. For Morico vide 3 Soc., 35; Bon., 49; 2 Cel., 3, 128; *Conform.* , 63b. —For the hospital vide Bon., 49; *Conform.* , 135a, 1; *Honorii III. opera,* Horoy, t. i., col. 206. Cf. Potthast, 7746; L. Auvray, *Registres de Grégoire IX.* , Paris, 1890, 4to, no. 209. For the Crucigeri in the time of St. Francis vide the interesting bull *Cum tu fili prior,* of July 8, 1203; Migne, *Inn. op.* , t. ii., col. 125 ff. Cf. Potthast, 1959, and *Cum pastoris,* April 5, 1204; Migne, *loc. cit.* , 319. Cf. Potthast, 2169 and 4474.

[8]   3 Soc., 55.

[9]   All this yet remains in its primitive state. The road which went from Assisi to the now ruined Abbey of Mount Subasio (almost on the summit of the mountain) passed the Carceri, where there was a little chapel built by the Benedictines.

[10]   *Illi qui religiose volunt stare in eremis sint tres aut quatuor ad plus. Duo ex ipsis sint matres, et habeant duos filios, vel unum ad minus. Illi duo teneant vitam Marthæ et alii duo vitam Mariæ Magdalenæ.* Assisi MS., 338, 43a-b; text given also in *Conf.*, 143a, 1, from which Wadding borrows it for his edition of the *Opuscules* of St. Francis. Cf. 2 Cel., 3, 113. It is possible that we have here a fragment of the Rule, which must have been composed toward 1217.

[11]   1 Cel., 42 and 43; 3 Soc., 55; Bon., 41.

[12]   1 Cel., 42-44.

[13]   2 Cel., 1, 15; Bon., 65. These two authors do not say where the event took place; but there appears to be no reason for suspecting the indication of Rivo-Torto given by the *Speculum*, fo. 21a.

[14]   2 Cel., 3, 110. Cf. *Spec.*, 22a.

[15]   1 Cel., 47; Bon., 43.

[16]   There are few events of the thirteenth century that offer more documents or are more obscure than this one. The chroniclers of the most different countries speak of it at length. Here is one of the shortest but most exact of the notices, given by an eye-witness (Annals of Genoa of the years 1197-1219, *apud Mon. Germ. hist. Script.*, t. 18): 1212 *in mense Augusti, die Sabbati, octava Kalendarum Septembris, intravit civitatem Janue quidam puer Teutonicus nomine Nicholaus peregrinationis causa, et cum eo multitudo maxima pelegrinorum defferentes cruces et bordonos atque scarsellas ultra septem millia arbitratu boni viri inter homines et feminas et puellos et puellas. Et die dominica sequenti de civitate exierunt.* — Cf. Giacomo di Viraggio: Muratori, t. ix., col. 46: *Dicebant quod mare debebat apud Januam siccari et sic ipsi debebant in Hierusalem proficisci. Multi autem inter eos erant filii Nobilium, quos ipsi etiam cum meretricibus destinarunt (!)* The most tragic

account is that of Alberic, who relates the fate of the company that embarked at Marseilles. *Mon. Ger. hist. Script.,* t. 23, p. 894.

[17]   The Benedictine chronicler, Albert von Stade (*Mon. Ger. hist. Script.,* t. 16, pp. 271-379), thus closes his notice of the children's crusade: *Adhuc quo devenerint ignorantur sed plurimi redierunt, a quibus cum quæreretur causa cursus dixerunt se nescire. Nudæ etiam mulieres circa idem tempus nihil loquentes per villas et civitates cucurrerunt. Loc. cit. ,* p. 355.

[18]   *Chron. Veronese, ann. 1238* (Muratori, *Scriptores Rer. Ital. ,* t. viii., p. 626). Cf. Barbarano de' Mironi: *Hist. Eccles. di Vicenza,* t. ii., pp. 79-84.

[19]   The Brothers were at first called *Viri pænitentiales de civitate Assisii* (3 Soc., 37); it appears that they had a momentary thought of calling themselves *Pauperes de Assisio,* but they were doubtless dissuaded from this at Rome, as too closely resembling that of the *Pauperes de Lugduno.* Vide *Burchardi chronicon. ,* p. 376; vide Introd., cap. 5.

[20]   Vide Rule of 1221, *cap.* 7. Cf. 1 Cel., 38, and Bon., 78.

[21]   1 Cel., 36.

[22]   *Storia d'Assisi,* t. i., pp. 123-129.

CHAPTER VIII

PORTIUNCULA

1211

It was doubtless toward the spring of 1211 that the Brothers quitted Rivo-Torto. They were engaged in prayer one day, when a peasant appeared with an ass, which he noisily drove before him into the poor shelter.

"Go in, go in! " he cried to his beast; "we shall be most comfortable here. " It appeared that he was afraid that if the Brothers remained there much longer they would begin to think this deserted place was their own. [1] Such rudeness was very displeasing to Francis, who immediately arose and departed, followed by his companions.

Now that they were so numerous the Brothers could no longer continue their wandering life in all respects as in the past; they had need of a permanent shelter and above all of a little chapel. They addressed themselves in vain first to the bishop and then to the canons of San Rufino for the loan of what they needed, but were more fortunate with the abbot of the Benedictines of Mount Subasio, who ceded to them in perpetuity the use of a chapel already very dear to their hearts, Santa Maria degli Angeli or the Portiuncula. [2]

Francis was enchanted; he saw a mysterious harmony, ordained by God himself, between the name of the humble sanctuary and that of his Order. The brethren quickly built for themselves a few huts; a quickset hedge served as enclosing wall, and thus in three or four days was organized the first Franciscan convent.

For ten years they were satisfied with this. These ten years are the heroic period of the Order. St. Francis, in full possession of his ideal, will seek to inculcate it upon his disciples and will succeed sometimes; but already the too rapid multiplication of the brotherhood will provoke some symptoms of relaxation.

The remembrance of the beginning of this period has drawn from the lips of Thomas of Celano a sort of canticle in honor of the monastic life. It is the burning and untranslatable commentary of the

Psalmist's cry: *"Behold how sweet and pleasant it is to be brethren and to dwell together. "*

Their cloister was the forest which then extended on all sides of Portiuncula, occupying a large part of the plain. There they gathered around their master to receive his spiritual counsels, and thither they retired to meditate and pray. [3] It would be a gross mistake, however, to suppose that contemplation absorbed them completely during the days which were not consecrated to missionary tours: a part of their time was spent in manual labor.

The intentions of St. Francis have been more misapprehended on this point than on any other, but it may be said that nowhere is he more clear than when he ordains that his friars shall gain their livelihood by the work of their hands. He never dreamed of creating a *mendicant* order, he created a *laboring* order. It is true we shall often see him begging and urging his disciples to do as much, but these incidents ought not to mislead us; they are meant to teach that when a friar arrived in any locality and there spent his strength for long days in dispensing spiritual bread to famished souls, he ought not to blush to receive material bread in exchange. To work was the rule, to beg the exception; but this exception was in nowise dishonorable. Did not Jesus, the Virgin, the disciples live on bread bestowed? Was it not rendering a great service to those to whom they resorted to teach them charity?

Francis in his poetic language gave the name of *mensa Domini*, the table of the Lord, to this table of love around which gathered the *little poor ones*. The bread of charity is the bread of angels; and it is also that of the birds, which reap not nor gather into barns.

We are far enough, in this case, from that mendicity which is understood as a means of existence and the essential condition of a life of idleness. It is the opposite extreme, and we are true and just to St. Francis and to the origin of the mendicant orders only when we do not separate the obligation of labor from the praise of mendicity. [4]

No doubt this zeal did not last long, and Thomas of Celano already entitles his chapters, *"Lament before God over the idleness and gluttony of the friars; "* but we must not permit this speedy and inevitable decadence to veil from our sight the holy and manly beauty of the origin.

With all his gentleness Francis knew how to show an inflexible severity toward the idle; he even went so far as to dismiss a friar who refused to work. [5] Nothing in this matter better shows the intentions of the Poverello than the life of Brother Egidio, one of his dearest companions, him of whom he said with a smile: "He is one of the paladins of my Round Table. "

Brother Egidio had a taste for great adventures, and is a living example of a Franciscan of the earliest days; he survived his master twenty-five years, and never ceased to obey the letter and spirit of the Rule with freedom and simplicity.

We find him one day setting out on a pilgrimage to the Holy Land. Arrived at Brindisi, he borrowed a water-jug that he might carry water while he was awaiting the departure of the ship, and passed a part of every day in crying through the streets of the city: "*Alla fresca! Alla fresca!* " like other water-carriers. But he would change his trade according to the country and the circumstances; on his way back, at Ancona, he procured willow for making baskets, which he afterward sold, not for money but for his food. It even happened to him to be employed in burying the dead.

Sent to Rome, every morning after finishing his religious duties, he would take a walk of several leagues, to a certain forest, whence he brought a load of wood. Coming back one day he met a lady who wanted to buy it; they agreed on a price, and Egidio carried it to her house. But when he arrived at the house she perceived him to be a friar, and would have given him more than the price agreed upon. "My good lady, " he replied, "I will not permit myself to be overcome by avarice, " and he departed without accepting anything at all.

In the olive season he helped in the gathering; in grape season he offered himself as vintager. One day on the Piazza di Roma, where men are hired for day's work, he saw a *padrone* who could not find a man to thrash his walnut tree; it was so high that no one dared risk himself in it. "If you will give me part of the nuts, " said Egidio, "I will do it willingly. " The bargain struck and the tree thrashed, there proved to be so many nuts that he did not know where to put his share. Gathering up his tunic he made a bag of it and full of joy returned to Rome, where he distributed them among all the poor whom he met.

Is not this a charming incident? Does it not by itself alone reveal the freshness, the youth, the kindness of heart of the first Franciscans? There is no end to the stories of the ingenuousness of Brother Egidio. All kinds of work seemed good to him provided he had time enough in the morning for his religious duties. Now he is in the service of the Cellarer of the Four Crowns at Rome, sifting flour and carrying water to the convent from the well of San Sisto. Now he is at Rieti, where he consents to remain with Cardinal Nicholas, bringing to every meal the bread which he had earned, notwithstanding the entreaties of the master of the house, who would gladly have provided for his wants. One day it rained so hard that Brother Egidio could not think of going out; the cardinal was already making merry over the thought that he would be forced to accept bread that he had not earned. But Egidio went to the kitchen, and finding that it needed cleaning he persuaded the cook to let him sweep it, and returned triumphant with the bread he had earned, which he ate at the cardinal's table. [6]

From the very beginning Egidio's life commanded respect; it was at once so original, so gay, so spiritual, [7] and so mystical, that even in the least exact and most expanded accounts his legend has remained almost free from all addition. He is, after St. Francis, the finest incarnation of the Franciscan spirit.

The incidents which are here cited are all, so to speak, illustrations of the Rule; in fact there is nothing more explicit than its commands with respect to work.

The Brothers, after entering upon the Order, were to continue to exercise the calling which they had when in the world, and if they had none they were to learn one. For payment they were to accept only the food that was necessary for them, but in case that was insufficient they might beg. In addition they were naturally permitted to own the instruments of their calling. [8] Brother Ginepro, whose acquaintance we shall make further on, had an awl, and gained his bread wherever he went by mending shoes, and we see St. Clara working even on her death-bed.

This obligation to work with the hands merits all the more to be brought into the light, because it was destined hardly to survive St. Francis, and because to it is due in part the original character of the first generation of the Order. Yet this was not the real reason for the being of the Brothers Minor. Their mission consisted above all in being the spouses of Poverty.

Terrified by the ecclesiastical disorders of the time, haunted by painful memories of his past life, Francis saw in money the special instrument of the devil; in moments of excitement he went so far as to execrate it, as if there had been in the metal itself a sort of magical power and secret curse. Money was truly for him the sacrament of evil.

This is not the place for asking if he was wrong; grave authors have demonstrated at length the economic troubles which would have been let loose upon the world if men had followed him. Alas! his madness, if madness it were, is a kind of which one need not fear the contagion.

He felt that in this respect the Rule could not be too absolute, and that if unfortunately the door was opened to various interpretations of it, there would be no stopping-point. The course of events and the periodical convulsions which shook his Order show clearly enough how rightly he judged.

I do not know nor desire to know if theologians have yet come to a scientific conclusion with regard to the poverty of Jesus, but it seems evident to me that poverty with the labor of the hands is the ideal held up by the Galilean to the efforts of his disciples.

Still it is easy to see that Franciscan poverty is neither to be confounded with the unfeeling pride of the stoic, nor with the stupid horror of all joy felt by certain devotees; St. Francis renounced everything only that he might the better possess everything. The lives of the immense majority of our contemporaries are ruled by the fatal error that the more one possesses the more one enjoys. Our exterior, civil liberties continually increase, but at the same time our inward freedom is taking flight; how many are there among us who are literally possessed by what they possess? [9]

Poverty not only permitted the Brothers to mingle with the poor and speak to them with authority, but, removing from them all material anxiety, it left them free to enjoy without hindrance those hidden treasures which nature reserves for pure idealists.

The ever-thickening barriers which modern life, with its sickly search for useless comfort, has set up between us and nature did not exist for these men, so full of youth and life, eager for wide spaces and the outer air. This is what gave St. Francis and his companions that quick susceptibility to Nature which made them thrill in mysterious harmony with her. Their communion with Nature was so intimate, so ardent, that Umbria, with the harmonious poetry of its skies, the joyful outburst of its spring-time, is still the best document from which to study them. The tie between the two is so indissoluble, that after having lived a certain time in company with St. Francis, one can hardly, on reading certain passages of his biographers, help *seeing* the spot where the incident took place, hearing the vague sounds of creatures and things, precisely as, when reading certain pages of a beloved author, one hears the sound of his voice.

The worship of Poverty of the early Franciscans had in it, then, nothing ascetic or barbarous, nothing which recalls the Stylites or the Nazirs. She was their bride, and like true lovers they felt no fatigues which they might endure to find and remain near her.

> La lor concordia e lor lieti sembianti,
> Amor e maraviglia e dolce sguardo
> Facean esser cagion de' pensier santi. [10]

To draw the portrait of an ideal knight at the beginning of the thirteenth century is to draw Francis's very portrait, with this difference, that what the knight did for his lady, he did for Poverty. This comparison is not a mere caprice; he himself profoundly felt it and expressed it with perfect clearness, and it is only by keeping it clearly present in the mind that we can see into the very depth of his heart. [11]

To find any other souls of the same nature one must come down to Giovanni di Parma and Jacoponi di Todi. The life of St. Francis as troubadour has been written; it would have been better to write it as knight, for this is the explanation of his whole life, and as it were the heart of his heart. From the day when, forgetting the songs of his friends and suddenly stopped in the public place of Assisi, he met Poverty, his bride, and swore to her faith and love, down to that evening when, naked upon the naked earth of Portiuncula, he breathed out his life, it may be said that all his thoughts went out to this lady of his chaste loves. For twenty years he served her without faltering, sometimes with an artlessness which would appear infantine, if something infinitely sincere and sublime did not arrest the smile upon the most sceptical lips.

Poverty agreed marvellously with that need which men had at that time, and which perhaps they have lost less than they suppose, the need of an ideal very high, very pure, mysterious, inaccessible, which yet they may picture to themselves in concrete form. Sometimes a few privileged disciples saw the lovely and pure Lady descend from heaven to salute her spouse, but, whether visible or not, she always kept close beside her Umbrian lover, as she kept close beside the Galilean; in the stable of the nativity, upon the cross at Golgotha, and even in the borrowed tomb where his body lay.

During several years this ideal was not alone that of St. Francis, but also of all the Brothers. In poverty the *gente poverelle* had found safety, love, liberty; and all the efforts of the new apostles are directed to the keeping of this precious treasure.

Their worship sometimes might seem excessive. They showed their spouse those delicate attentions, those refinements of courtesy so frequent in the morning light of a betrothal, but which one gradually forgets till they become incomprehensible. [12]

The number of disciples continually increased; almost every week brought new recruits; the year 1211 was without doubt devoted by Francis to a tour in Umbria and the neighboring provinces. His sermons were short appeals to conscience; his heart went out to his hearers in ineffable tones, so that when men tried to repeat what they had heard they found themselves incapable. [13] The Rule of 1221 has preserved for us a summary of these appeals:

> "Here is an exhortation which all the Brothers may make when they think best: Fear and honor God, praise and bless him. Give thanks unto him. Adore the Lord, Almighty God, in Trinity and unity, the Father, the Son, and the Holy Ghost. Repent and make fruits meet for repentance, for you know that we shall soon die. Give, and it shall be given unto you. Forgive, and you shall be forgiven; for if you forgive not, God will not forgive you. Blessed are they who die repenting, for they shall be in the kingdom of heaven.... Abstain carefully from all evil, and persevere in the good until the end. "[14]

We see how simple and purely ethical was the early Franciscan preaching. The complications of dogma and scholasticism are entirely absent from it. To understand how new this was and how refreshing to the soul we must study the disciples that came after him.

With St. Anthony of Padua ([Cross] June 13, 1231; canonized in 1233[15]), the most illustrious of them all, the descent is immense. The distance between these two men is as great as that which separates Jesus from St. Paul.

I do not judge the disciple; he was of his time in not knowing how to say simply what he thought, in always desiring to subtilize it, to extract it from passages in the Bible turned from their natural meaning by efforts at once laborious and puerile; what the alchemists did in their continual making of strange mixtures from which they fancied that they should bring out gold, the preachers did to the texts, in order to bring out the truth.

The originality of St. Francis is only the more brilliant and meritorious; with him gospel simplicity reappeared upon the earth. [16] Like the lark with which he so much loved to compare himself, [17] he was at his ease only in the open sky. He remained thus until his death. The epistle to all Christians which he dictated in the last weeks of his life repeats the same ideas in the same terms, perhaps with a little more feeling and a shade of sadness. The evening breeze which breathed upon his face and bore away his words was their symbolical accompaniment.

"I, Brother Francis, the least of your servants, pray and conjure you by that Love which is God himself, willing to throw myself at your feet and kiss them, to receive with humility and love these words and all others of our Lord Jesus Christ, to put them to profit and carry them out. "

This was not a more or less oratorical formula. Hence conversions multiplied with an incredible rapidity. Often, as formerly with Jesus, a look, a word sufficed Francis to attach to himself men who would follow him until their death. It is impossible, alas! to analyze the best of this eloquence, all made of love, intimate apprehension, and fire. The written word can no more give an idea of it than it can give us an idea of a sonata of Beethoven or a painting by Rembrandt. We are often amazed, on reading the memoirs of those who have been great conquerors of souls, to find ourselves remaining cold, finding in them all no trace of animation or originality. It is because we have only a lifeless relic in the hand; the soul is gone. It is the white wafer of the sacrament, but how shall that rouse in us the emotions of the beloved disciple lying on the Lord's breast on the night of the Last Supper?

The class from which Francis recruited his disciples was still about the same; they were nearly all young men of Assisi and its environs, some the sons of agriculturists, and others nobles; the School and the Church was very little represented among them. [18]

Everything still went on with an unheard-of simplicity. In theory, obedience to the superior was absolute; in practice, we can see Francis continually giving his companions complete liberty of action. [19] Men entered the Order without a novitiate of any sort; it sufficed to say to Francis that they wanted to lead with him a life of evangelical perfection, and to prove it by giving all that they possessed to the poor. The more unpretending were the neophytes, the more tenderness he had for them. Like his Master, he had a partiality for those who were lost, for men whom regular society casts out of its limits, but who with all their crimes and scandals are nearer to sainthood than mediocrities and hypocrites.

> One day St. Francis, passing by the desert of Borgo San Sepolcro came to a place called Monte-Casale, [20] and behold a noble and refined young man came to him. "Father, " he said, "I would gladly be one of your disciples. "
>
> "My son, " said St. Francis, "you are young, refined, and noble; you will not be able to follow poverty and live wretched like us. "
>
> "But, my father, are not you men like me? What you do I can do with the grace of Jesus. " This reply was well-pleasing to St. Francis, who, giving him his blessing, incontinently received him into the Order under the name of Brother Angelo.
>
> He conducted himself so well that a little while after he was made guardian[21] of Monte-Casale. Now, in those times there were three famous robbers who did much evil in the country. They came to the hermitage one day to beg Brother

Angelo to give them something to eat; but he replied to them with severe reproaches: "What! robbers, evil-doers, assassins, have you not only no shame for stealing the goods of others, but you would farther devour the alms of the servants of God, you who are not worthy to live, and who have respect neither for men nor for God your Creator. Depart, and let me never see you here again!"

They went away full of rage. But behold, the Saint returned, bringing a wallet of bread and a bottle of wine which had been given him, and the guardian told him how he had sent away the robbers; then St. Francis reproved him severely for showing himself so cruel.... "I command thee by thine obedience," said he, "to take at once this loaf and this wine and go seek the robbers by hill and dell until you have found them, to offer them this as from me, and to kneel there before them and humbly ask their pardon, and pray them in my name no longer to do wrong but to fear God; and if they do it, I promise to provide for all their wants, to see that they always have enough to eat and drink. After that you may humbly return hither."

Brother Angelo did all that had been commanded him, while St. Francis on his part prayed God to convert the robbers. They returned with the brother, and when St. Francis gave them the assurance of the pardon of God, they changed their lives and entered the Order, in which they lived and died most holily. [22]

What has sometimes been said of the voice of the blood is still more true of the voice of the soul. When a man truly wakens another to moral life, he gains for himself an unspeakable gratitude. The word *master* is often profaned, but it can express the noblest and purest of earthly ties.

Who are those among us, who in the hours of manly innocence when they examine their own consciences, do not see rising up before them from out of the past the ever beloved and loving face of one who, perhaps without knowing it, initiated them into spiritual things? At such a time we would throw ourselves at the feet of this father, would tell him in burning words of our admiration and gratitude. We cannot do it, for the soul has its own bashfulness; but who knows that our disquietude and embarrassment do not betray us, and unveil, better than words could do, the depths of our heart? The air they breathed at Portiuncula was all impregnated with joy and gratitude like this.

To many of the Brothers, St. Francis was truly a saviour; he had delivered them from chains heavier than those of prisons. And therefore their greatest desire was in their turn to call others to this same liberty.

We have already seen Brother Bernardo on a mission to Florence a few months after his entrance into the Order. Arrived at maturity when he put on the habit, he appears in some degree the senior of this apostolic college. He knew how to obey St. Francis and remain faithful to the very end to the ideal of the early days; but he had no longer that privilege of the young—of Brother Leo, for example—of being able to transform himself almost entirely into the image of him whom he admired. His physiognomy has not that touch of juvenile originality, of poetic fancy, which is so great a charm of the others.

Toward this epoch two Brothers entered the Order, men such as the successors of St. Francis never received, whose history throws a bright light on the simplicity of the early days. It will be remembered with what zeal Francis had repaired several churches; his solicitude went further; he saw a sort of profanation in the negligence with which most of them were kept; the want of cleanliness of the sacred objects, ill-concealed by tinsel, gave him a sort of pain, and it often happened that when he was going to preach somewhere he secretly called together the priests of the locality and implored them to look after the decency of the service. But even in these cases he was not content to preach only in words; binding together some stalks of heather he would make them into brooms for sweeping out the churches.

One day in the suburbs of Assisi he was performing this task when a peasant appeared, who had left his oxen and cart out in the fields while he came to gaze at him.

"Brother, " said he on entering, "give me the broom. I will help you, " and he swept out the rest of the church.

When he had finished, "Brother, " he said to Francis, "for a long time I have decided to serve God, especially when I heard men speak of you. But I never knew how to find you.

Now it has pleased God that we should meet, and henceforth I shall do whatever you may please to command me. "

Francis seeing his fervor felt a great joy; it seemed to him that with his simplicity and honesty he would become a good friar.

It appears indeed that he had only too much simplicity, for after his reception he felt himself bound to imitate every motion of the master, and when the latter coughed, spat, or sighed, he did the same. At last Francis noticed it and gently reproved him. Later he became so perfect that the other friars admired him greatly, and after his death, which took place not long after, St. Francis loved to relate his conversion, calling him not Brother John, but Brother St. John. [23]

Ginepro is still more celebrated for his holy follies.

One day he went to see a sick Brother and offered him his services. The patient confessed that he had a great longing to eat a pig's foot; the visitor immediately rushed out, and armed with a knife ran to the neighboring forest, where, espying a troop of pigs, he cut off a foot of one of them, returning to the monastery full of pride over his trophy.

The owner of the pigs shortly followed, howling like mad, but Ginepro went straight to him and pointed out with so much volubility that he had done him a great service, that the man, after overwhelming him with reproaches, suddenly begged pardon, killed the pig and invited all the Brothers to feast upon it. Ginepro was probably less mad than the story would lead us to suppose; Franciscan humility never had a more sincere disciple; he could not endure the tokens of admiration which the populace very early lavished on the growing Order, and which by their extravagance contributed so much to its decadence.

One day, as he was entering Rome, the report of his arrival spread abroad, and a great crowd came out to meet him. To escape was impossible, but he suddenly had an inspiration; near the gate of the city some children were playing at see-saw; to the great amazement of the Romans Ginepro joined them, and, without heeding the salutations addressed to him, remained so absorbed in his play that at last his indignant admirers departed. [24]

It is clear that the life at Portiuncula must have been very different from that of an ordinary convent. So much youth, [25] simplicity, love, quickly drew the eyes of men toward it. From all sides they were turned to those thatched huts, where dwelt a spiritual family whose members loved one another more than men love on earth, leading a life of labor, mirth, and devotion. The humble chapel seemed a new Zion destined to enlighten the world, and many in their dreams beheld blind humanity coming to kneel there and recover sight. [26]

Among the first disciples who joined themselves to St. Francis we must mention Brother Silvestro, the first priest who entered the Order, the very same whom we have already seen the day that Bernardo di Quintevalle distributed his goods among the poor. Since then he had not had a moment's peace, bitterly reproaching himself for his avarice; night and day he thought only of that, and in his dreams he saw Francis exorcising a horrid monster which infested all the region. [27]

By his age and the nature of the memory he has left behind him Silvestro resembles Brother Bernardo. He was what is usually understood by a holy priest, but nothing denotes that he had the truly Franciscan love of great enterprises, distant journeys, perilous missions. Withdrawn into one of the grottos of the Carceri, absorbed in the contemplative life, he gave spiritual counsels to his brethren as occasion served. [28]

The typical Franciscan priest is Brother Leo. The date of his entrance into the Order is not exactly known, but we are probably not far from the truth in placing it about 1214. Of a charming simplicity, tender, affectionate, refined, he is, with Brother Elias, the one who plays the noblest part during the obscure years in which the new reform was being elaborated. Becoming Francis's confessor and secretary, treated by him as his favorite son, he excited much opposition, and was to the end of his long life the head of the strict observance. [29]

> One winter's day, St. Francis was going with Brother Leo from Perugia to Santa Maria degli Angeli, and the cold, being intense, made them shiver; he called Brother Leo, who was walking a little in advance, and said: "O Brother Leo, may it please God that the Brothers Minor all over the world may give a great example of holiness and edification; write,

however, and note with care, that not in this is the perfect joy."

St. Francis, going on a little farther, called him a second time: "O Brother Leo, if the Brothers Minor gave sight to the blind, healed the infirm, cast out demons, gave hearing to the deaf, or even what is much more, if they raised the four days dead, write that not in this is the perfect joy."

Going on a little farther he cried: "O Brother Leo, if the Brother Minor knew all languages, all science, and all scriptures, if he could prophesy and reveal not only future things but even the secrets of consciences and of souls, write that not in this consists the perfect joy."

Going a little farther St. Francis called to him again: "O Brother Leo, little sheep of God, if the Brother Minor could speak the language of angels, if he knew the courses of the stars and the virtues of plants, if all the treasures of earth were revealed to him, and he knew the qualities of birds, fishes, and all animals, of men, trees, rocks, roots, and waters, write that not in these is the perfect joy."

And advancing still a little farther St. Francis called loudly to him: "O Brother Leo, if the Brother Minor could preach so well as to convert all infidels to the faith of Christ, write that not in this is the perfect joy."

While speaking thus they had already gone more than two miles, and Brother Leo, full of surprise, said to him: "Father, I pray you in God's name tell me in what consists the perfect joy."

And St. Francis replied: "When we arrive at Santa Maria degli Angeli, soaked with rain, frozen with cold, covered with mud, dying of hunger, and we knock and the porter comes in a rage, saying, 'Who are you?' and we answer, 'We are two of your brethren,' and he says, 'You lie, you are two lewd fellows who go up and down corrupting the world and stealing the alms of the poor. Go away from here!' and he does not open to us, but leaves us outside shivering in the snow and rain, frozen, starved, till night; then, if thus maltreated and turned away, we patiently endure all without murmuring against him, if we think with humility and charity that this porter really knows us truly and that God makes him speak thus to us, then, O Brother Leo, write that in this is the perfect joy.... Above all the graces and all the gifts which the Holy Spirit gives to his friends is the grace to conquer oneself, and willingly to suffer pain, outrages, disgrace, and evil treatment, for the love of Christ! "[30]

Although by its slight and somewhat playful character this story recalls the insipid statues of the fourteenth century, it has justly become celebrated, its spirit is thoroughly Franciscan; that transcendent idealism, which sees in perfection and joy two equivalent terms, and places perfect joy in the pure and serene region of the perfecting of oneself; that sublime simplicity which so easily puts in their true place the miracle-worker and the scholar, these are perhaps not entirely new; [31] but St. Francis must have had singular moral strength to impose upon his contemporaries ideas in such absolute contradiction to their habits and their hopes; for the intellectual aristocracy of the thirteenth century with one accord found the perfect joy in knowledge, while the people found it in miracles.

Doubtless we must not forget those great mystical families, which, all through the Middle Ages, were the refuge of the noblest souls; but they never had this fine simplicity. The School is always more or less the gateway to mysticism; it is possible only to an elect of subtile minds; a pious peasant seldom understands the Imitation.

It may be said that all St. Francis's philosophy is contained in this chapter of the Fioretti. [32] From it we foresee what will be his attitude toward learning, and are helped to understand how it happens that this famous saint was so poor a miracle-worker.

Twelve centuries before, Jesus had said, "Blessed are the poor in spirit. Blessed are they who suffer. " The words of St. Francis are only a commentary, but this commentary is worthy of the text.

It remains to say a word concerning two disciples who were always closely united with Brother Leo in the Franciscan memorials—Rufino and Masseo.

Born of a noble family connected with that of St. Clara, the former was soon distinguished in the Order for his visions and ecstasies, but his great timidity checked him as soon as he tried to preach: for this reason he is always to be found in the most isolated hermitages— Carceri, Verna, Greccio. [33]

Masseo, of Marignano, a small village in the environs of Assisi, was his very opposite; handsome, well made, witty, he attracted attention by his fine presence and his great facility of speech; he occupies a special place in popular Franciscan tradition. He deserves it. St. Francis, to test his humility, made him the porter and cook of the hermitage, [34] but in these functions Masseo showed himself to be so perfectly a *Minor* that from that time the master particularly loved to have him for companion in his missionary journeys.

One day they were travelling together, when they arrived at the intersection of the roads to Sienna, Arezzo, and Florence.

"Which one shall we take? " asked Masseo.

"Whichever one God wills. "

"But how shall we know which one God wills? "

"You shall see. Go and stand at the crossing of the roads, turn round and round as the children do, and do not stop until I bid you. "

Brother Masseo began to turn; seized with a vertigo, he was nearly falling, but caught himself up at once. Finally Francis called out, "Stop! which way are you facing? "

"Toward Sienna. "

"Very well; God wills that we go to Sienna. "[35]

Such a method of making up one's mind is doubtless not for the daily needs of life, but Francis employed still others, like it, if not in form at least in fact.

Up to this time we have seen the brethren living together in their hermitages or roving the highways, preaching repentance. It would, however, be a mistake to think that their whole lives were passed thus. To understand the first Franciscans we must absolutely forget what they may have been since that time, and what monks are in general; if Portiuncula was a monastery it was also a workshop, where each brother practised the trade which had been his before entering the Order; but what is stranger still to our ideas, the Brothers often went out as servants. [36]

Brother Egidio's case was not an exception, it was the rule. This did not last long, for very soon the friars who entered a house as domestics came to be treated as distinguished guests; but in the beginning they were literally servants, and took upon themselves the most menial labors. Among the works which they might undertake Francis recommended above all the care of lepers. We have already seen the important part which these unfortunates played in his conversion; he always retained for them a peculiar pity, which he sought to make his disciples share.

For several years the Brothers Minor may be said to have gone from lazaretto to lazaretto, preaching by day in the towns and villages, and retiring at night to these refuges, where they rendered to these *patients of God* the most repugnant services.

The Crucigeri, who took charge of the greater number of leper-houses, always welcomed these kindly disposed aides, who, far from asking any sort of recompense, were willing to eat whatever the patients might have left. [37] In fact, although created solely for the care of lepers, the Brothers of this Order sometimes lost patience when the sufferers were too exacting, and instead of being grateful had only murmurs or even reproaches for their benefactors. In these desperate cases the intervention of Francis and his disciples was especially precious. It often happened that a Brother was put in special charge of a single leper, whose companion and servant he continued to be, sometimes for a long period. [38]

The following narrative shows Francis's love for these unfortunates, and his method with them. [39]

It happened one time that the Brothers were serving the lepers and the sick in a hospital, near to the place where St. Francis was. Among them was a leper who was so impatient, so cross-grained, so unendurable, that everyone believed him to be possessed by the devil, and rightly enough, for he heaped insults and blows upon those who waited upon him, and what was worse, he continually insulted and blasphemed the blessed Christ and his most holy Mother the Virgin Mary, so that there was no longer anyone who could or would wait upon him. The Brothers would willingly have endured the insults and abuse which he lavished upon them, in order to augment the merit of their patience, but their souls could not consent to hear those which he uttered against Christ and his Mother. They therefore resolved to abandon this leper, but not without having told the whole story exactly to St. Francis, who at that time was dwelling not far away.

When they told him St. Francis betook himself to the wicked leper; "May God give thee peace, my most dear brother, " he said to him as he drew near.

"And what peace, " asked the leper, "can I receive from God, who has taken away my peace and every good thing, and has made my body a mass of stinking and corruption? "

St. Francis said to him: "My brother, be patient, for God gives us diseases in this world for the salvation of our souls, and when we endure them patiently they are the fountain of great merit to us. "

"How can I endure patiently continual pains which torture me day and night? And it is not only my disease that I suffer from, but the friars that you gave me to wait upon me are unendurable, and do not take care of me as they ought. "

Then St. Francis perceived that this leper was possessed by the spirit of evil, and he betook himself to his knees in order to pray for him. Then returning he said to him: "My son, since you are not satisfied with the others, I will wait upon you. "

"That is all very well, but what can you do for me more than they? "

"I will do whatever you wish. "

"Very well; I wish you to wash me from head to foot, for I smell so badly that I disgust myself. "

Then St. Francis made haste to heat some water with many sweet-smelling herbs; next he took off the leper's clothes and began to bathe him, while a Brother poured out the water. And behold, by a divine miracle, wherever St. Francis touched him with his holy hands the leprosy disappeared and the flesh became perfectly sound. And in proportion as the flesh was healed the soul of the wretched man was also healed, and he began to feel a lively sorrow for his sins, and to weep bitterly.... And being completely healed both in body and soul, he cried with all his might: "Woe unto me, for I have deserved hell for the abuses and outrages which I have said and done to the Brothers, for my impatience and my blasphemies. "

One day, Brother John, whose simplicity we have already seen, and who had been especially put in charge of a certain leper, took him for a walk to Portiuncula, as if he had not been the victim of a contagious malady. Reproaches were not spared him; the leper heard them and could not hide his sadness and distress; it seemed to him like being a second time banished from the world. Francis was quick to remark all this and to feel sharp remorse for it; the thought of having saddened one of *God's patients* was unendurable; he not only begged his pardon, but he caused food to be served, and sitting down beside him he shared his repast, eating from the same porringer. [40] We see with what perseverance he pursued by every means the realization of his ideal.

The details just given show the Umbrian movement, as it appears to me, to be one of the most humble and at the same time the most sincere and practical attempts to realize the kingdom of God on earth. How far removed we are here from the superstitious vulgarity of the mechanical devotion, the deceitful miracle-working of certain Catholics; how far also from the commonplace, complacent, quibbling, theorizing Christianity of certain Protestants!

Francis is of the race of mystics, for no intermediary comes between God and his soul; but his mysticism is that of Jesus leading his disciples to the Tabor of contemplation; but when, overflooded with joy, they long to build tabernacles that they may remain on the heights and satiate themselves with the raptures of ecstasy, "Fools, " he says to them, "ye know not what ye ask, " and directing their gaze to the crowds wandering like sheep having no shepherd, he leads them back to the plain, to the midst of those who moan, who suffer, who blaspheme.

The higher the moral stature of Francis the more he was exposed to the danger of being understood only by the very few, and disappointed by those who were nearest to him. Reading the Franciscan authors, one feels every moment how the radiant beauty of the model is marred by the awkwardness of the disciple. It could not have been otherwise, and this difference between this master and the companions is evident from the very beginnings of the Order. The greater number of the biographers have drawn the veil of oblivion over the difficulties created by certain Brothers as well as those which came from the ecclesiastical hierarchy, but we must not allow ourselves to be deceived by this almost universal silence.

Here and there we find indications all the more precious for being, so to say, involuntary. Brother Rufino, for example, the same who was destined to become one of the intimates of Francis's later days, assumed an attitude of revolt shortly after his entrance into the Order. He thought it foolish in Francis when, instead of leaving the friars to give themselves unceasingly to prayer, he sent them out in all directions to wait upon lepers. [41] His own ideal was the life of the hermits of the Thebaïde, as it is related in the then popular legends of St. Anthony, St. Paul, St. Paconius, and twenty others. He once passed Lent in one of the grottos of the Carceri. Holy Thursday having arrived, Francis, who was also there, summoned all the brethren who were dispersed about the neighborhood, whether in grottos or huts, to observe with him the memories to which this day was consecrated. Rufino refused to come; "For that matter, " he added, "I have decided to follow him no longer; I mean to remain here and live solitary, for in this way I shall be more surely saved than by submitting myself to this man and his nonsense. "

Young and enthusiastic for the most part, it was not always without difficulty that the Brothers formed the habit of keeping their work in the background. Agreeing with their master as to fundamentals, they would have liked to make more of a stir, attract public attention by more obvious devotion; there were some among them whom it did not satisfy to be saints, but who also wished to appear such.

FOOTNOTES:

[1]   1 Cel., 44; 3 Soc., 55.

[2]   3 Soc., 56; *Spec.* , 32b; *Conform.* , 217b, 1; *Fior. Bibl. Angel.* , Amoni, p. 378.

[3]   This forest has disappeared. Some of Francis's counsels have been collected in the Admonitions. See 1 Cel., 37-41.

[4]   Vide Angelo Clareno, *Tribul.* cod. Laur., 3b.

[5]   2 Cel., 3, 97 and 98. The Conformities, 142a, 1, cite textually 97 as coming from the *Legenda Antiqua*. Cf. *Spec.* , 64b. —2 Cel., 3, 21. Cf. *Conform.* , 171a, 1; *Spec.* , 19b. See especially Rule of 1221, *cap.* 7; Rule of 1223, *cap.* 5; the Will and 3 Soc. 41. The passage, *liceat eis habere ferramenta et instrumenta suis artibus necessaria,* sufficiently proves that certain friars had real trades.

[6]   A. SS., Aprilis, t. iii., pp. 220-248; *Fior. Vita d'Egidio*; *Spec.* , 158 ff; *Conform.* , 53-60.

[7]   Other examples will be found below; it may suffice to recall here his sally: "The glorious Virgin Mother of God had sinners for parents, she never entered any religious order, and yet she is what she is! " A. SS., *loc. cit.* , p. 234.

[8]   The passage of the Will, *firmiter volo quod omnes laborent,...* has a capital importance because it shows Francis renewing in the most solemn manner injunctions already made from the origin of the Order. Cf. 1 Cel., 38 and 39; *Conform.* , 219b. 1: *Juvabant Fratres pauperes homines in agris eorum et ipsi dabant postea eis de pane amore Dei. Spec.* , 34; 69. Vide also *Archiv.* , t. ii., pp. 272 and 299; Eccleston, 1 and 15; 2 Cel., 1, 12.

[9]   *Nihil volebat proprietatis habere ut omnia plenius posset in Domino possidere.* B. de Besse, 102a.

[10]   Their concord and their joyous semblances The love, the wonder and the sweet regard They made to be the cause of holy thought.

        DANTE: Paradiso, canto xi., verses 76-78. Longfellow's translation.

[11]   *Amor factus... castis eam, stringit amplexibus nec ad horam patitur non esse muritus.* 2 Cel., 3, 1; cf. 1 Cel., 35; 51; 75; 2 Cel., 3, 128; 3 Soc., 15; 22; 33; 35; 50; Bon., 87; *Fior.* 13.

[12]   Bon., 93. —*Prohibuit fratrem qui faciebat coquinam ne poneret legumina de sero in aqua calida quæ debebat dare fratribus ad manducandum die sequenti ut observaverint illud verbum Evangelii: Nolite solliciti esse de crastino. Spec.* , 15.

[13]   2 Cel., 3, 50.

[14]   *Cap.* , 21. Cf. *Fior., I. consid.* , 18; 30; *Conform.* , 103a, 2; 2 Cel., 3, 99; 100; 121. Vide Müller, *Anfänge*, p. 187.

[15]   Vide his *Opera omnia postillis illustrata*, by Father de la Haye, 1739, f^o. For his life, Surius and Wadding arranged and mutilated the sources to which they had access; the Bollandists had only a legend of the fifteenth century. The Latin manuscript 14,363 of the Bibliothèque Nationale gives one which dates from the thirteenth. Very Rev. Father Hilary, of Paris: *Saint Antoine de Padone, sa légende primitive*, Montreuil-sur-Mer, Imprimerie Notre-Dame-des-Prés, 1890, 1 vol., 8vo. Cf. *Legenda seu vita et miracula S. Antonii sæculo xiii concinnata ex cod. memb. antoniæ bibliothecæ* a P. M. Antonio Maria Josa min. comv. Bologna, 1883, 1 vol., 8vo.

[16]   This evangelical character of his mission is brought out in relief by all his biographers. 1 Cel., 56; 84; 89; 3 Soc. 25; 34; 40; 43; 45; 48; 51; 57; 2 Cel., 3, 8; 50; 93.

[17]   *Spec.* , 134; 2 Cel., 3, 128.

[18]   The Order was at first essentially lay (at the present time it is, so far as I know, the only one in which there is no difference of costume between laymen and priests). Vide Ehrle, *Archiv.* , iii., p. 563. It is the influence of the friars from northern countries which has especially changed it in this matter. General Aymon, of Faversham (1240-1243), decided that laymen should be excluded from all charges; *laicos ad officia inhabilitavit, quæ usque tunc ut clerici exercebant.* (*Chron.* xxiv. *gen.* cod. Gadd. relig., 53, f° 110a). Among the early Brothers who refused ordination there were surely some who did so from humility, but this sentiment is not enough

to explain all the cases. There were also with certain of them revolutionary desires and as it were a vague memory of the prophecies of Gioacchino di Fiore upon the age succeeding that of the priests: *Fior.* , 27. *Frate Pellegrino non volle mai andare come chierico, ma come laico, benche fassi molto litterato e grande decretalista.* Cf. *Conform.* , 71a., 2. *Fr. Thomas Hibernicus sibi pollecem amputavit ne ad sacerdotium cogeretur. Conform.* , 124b, 2.

[19]   See, for example, the letter to Brother Leo. Cf. *Conform.* , 53b, 2. *Fratri Egidio dedit licentiam liberam ut iret quocumque vellet et staret ubicumque sibi placeret.*

[20]   The hermitage of Monte-Casale, at two hours walk northeast from Borgo San Sepolero, still exists in its original state. It is one of the most significant and curious of the Franciscan deserts.

[21]   The office of guardian (superior of a monastery) naturally dates from the time when the Brothers stationed themselves in small groups in the villages of Umbria—that is to say, most probably from the year 1211. A few years later the monasteries were united to form a custodia. Finally, about 1215, Central Italy was divided unto a certain number of provinces with provincial ministers at their head. All this was done little by little, for Francis never permitted himself to regulate what did not yet exist.

[22]   *Fior.* , 26; Conform., 119b, 1. Cf. Rule of 1221, cap. vii. *Quicumque ad eos (fratres) venerint, amicus vel adversarius, fur vel latro benigne recipiatur.*

[23]   2 Cel., 3, 120; *Spec.* , 37; *Conform.* , 53a, 1. See below, p. 385, n. 1.

[24]   *Fior.* , Vita di fra Ginepro; *Spec.* , 174-182; *Conform.* , 62b.

[25]   A. SS., p. 600.

[26]   3 Soc., 56; 2 Cel., 1, 13; Bon., 24.

[27]   Bon., 30; 3 Soc., 30, 31; 2 Cel., 3, 52. Cf. *Fior.* , 2. The dragon of this dream perhaps symbolizes heresy.

[28] Bon., 83; 172; *Fior.* , 1, 16; *Conform.* , 49a, 1, and 110b, 1; 2 Cel., 3, 51.

[29] Bernard de Besse, *De laudibus,* Turin MS., f°. 102b and 96a. He died November 15, 1271. A. SS., Augusti, t. ii., p. 221.

[30] *Fior.* , 8; *Spec.* , 89b ff. ; *Conform.* , 30b, 2, and 140a, 2.

[31] I need not here point out the analogy in form between this chapter and St. Paul's celebrated song of love, 1 Cor. xiii.

[32] We find the same thoughts in nearly the same terms in *cap.* v. of the *Verba sacræ admonitionis.*

[33] He is the second of the Three Companions. 3 Soc., 1; cf. 1 Cel., 95; *Fior.* , 1; 29, 30, 31; Eccleston, 12; *Spec.* , 110a-114b; *Conform.* , 51b ff. ; cf. 2 Cel., 2, 4.

[34] Very probably that of the Carceri, though the name is not indicated Vide 3 Soc., 1; *Fior.* , 4; 10; 11; 12; 13; 16; 27; 32; *Conform.* , 51b, 1 ff; *Tribul. Archiv.* , t. ii., p. 263.

[35] *Fior.* , 11; *Conform.* , 50b, 2; *Spec.* , 104a.

[36] Rule of 1221, chap. 7. *Omnes fratres, in quibuscumque locis fuerint apud aliquos ad serviendum, vel ad laborandum, non sint camerarii, nec cellarii, nec præsint in domibus corum quibus serviunt.* Cf. 1 Cel., 38 and 40; A. SS., p. 606.

[37] 1 Cel., 103; 39; *Spec.* , 28; Reg. 1221, ix. ; *Giord.* , 33 and 39.

[38] Vide *Spec.* , 34b. ; *Fior.* , 4.

[39] All the details of this story lead me to think that it refers to Portiuncula and the hospital *San Salvatore delle Pareti.* The story is given by the *Conform.* , 174b, 2, as taken from the *Legenda Antiqua.* Cf. *Spec.* , 56b; *Fior.* , 25.

[40] In the *Speculum,* f° 41a, this story ends with the phrase: *Qui vidit hæc scripsit et testimonium perhibet de hiis.* The brother is here called *Frater Jacobus simplex.* Cf. *Conform.* , 174b.

[41] *Conform.* , 51b, 1. Cf. 2 Cel., 2, 4; *Spec.* , 110b; *Fior.* , 29.

CHAPTER IX

SANTA CLARA

Popular piety in Umbria never separates the memory of St. Francis from that of Santa Clara. It is right.

Clara[1] was born at Assisi in 1194, and was consequently about twelve years younger than Francis. She belonged to the noble family of the Sciffi. At the age when a little girl's imagination awakes and stirs, she heard the follies of the son of Bernardone recounted at length. She was sixteen when the Saint preached for the first time in the cathedral, suddenly appearing like an angel of peace in a city torn by intestine dissensions. To her his appeals were like a revelation. It seemed as if Francis was speaking for her, that he divined her secret sorrows, her most personal anxieties, and all that was ardent and enthusiastic in the heart of this young girl rushed like a torrent that suddenly finds an outlet into the channel indicated by him. For saints as for heroes the supreme stimulus is woman's admiration.

But here, more than ever, we must put away the vulgar judgment which can understand no union between man and woman where the sexual instinct has no part. That which makes the union of the sexes something almost divine is that it is the prefiguration, the symbol, of the union of souls. Physical love is an ephemeral spark, designed to kindle in human hearts the flame of a more lasting love; it is the outer court of the temple, but not the most holy place; its inestimable value is precisely that it leaves us abruptly at the door of the holiest of all as if to invite us to step over the threshold.

The mysterious sigh of nature goes out for the union of souls. This is the unknown God to whom debauchees, those pagans of love, offer their sacrifices, and this sacred imprint, even though effaced, though soiled by all pollutions, often saves the man of the world from inspiring as much disgust as the drunkard and the criminal.

But sometimes—more often than we think—there are souls so pure, so little earthly, that on their first meeting they enter the most holy place, and once there the thought of any other union would be not merely a descent, but an impossibility. Such was the love of St. Francis and St. Clara.

But these are exceptions. There is something mysterious in this supreme purity; it is so high that in holding it up to men one risks speaking to them in an unknown tongue, or even worse.

The biographers of St. Francis have clearly felt the danger of offering to the multitude the sight of certain beauties which are far beyond them, and this is for us the great fault of their works. They try to give us not so much the true portrait of Francis as that of the perfect minister-general of the Order such as they conceive it, such as it must needs be to serve as a model for his disciples; thus they have made this model somewhat according to the measure of those whom it is to serve, by omitting here and there features which, stupidly interpreted, might have furnished material for the malevolence of unscrupulous adversaries, or from which disciples little versed in spiritual things could not have failed to draw support for permitting themselves dangerous intimacies. Thus the relations of St. Francis with women in general and St. Clara in particular, have been completely travestied by Thomas of Celano. It could not have been otherwise, and we must not bear him a grudge for it. The life of the founder of an Order, when written by a monk, in the very nature of things becomes always a sort of appendix to or illustration of the Rule. And the Rule, especially if the Order has its thousands of members, is necessarily made not for the elect, but for the average, for the majority of the flock. [2]

Hence this portrait, in which St. Francis is represented as a stern ascetic, to whom woman appears to be a sort of incarnate devil! The biographers even go so far as to assure us that he knew only two women by sight. These are manifest exaggerations, or rather the opposite of the truth. [3]

We are not reduced to conjecture to discover the true attitude of the Umbrian prophet in this matter. Without suspecting it, Celano himself gives details enough for the correction of his own errors, and there are besides a number of other documents whose scattered hints correspond and agree with one another in a manner all the more marvellous that it is entirely unintentional, giving, when they are brought together, almost all one could desire to know of the intercourse of these two beautiful souls.

After the sermons of Francis at St. Rufino, Clara's decision was speedily taken; she would break away from the trivialities of an idle and luxurious life and make herself the servant of the poor; all her efforts should be bent to make each day a new advance in the royal way of love and poverty; and for this she would have only to obey him who had suddenly revealed it to her.

She sought him out and opened to him her heart. With that exaltation, a union of candor and delicacy, which is woman's fine endowment, and to which she would more readily give free course if she did not too often divine the pitfalls of base passion and incredulity, Clara offered herself to Francis.

It is one of the privileges of saints to suffer more than other men, for they feel in their more loving hearts the echo of all the sorrows of the world; but they also know joys and delights of which common men never taste. What an inexpressible song of joy must have burst forth in Francis's heart when he saw Clara on her knees before him, awaiting, with his blessing, the word which would consecrate her life to the gospel ideal.

Who knows if this interview did not inspire another saint, Fra Angelico, to introduce into his masterpiece those two elect souls who, already radiant with the light of the heavenly Jerusalem, stop to exchange a kiss before crossing its threshold?

Souls, like flowers, have a perfume of their own which never deceives. One look had sufficed for Francis to go down into the depths of this heart; he was too kind to submit Clara to useless tests, too much an idealist to prudently confine himself to custom or arbitrary decorum; as when he founded the Order of Friars, he took counsel only of himself and God. In this was his strength; if he had hesitated, or even if he had simply submitted himself to ecclesiastical rules, he would have been stopped twenty times before he had done anything. Success is so powerful an argument that the biographers appear not to have perceived how determined Francis was to ignore the canonical laws. He, a simple deacon, arrogated to himself the right to receive Clara's vows and admit her to the Order without the briefest novitiate. Such an act ought to have drawn down upon its author all the censures of the Church, but Francis was already one of those powers to whom much is forgiven, even by those who speak in the name of the holy Roman Church.

Francis had decided that on the night between Palm Sunday and Holy Monday (March 18-19, 1212) Clara should secretly quit the paternal castle and come with two companions to Portiuncula, where he would await her, and would give her the veil. She arrived just as the friars were singing matins. They went out, the story goes, carrying candles in their hands, to meet the bride, while from the woods around Portiuncula resounded songs of joy over this new bridal. Then Mass was begun at that same altar where, three years before, Francis had heard the decisive call of Jesus; he was kneeling in the same place, but surrounded now with a whole spiritual family.

It is easy to imagine Clara's emotion. The step which she had just taken was simply heroic, for she knew to what persecutions from her family she was exposing herself, and what she had seen of the life of the Brothers Minor was a sufficient warning of the distresses to which she was exposing herself in espousing poverty. No doubt she interpreted the words of the service in harmony with her own thoughts:

> "Surely they are my people, " said Jehovah.
> "Children who will not be faithless! "
> And he was for them a saviour.
> In none of their afflictions were they without succor.
> And the angel that is before his face saved them. [4]

Then Francis read again the words of Jesus to his disciples; she vowed to conform her life to them; her hair was cut off; all was finished. A few moments after, Francis conducted her to a house of Benedictine nuns[5] at an hour's distance, where she was to remain provisionally and await the progress of events.

The very next morning Favorino, her father, arrived with a few friends, inveighing, supplicating, abusing everybody. She was unmovable, showing so much courage that at last they gave up the thought of carrying her off by main force.

She was not, however, at the end of her tribulations. Had this scene frightened the Benedictines? We cannot tell, but less than a fortnight after we find her in another convent, that of Sant-Angelo in Panso, at Assisi. [6] A week after Easter, Agnes, her younger sister, joined her there, decided in her turn to serve poverty. Francis received her into the Order. This time the father's fury was horrible. With a band of relatives he invaded the convent, but neither abuse nor blows could subdue this child of fourteen. In spite of her cries they dragged her away. She fainted, and the little inanimate body suddenly seemed to them so heavy that they abandoned it in the midst of the fields, some laborers looking with pity on the painful scene, until Clara, whose cry God had heard, hastened to succor her sister.

Their sojourn in this convent was of very short duration. It appears that they did not carry away a very pleasant impression of it. [7] Francis knew that several others were burning to join his two women friends; he therefore set himself to seek out a retreat where they could live under his direction and in all liberty practise the gospel rule.

He had not long to seek; the Benedictine monks of Mount Subasio always seized every possible opportunity to make themselves popular. They belonged to that congregation of Camaldoli, whom the common people appear to have particularly detested, and several of whose convents had lately been pillaged. [8] The abbey no longer counted more than eight monks, who were trying to save the wreck of their riches and privileges by partial sacrifices; on the 22d of April, 1212, they had given to the commune of Assisi for a communal house a monument which is standing this day, the temple of Minerva. [9]

Francis, who already was their debtor for Portiuncula, once more addressed himself to them. Happy in this new opportunity to render service to one who was the incarnation of popular claims, they gave him the chapel of St. Damian; perhaps they were well pleased, by favoring the new Order, to annoy Bishop Guido, of whom they had reason to complain. [10] However this may be, in this hermitage, so well adapted for prayer and meditation, Francis installed his spiritual daughters. [11] In this sanctuary, repaired by his own hands, at the feet of this crucifix which had spoken to him, Clara was henceforward to pray. It was the house of God; it was also in good measure that of Francis. Crossing its threshold, Clara doubtless experienced that feeling, at once so sweet and so poignant, of the wife who for the first time enters her husband's house, trembling with emotion at the radiant and confused vision of the future.

If we are not entirely to misapprehend these beginnings, we must remember with what rapidity external influences transformed the first conception of St. Francis. At this moment he no more expected to found a second order than he had desired to found the first one. In snatching Clara from her family he had simply acted like a true knight who rescues an oppressed woman, and takes her under his protection. In installing her at St. Damian he was preparing a refuge for those who desired to imitate her and apart from the world practise the gospel Rule. But he never thought that the perfection of which he and his disciples were the apostles and missionaries, and which Clara and her companions were to realize in celibacy, was not practicable in social positions also; thence comes what is wrongly called the *Tertiari*, or Third Order, and which in its primitive thought was not separated from the first. This Third Order had no need to be instituted in 1221, for it existed from the moment when a single conscience resolved to practise his teachings, without being able to follow him to Portiuncula. [12] The enemy of the soul for him as for Jesus was avarice, understood in its largest sense — that is to say, that blindness which constrains men to consecrate their hearts to material preoccupations, makes them the slave of a few pieces of gold or a few acres of land, renders them insensible to the beauties of nature, and deprives them of infinite joys which they alone can know who are the disciples of poverty and love.

Whoever was free at heart from all material servitude, whoever was decided to live without hoarding, every rich man who was willing to labor with his hands and loyally distribute all that he did not consume in order to constitute the common fund which St. Francis called *the Lord's table*, every poor man who was willing to work, free to resort, in the strict measure of his wants, to this table of the Lord, these were at that time true Franciscans.

It was a social revolution.

There was then at that time neither one Order nor several. [13] The gospel of the Beatitudes had been found again, and, as twelve centuries before, it could accommodate itself to all situations.

Alas! the Church, personified by Cardinal Ugolini, was about, if not to cause the Franciscan movement to miscarry, at least so well to hedge about it that a few years later it would have lost nearly its whole original character.

As has been seen, the word poverty expresses only very imperfectly St. Francis's point of view, since it contains an idea of renunciation, of *abstinence*, while in thought the vow of poverty is a vow of liberty. Property is the cage with gilded wires, to which the poor larks are sometimes so thoroughly accustomed that they no longer even think of getting away in order to soar up into the blue. [14]

From the beginning St. Damian was the extreme opposite to what a convent of Clarisses of the strict observance is now; it is still to-day very much as Francis saw it. We owe thanks to the Brothers Minor for having preserved intact this venerable and charming hermitage, and not spoiling it with stupid embellishments. This little corner of Umbrian earth will be for our descendants like Jacob's well whereon Christ sat himself down for an instant, one of the favorite courts of the worship in spirit and in truth.

In installing Clara there Francis put into her hands the Rule which he had prepared for her, [15] which no doubt resembled that of the Brothers save for the precepts with regard to the missionary life. He accompanied it with the engagement[16] taken by himself and his brothers to supply by labor or alms all the needs of Clara and her future companions. In return they also were to work and render to the Brothers all the services of which they might be capable. We have seen the zeal which Francis had brought to the task of making the churches worthy of the worship celebrated in them; he could not endure that the linen put to sacred uses should be less than clean. Clara set herself to spinning thread for the altar-cloths and corporals which the Brothers undertook to distribute among the poor churches of the district. [17] In addition, during the earlier years, she also nursed the sick whom Francis sent to her, and St. Damian was for some time a sort of hospital. [18]

One or two friars, who were called *Zealots of the Poor Ladies*, were especially charged with the care of the Sisters, making themselves huts beside the chapel, after the model of those of Portiuncula. Francis was also near at hand; a sort of terrace four paces long overlooks the hermitage; Clara made there a tiny garden, and when, at twilight, she went thither to water her flowers, she could see, hardly half a league distant, Portiuncula standing out against the aureola of the western sky.

For several years the relations between the two houses were continual, full of charm and freedom. The companions of Francis who received Brothers received Sisters also, at times returning from their preaching tours with a neophyte for St. Damian. [19]

But such a situation could not last long. The intimacy of Francis and Clara, the familiarity of the earlier friars and Sisters would not do as a model for the relations of the two Orders when each had some hundreds of members. Francis himself very soon perceived this, though not so clearly as his sister-friend. Clara survived him nearly twenty-seven years, and thus had time to see the shipwreck of the Franciscan ideal among the Brothers, as well as in almost every one of the houses which had at first followed the Rule of St. Damian. She herself was led by the pressure of events to lay down rules for her own convent, but to her very death-bed she contended for the defence of the true Franciscan ideas, with a heroism, a boldness, at once intense and holy, by which she took a place in the first rank of witnesses for conscience.

Is it not one of the loveliest pictures in religious history, that of this woman who for more than half a century sustains moment by moment a struggle with all the popes who succeed one another in the pontifical throne, remaining always equally respectful and immovable, not consenting to die until she has gained her victory? [20]

To relate her life is to relate this struggle; the greater number of its vicissitudes may be found in the documents of the Roman *curia*. Francis had warded off many a danger from his institution, but he had given himself guardians who were little disposed to yield any of their rights; Cardinal Ugolini in particular, the future Gregory IX., took a part in these matters which is very difficult to understand. We see him continually lavishing upon Francis and Clara expressions of affection and admiration which appear to be absolutely sincere; and yet the Franciscan ideal—regarded as the life of love at which one arrives by freeing himself from all servitude to material things—has hardly had a worse adversary than he.

In the month of May, 1228, Gregory IX. went to Assisi for the preliminaries of the canonization of St. Francis. Before entering the city he turned out of his way to visit St. Damian and to see Clara, whom he had known for a long time, and to whom he had addressed letters burning with admiration and paternal affection. [21]

How can we understand that at this time, the eve of the canonization (July 16, 1228), the pontiff could have had the idea of urging her to be faithless to her vows?

He represented to her that the state of the times made life impossible to women who possess nothing, and offered her certain properties. As Clara gazed at him in astonishment at this strange proposition, he said, "If it is your vows which prevent you, we will release you from them. "

"Holy Father, " replied the Franciscan sister, "absolve me from my sins, but I have no desire for a dispensation from following Christ. "[22]

Noble and pious utterance, artless cry of independence, in which the conscience proudly proclaims its autonomy! In these words is mirrored at full length the spiritual daughter of the Poverello.

By one of those intuitions which often come to very enthusiastic and very pure women, she had penetrated to the inmost depths of Francis's heart, and felt herself inflamed with the same passion which burned in him. She remained faithful to him to the end, but we perceive that it was not without difficulty.

This is not the place in which to ask whether Gregory IX. was right in desiring that religious communities should hold estates; he had a right to his own views on the subject; but there is something shocking, to say no more, in seeing him placing Francis among the saints at the very moment when he was betraying his dearest ideals, and seeking to induce those who had remained faithful to betray them.

Had Clara and Francis foreseen the difficulties which they would meet? We may suppose so, for already under the pontificate of Innocent III. she had obtained a grant of the privilege of poverty. The pope was so much surprised at such a request that he desired to write with his own hands the opening lines of this patent, the like of which had never been asked for at the court of Rome. [23]

Under his successor, Honorius III., the most important personage of the curia was this very Cardinal Ugolini. Almost a septuagenarian in 1216 he inspired awe at first sight by the aspect of his person. He had that singular beauty which distinguishes the old who have escaped the usury of life; pious, enlightened, energetic, he felt himself made for great undertakings. There is something in him which recalls Cardinal Lavigerie and all the prelates whose red robes cover a soldier or a despot rather than a priest. [24]

The Franciscan movement was attacked with violence[25] in various quarters; he undertook to defend it, and a very long time before the charge of protector of the Order was officially confided to him, he exercised it with devouring zeal. [26] He felt an unbounded admiration for Francis and Clara, and often manifested it in a touching manner. If he had been a simple man he might have loved them and followed them. Perhaps he even had thought of doing so. [27] Alas! he was a prince of the Church; he could not help thinking of what he would do in case he should be called to guide the ship of St. Peter.

He acted accordingly; was it calculation on his part or simply one of those states of conscience in which a man absorbed in the end to be attained hardly discusses the ways and means? I do not know, but we see him immediately on the death of Innocent III., under pretext of protecting the Clarisses, take their direction in hand, give them a Rule, and substitute his own ideas for those of St. Francis. [28]

In the privilege which as legate he gave in favor of Monticelli, July 27, 1219, neither Clara nor Francis is named, and the Damianites become as a congregation of Benedictines. [29]

We shall see farther on the wrath of Francis against Brother Philip, a Zealot of the Poor Ladies, who had accepted this privilege in his absence. His attitude was so firm that other documents of the same nature granted by Ugolini at the same epoch were not indorsed by the pope until three years later.

The cardinal's ardor to profit by the enthusiasm which the Franciscan ideas everywhere excited was so great that we find, in the register of his legation of 1221, a sort of formula all prepared for those who would found convents like those of the Sisters of St. Damian; but even there we search in vain for the name of Francis or Clara. [30]

This old man had, however, a truly mystical passion for the young abbess; he wrote to her, lamenting the necessity of being far from her, in words which are the language of love, respect, and admiration. [31] There were at least two men in Ugolini: the Christian, who felt himself subdued before Clara and Francis; the prelate, that is, a man whom the glory of the Church sometimes caused to forget the glory of God.

Francis, though almost always resisting him, appears to have kept a feeling of ingenuous gratitude toward him to the very end. Clara, on the contrary, had too long a struggle to be able to keep any illusions as to the attitude of her protector. After 1230 there is no trace of any relations between them.

All the efforts of the pope to mitigate the rigor of Clara's vow of poverty had remained vain. Many other nuns desired to practise strictly the Rule of St. Francis. Among them was the daughter of the King of Bohemia, Ottokar I., who was in continual relations with Clara. But Gregory IX., to whom she addressed herself, was inflexible. While pouring eulogies upon her he enjoined upon her to follow the Rule which he sent to her—that is, the one which he had composed while he was yet cardinal. The Rule of the Poverello was put among the utopias, not to say heresies. [32] He never, however, could induce St. Clara to completely submit herself. One day, indeed, she rebelled against his orders, and it was the pope who was obliged to yield: he had desired to bring about a wider separation between the friars and the Sisters than had formerly prevailed; for a long time after the death of Francis a certain familiarity had continued between St. Damian and Portiuncula; Clara especially loved these neighborly relations, and often begged one or another Brother to come and preach. The pope thought ill of this, and forbade, under the severest penalty, that any friar of Portiuncula should go to St. Damian without express permission of the Holy See.

This time Clara became indignant. She went to the few friars attached to her monastery, and thanking them for their services, "Go, " she said; "since they deprive us of those who dispense to us spiritual bread, we will not have those who procure for us our material bread. " He who wrote that *the necks of kings and princes are bowed at the feet of the priests*" was obliged to bow before this woman and raise his prohibition. [33]

St. Damian had too often echoed with St. Francis's hymns of love and liberty to forget him so soon and become an ordinary convent. Clara remained surrounded with the master's early companions; Egidio, Leo, Angelo, Ginepro never ceased to be assiduous visitors. These true lovers of poverty felt themselves at home there, and took liberties which would elsewhere have given surprise. One day an English friar, a celebrated theologian, came according to the minister's orders to preach at St. Damian. Suddenly Egidio, though a simple layman, interrupted him: "Stop, brother, let me speak, " he said to him. And the master in theology, bowing his head, covered himself with his cowl as a sign of obedience, and sat down to listen to Egidio.

Clara felt a great joy in this; it seemed to her that she was once again living in St. Francis's days. [34] The little coterie was kept up until her death; she expired in the arms of Brothers Leo, Angelo, and Ginepro. In her last sufferings and her dying visions she had the supreme happiness of being surrounded by those who had devoted their lives to the same ideal as she. [35]

In her will her life shows itself that which we have seen it—a daily struggle for the defence of the Franciscan idea. We see how courageous and brave was this woman who has always been represented as frail, emaciated, blanched like a flower of the cloister. [36]

She defended Francis not only against others, but also against himself. In those hours of dark discouragement which so often and so profoundly disturb the noblest souls and sterilize the grandest efforts, she was beside him to show him his way. When he doubted his mission and thought of fleeing to the heights of repose and solitary prayer, it was she who showed him the ripening harvest with no reapers to gather it in, men going astray with no shepherd to lead them, and drew him once again into the train of the Galilean, into the number of those who *give their lives a ransom for many*. [37]

Yet this love with which at St. Damian Francis felt himself surrounded frightened him at times. He feared that his death, making too great a void, would imperil the institution itself, and he took pains to remind the sisters that he would not be always with them. One day when he was to preach to them, instead of entering the pulpit he caused some ashes to be brought, and after having spread them around him and scattered some on his head, he intoned the *Miserere*, thus reminding them that he was but dust and would soon return to dust. [38]

But in general it is at St. Damian that St. Francis is the most himself; it is under the shade of its olive-trees, with Clara caring for him, that he composes his finest work, that which Ernest Renan called the most perfect utterance of modern religious sentiment, the "Canticle of the Sun. "

FOOTNOTES:

[1]   Easy as it is to seize the large outlines of her life, it is with difficulty that one makes a detailed and documentary study

of it. There is nothing surprising in this, for the Clarisses felt the rebound of the struggles which divided and rapidly transformed the Order of the Brothers Minor. The greater number of the documents have disappeared; we give summary indication of those which will most often be cited: 1. Life of St. Clara by an anonymous author. A. SS., *Aug.* , t. ii., pp. 739-768. 2. Her Will, given by Wadding (*Annales*, 1253, No. 5), but which does not appear to be free from alteration. (Compare, for example, the opening of this will with Chapter VI. of the Rule of the Damianites approved by Innocent IV., August 8, 1253.) 3. The bull of canonization, given September 26, 1255—that is to say, two years after Clara's death; it is much longer than these documents ordinarily are, and relates the principal incidents of her life. A. SS., *loc. cit.* , p. 749; Potthast, 16,025. 4. Her correspondence. Unhappily we have only fragments of it; the Bollandists, without saying whence they drew them, have inserted four of her letters in the *Acta* of St. Agnes of Bohemia, to whom they were addressed. (A. SS., *Martii*, t. i., pp. 506-508.)

[2]   Reading the Chronicle of Fra Salimbeni, which represents the average Franciscan character about 1250, one sees with what reason the Rule had multiplied minute precautions for keeping the Brothers from all relations with women.

The desire of Celano to present the facts in the life of Francis as the norm of the acts of the friars appears still more in the chapters concerning St. Clara than in all the others. Vide 2 Cel., 3, 132: *Non credatis, charissimi (dixit Franciscus), quodeas perfecte non diligam.... Sed exemplum do vobis, ut quemadmodum ego facio, ita et vos faciatis.* Cf. ibid., 134.

[3]   2 Cel., 3, 55. *Fateor veritatem... nullam me si aspicerem recogniturum in facie nisi duas.* This chapter and the two following give us a sort of caricature, in which Francis is represented as so little sure of himself that he casts down his eyes for fear of yielding to desire. The stories of Francis and Jacqueline of Settesoli give a very different picture of the relations between the Brothers and the women in the origin of the Order from that which was given later. Bernard de Besse (Turin MS., f°. 113) relates at length the coming of Jacqueline to Portiuncula to be present at St. Francis's death.

Cf. *Spec.* , 107; 133; Bon., 112. Also Clara's repast at Portiuncula. *Fior.* , 15; *Spec.* , 139b. ; A. SS. *Aug. Vita Clar.* , No. 39 ff.

[4]   Isaiah, lxiii., 8 and 9 (Ségond's [French] translation). At the Mass on Holy Monday Isaiah lxiii. is read for the Epistle and Mark xiv. for the Gospel.

[5]   San Paolo on the Chiasco, near Bastia.

[6]   At the present day diocesan seminary of Assisi, *"Seminarium seraphicum. "* In the thirteenth century the north gate of the city was there. The houses which lie between there and the Basilica form the new town, which is rapidly growing and will unite the city with Sacro Convento.

[7]   *Nam steteramus in alio loco, licet parum. Test. Clar.* It is truly strange that there is not a word here for the house where the first days of her religious life were passed. Cf. *Vit.* , no. 10: *S. Angelus de Panse... ubi cum non plene mens ejus quiesceret.*

[8]   Mittarelli, *Annales Camaldulenses* (Venice, 1755-1773, 9 vols., f^o.), t. iv., app. 431 and 435. Cf. 156.

[9]   The act of donation is still in the archives of Assisi. An analysis of it will be found in Cristofani, t. i., p. 133. Their munificence remained without result; the bull *Ab Ecclesia* of July 27, 1232, shows that they were suppressed less than twenty years after. *Sbaralea*, t. 1, p. 81. Potthast, 8984. Cf., ib., p. 195, note c, and 340, note a, and the bulls which are there indicated.

[10]   See p. 81, note ii.

[11]   1 Cel., 18; 21; 3 Soc., 24; 2 Cel., 1, 8.

[12]   *An. Perus.* , A. SS., p. 600. Cf. 3 Soc., 60. The three Orders are contemporary, one might even say, the four, including among them the one that miscarried among the secular priests (see below).

In a letter St. Clara speaks of her Order as making only a part with that of the Brothers: *Sequaris consilia Reverendi*

Patris nostri fratris Eliæ Ministri generalis totius ordinis. A. SS., Martii, t. i., p. 507.

[13]   This point of view is brought into relief by an anecdote in the *De laudibus* of Bernard of Besse (Turin MS., 113a). This is how he ends chap. vii. on the three Orders: *Nec Santus his contentus ordinibus satagebat omnium generi salutis et penitentiæ viam dare. Unde parochiali cuidam sacerdoti dicenti sibi quod vellet suus, retenta tamen ecclesia. Frater esse, dato vivendi et induendi modo, dicitur indixisse ut annuatim, collectis Eclesiæ fructibus daret pro Deo, quod de præteritis superesset.*

[14]   See the lovely story in the *Fior.* , 13. Cf. *Spec.* , 65a; *Conform.* , 168b. 1.

[15]   The text of it was doubtless formerly inserted in chapter vi. of the Rule granted to the Clarisses of St. Damian, August 9, 1253, by the bull *Solet annuere.* Potthast, 15,086. But this chapter has been completely changed in many editions. The text of the *Speculum*, Morin, Rouen 1509, should be read. *Tract* iii., 226b. The critical study to be made upon this text by comparing the indications given by the bull *Angelis guadium* of May 11, 1238, Sbaralea, i., p. 242, is too long to find a place here.

[16]   2 Cel., 3, 132. Cf. *Test. B. Clar.*

[17]   *In illa gravi infirmitate... faciebat se erigi... et sedens filabat.* A. SS., 760e. *Sic vult eas [sorores] operare manibus suis.* Ib. 762a.

[18]   *Fior.* 33.

[19]   Rule of 1221, chap xii. *Et nulla penitus mulier ab aliquo frater recipiatur ad obedientiam, sed dato sibi consilio spirituali, ubi voluerit agat penitentiam.*   Cf. below, p. 252, note 1, the remainder of this chapter and the indication of the sources. This proves, 1, that the friars had received women into the Order; 2, that at the beginning they said The Order in the singular, and under this appellation included Sisters as well as Brothers. We see how far the situation was, even at the end of 1221, from being what it became a few years later. It is to be noted that in all the reforming sects of the commencement of the thirteenth century the two sexes were

closely united. (Vide *Burchardi chronicon*, Pertz, 1, 23, p. 376. Cf. Potthast, 2611, bull *Cum otim* of Nov. 25, 1205.)

On the 7th of June, 1201 (bull *Incunubit nobis*), Innocent III. had approved the Rule of the Humiliants. This was a religious association whose members continued to live in their own homes, and who offer surprising points of contact with the Franciscan Order, though they took no vow of poverty. From them issued a more restricted association which founded convents where they worked in wool; these convents received both men and women. Vide Jacques de Vitry, *Hist. Occidentalis*, cap. 28. *De religione et regula Humiliatorum* (Douai, 1597, pp. 334-337). The time came when from these two Orders issued a third, composed solely of priests. These *Humiliati* are too little known, though they have had a historian whose book is one of the noble works of the eighteenth century: Tiraboschi, *Vetera Humiliatorum monumenta* (Milan, 3 vols., 4to, 1766-1768). Toward 1200 they had monopolized *l'arte della lana* in all upper Italy as far as to Florence; it is evident, therefore, that Francis's father must have had relations with them.

[20]   The bull approving the Rule of St. Damian is of August 9, 1253. Clara died two days later.

[21]   1 Cel., 122. Cf. Potthast, 8194 ff. ; cf. ib., 709.

[22]   A. SS., *Vita Cl.* , p. 758. Cf. bull of canonization.

[23]   *Vit. S. Clar.* , A. SS., p. 758. This petition was surely made by the medium of Francis; and there are several indications of his presence in Perugia in the latter part of the life of Innocent III. *In obitu suo [Alexandri papæ] omnes familiares sui deseruerunt eum præter fratres Minores. Et similiter Papam Gregorium et Honorium et Innocentium in cujus obitu fuit præsentialiter S. Franciscus.* Eccl. xv. Mon. Germ. hist. Script. , t. 28 p. 568. Sbaralea puts forth doubts as to the authenticity of this privilege, the text of which he gives; wrongly, I think, for Clara alludes to it in her will, A. SS., p. 747.

[24]   He was born about 1147, created cardinal in 1198. Vide Raynald, *ann.* , 1217, § 88, the eulogy made upon him by Honorius III. *Forma decorus et venustus aspectu... zelator fidei,*

disciplina virtutis,... castitatis amator et totius sanctitatis exemplar: Muratori, *Scriptores rer. Ital.* , iii., 1, 575.

[25]   1 Cel., 74.

[26]   The bull *Litteræ tuæ* of August 27, 1218, shows him already favoring the Clarisses. Sbaralea, i., p. 1. Vide 3 Soc., 61. *Offero me ipsum, dixit Hugolinus, vobis, auxilium et consilium, atque protectionem paratus impendere.*

[27]   In the Conformities, 107a, 2, there is a curious story which shows Ugolini going to the Carceri to find Francis, and asking him if he ought to enter his Order. Cf. *Spec.* , 217.

[28]   He succeeded so well that Thomas of Celano himself seems to forget that, at least at St. Damian, the Clarisses followed the Rule given by St. Francis himself: *Ipsorum vita mirifica et institutio gloriosa a domino Papa Gregorio, tunc Hostiensi episcopo.* 1 Cel. 20. Cf. *Honorii Opera* Horoy, t. iii., col. 363; t. iv., col. 218; Potthast, 6179 and 6879 ff.

[29]   This privilege is inserted in the bull *Sacrosancta* of December 9, 1219. *Honorii opera*, Horoy, t. iii., col. 363 ff.

[30]   G. Levi, *Registri dei Cardinali*, no. 125. Vide below, p. 400. Cf. Campi, *Hist. eccl. di Piacenza*, ii., 390.

[31]   See, for example, the letter given by Wadding: Annals, ii., p. 16 (Rome, 1732). *Tanta me amaritudo cordis, abundantia lacrymarum et immanitas doloris invasit, quod nisi ad pedes Jesu, consolationem solitæ pietatis invenirem, spiritus meus forte deficeret et penitus anima liquefieret.* Wadding's text should be corrected by that of the Riccardi MS., 279. f° 80a and b. Cf. Mark of Lisbon, t. i., p. 185; Sbaralea, i., p. 37.

[32]   Bull *Angelis gaudium* of May 11, 1238; it may be found in Sbaralea, i., p. 242. Cf. Palacky, *Literarische Reise nach Italien*, Prague, 1838, 4to, no. 147. Potthast, 10,596; cf. 11,175.

[33]   A. SS., *Vit. Clar.* , p. 762. Cf. *Conform.* , 84b, 2.

[34]   A. SS., *Aprilis*, t. iii., p. 239a; *Conform.* , 54a, 1; 177a, 2.

[35]   A. SS., *Vit. Clar.*, p. 764d.

[36]   The bull of canonization says nothing of the Saracens whom she put to flight. Her life in the A. SS. relates the fact, but shows her simply in prayer before the Holy Sacrament. Cf. *Conform.*, 84b, 1. Mark of Lisbon t. i., part 2, pp. 179-181. None of these accounts represents Clara as going to meet them with a monstrance.

[37]   Bon., 173; *Fior.* 16; *Spec.*, 62b; *Conform.*, 84b, 2; 110b 1; 49a, 1. With these should be compared *Spec.*, 220b: *Frater Leo narravit quod Sanctus Franciscus surgens orare* (sic) *venit ad fratres suos dicens: "Ite ad sæculum et dimittatis habitum, licentio vos."*

[38]   2 Cel., 3, 134.

CHAPTER X

FIRST ATTEMPTS TO REACH THE INFIDELS

Autumn, 1212-Summer, 1215

The early Brothers Minor had too much need of the encouragement and example of Francis not to have very early agreed with him upon certain fixed periods when they would be sure to find him at Portiuncula. Still it appears probable that these meetings did not become true Chapters-General until toward 1216. There were at first two a year, one at Whitsunday, the other at Michaelmas (September 29th). Those of Whitsunday were the most important; all the Brothers came together to gain new strength in the society of Francis, to draw generous ardor and grand hopes from him with his counsels and directions.

The members of the young association had everything in common, their joys as well as their sorrows; their uncertainties as well as the results of their experiences. At these meetings they were particularly occupied with the Rule, the changes that needed to be made in it, and above all, how they might better and better observe it; [1] then, in perfect harmony, they settled the allotment of the friars to the various provinces.

One of Francis's most frequent counsels bore upon the respect due to the clergy; he begged his disciples to show a very particular deference to the priests, and never to meet them without kissing their hands. He saw only too well that the Brothers, having renounced everything, were in danger of being unjust or severe toward the rich and powerful of the earth; he, therefore, sought to arm them against this tendency, often concluding his counsels with these noble words: "There are men who to-day appear to us to be members of the devil who one day shall be members of Christ. "

"Our life in the midst of the world, " said he again, "ought to be such that, on hearing or seeing us, every one shall feel constrained to praise our heavenly Father. You proclaim peace; have it in your hearts. Be not an occasion of wrath or scandal to anyone, but by your gentleness may all be led to peace, concord, and good works. "

It was especially when he undertook to cheer his disciples, to fortify them against temptations and deliver them from their power, that Francis was most successful. However anxious a soul might be, his words brought it back to serenity. The earnestness which he showed in calming sadness became fiery and terrible in reproving those who fell away, but in these days of early fervor he seldom had occasion to show severity; more often he needed gently to reprove the Brothers whose piety led them to exaggerate penances and macerations.

When all was finished and each one had had his part in this banquet of love, Francis would bless them, and they would disperse in all directions like strangers and travellers. They had nothing, but already they thought they saw the signs of the grand and final regeneration. Like the exile on Patmos they saw "the holy city, the new Jerusalem, coming down from God out of heaven, like a bride adorned for her husband... and the throne upon which is seated the Desired of all nations, the Messiah of the new times, he who is to make all things new. "[2]

Yet all eyes were turned toward Syria, where a French knight, Jean de Brienne, had just been declared King of Jerusalem (1210), and toward which were hastening the bands of the children's crusade.

The conversion of Francis, radical as it was, giving a new direction to his thoughts and will, had not had power to change the foundation of his character. "In a great heart everything is great. " In vain is one changed at conversion—he remains the same. That which changes is not he who is converted, but his surroundings; he is suddenly introduced into a new path, but he runs in it with the same ardor. Francis still remained a knight, and it is perhaps this which won for him in so high a degree the worship of the finest souls of the Middle Ages. There was in him that longing for the unknown, that thirst for adventures and sacrifices, which makes the history of his century so grand and so attractive, in spite of many dark features.

Those who have a genius for religion have generally the privilege of illusion. They never quite see how large the world is. When their faith has moved a mountain they thrill with rapture, like the old Hebrew prophets, and it seems to them that they see the dawning of the day "when the glory of the Lord will appear, when the wolf and the lamb will feed together. " Blessed illusion, that fires the blood like a generous wine, so that the soldiers of righteousness hurl themselves against the most terrific fortresses, believing that these once taken the war will be ended.

Francis had found such joys in his union with poverty that he held it for proven that one needed only to be a man to aspire after the same happiness, and that the Saracens would be converted in crowds to the gospel of Jesus, if only it were announced to them in all its simplicity. He therefore quitted Portiuncula for this new kind of crusade. It is not known from what port he embarked. It was probably in the autumn of 1212. A tempest having cast the ship upon the coast of Slavonia, he was obliged to resign himself either to remain several months in those parts or to return to Italy; he decided to return, but found much difficulty in securing a passage on a ship which was about to sail for Ancona. He had no ill-will against the sailors, however, and the stock of food falling short he shared with them the provisions with which his friends had overloaded him.

No sooner had he landed than he set out on a preaching tour, in which souls responded to his appeals[3] with even more eagerness than in times past. We may suppose that he returned from Slavonia in the winter of 1212-1213, and that he employed the following spring in evangelizing Central Italy. It was perhaps during this Lent that he retired to an island in Lake Trasimeno, making a sojourn there which afterward became famous in his legend. [4] However that may be, a perfectly reliable document shows him to have been in the Romagna in the month of May, 1213. [5] One day Francis and his companion, perhaps Brother Leo, arrived at the chateau of Montefeltro, [6] between Macerata and San Marino. A grand fête was being given for the reception of a new knight, but the noise and singing did not affright them, and without hesitation they entered the court, where all the nobility of the country was assembled. Francis then taking for his text the two lines,

> Tanto è il bene ch' aspetto
> Ch'ogni pena m'è diletto, [7]

preached so touching a sermon that several of those present forgot for a moment the tourney for which they had come. One of them, Orlando dei Cattani, Count of Chiusi in Casentino, was so much moved that, drawing Francis aside, "Father, " he said to him, "I desire much to converse with you about the salvation of my soul. " "Very willingly, " replied Francis; "but go for this morning, do honor to those friends who have invited you, eat with them, and after that we will converse as much as you please. "

So it was done. The count came back and concluded the interview by saying, "I have in Tuscany a mountain especially favorable to contemplation; it is entirely isolated and would well suit anyone who desired to do penance far from the noises of the world; if it pleased you I would willingly give it to you and your brethren for the salvation of my soul. "

Francis accepted it joyfully, but as he was obliged to be at Portiuncula for the Whitsunday chapter he postponed the visit to the Verna[8] to a more favorable time.

It was perhaps in this circuit that he went to Imola; at least nothing forbids the supposition. Always courteous, he had gone immediately on his arrival to present himself to the bishop, and ask of him authority to preach. "I am not in need of anyone to aid me in my task, " replied the bishop dryly. Francis bowed and retired, more polite and even more gentle than usual. But in less than hour he had returned. "What is it, brother, what do you want of me again? " "Monsignor, " replied Francis, "when a father drives his son out at the door he returns by the window. "

The bishop, disarmed by such pious persistence, gave the desired authorization. [9]

The aim of Francis at that time, however, was not to evangelize Italy; his friars were already scattered over it in great numbers; and he desired rather to gain them access to new countries.

Not having been able to reach the infidels in Syria, he resolved to seek them in Morocco. Some little time before (July, 1212), the troops of the Almohades had met an irreparable defeat in the plains of Tolosa; beaten by the coalition of the Kings of Aragon, Navarre, and Castile, Mohammed-el-Naser had returned to Morocco to die. Francis felt that this victory of arms would be nothing if it were not followed by a peaceful victory of the gospel spirit.

He was so full of his project, so much in haste to arrive at the end of his journey, that very often he would forget his companion, and hastening forward would leave him far behind. The biographers are unfortunately most laconic with regard to this expedition; they merely say that on arriving in Spain he was so seriously ill that a return home was imperative. Beyond a few local legends, not very well attested, we possess no other information upon the labors of the Saint in this country, nor upon the route which he followed either in going or returning. [10]

This silence is not at all surprising, and ought not to make us undervalue the importance of this mission. The one to Egypt, which took place six years later, with a whole train of friars, and at a time when the Order was much more developed, is mentioned only in a few lines by Thomas of Celano; but for the recent discovery of the Chronicle of Brother Giordano di Giano and the copious details given by Jacques de Vitry, we should be reduced to conjectures upon that journey also. The Spanish legends, to which allusion has just been made, cannot be altogether without foundation, any more than those which concern the journey of St. Francis through Languedoc and Piedmont; but in the actual condition of the sources it is impossible to make a choice, with any sort of authority, between the historic basis and additions to it wholly without value.

The mission in Spain doubtless took place between the Whitsunday of 1214 and that of 1215. [11] Francis, I think, had passed the previous year[12] in Italy. Perhaps he was then going to see the Verna. The March of Ancona and the Valley of Rieti would naturally have attracted him equally about this epoch, and finally the growth of the two branches of the Order must have made necessary his presence at Portiuncula and St. Damian. The rapidity and importance of these missions ought in no sense to give surprise, nor awaken exaggerated critical doubts. It took only a few hours to become a member of the fraternity, and we may not doubt the sincerity of these vocations, since their condition was the immediate giving up of all property of whatever kind, for the benefit of the poor. The new friars were barely received when they in their turn began to receive others, often becoming the heads of the movement in whatever place they happened to be. The way in which we see things going on in Germany in 1221, and in England in 1224, gives a very living picture of this spiritual germination.

To found a monastery it was enough that two or three Brothers should have at their disposition some sort of a shelter, whence they radiated out into the city and the neighboring country. It would, therefore, be as much an exaggeration to describe St. Francis as a man who passed his life in founding convents, as to deny altogether the local traditions which attribute to him the erection of a hundred monasteries. In many cases a glance is enough to show whether these claims of antiquity are justified; before 1220 the Order had only hermitages after the pattern of the Verna or the Carceri, solely intended for the Brothers who desired to pass some time in retreat.

Returned to Assisi, Francis admitted to the Order a certain number of learned men, among whom was perhaps Thomas of Celano. The latter, in fact, says that God at that time mercifully remembered him, and he adds further on: "The blessed Francis was of an exquisite nobility of heart and full of discernment; with the greatest care he rendered to each one what was due him, with wisdom considering in each case the degree of their dignities. "

This does not harmonize very well with the character of Francis as we have sketched it; one can hardly imagine him preserving in his Order such profound distinctions as were at that time made between the different social ranks, but he had that true and eternal politeness which has its roots in the heart, and which is only an expression of tact and love. It could not be otherwise with a man who saw in courtesy one of the qualities of God.

We are approaching one of the most obscure periods of his life. After the chapter of 1215 he seems to have passed through one of those crises of discouragement so frequent with those who long to realize the ideal in this world. Had he discovered the warning signs of the misfortunes which were to come upon his family? Had he come to see that the necessities of life were to sully and blight his dream? Had he seen in the check of his missions in Syria and Morocco a providential indication that he had to change his method? We do not know. But about this time he felt the need of turning to St. Clara and Brother Silvestro for counsel on the subject of the doubts and hesitations which assailed him; their reply restored to him peace and joy. God by their mouth commanded him to continue his apostolate. [13]

Immediately he rose and set forth in the direction of Bevagna, [14] with an ardor which he had never yet shown. In encouraging him to persevere Clara had in some sort inoculated him with a new enthusiasm. One word from her had sufficed to give him back all his courage, and from this point in his life we find in him more poetry, more love, than ever before.

Full of joy, he was going on his way when, perceiving some flocks of birds, he turned aside a little from the road to go to them. Far from taking flight, they flocked around him as if to bid him welcome. "Brother birds, " he said to them then, "you ought to praise and love your Creator very much. He has given you feathers for clothing, wings for flying, and all that is needful for you. He has made you the noblest of his creatures; he permits you to live in the pure air; you have neither to sow nor to reap, and yet he takes care of you, watches over you and guides you. " Then the birds began to arch their necks, to spread out their wings, to open their beaks, to look at him, as if to thank him, while he went up and down in their midst stroking them with the border of his tunic, sending them away at last with his blessing. [15]

In this same evangelizing tour, passing through Alviano, [16] he spoke a few exhortations to the people, but the swallows so filled the air with their chirping that he could not make himself heard. "It is my turn to speak, " he said to them; "little sister swallows, hearken to the word of God; keep silent and be very quiet until I have finished. "[17]

We see how Francis's love extended to all creation, how the diffused life shed abroad upon all things inspired and moved him. From the sun to the earthworm which we trample under foot, everything breathed in his ear the ineffable sigh of beings that live and suffer and die, and in their life as in their death have a part in the divine work.

"Praised be thou, Lord, with all thy creatures, especially for my brother Sun which gives us the day and by him thou showest thy light. He is beautiful and radiant with great splendor; of thee, Most High, he is the symbol. "

Here again, Francis revives the Hebrew inspiration, the simple and grandiose view of the prophets of Israel. "Praise the Lord! " the royal Psalmist had sung, "praise the Lord, fire and frost, snow and mists, stormy winds that do his will, mountains and all hills, fruit-trees and all cedars, beasts and all cattle, creeping things and fowls with wings, kings of the earth and all peoples, princes and all judges of the earth, young men and maidens, old men and children, praise the Lord, praise ye the Lord! "

The day of the birds of Bevagna remained in his memory as one of the most beautiful of his whole life, and though usually so reserved he always loved to tell of it; [18] it was because he owed to Clara these pure ardors which brought him into a secret and delicious communion with all beings; it was she who had revived him from sadness and hesitation; in his heart he bore an immense gratitude to her who, just when he needed it, had known how to return to him love for love, inspiration for inspiration.

Francis's sympathy for animals, as we see it shining forth here, has none of that sentimentalism, so often artificial and exclusive of all other love, which certain associations of his time noisily displayed; in him it is only a manifestation of his feeling for nature, a deeply mystical, one might say pantheistic, sentiment, if the word had not a too definitely philosophical sense, quite opposite to the Franciscan thought.

This sentiment, which in the poets of the thirteenth century is so often false and affected, was in him not only true, but had in it something alive, healthy, robust. [19] It is this vein of poetry which awoke Italy to self-consciousness, made her in a few years forget the nightmare of Catharist ideas, and rescued her from pessimism. By it Francis became the forerunner of the artistic movement which preceded the Renaissance, the inspirer of that group of Pre-Raphaelites, awkward, grotesque in drawing though at times they were, to whom we turn to-day with a sort of piety, finding in their ungraceful saints an inner life, a moral feeling which we seek for elsewhere in vain.

If the voice of the Poverello of Assisi was so well understood it was because in this matter, as in all others, it was entirely unconventional. How far we are, with him, from the fierce or Pharisaic piety of those monks which forbids even the females of animals to enter their convent! His notion of chastity in no sense resembles this excessive prudery. One day at Sienna he asked for some turtle-doves, and holding them in the skirt of his tunic, he said: "Little sisters turtle-doves, you are simple, innocent, and chaste; why did you let yourselves be caught? I shall save you from death, and have nests made for you, so that you may bring forth young and multiply according to the commandment of our Creator. "

And he went and made nests for them all, and the turtle-doves began to lay eggs and bring up their broods under the eyes of the Brothers. [20]

At Rieti a family of red-breasts were the guests of the monastery, and the young birds made marauding expeditions on the very table where the Brothers were eating. [21] Not far from there, at Greccio, [22] they brought to Francis a leveret that had been taken alive in a trap. "Come to me, brother leveret, " he said to it. And as the poor creature, being set free, ran to him for refuge, he took it up, caressed it, and finally put it on the ground that it might run away; but it returned to him again and again, so that he was obliged to send it to the neighboring forest before it would consent to return to freedom. [23]

One day he was crossing the Lake of Rieti. The boatman in whose bark he was making the passage offered him a tench of uncommon size. Francis accepted it with joy, but to the great amazement of the fisherman put it back into the water, bidding it bless God. [24]

We should never have done if we were to relate all the incidents of this kind, [25] for the sentiment of nature was innate with him; it was a perpetual communion which made him love the whole creation. [26] He is ravished with the witchery of great forests; he has the terrors of a child when he is alone at prayer in a deserted chapel, but he tastes ineffable joy merely in inhaling the perfume of a flower, or gazing into the limpid water of a brook. [27]

This perfect lover of poverty permitted one luxury—he even commanded it at Portiuncula—that of flowers; the Brother was bidden not to sow vegetables and useful plants only; he must reserve one corner of good ground for our sisters, the flowers of the fields. Francis talked with them also, or rather he replied to them, for their mysterious and gentle language crept into the very depth of his heart. [28]

The thirteenth century was prepared to understand the voice of the Umbrian poet; the sermon to the birds[29] closed the reign of Byzantine art and of the thought of which it was the image. It is the end of dogmatism and authority; it is the coming in of individualism and inspiration; very uncertain, no doubt, and to be followed by obstinate reactions, but none the less marking a date in the history of the human conscience. [30] Many among the companions of Francis were too much the children of their century, too thoroughly imbued with its theological and metaphysical methods, to quite understand a sentiment so simple and profound. [31] But each in his degree felt its charm. Here Thomas of Celano's language rises to an elevation which we find in no other part of his works, closing with a picture of Francis which makes one think of the Song of Songs. [32]

Of more than middle height, Francis had a delicate and kindly face, black eyes, a soft and sonorous voice. There was in his whole person a delicacy and grace which made him infinitely lovely. All these characteristics are found in the most ancient portraits. [33]

FOOTNOTES:

[1]   3 Soc., 57; cf. *An. Perus.* , A. SS., p. 599.

[2]   Rev. xxi. ; 1 Cel., 46; 3 Soc., 57-59; *An. Perus.* , A. SS., p. 600.

[3]   1 Cel., 55 and 56; Bon., 129-132.

[4]   *Fior.* , 7; *Spec.* , 96; *Conform.* , 223a, 2. The fact of Francis's sojourn on an island in this lake is made certain by 1 Cel., 60.

[5]   Vide below, p. 400. Cf. A. SS., pp. 823 f.

[6]   At present Sasso-Feltrio, between Conca and Marecchio, south of and about two hours' walk from San Marino.

[7]   The happiness that I expect is so great that all pain is joyful to me. All the documents give Francis's text in Italian, which is enough to prove that it was the language not only of his poems but also of his sermons. *Spec.* 92a ff. *Conform.* 113a, 2; 231a, 1; *Fior., Prima consid.*

[8]   See p. 400.

[9]   2 Cel., 3, 85; Bon., 82.

[10]   1 Cel., 56; Bon., 132.

[11]   Vide Wadding, *ann. 1213-1215.* Cf. A. SS., pp. 602, 603, 825-831. Mark of Lisbon, *lib.* i., *cap.* 45, pp. 78-80; Papini, *Storia di S. Francesco,* i., p. 79 ff. (Foligno, 1825, 2 vols., 4to). It is

surprising to see Father Suysken giving so much weight to the *argumentum a silentio*.

[12]   From Pentecost, 1213, to that of 1214. —*Post non multum vero temporis versus Marochium iter arripuit*, says Thomas of Celano (1 Cel., 56), after having mentioned the return from Slavonia. Taking into account the author's *usus loquendi* the phrase appears to establish a certain interval between the two missions.

[13]   *Conform.*, 110b, 1; *Spec.*, 62b; *Fior.*, 16; Bon., 170-174.

[14]   Village about two leagues S. W. from Assisi. The time is indirectly fixed by Bon., 173, and 1 Cel., 58.

[15]   1 Cel. 58; Bon., 109 and 174; *Fior.*, 16; *Spec.*, 62b; *Conform.*, 114b, 2.

[16]   About halfway between Orvieto and Narni.

[17]   1 Cel., 59; Bon., 175.

[18]   *Ad hæc, ut ipse dicebat...* 1 Cel., 58.

[19]   Francis has been compared in this regard to certain of his contemporaries, but the similarity of the words only makes more evident the diversity of inspiration. Honorius III. may say: *Forma rosæ est inferius angusta, superius ampla et significat quod Christus pauper fuit in mundo, sed est Dominus super omnia et implet universa. Nam sicut forma rosæ*, etc. (Horoy, t. i., col. xxiv. and 804), and make a whole sermon on the symbolism of the rose; these overstrained dissertations have nothing to do with the feeling for nature. It is the arsenal of mediæval rhetoric used to dissect a word. It is an intellectual effort, not a song of love. The Imitation would say: *If thy heart were right all creatures would be for thee a mirror of life and a volume of holy doctrine*, lib. ii., cap. 2. The simple sentiment of the beauty of creation is absent here also; the passage is a pedagogue in disguise.

[20]   *Spec.*, 157. *Fior.*; 22.

[21]   2 Cel., 2, 16; *Conform.* , 148a, 1, 183b, 2. Cf. the story of the sheep of Portiuncula: Bon., 111.

[22]   Village in the valley of Rieti, two hours' walk from that town, on the road to Terni.

[23]   1 Cel., 60; Bon., 113.

[24]   1 Cel., 61; Bon., 114.

[25]   2 Cel., 3, 54; Bon., 109; 2 Cel., 3; 103 ff. ; Bon., 116 ff. ; Bon., 110; 1 Cel., 61; Bon., 114, 113, 115; 1 Cel., 79; *Fior.* , 13, etc.

[26]   2 Cel., 3, 101 ff. ; Bon., 123.

[27]   2 Cel., 3, 59; 1 Cel., 80 and 81.

[28]   2 Cel., 3, 101; *Spec.* , 136a; 1 Cel., 81.

[29]   This is the scene in his life most often reproduced by the predecessors of Giotto. The unknown artist who (before 1236) decorated the nave of the Lower Church of Assisi gives five frescos to the history of Jesus and five to the life of St. Francis. Upon the latter he represents: 1, the renunciation of the paternal inheritance; 2, Francis upholding the Lateran church; 3, the sermon to the birds; 4, the stigmata; 5, the funeral. This work, unhappily very badly lighted, and about half of it destroyed at the time of the construction of the chapels of the nave, ought to be engraved before it completely disappears. The history of art in the time of Giunta Pisano is still too much enveloped in obscurity for us to neglect such a source of information. M. Thode (*Franz von Assisi und die Anfänge der Kunst*, Berlin, 1885, 8vo. illust.) and the Rev. Father Fratini (*Storia della Basilica d'Assisi*, Prato, 1882, 8vo) are much too brief so far as these frescos are concerned.

[30]   It is needless to say that I do not claim that Francis was the only initiator of this movement, still less that he was its creator; he was its most inspired singer, and that may suffice for his glory. If Italy was awakened it was because her sleep was not so sound as in the tenth century; the mosaics of the façade of the Cathedral of Spoleto (the Christ between the

Virgin and St. John) already belong to the new art. Still, the victory was so little final that the mural paintings of St. Lawrence without the walls and of the Quattro Coronate, which are subsequent to it by half a score of years, relapse into a coarse Byzantinism. See also those of the Baptistery of Florence.

[31] Hence the more or less subtile explanations with which they adorn these incidents. —As to the part of animals in thirteenth century legends consult Cæsar von Heisterbach, Strange's edition, t. ii., pp. 257 ff.

[32] 1 Cel., 80-83.

[33] 1 Cel., 83; *Conform.* , 111a. M. Thode (*Anfänge*, pp. 76-94) makes a study of some thirty portraits. The most important are reproduced in *Saint François* (1 vol., 4to, Paris, 1885); 1, contemporary portrait, by Brother Eudes, now at Subiaco (*loc. cit.* , p. 30); 2, portrait dating about 1230, by Giunta Pisano (?); preserved at Portiuncula (*loc. cit.* , p. 384); 3, finally, portrait dated 1235, by Bon. Berlinghieri, and preserved at Pescia, in Tuscany (*loc. cit.* , p. 277). In 1886 Prof. Carattoli studied with great care a portrait which dates from about those years and of which he gives a picture (also preserved of late years at Portiuncula). *Miscellanea francescana* t. i., pp. 44-48; cf. pp. 160, 190, and 1887, p. 32. M. Bonghi has written some interesting papers on the iconography of St. Francis (*Francesco di Assisi*, 1 vol., 12mo, Citta di Castello, Lapi, 1884. Vide pp. 103-113).

CHAPTER XI

THE INNER MAN AND WONDER-WORKING

The missionary journey, undertaken under the encouragement of St. Clara and so poetically inaugurated by the sermon to the birds of Bevagna, appears to have been a continual triumph for Francis. [1] Legend definitively takes possession of him; whether he will or no, miracles burst forth under his footsteps; quite unawares to himself the objects of which he has made use produce marvellous effects; folk come out from the villages in procession to meet him, and the biographer gives us to hear the echo of those religious festivals of Italy—merry, popular, noisy, bathed in sunshine—which so little resemble the fastidiously arranged festivals of northern peoples.

From Alviano Francis doubtless went to Narni, one of the most charming little towns in Umbria, busy with building a cathedral after the conquest of their communal liberties. He seems to have had a sort of predilection for this city as well as for its surrounding villages. [2] From thence he seems to have plunged into the valley of Rieti, where Greccio, Fonte-Colombo, San Fabiano, Sant-Eleuthero, Poggio-Buscone retain even stronger traces of him than the environs of Assisi.

Thomas of Celano gives us no particulars of the route followed, but, on the other hand, he goes at length into the success of the apostle in the March of Ancona, and especially at Ascoli. Did the people of these districts still remember the appeals which Francis and Egidio had made to them six years before (1209), or must we believe that they were peculiarly prepared to understand the new gospel? However this may be, nowhere else was a like enthusiasm shown; the effect of the sermons was so great that some thirty neophytes at once received the habit of the Order.

The March of Ancona ought to be held to be the Franciscan province *par excellence*. There are Offida, San-Severino, Macerata, Fornaro, Cingoli, Fermo, Massa, and twenty other hermitages where, during more than a century, poverty was to find its heralds and its martyrs; from thence came Giovanni della Verna, Jacopo di Massa, Conrad di Offida, Angelo Clareno, and those legions of nameless revolutionists, dreamers, and prophets, who since the *extirpés* in 1244 by the general of the Order, Crescentius of Jesi, never ceased to make new recruits, and by their proud resistance to all powers filled one of the finest pages of religious history in the Middle Ages.

This success, which bathed the soul of Francis with joy, did not arouse in him the smallest movement of pride. Never has man had a greater power over hearts, because never preacher preached himself less. One day Brother Masseo desired to put his modesty to the test.

"Why thee? Why thee? Why thee? " he repeated again and again, as if to make a mock of Francis. "What are you saying? " cried Francis at last. "I am saying that everybody follows thee, everyone desires to see thee, hear thee, and obey thee, and yet for all that thou art neither beautiful, nor learned, nor of noble family. Whence comes it, then, that it should be thee whom the world desires to follow? "

On hearing these words the blessed Francis, full of joy, raised his eyes to heaven, and after remaining a long time absorbed in contemplation he knelt, praising and blessing God with extraordinary fervor. Then turning toward Masseo, "Thou wishest to know why it is I whom men follow? Thou wishest to know? It is because the eyes of the Most High have willed it thus; he continually watches the good and the wicked, and as his most holy eyes have not found among sinners any smaller man, nor any more insufficient and more sinful, therefore he has chosen me to accomplish the marvellous work which God has undertaken; he chose me because he could find no one more worthless, and he wished here to confound the nobility and grandeur, the strength, the beauty, and the learning of this world. "

This reply throws a ray of light upon St. Francis's heart; the message which he brought to the world is once again the glad tidings announced to the poor; its purpose is the taking up again of that Messianic work which the Virgin of Nazareth caught a glimpse of in her *Magnificat*, that song of love and liberty, the sighs of which breathe the vision of a new social state. He comes to remind the world that the welfare of man, the peace of his heart, the joy of his life, are neither in money, nor in learning, nor in strength, but in an upright and sincere will. Peace to men of good will.

The part which he had taken at Assisi in the controversies of his fellow-citizens he would willingly have taken in all the rest of Italy, for no man has ever dreamed of a more complete renovation; but if the end he sought was the same as that of many revolutionaries who came after him, their methods were completely different; his only weapon was love.

The event has decided against him. Apart from the *illuminati* of the March of Ancona and the *Fraticelli* of our own Provence his disciples have vied with one another to misunderstand his thought. [3]

Who knows if some one will not arise to take up his work? Has not the passion for worm-eaten speculations yet made victims enough? Are there not many among us who perceive that luxury is a delusion, that if life is a battle, it is not a slaughter-house where ferocious beasts wrangle over their prey, but a wrestling with the divine, under whatever form it may present itself—truth, beauty, or love? Who knows whether this expiring nineteenth century will not arise from its winding-sheet to make *amende honorable* and bequeath to its successor one manly word of faith?

Yes, the Messiah will come. He who was announced by Gioacchino di Fiore and who is to inaugurate a new epoch in the history of humanity will appear. *Hope maketh not ashamed.* In our modern Babylons and in the huts on our mountains are too many souls who mysteriously sigh the hymn of the great vigil, *Rorate coeli desuper et nubes pluant Justum,* [4] for us not to be on the eve of a divine birth.

All origins are mysterious. This is true of matter, but yet more true of that life, superior to all others, which we call holiness; it was in prayer that Francis found the spiritual strength which he needed; he therefore sought for silence and solitude. If he knew how to do battle in the midst of men in order to win them to the faith, he loved, as Celano says, to fly away like a bird going to make its nest upon the mountain. [5]

With men truly pious the prayer of the lips, the formulated prayer, is hardly other than an inferior form of true prayer. Even when it is sincere and attentive, and not a mechanical repetition, it is only a prelude for souls not dead of religious materialism.

Nothing resembles piety so much as love. Formularies of prayer are as incapable of speaking the emotions of the soul as model love-letters of speaking the transports of an impassioned heart. To true piety as well as to profound love, the formula is a sort of profanation.

To pray is to talk with God, to lift ourselves up to him, to converse with him that he may come down to us. It is an act of meditation, of reflection, which presupposes the effort of all that is most personal in us.

Looked at in this sense, prayer is the mother of all liberty and all freedom.

Whether or no it be a soliloquy of the soul with itself, the soliloquy would be none the less the very foundation of a strong individuality.

With St. Francis as with Jesus, prayer has this character of effort which makes of it the greatest moral act. In order to truly know such men one must have been able to go with them, to follow Jesus up to the mountain where he passed his nights. Three favored ones, Peter, James, John, followed him thither one day; but to describe what they saw, all that a manly *sursum corda* added to the radiance and the mysterious grandeur of him whom they adored, they were obliged to resort to the language of symbols.

It was so with St. Francis. For him as for his Master the end of prayer is communion with the heavenly Father, the accord of the divine with the human; or rather it is man who puts forth his strength to do the work of God, not saying to him a mere passive, resigned, powerless *Fiat*, but courageously raising his head: "Behold me, Lord, I delight to do thy will. "

"There are unfathomable depths in the human soul, because at the bottom is God himself. " Whether this God be transcendent or immanent, whether he be One, the Creator, the eternal and immutable Principle, or whether he be, as say the doctors beyond the Rhine, the ideal objectivation of our Me, is not the question for the heroes of humanity. The soldier in the thick of battle does not philosophize as to how much truth or falsehood there is in the patriotic sentiment; he takes his arms and fights at the peril of his life. So the soldiers of spiritual conflicts seek for strength in prayer, in reflection, contemplation, inspiration; all, poets, artists, teachers, saints, legislators, prophets, leaders of the people, learned men, philosophers, all draw from this same source.

But it is not without difficulty that the soul unites itself to God, or if one prefers, that it finds itself. A prayer ends at last in divine communion only when it began by a struggle. The patriarch of Israel, asleep near Bethel, had already divined this: the God who passes by tells his name only to those who stop him and do him violence to learn it. He blesses only after long hours of conflict.

The gospel has found an untranslatable word to characterize the prayers of Jesus, it compares the conflict which preceded the voluntary immolation of Christ to the death-struggle: *Factus in agonia.* [6] We might say of his life that it had been a long temptation, a struggle, a prayer, since these words only express different moments of spiritual activity.

Like their Master, the disciples and successors of Christ can conquer their own souls only through perseverance. But these words, empty of meaning for devout conventicles, have had a tragic sense for men of religious genius.

Nothing is more false, historically, than the saints that adorn our churches, with their mincing attitude, their piteous expression, that indescribably anæmic and emaciated—one may almost say emasculated—air which shows in their whole nature; they are pious seminarists brought up under the direction of St. Alphonso di Liguori or of St Louis di Gonzaga; they are not saints, not the violent who take the kingdom of heaven by force.

We have come to one of the most delicate features of the life of Francis—his relations with diabolical powers. Customs and ideas have so profoundly changed in all that concerns the existence of the devil and his relations with men, that it is almost impossible to picture to oneself the enormous place which the thought of demons occupied at that time in the minds of men.

The best minds of the Middle Ages believed without a doubt in the existence of the perverse spirit, in his perpetual transformations in the endeavor to tempt men and cause them to fall into his snares. Even in the sixteenth century, Luther, who undermined so many beliefs, had no more doubt of the personal existence of Satan than of sorcery, conjurations, or possessions. [7]

Finding in their souls a wide background of grandeur and wretchedness, whence they sometimes heard a burst of distant harmonies calling them to a higher life, soon to be overpowered by the clamors of the brute, our ancestors could not refrain from seeking the explanation of this duel. They found it in the conflict of the demons with God.

The devil is the prince of the demons, as God is the prince of the angels; capable of all transformations, they carry on to the end of time terrible battles which will end in the victory of God, but meantime each man his whole life long is contended for by these two adversaries, and the noblest souls are naturally the most disputed.

This is how St. Francis, with all men of his time, explained the disquietudes, terrors, anguish, with which his heart was at times assailed, as well as the hopes, consolations, joys in which in general his soul was bathed. Wherever we follow his steps local tradition has preserved the memory of rude assaults of the tempter which he had to undergo.

It is no doubt useless to recall here the elementary fact that if manners change with the times, man himself is quite as strangely modified. If, according to education, and the manner of life, such or such a sense may develop an acuteness which confounds common experience—hearing in the musician, touch with the blind, etc. —we may estimate by this how much sharper certain senses may have been then than now. Several centuries ago visual delusion was with adults what it is now with children in remotest country parts. A quivering leaf, a nothing, a breath, an unexplained sound creates an image which they see and in the reality of which they believe absolutely. Man is all of a piece; the hyperæsthesia of the will presupposes that of the sensibility, one is conditioned on the other, and it is this which makes men of revolutionary epochs so much greater than nature. It would be absurd under pretext of truth to try to bring them back to the common measures of our contemporary society, for they were veritably demigods for good as for evil.

Legends are not always absurd. The men of '93 are still near to us, but it is nevertheless with good right that legend has taken possession of them, and it is pitiable to see these men who, ten times a day, had to take resolutions where everything was at stake—their destiny, that of their ideas, and sometimes that of their country— judged as if they had been mere worthy citizens, with leisure to discuss at length every morning the garments they were to wear or the *menu* of a dinner. Most of the time historians have perceived only a part of the truth about them; for not only were there two men in them, almost all of them are at the same time poets, demagogues, prophets, heroes, martyrs. To write history, then, is to translate and transpose almost continually. The men of the thirteenth century could not bring themselves to not refer to an exterior cause the inner motions of their souls. In what appears to us as the result of our own reflections they saw inspiration; where we say desires, instincts, passions, they said temptation, but we must not permit these differences of language to make us overlook or tax with trickery a part of their spiritual life, bringing us thus to the conclusions of a narrow and ignorant rationalism.

St. Francis believed himself to have many a time fought with the devil; the horrible demons of the Etruscan Inferno still haunted the forests of Umbria and Tuscany; but while for his contemporaries and some of his disciples apparitions, prodigies, possessions, are daily phenomena, for him they are exceptional, and remain entirely in the background. In the iconography of St. Benedict, as in that of most of the popular saints, the devil occupies a preponderant place; in that of St. Francis he disappears so completely that in the long series of Giotto's frescos at Assisi he is not seen a single time. [8]

In the same way all that is magic and miracle-working occupies in his life an entirely secondary rank. Jesus in the Gospels gave his apostles power to cast out evil spirits, and to heal all sickness and all infirmity. [9] Francis surely took literally these words, which made a part of his Rule. He believed that he could work miracles, and he willed to do so; but his religious thought was too pure to permit him to consider miracles otherwise than as an entirely exceptional means of relieving the sufferings of men. Not once do we see him resorting to miracle to prove his apostolate or to bolster up his ideas. His tact taught him that souls are worthy of being won by better means. This almost complete absence of the marvellous[10] is by so much the more remarkable that it is in absolute contradiction with the tendencies of his time. [11]

Open the life of his disciple, St. Anthony of Padua ([Cross] 1231); it is a tiresome catalogue of prodigies, healings, resurrections. One would say it was rather the prospectus of some druggist who had invented a new drug than a call to men to conversion and a higher life. It may interest invalids or devotees, but neither the heart nor the conscience is touched by it. It must be said in justice to Anthony of Padua that his relations with Francis appear to have been very slight. Among the earliest disciples who had time to fathom their master's thought to the very depths we find traces of this noble disdain of the marvellous; they knew too well that the perfect joy is not to astound the world with prodigies, to give sight to the blind, nor even to revive those who have been four days dead, but that it lives in the love that goes even to self-immolation. *Mihi absit gloriari nisi in cruce Domini.* [12]

Thus Brother Egidio asked of God grace not to perform miracles; he saw in them, as in the passion for learning, a snare in which the proud would be taken, and which would distract the Order from its true mission. [13]

St. Francis's miracles are all acts of love; the greater number of them are found in the healing of nervous maladies, those apparently inexplicable disquietudes which are the cruel afflictions of critical times. His gentle glance, at once so compassionate and so strong, which seemed like a messenger from his heart, often sufficed to make those who met it forget all their suffering.

The evil eye is perhaps a less stupid superstition than is generally fancied. Jesus was right in saying that a look sufficed to make one an adulterer; but there is also a look—that of the contemplative Mary, for example—which is worth all sacrifices, because it includes them all, because it gives, consecrates, immolates him who looks.

Civilization dulls this power of the glance. A part of the education the world gives us consists in teaching our eyes to deceive, in making them expressionless, in extinguishing their flames; but simple and straightforward natures never give up using this language of the heart, "which brings life and health in its beams. "

"A Brother was suffering unspeakable tortures; sometimes he would roll upon the ground, striking against whatever lay in his way, frothing at the mouth, horrible to see; at times he would become rigid, and again, after remaining stark outstretched for a moment, would roll about in horrible contortions; sometimes lying in a heap on the ground, his feet touching his head, he would bound upward as high as a man's head. " Francis came to see him and healed him. [14]

But these are exceptions, and the greater part of the time the Saint withdrew himself from the entreaties of his companions when they asked miracles at his hands.

To sum up, if we take a survey of the whole field of Francis's piety, we see that it proceeds from the secret union of his soul with the divine by prayer; this intuitive power of seeing the ideal classes him with the mystics. He knew, indeed, both the ecstasy and the liberty of mysticism, but we must not forget those features of character which separate him from it, particularly his apostolic fervor. Besides this his piety had certain peculiar qualities which it is necessary to point out.

And first, liberty with respect of observances: Francis felt all the emptiness and pride of most religious observance. He saw the snare that lies hidden there, for the man who carefully observes all the minutiæ of a religious code risks forgetting the supreme law of love. More than this, the friar who lays upon himself a certain number of supererogatory facts gains the admiration of the ignorant, but the pleasure which he finds in this admiration actually transforms his pious act into sin. Thus, strangely enough, contrary to other founders of orders, he was continually easing the strictness of the various rules which he laid down. [15] We may not take this to be a mere accident, for it was only after a struggle with his disciples that he made his will prevail; and it was precisely those who were most disposed to relax their vow of poverty who were the most anxious to display certain bigoted observances before the public eye.

"The sinner can fast, " Francis would say at such times; "he can pray, weep, macerate himself, but one thing he cannot do, he cannot be faithful to God. " Noble words, not unworthy to fall from the lips of him who came to preach a worship in spirit and in truth, without temple or priest; or rather that every fireside shall be a temple and every believer a priest.

Religious formalism, in whatever form of worship, always takes on a forced and morose manner. Pharisees of every age disfigure their faces that no one may be unaware of their godliness. Francis not merely could not endure these grimaces of false piety, he actually counted mirth and joy in the number of religious duties.

How shall one be melancholy who has in the heart an inexhaustible treasure of life and truth which only increases as one draws upon it? How be sad when in spite of falls one never ceases to make progress? The pious soul which grows and develops has a joy like that of the child, happy in feeling its weak little limbs growing strong and permitting it every day a further exertion.

The word joy is perhaps that which comes most often to the pen of the Franciscan authors; [16] the master went so far as to make it one of the precepts of the Rule. [17] He was too good a general not to know that a joyous army is always a victorious army. In the history of the early Franciscan missions there are bursts of laughter which ring out high and clear. [18]

For that matter, we are apt to imagine the Middle Ages as much more melancholy than they really were. Men suffered much in those days, but the idea of grief being never separated from that of penalty, suffering was either an expiation or a test, and sorrow thus regarded loses its sting; light and hope shine through it.

Francis drew a part of his joy from the communion. He gave to the sacrament of the eucharist that worship imbued with unutterable emotion, with joyful tears, which has aided some of the noblest of human souls to endure the burden and heat of the day. [19] The letter of the dogma was not fixed in the thirteenth century as it is to-day, but all that is beautiful, true, potent, eternal in the mystical feast instituted by Jesus was then alive in every heart.

The eucharist was truly the viaticum of the soul. Like the pilgrims of Emmaus long ago, in the hour when the shades of evening fall and a vague sadness invades the soul, when the phantoms of the night awake and seem to loom up behind all our thoughts, our fathers saw the divine and mysterious Companion coming toward them; they drank in his words, they felt his strength descending upon their hearts, all their inward being warmed again, and again they whispered, "Abide with us, Lord, for the day is far spent and the night approacheth."

And often their prayer was heard.

FOOTNOTES:

[1]   1 Cel., 62.

[2]   1 Cel., 66; cf. Bon., 180; 1 Cel., 67; cf. Bon., 182; 1 Cel., 69; Bon., 183. After St. Francis's death the Narniates were the first to come to pray at his tomb. 1 Cel., 128, 135, 136, 138, 141; Bon., 275.

[3]   As concerning: 1, fidelity to Poverty; 2, prohibition of modifying the Rule; 3, the equal authority of the Will and the Rule; 4, the request for privileges at the court of Rome; 5, the elevation of the friars to high ecclesiastical charges; 6, the absolute prohibition of putting themselves in opposition to the secular clergy; 7, the interdiction of great churches and rich convents. On all these points and many others infidelity to Francis's will was complete in the Order less than twenty-five years after his death. We might expatiate on all this; the Holy See in interpreting the Rule had canonical right on its side, but Ubertino di Casali in saying that it was perfectly clear and had no need of interpretation had good sense on his side; let that suffice! *Et est stupor quare queritur expositio super litteram sic apertam quia nulla est difficultas in regulæ intelligentia. Arbor vitæ crucifixæ,* Venice, 1485. lib. v., cap. 3. *Sanctus vir Egidius tanto ejulatu clamabat super regulæ destructionem quam videbat quod ignorantibus viam spiritus quasi videbatur insanus. Id. ibid.*

[4]   *Heavens drop down your dew, and let the clouds rain down the Just One.* Anthem for Advent.

[5]   *In foramibus petræ nidificabat.* 1 Cel., 71. Upon the prayers of Francis vide ibid., 71 and 72; 2 Cel., 3, 38-43; Ben., 139-148. Cf. 1 Cel., 6; 91; 103; 3 Soc., 8; 12; etc.

[6]   Luke, xxii. 44.

[7]   Felix Kuhn: *Luther, sa vie et son oeuvre,* Paris, 1883, 3 vols., 8vo. t. i., p. 128; t. ii., p. 9; t. iii., p. 257. Benvenuto Cellini does not hesitate to describe a visit which he made one day to the Coliseum in company with a magician whose words evoked clouds of devils who filled the whole place. B. Cellini, *La vita scritta da lui medesimo,* Bianchi's edition, Florence, 1890, 12mo, p. 33.

[8]   On the devil and Francis vide 1 Cel., 68, 72; 3 Soc., 12; 2 Cel., 1, 6; 3, 10; 53; 58-65; Bon., 59-62. Cf. Eccl., 3; 5; 13; *Fior.* , 29; *Spec.* , 110b. To form an idea of the part taken by the devil in the life of a monk at the beginning of the thirteenth century, one must read the *Dialogus miraculorium* of Cæsar von Heisterbach.

[9]   Matthew, x. 1.

[10]   Miracles occupy only ten paragraphs (61-70) in 1 Cel., and of this number there are several which can hardly be counted as Francis's miracles, since they were performed by objects which had belonged to him.

[11]   Heretics often took advantage of this thirst for the marvellous to dupe the catholics. The Cathari of Moncoul made a portrait of the Virgin representing her as one eyed and toothless, saying that in his humility Christ had chosen a very ugly woman for mother. They had no difficulty in healing several cases of disease by its means; the image became famous, was venerated almost everywhere, and accomplished many miracles until the day when the heretics divulged the deception, to the great scandal of the faithful. Egbert von Schönau, *Contra Catharos*. Serm. I. cap. 2. (Patrol. lat. Migne t. 195.) Cf. Heisterbach, *loc. cit.* , v. 18. Luc de Tuy, *De altera Vita*, lib. ii. 9; iii. 9, 18 (Patrol. Migne., 208).

[12]   "But God forbid that I should glory save in the cross of our Lord Jesus Christ. " Gal. vi. 14. This is to this day the motto of the Brothers Minor.

[13]   *Spec.* , 182a; 200a; 232a. Cf. 199a.

[14]   1 Cel., 67.

[15]   *Secundum primam regulam fratres feria quarta et sexta et per licentiam beati Francisci feria secunda et sabbato jejunabant. Giord. 11. cf. Reg. 1221, cap. 3* and *Reg. 1223, cap. 3*, where Friday is the only fast day retained.

[16]   1 Cel., 10; 22; 27; 31; 42; 80; 2 Cel., 1, 1; 3, 65-68; Eccl., 5; 6; *Giord.* , 21; *Spec.* , 119a; *Conform.* , 143a, 2.

[17]   *Caveant fratres quod non ostendant se tristes extrinsecus nubilosos et hypocritas; sed ostendant se gaudentis in Domine, hilares et convenientes gratiosos.*

[18]   Eccl., *loc. cit.* ; Giord., *loc. cit.*

[19]   Vide *Test.* ; 1 Cel., 46; 62; 75; 2 Cel., 3, 129; *Spec.* , 44a.

CHAPTER XII

THE CHAPTER-GENERAL OF 1217[1]

After Whitsunday of 1217 chronological notes of Francis's life are numerous enough to make error almost impossible. Unhappily, this is not the case for the eighteen months which precede it (autumn of 1215-Whitsunday, 1217). For this period we are reduced to conjecture, or little better.

As Francis at that time undertook no foreign mission, he doubtless employed his time in evangelizing Central Italy and in consolidating the foundations of his institution. His presence at Rome during the Lateran Council (November 11-30, 1215) is possible, but it has left no trace in the earliest biographies. The Council certainly took the new Order into consideration, [2] but it was to renew the invitation made to it five years before by the supreme pontiff, to choose one of the Rules already approved by the Church. [3] St. Dominic, who was then at Rome to beg for the confirmation of his institute, received the same counsel and immediately conformed to it. The Holy See would willingly have conceded special constitutions to the Brothers Minor, if they had adopted for a base the Rule of St. Benedict; thus the Clarisses, except those of St. Damian, while preserving their name and a certain number of their customs, were obliged to profess the Benedictine rule.

In spite of all solicitations, Francis insisted upon retaining his own Rule. One is led to believe that it was to confer upon these questions that we find him at Perugia in July, 1216, when Innocent III. died. [4]

However this may be, about this epoch the chapters took on a great importance. The Church, which had looked on at the foundation of the Order with somewhat mixed feelings, could no longer rest content with being the mere spectator of so profound a movement; it saw the need of utilizing it.

Ugolini was marvellously well prepared for such a task. Giovanni di San Paolo, Bishop of the Sabine, charged by Innocent III. to look after the Brothers, died in 1216, and Ugolini was not slow to offer his protection to Francis, who accepted it with gratitude. This extraordinary offer is recounted at length by the Three Companions.

[5] It must certainly be fixed in the summer of 1216[6] immediately after the death of Giovanni di San Paolo.

It is very possible that the first chapter held in the presence of this cardinal took place on May 29, 1216. By an error very common in history, most of the Franciscan writers have referred to a single date all the scattered incidents concerning the first solemn assizes of the Order, and have called this typical assembly the *Chapter of the Mats*. In reality for long years all the gatherings of the Brothers Minor deserved this name. [7]

Coming together at the season of the greatest heat, they slept in the open air or sheltered themselves under booths of reeds. We need not pity them. There is nothing like the glorious transparency of the summer night in Umbria; sometimes in Provence one may enjoy a foretaste of it, but if at Baux, upon the rock of Doms, or at St. Baume, the sight is equally solemn and grandiose, it still wants the caressing sweetness, the effluence of life which in Umbria give the night a bewitching charm.

The inhabitants of the neighboring towns and villages flocked to these meetings in crowds, at once to see the ceremonies, to be present when their relatives or friends assumed the habit, to listen to the appeals of the Saint and to furnish to the friars the provisions of which they might have need. All this is not without some analogy with the camp-meeting so dear to Americans. As to the figures of several thousands of attendants given in the legends, and furnishing even to a Franciscan, Father Papini, the occasion for pleasantries of doubtful taste, it is perhaps not so surprising as might be supposed. [8]

These first meetings, to which all the Brothers eagerly hastened, held in the open air in the presence of crowds come together from distant places, have then nothing in common with the subsequent chapters-general, which were veritable conclaves attended by a small number of delegates, and the majority of the work of which, done in secret, was concerned only with the affairs of the Order.

During Francis's lifetime the purpose of these assemblies was essentially religious. Men attended them not to talk business, or proceed to the nomination of the minister-general, but in mutual communion to gain new strength from the joys, the example, and the sufferings of the other brethren. [9]

The four years which followed the Whitsunday of 1216 form a stage in the evolution of the Umbrian movement; that during which Francis was battling for autonomy. We find here pretty delicate shades of distinction, which have been misunderstood by Church writers as much as by their adversaries, for if Francis was particular not to put himself in the attitude of revolt, he would not compromise his independence, and he felt with an exquisite divination that all the privileges which the court of Rome could heap upon him were worth nothing in comparison with liberty. Alas, he was soon forced to resign himself to these gilded bonds, against which he never ceased to protest, even to his last sigh; [10] but to shut one's eyes to the moral violence which the papacy did him in this matter is to condemn oneself to an entire misapprehension of his work.

A glance over the collection of bulls addressed to the Franciscans suffices to show with what ardor he struggled against favors so eagerly sought by the monastic orders. [11]

A great number of legendary anecdotes put Francis's disdain of privileges in the clearest light. Even his dearest friends did not always understand his scruples.

> "Do you not see, " they said to him one day, "that often the bishops do not permit us to preach, and make us remain several days without doing anything before we are permitted to proclaim the word of God? It would be better worth while to obtain for this end a privilege from the pope, and it would be for the good of souls. "

> "I would first convert the prelates by humility and respect, " he replied quickly; "for when they have seen us humble and respectful toward them, they themselves will beg us to preach and convert the people. As for me, I ask of God no privilege unless it be that I may have none, to be full of respect for all men, and to convert them, as our Rule ordains, more by our example than by our speech. "[12]

The question whether Francis was right or wrong in his antipathy to the privileges of the curia does not come within the domain of history; it is evident that this attitude could not long continue; the Church knows only the faithful and rebels. But the noblest hearts often make a stand at compromises of this kind; they desire that the future should grow out of the past without convulsion and without a crisis.

The chapter of 1217 was notable for the definitive organization of the Franciscan missions. Italy and the other countries were divided off into a certain number of *provinces*, having each its provincial minister. Immediately upon his accession Honorius III. had sought to revive the popular zeal for the crusades. He had not stopped at preaching it, but appealed to prophecies which had proclaimed that under his pontificate the Holy Land would be reconquered. [13] The renewal of fervor which ensued, and of which the rebound was felt as far as Germany, had a profound influence on the Brothers Minor. This time Francis, perhaps from humility, did not put himself at the head of the friars charged with a mission to Syria; for leader he gave them the famous Elias, formerly at Florence, where he had had opportunity to show his high qualities. [14]

This Brother, who from this time appears in the foreground of this history, came from the most humble ranks of society; the date and the circumstances of his entrance into the Order are unknown, and hence conjecture has come to see in him that friend of the grotto who had been Francis's confidant shortly before his decisive conversion. However this may be, in his youth he had earned his living in Assisi, making mattresses and teaching a few children to read; then he had spent some time in Bologna as *scriptor*; then suddenly we find him among the Brothers Minor, charged with the most difficult missions.

His adversaries vie with one another in asserting that he was the finest mind of his century, but unhappily it is very difficult, in the existing state of the documents, to pronounce as to his actions; learned and energetic, eager to play the leading part in the work of the reformation of religion, and having made his plan beforehand as to the proper mode of realizing it, he made straight for his goal, half political, half religious. Full of admiration for Francis and gratitude toward him, he desired to regulate and consolidate the movement for renovation. In the inner Franciscan circle, where Leo, Ginepro, Egidio, and many others represent the spirit of liberty, the religion of the humble and the simple, Elias represents the scientific and ecclesiastical spirit, prudence and reason.

He had great success in Syria and received into the Order one of the disciples most dear to Francis, Cæsar of Speyer, who later on was to make the conquest of all Southern Germany in less than two years

(1221-1223), and who in the end sealed with his blood his fidelity to the strict observance, which he defended against the attacks of Brother Elias himself. [15]

Cæsar of Speyer offers a brilliant example of those suffering souls athirst for the ideal, so numerous in the thirteenth century, who everywhere went up and down, seeking first in learning, then in the religious life, that which should assuage the mysterious thirst which tortured them. Disciple of the scholastic Conrad, he had felt himself overpowered with the desire to reform the Church; while still a layman he had preached his ideas, not without some success, since a certain number of ladies of Speyer had begun to lead a new life; but their husbands disapproving, he was obliged to escape their vengeance by taking refuge at Paris, and thence he went to the East, where in the preaching of the Brothers Minor he found again his hopes and his dreams. This instance shows how general was the waiting condition of souls when the Franciscan gospel blazed forth, and how its way had been everywhere prepared.

But it is time to return to the chapter of 1217: the friars who went to Germany under conduct of Giovanni di Penna were far from having the success of Elias and his companions; they were completely ignorant of the language of the country which they had undertaken to evangelize. Perhaps Francis had not taken into account the fact that though Italian might, in case of need, suffice in all the countries bathed by the Mediterranean, this could not be the case in Central Europe. [16]

The lot of the party going to Hungary was not more happy. Very often it came to pass that the missionaries were fain to give up their very garments in the effort to appease the peasants and shepherds who maltreated them. But no less incapable of understanding what was said to them than of making themselves understood, they were soon obliged to think of returning to Italy. We may thank the Franciscan authors for preserving for us the memory of these checks, and not attempting to picture the friars as suddenly knowing all languages by a divine inspiration, as later on was so often related. [17]

Those who had been sent to Spain had also to undergo persecutions. This country, like the south of France, was ravaged by heresy; but already at that time it was vigorously repressed. The Franciscans, suspected of being false Catholics and therefore eagerly hunted out, found a refuge with Queen Urraca of Portugal, who permitted them to establish themselves at Coimbra, Guimarraens, Alenquero, and Lisbon. [18]

Francis himself made preparations for going to France. [19] This country had a peculiar charm for him because of his fervent love of the Holy Sacrament. Perhaps also he was unwittingly drawn toward this country to which he owed his name, the chivalrous dreams of his youth, all of poetry, song, music, delicious dream that had come into his life.

Something of the emotion that thrilled through him on undertaking this new mission has passed into the story of his biographers; one feels there the thrill at once sweet and agonizing, the heart-throb of the brave knight who goes forth all harnessed in the early dawn to scan the horizon, dreading the unknown and yet overflowing with joy, for he knows that the day will be consecrated to love and to the right.

The Italian poet has given the one name of "pilgrimages of love" to the farings forth of chivalry and the journeys undertaken by dreamers, artists, or saints to those parts of the earth which forever mirror themselves before their imagination and remain their chosen fatherland. [20] Such a pilgrimage as this was Francis undertaking.

> "Set forth, " said he to the Brothers who accompanied him, "and walk two and two, humble and gentle, keeping silence until after tierce, praying to God in your hearts, carefully avoiding every vain or useless word. Meditate as much while on this journey as if you were shut up in a hermitage or in your cell, for wherever we are, wherever we go, we carry our cell with us; Brother body is our cell, and the soul is the hermit who dwells in it, there to pray to the Lord and to meditate. "

Arrived at Florence he found there Cardinal Ugolini, sent by the pope as legate to Tuscany to preach the crusade and take all needful measures for assuring its success. [21] Francis was surely far from expecting the reception which the prelate gave him. Instead of encouraging him, the cardinal urged him to give up his project.

> "I am not willing, my brother, that you should cross the mountains; there are many prelates who ask nothing better than to stir up difficulties for you with the court of Rome.

But I and the other cardinals who love your Order desire to protect and aid you, on the condition, however, that you do not quit this province. "

"But, monsignor, it would be a great disgrace for me to send my brethren far away while I remained idly here, sharing none of the tribulations which they must undergo. "

"Wherefore, then, have you sent your brethren so far away, exposing them thus to starvation and all sorts of perils? "

"Do you think, " replied Francis warmly, and as if moved by prophetic inspiration, "that God raised up the Brothers for the sake of this country alone? Verily, I say unto you, God has raised them up for the awakening and the salvation of all men, and they shall win souls not only in the countries of those who believe, but also in the very midst of the infidels. "[22]

The surprise and admiration which these words awoke in Ugolini were not enough to make him change his mind. He insisted so strongly that Francis turned back to Portiuncula, the inspiration of his work not even shaken. Who knows whether the joy which he would have felt in seeing France did not confirm him in the idea that he ought to renounce this plan? Souls athirst with the longing for sacrifice often have scruples such as these; they refuse the most lawful joys that they may offer them to God. We cannot tell whether it was immediately after this interview or not till the following year that Francis put Brother Pacifico at the head of the missionaries sent into France. [23]

Pacifico, who was a poet of talent, had before his conversion been surnamed Prince of Poesy and crowned at the capital by the emperor. One day while visiting a relative who was a nun at San Severino in the March of Ancona, Francis also arrived at the monastery, and preached with such a holy impetuosity that the poet felt himself pierced with the sword of which the Bible speaks, which penetrates between the very joints and marrow, and discerns the thoughts and intents of the heart. [24] On the morrow he assumed the habit and received his symbolical surname. [25]

He was accompanied to France by Brother Agnello di Pisa, who was destined to be put at the head of the first mission to England in 1224. [26]

Francis, on sending them forth, was far from dreaming that from this country, which exerted such a fascination over him, was to come forth the influence which was to compromise his dream — that Paris would be the destruction of Assisi; and yet the time was not very far distant; a few years more and the Poverello would see a part of his spiritual family forgetting the humility of their name, their origin, and their aspirations, to run after the ephemeral laurels of learning.

We have already seen that the habit of the Franciscans of this time was to make their abode within easy reach of great cities; Pacifico and his companions established themselves at St. Denis. [27] We have no particulars of their work; it was singularly fruitful, since it permitted them a few years later to attack England with full success.

Francis passed the following year (1218) in evangelizing tours in Italy. It is naturally impossible to follow him in these travels, the itinerary of which was fixed by his daily inspirations, or by indications as fanciful as the one which had formerly determined his going to Sienna. Bologna, [28] the Verna, the valley of Rieti, the Sacro-Speco of St. Benedict at Subiaco, [29] Gaeta; [30] San Michele on Mount Gargano[31] perhaps received him at this time, but the notes of his presence in these places are too sparse and vague to permit their being included in any scheme of history.

It is very possible that he also paid a visit to Rome during this time; his communications with Ugolini were much more frequent than is generally supposed. We must not permit the stories of biographers to deceive us in this matter; it is a natural tendency to refer all that we know of a man to three or four especially striking dates. We forget entire years of the life of those whom we have known the best and loved the most and group our memories of them around a few salient events which shine all the more brilliantly the deeper we make the surrounding obscurity. The words of Jesus spoken on a hundred different occasions came at last to be formed into a single discourse, the Sermon on the Mount. It is in such cases that criticism needs to be delicate, to mingle a little divination with the heavy artillery of scientific argument.

The texts are sacred, but we must not make fetiches of them; notwithstanding St. Matthew, no one to-day dreams of representing Jesus as uttering the Sermon on the Mount all at one time. In the same way, in the narratives concerning the relations between St. Francis and Ugolini, we find ourselves every moment shut up in no-thoroughfares, coming up against contradictory indications, just so long as we try to refer everything to two or three meetings, as we are at first led to do.

With a simple act of analysis these difficulties disappear and we find each of the different narratives bringing us fragments which, being pieced together, furnish an organic story, living, psychologically true.

From the moment at which we have now arrived, we must make a much larger place for Ugolini than in the past; the struggle has definitively opened between the Franciscan ideal — chimerical, perhaps, but sublime — and the ecclesiastical policy, to go on until the day when, half in humility, half in discouragement, Francis, heartsick, abdicates the direction of his spiritual family.

Ugolini returned to Rome at the end of 1217. During the following winter his countersign is found at the bottom of the most important bulls; [32] he devoted this time to the special study of the question of the new orders, and summoned Francis before him. We have seen with what frankness he had declared to him at Florence that many of the prelates would do anything to discredit him with the pope. [33] It is evident the success of the Order, its methods, which in spite of all protestations to the contrary seemed to savor of heresy, the independence of Francis, who had scattered his friars in all the four corners of the globe without trying to gain a confirmation of the verbal and entirely provisional authorization accorded him by Innocent III. — all these things were calculated to startle the clergy.

Ugolini, who better than any one else knew Umbria, Tuscany, Emilia, the March of Ancona, all those regions where the Franciscan preaching had been most successful, was able by himself to judge of the power of the new movement and the imperious necessity of directing it; he felt that the best way to allay the prejudices which the pope and the sacred college might have against Francis was to present him before the curia.

Francis was at first much abashed at the thought of preaching before the Vicar of Jesus Christ, but upon the entreaties of his protector he consented, and for greater security he learned by heart what he had to say.

Ugolini himself was not entirely at ease as to the result of this step; Thomas of Celano pictures him as devoured with anxiety; he was troubled about Francis, whose artless eloquence ran many a risk in the halls of the Lateran Palace; he was also not without some more personal anxieties, for the failure of his *protégé* might be most damaging to himself. He was in all the greater anxiety when, on arriving at the feet of the pontiff, Francis forgot all he had intended to say; but he frankly avowed it, and seeking a new discourse from the inspiration of the moment, spoke with so much warmth and simplicity that the assembly was won. [34]

The biographers are mute as to the practical result of this audience. We are not to be surprised at this, for they write with the sole purpose of edification. They wrote after the apotheosis of their master, and would with very bad grace have dwelt upon the difficulties which he met during the early years. [35]

The Holy See must have been greatly perplexed by this strange man, whose faith and humility were evident, but whom it was impossible to teach ecclesiastical obedience.

St. Dominic happened to be in Rome at the same time, [36] and was overwhelmed with favors by the pope. It is a matter of history that Innocent III. having asked him to choose one of the Rules already approved by the Church, he had returned to his friars at Notre Dame de Prouille, and after conferring with them had adopted that of St. Augustine; Honorius therefore was not sparing of privileges for him. It is hardly possible that Ugolini did not try to use the influence of his example with St. Francis.

The curia saw clearly that Dominic, whose Order barely comprised a few dozen members, was not one of the moral powers of the time, but its sentiments toward him were by no means so mixed as those it experienced with regard to Francis.

To unite the two Orders, to throw over the shoulders of the Dominicans the brown cassock of the Poor Men of Assisi, and thus make a little of the popularity of the Brothers Minor to be reflected upon them, to leave to the latter their name, their habit, and even a semblance of their Rule, only completing it with that of St. Augustine, such a project would have been singularly pleasing to Ugolini, and with Francis's humility would seem to have some chance of success.

One day Dominic by dint of pious insistance induced Francis to give him his cord, and immediately girded himself with it. "Brother, " said he, "I earnestly long that your Order and mine might unite to form one sole and same institute[37] in the Church. " But the Brother Minor wished to remain as he was, and declined the proposition. So truly was he inspired with the needs of his time and of the Church that less than three years after this Dominic was drawn by an irresistible influence to transform his Order of Canons of St. Augustine into an order of mendicant monks, whose constitutions were outlined upon those of the Franciscans. [38]

A few years later the Dominicans took, so to speak, their revenge, and obliged the Brothers Minor to give learning a large place in their work. Thus, while hardly come to youth's estate, the two religious families rivalled one another, impressed, influenced one another, yet never so much so as to lose all traces of their origin—summed up for the one in poverty and lay preaching, for the other in learning and the preaching of the clergy.

FOOTNOTES:

[1]   The commencement of the great missions and the institution of provincial ministers is usually fixed either at 1217 or 1219, but both these dates present great difficulties. I confess that I do not understand the vehemence with which partisans of either side defend their opinions. The most important text is a passage in the 3 Soc., 62: *Expletis itaque undecim annis ab inceptione religionis, et multiplicatis numero et merito fratribus, electi fuerant ministri, et missi cum aliquot fratribus quasi per universas mundi provincias in quibus fides catholica colitur et servatur.* What does this expression, *inceptio religionis*, mean? At a first reading one unhesitatingly takes it to refer to the foundation of the Order, which occurred in April, 1209, by the reception of the first Brothers; but on adding eleven full years to this date we reach the summer of 1220. This is manifestly too late, for the 3 Soc. say that the brethren who went out were persecuted in most of the countries beyond

the mountains, as being accredited by no pontifical letter; but the bull *Cum dilecti*, bears the date of June 11, 1219. We are thus led to think that the eleven years are not to be counted from the reception of the first Brothers, but from Francis's conversion, which the authors might well speak of as *inceptio religionis*, and 1206 + 11 = 1217. The use of this expression to designate conversion is not entirely without example. Glassberger says (*An. fr.* , p. 9): *Ordinem minorum incepit anno 1206.* Those who admit 1219 are obliged (like the Bollandists, for example), to attribute an inaccuracy to the text of the 3 Soc., that of having counted eleven years as having passed when there had been only ten. We should notice that in the two other chronological indications given by the 3 Soc. (27 and 62) they count from the conversion, that is from 1206, as also Thomas of Celano, 88, 105, 119, 97, 88, 57, 55, 21. Curiously, the Conformities reproduce the passage of the 3 Soc. (118b, 1), but with the alteration: *Nono anno ab inceptione religionis.* Giordano di Giano opens the door to many scruples: *Anno vero Domini* 1219 *et anno conversionis ejus decimo frater Franciscus... misit fratres in Franciam, in Theutoniam, in Hungariam, in Hespaniam*, Giord., 3. As a little later the same author properly harmonizes 1219 with the thirteenth year from Francis's conversion, everyone is in agreement in admitting that the passage cited needs correction; we have unfortunately only one manuscript of this chronicle. Glassberger, who doubtless had another before him, substitutes 1217, but he may have drawn this date from another document. It is noteworthy that Brother Giordano gives as simultaneous the departure of the friars for Germany, Hungary, and France; but, as to the latter country, it certainly took place in 1217. So the Speculum, 44a.

The chronicle of the xxiv. generals and Mark of Lisbon (Diola's ed., t. i., p. 82) holds also to 1217, so that, though not definitely established, it would appear that this date should be accepted until further information. Starting from slightly different premises, the learned editors of the *Analecta* arrive at the same conclusion (t. ii., pp. 25-36). Cf. Evers, *Analecta ad Fr. Minorum historiam*, Leipsic, 1882, 4to, pp. 7 and 11. That which appears to me decidedly to tip the balance in favor of 1217, is the fact that the missionary friars were persecuted because they had no document of legitimation; and in 1219 they would have had the bull *Cum dilecti*, from June 11th of that year. The Bollandists, who hold for 1219, have so clearly seen this argument that they have been obliged to deny the authenticity of the bull (or at least to suppose it wrongly dated). A. SS., p. 839.

[2]   Vide A. SS., p. 604. Cf. Angelo Clareno, *Tribul. Archiv.* , i., p. 559. *A papa Innocentis fuit omnibus annuntiatum in concilio generali... sicut sanctus vir fr. Leo scribit et fr. Johannes de Celano.* These lines have not perhaps the significance which one would be led to give them at the first glance, their author having perhaps confounded *consilium* and *consistorium*. The Speculum, 20b says: *Eam (Regulam Innocentius) approvabit et concessit et postea in consistorio omnibus annuntiavit.*

[3]   *Ne nimia Religionem diversitas gravem in Ecclesia Dei confusionem inducat, firmiter prohibemus, ne quis de coetero novam Religionem inveniat; sed quicumque voluerit ad Religionem converti, unam de approbatis assumat.* Labbé and Cossart: *Sacrosancta concilia,* Paris, 1672, t. xi., col. 165.

[4]   Eccl., 15 (*An. franc.* , t. 1, p. 253): *Innocentium in cujus obitu fuit presentialiter S. Franciscus.*

[5]   3 Soc., 61; cf. *An. Perus.* , A. SS., p. 606f.

[6]   Thomas of Celano must be in error when he declares that Francis was not acquainted with Cardinal Ugolini before the visit which he made him at Florence (summer of 1217): *Nondum alter alteri erat præcipua familiaritate conjunctus* (1 Cel., 74 and 75). The Franciscan biographer's purpose was not historic; chronological indications are given in profusion; what he seeks is the *apta junctura*. Tradition has preserved the memory of a chapter held at Portiuncula in presence of Ugolini during a stay of the curia at Perugia (*Spec.* , 137b. ; *Fior.*, 18; *Conform.* , 207a; 3 Soc., 61). But the curia did not come back to Perugia between 1216 and Francis's death. It is also to be noted that according to Angelo Clareno, Ugolini was with Francis in 1210, supporting him in the presence of Innocent III. Vide below, p. 413. Finally the bull *Sacrosancta* of December 9, 1219, witnesses that already during his legation in Florence (1217) Ugolini was actually interesting himself for the Clarisses.

[7]   See, for example, the description of the chapter of 1221 by Brother Giordano. Giord., 16.

[8]   With regard to the figure of five thousand attendants given by Bonaventura (Bon., 59) Father Papini writes: *Io non credo stato capace alcuno di dare ad intendere al S. Dottore simil fanfaluca, ne capace lui di crederla.*

        ... In somma il numero quinque millia et ultra non è del Santo, incapace di scrivere una cosa tanto improbabile e relativamente impossibile. Storia di S. Fr. , i., pp. 181 and 183. This figure, five thousand, is also indicated by Eccl., 6. All this may be explained and become possible by admitting the presence of the Brothers of Penitence, and it seems very difficult to contest it, since in the Order of the Humiliants, which much resembles that of the Brothers Minor (equally composed of three branches approved by three bulls given June, 1201), the chapters-general annually held were frequented by the brothers of the three Orders. Tiraboschi t. ii., p. 144. Cf. above, p. 158.

[9]   Vide 2 Cel., 3, 121; *Spec.* , 42b; 127b.

[10]   *Præcipio firmiter per obedientiam fratribus universis quod ubicunque sunt, non audeant petere aliquam litteram in Curia Romana. Test. B. Fr.*

[11]   A comparison with the Bullary of the Preaching Friars is especially instructive: from their first chapter at Notre Dame de Prouille, in 1216, they are about fifteen; we find there at this time absolutely nothing that can be compared to the Franciscan movement, which was already stirring up all Italy. But while the first bull in favor of the Franciscans bears the date of June 11, 1219, and the approbation properly so called that of November 29, 1223, we find Honorius already in the end of 1216 lavishing marks of affection upon the Dominicans; December 22, 1216, *Religiosam vitam.* Cf. Pressuti, *I regesti, del Pontefice Onorio III.* , Roma, 1884, t. i., no. 175; same date; *Nos attendentes,* ibid., no. 176; January 21, 1217, *gratiarum omnium,* ib., no. 243. Vide 284, 1039, 1156, 1208. It is needless to continue this enumeration. Very much the same could be done for the other Orders; whence the conclusion that if the Brothers Minor alone are forgotten in

this shower of favors, it is because they decidedly wished to be. It must be admitted that immediately upon Francis's death they made up for lost time.

[12]   The authenticity of this passage is put beyond doubt by Ubertino di Casal's citation. *Archiv.* , iii., p. 53. Cf. *Spec.* , 30a; *Conform.* , 111b, 1; 118b, 1; Ubertino, *Arbor vitæ cruc.* , iii., 3.

[13]   *Burchardi chronicon ann. 1217, loc. cit.* , p. 377. See also the bulls indicated by Potthast, 5575, 5585-92.

[14]   Before 1217 the office of minister virtually existed, though its definitive institution dates only from 1217. Brother Bernardo in his mission to Bologna, for example (1212?), certainly held in some sort the office of minister.

[15]   Imprisoned by order of Elias, he died in consequence of blows given him one day when he was taking the air outside of his prison. *Tribul.* , 24a.

[16]   Giord., 5 and 6; 3 Soc., 62.

[17]   Of Giovanni di Parma, Clareno, Anthony of Padua, etc.

[18]   Mark of Lisbon, t. l., p. 82. Cf. p. 79, t. ii., p. 86, Glassberger *ann.* , 1217. *An. fr.* , ii., pp. 9 ff. ; *Chron xxiv. gen.* , MS. of Assisi, no. 328, f° 2b.

[19]   *Spec.* , 44a. ; *Conform.* , 119a, 2; 135a; 181b, 1; 1 Cel., 74 and 75.

[20]   Cel., 3, 129. *Diligebat Franciam... volebat in ea mori.*

[21]   V. bull of January 23, 1217, *Tempus acceptabile*, Potthast, no. 5430, given in Horoy, t. ii., col. 205 ff. ; cf. Pressuti, i., p. 71. This bull and those following fix without question the time of the journey to Florence. Potthast, 5488, 5487, and page 495.

[22]   It is superfluous to point out the error of the Bollandist text in the phrase *Monuit (Cardinalis Franciscum) coeptum non perficere iter*, where the *non* is omitted, A. SS., p. 704. Cf., p. 607 and 835, which has led Suysken into several other errors.

[23]   Bon., 51. Cf. Glassberger, *ann.* 1217; *Spec.* , 45b.

[24]   Heb., iv., 12; 2 Cel., 3, 49; Bon., 50 and 51.

[25]   Brother Pacifico interests us [the French people] particularly
         as the first minister of the Order in France; information
         about him is abundant: Bon., 79; 2 Cel., 3, 63; *Spec.* , 41b. :
         Conform. , 38a, 1; 43a, 1; 71b; 173b, 1, and 176; 2 Cel., 8, 27;
         Spec. , 38b; *Conform.* , 181b; 2 Cel., 3, 76; *Fior.* , 46; *Conform.* ,
         70a. I do not indicate the general references found in
         Chevalier's Bibliography. The Miscellanea, t. ii. (1887), p.
         158, contains a most precise and interesting column about
         him. Gregory IX. speaks of him in the bull *Magna sicut dicitur*
         of August 12, 1227. Sbaralea, Bull, fr., i., p. 33 (Potthast,
         8007). Thomas of Tuscany, *socius* of St. Bonaventura, knew
         him and speaks of him in his *Gesta Imperatorum (Mon. germ.
         hist. script.* , t. 22, p. 492).

[26]   Eccl., 1; *Conform.* , 113b, 1.

[27]   Toward 1224 the Brothers Minor desired to draw nearer and
         build a vast convent near the walls of Paris in the grounds
         called Vauvert, or Valvert (now the Luxembourg Garden),
         (Eccl., 10; cf. *Top. hist. du vieux Paris*, by Berty and Tisserand,
         t. iv., p. 70). In 1230 they received at Paris from the
         Benedictines of Saint-Germain-des-Prés a certain number of
         houses *in parocchia SS. Cosmæ et Damiani infra muros domini
         regis prope portam de Gibardo (Chartularium Universitatis
         Parisiensis*, no. 76. Cf. *Topographie historique du vieux Paris;
         Région occid. de l'univ.* , p. 95; Félibien, *Histoire de la ville de
         Paris*, i., p. 115). Finally, St. Louis installed them in the
         celebrated Convent of the Cordeliers, the refectory of which
         still exists, transformed into the Dupuytren Museum. The
         Dominicans, who arrived in Paris September 12, 1217, went
         straight to the centre of the city, near the bishop's palace on
         the *Ile de la Cité*, and on August 6, 1218, were installed in the
         Convent of St. Jacques.

[28]   *Fior.* , 27; *Spec.* , 148b; *Conform.* , 71a and 113a, 2; Bon., 182.

[29]   The traces of Francis's visit here are numerous. A Brother
         Eudes painted his portrait here.

[30]   Bon., 177.

[31]   Vide A. SS., pp. 855 and 856. Cf. 2 Cel., 3, 136.

[32]   Among others those of December 5, 1217, Potthast, 5629;
         February 8, March 30, April 7, 1218, Potthast, 5695, 5739,
         5747.

[33]   1 Cel., 74. *O quanti maxime in principio cum hæc agerentur
         novellæ plantationi ordinis insidiabantur ut perderent.* Cf. 2 Cel.,
         1, 16. *Videbat Franciscus luporum more sevire quamplures.*

[34]   1 Cel., 73 (cf. 2 Cel., 1, 17; *Spec.* , 102a); 3 Soc., 64; Bon., 78.
         The fixing of this scene in the winter of 1217-1218 seems
         hardly to be debatable; Giordano's account (14) in fact
         determines the date at which Ugolini became *officially*
         protector of the Order; it supposes earlier relations between
         Honorius, Francis, and Ugolini. We are therefore led to seek
         a date at which these three personages may have met in
         Rome, and we arrive thus at the period between December,
         1217, and April, 1218.

[35]   A word of Brother Giordano's opens the door to certain
         conjectures. "My lord, " said Francis to Honorius III., in
         1220, "you have given me many fathers (popes) give me a
         single one to whom I may turn with the affairs of my Order. "
         (Giord., 14, *Multos mihi papas dedisti da unum,...* etc.)

         Does not this suggest the idea that the pontiff had perhaps
         named a commission of cardinals to oversee the Brothers
         Minor? Its deliberations and the events to be related in the
         following chapter might have impelled him to issue the bull
         Cum dilecti of June 11, 1219, which was not an approbation
         properly so called, but a safe-conduct in favor of the
         Franciscans.

[36]   He took possession of St. Sabine on February 28, 1218.

[37]   2 Cel., 3, 87. The literal meaning of the phrase is somewhat
         ambiguous. The text is: *Vellem, frater Francisce, unam fieri
         religionem tuam et meam et in Ecclesia pari forma nos vivere.*
         Spec. 27b. The echo of this attempt is found in Thierry
         d'Apolda, *Vie de S. Dominique* (A. SS., Augusti, t. i., p. 572 d):
         *S. Dominicus in oscula sancta ruens et sinceros amplexus, dixit:
         Tu es socius meus, tu curres pariter mecum, stemus simul, nullus*

adversarius prævalebit. Bernard of Besse says: *B. Dominicus tanta B. Francisco devotione cohesit ut optatam ab eo cordam sub inferiori tunica devotissimi cingeret, cujus et suam Religionem unam velle fieri diceret, ipsumque pro sanctitate cæteris sequendem religiosis assereret.* Turin MS., 102b.

[38]   At the chapter held at Bologna at Whitsunday, 1220. The bull *Religiosam vitam* (Privilege of Notre Dame de Prouille) of March 30, 1218, enumerates the possessions of the Dominicans. Ripolli, *Bull. Præd.* , t. i., p. 6. Horoy, *Honorii opera,* t. ii., col. 684.

CHAPTER XIII

ST. DOMINIC AND ST. FRANCIS

The Egyptian Mission. Summer 1218-Autumn 1220

Art and poetry have done well in inseparably associating St. Dominic and St. Francis; the glory of the first is only a reflection of that of the second, and it is in placing them side by side that we succeed best in understanding the genius of the Poverello. If Francis is the man of inspiration, Dominic is that of obedience to orders; one may say that his life was passed on the road to Rome, whither he continually went to ask for instructions. His legend was therefore very slow to be formed, although nothing forbade it to blossom freely; but neither the zeal of Gregory IX. for his memory nor the learning of his disciples were able to do for the *Hammer of heretics* that which the love of the people did for the *Father of the poor*. His legend has the two defects which so soon weary the readers of hagiographical writings, when the question is of the saints whose worship the Church has commanded. [1] It is encumbered with a spurious supernaturalism, and with incidents borrowed right and left from earlier legends. The Italian people, who hailed in Francis the angel of all their hopes, and who showed themselves so greedy for his relics, did not so much as dream of taking up the corpse of the founder of the Order of Preaching Friars, and allowed him to wait twelve years for the glories of canonization. [2]

We have already seen the efforts of Cardinal Ugolini to unite the two Orders, and the reasons he had for this course. He went to the Whitsunday chapter-general which met at Portiuncula (June 3, 1218), to which came also St. Dominic with several of his disciples. The ceremonial of these solemnities appears to have been always about the same since 1216; the Brothers Minor went in procession to meet the cardinal, who immediately dismounted from his horse and lavished expressions of affection upon them. An altar was set up in the open air, at which he said mass, Francis performing the functions of deacon. [3]

It is easy to imagine the emotion which overcame those present when in its beautiful setting of the Umbrian landscape burst forth that part of the Pentecostal service, that most exciting, the most apocalyptic of the whole Catholic liturgy, the anthem *Alleluia,*

Alleluia, Emitte Spiritum tuum et creabuntur, et renovabis faciem terræ. Alleluia, [4] does not this include the whole Franciscan dream?

But what especially amazed Dominic was the absence of material cares. Francis had advised his brethren not to disquiet themselves in any respect about food and drink; he knew by experience that they might fearlessly trust all that to the love of the neighboring population. This want of carefulness had greatly surprised Dominic, who thought it exaggerated; he was able to reassure himself, when meal-time arrived, by seeing the inhabitants of the district hastening in crowds to bring far larger supplies of provisions than were needed for the several thousands of friars, and holding it an honor to wait upon them.

The joy of the Franciscans, the sympathy of the populace with them, the poverty of the huts of Portiuncula, all this impressed him deeply; so much was he moved by it that in a burst of enthusiasm he announced his resolution to embrace gospel poverty. [5]

Ugolini, though also moved, even to tears, [6] did not forget his former anxieties; the Order was too numerous not to include a group of malcontents; a few friars who before their conversion had studied in the universities began to condemn the extreme simplicity laid upon them as a duty. To men no longer sustained by enthusiasm the short precepts of the Rule appeared a charter all too insufficient for a vast association; they turned with envy toward the monumental abbeys of the Benedictines, the regular Canons, the Cistercians, and toward the ancient monastic legislations. They had no difficulty in perceiving in Ugolini a powerful ally, nor in confiding their observations to him.

The latter deemed the propitious moment arrived, and in a private conversation with Francis made a few suggestions: Ought he not give to his disciples, especially to the educated among them, a greater share of the burdens? consult them, gain inspiration from their views? was there not room to profit by the experience of the older orders? Though all this was said casually and with the greatest possible tact, Francis felt himself wounded to the quick, and without answering he drew the cardinal to the very midst of the chapter.

"My brothers, " said he with fire, "the Lord has called me into the ways of simplicity and humility. In them he has shown me the truth for myself and for those who desire to believe and follow me; do not, then, come speaking to me of the Rule of St. Benedict, of St. Augustine, of St. Bernard, or of any other, but solely of that which God in his mercy has seen fit to show to me, and of which he has told me that he would, by its means, make a new covenant with the world, and he does not will that we should have any other. But by your learning and your wisdom God will bring you to confusion. For I am persuaded that God will chastise you; whether you will or no you will be forced to come to repentance, and nothing will remain for you but confusion. "[7]

This warmth in defending and affirming his ideas profoundly astonished Ugolini, who added not a word. As to Dominic, what he had just seen at Portiuncula was to him a revelation. He felt, indeed, that his zeal for the Church could not be greater, but he also perceived that he could serve her with more success by certain changes in his weapons.

Ugolini no doubt only encouraged him in this view, and Dominic, beset with new anxieties, set out a few months later for Spain. The intensity of the crisis through which he passed has not been sufficiently noticed; the religious writers recount at length his sojourn in the grotto of Segovia, but they see only the ascetic practices, the prayers, the genuflexions, and do not think of looking for the cause of all this. From this epoch it might be said that he was unceasingly occupied in copying Francis, if the word had not a somewhat displeasing sense. Arrived at Segovia he follows the example of the Brothers Minor, founds a hermitage in the outskirts of the city, hidden among the rocks which overlook the town, and thence he descends from time to time to preach to the people. The transformation in his mode of life was so evident that several of his companions rebelled and refused to follow him in the new way.

Popular sentiment has at times its intuitions; a legend grew up around this grotto of Segovia, and it was said that St. Dominic there received the stigmata. Is there not here an unconscious effort to translate into an image within the comprehension of all, that which actually took place in this cave of the Sierra da Guaderrama? [8]

Thus St. Dominic also arrived at the poverty of the gospel, but the road by which he reached it was different indeed from that which St. Francis had followed; while the latter had soared to it as on wings, had seen in it the final emancipation from all the anxieties which debase this life, St. Dominic considered it only as a means; it was for him one more weapon in the arsenal of the host charged with the defence of the Church. We must not see in this a mere vulgar calculation; his admiration for him whom he thus imitated and followed afar off was sincere and profound, but genius is not to be copied. This sacred malady was not his; he has transmitted to his sons a sound and robust blood, thanks to which they have known nothing of those paroxysms of hot fever, those lofty flights, those sudden returns which make the story of the Franciscans the story of the most tempest-tossed society which the world has ever known, in which glorious chapters are mingled with pages trivial and grotesque, sometimes even coarse.

At the chapter of 1218 Francis had other causes for sadness than the murmurs of a group of malcontents; the missionaries sent out the year before to Germany and Hungary had returned completely discouraged. The account of the sufferings they had endured produced so great an effect that from that time many of the friars added to their prayers the formula: "Lord preserve us from the heresy of the Lombards and the ferocity of the Germans. "[9]

This explains how Ugolini at last succeeded in convincing Francis of his duty to take the necessary measures no longer to expose the friars to be hunted down as heretics. It was decided that at the end of the next chapter the missionaries should be armed with a papal brief, which should serve them as ecclesiastical passport. Here is the translation of this document:

> Honorius, bishop, servant of the servants of God, to the archbishops, bishops, abbots, deacons, archdeacons, and other ecclesiastical superiors, salutation and the apostolic blessing.

> Our dear son, brother Francis, and his companions of the life and the Order of the Brothers Minor, having renounced the vanities of this world to choose a mode of life which has merited the approval of the Roman Church, and to go out after the example of the Apostles to cast in various regions the seed of the word of God, we pray and exhort you by these apostolic letters to receive as good catholics the friars of the above mentioned society, bearers of these presents, warning you to be favorable to them and treat them with kindness for the honor of God and out of consideration for us.

Given (at Rieti) this third day of the ides of June (June 11, 1219), in the third year of our pontificate. [10]

It is evident that this bull was calculated to avoid awakening Francis's susceptibilities. To understand precisely in what it differs from the first letters usually accredited to new Orders it is necessary to compare it with them; that which had instituted the Dominicans had been, like the others, a veritable privilege; [11] here there is nothing of the kind.

The assembly which was opened at Whitsunday of 1219 (May 26) was of extreme importance. [12] It closed the series of those primitive chapters in which the inspiration and fancy of Francis were given free course. Those which followed, presided over by the vicars, have neither the same cheerfulness nor the same charm; the crude glare of full day has driven away the hues of dawn and the indescribable ardors of nature at its awakening.

The summer of 1219 was the epoch fixed by Honorius III. for making a new effort in the East, and directing upon Egypt all the forces of the Crusaders. [13] Francis thought the moment arrived for realizing the project which he had not been able to execute in 1212. Strangely enough, Ugolini who, two years before had hindered his going to France, now left him in entire liberty to carry out this new expedition. [14] Several authors have deemed that Francis, having found in him a true protector, felt himself reassured as to the future of the Order; he might indeed have thought thus, but the history of the troubles which burst out immediately after his departure, the astounding story of the kind reception given by the court of Rome to some meddlers who took the opportunity of his absence to imperil his Order, would suffice to show how much the Church was embarrassed by him, and with what ardor she longed for the transformation of his work. We shall find later on the detailed account of these facts.

It appears that a Romagnol brother Christopher was at this same chapter nominated provincial of Gascony; he lived there after the customs of the early Franciscans, working with his hands, living in a narrow cell made of the boughs of trees and potter's earth. [15]

Egidio set out for Tunis with a few friars, but a great disappointment awaited them there; the Christians of this country, in the fear of being compromised by their missionary zeal, hurried them into a boat and constrained them to recross the sea. [16]

If the date of 1219 for these two missions has little other basis than conjecture, the same is not the case as to the departure of the friars who went to Spain and Morocco. The discovery has recently been made of the account of their last preachings and of their tragic death, made by an eye-witness. [17] This document is all the more precious because it confirms the general lines of the much longer account given by Mark of Lisbon. It would be out of place to give a summary of it here, because it but very indirectly concerns the life of St. Francis, but we must note that these *acta* have beyond their historic value a truly remarkable psychological—one must almost say pathological—significance; never was the mania for martyrdom better characterized than in these long pages, where we see the friars forcing the Mahometans to pursue them and make them win the heavenly palm. The forbearance which Miramolin as well as his fellow religionists at first show gives an idea of the civilization and the good qualities of these infidels, all the higher that very different sentiments would be natural in the vanquished ones of the plains of Tolosa.

It is impossible to call by the name of sermons the collections of rude apostrophes which the missionaries addressed to those whom they wished to convert; at this paroxysm the thirst for martyrdom becomes the madness of suicide. Is this to say that friars Bernard, Pietro, Adjutus, Accurso, and Otho have no right to the admiration and worship with which they have been surrounded? Who would dare say so? Is not devotion always blind? That a furrow should be fecund it must have blood, it must have tears, such tears as St. Augustine has called the blood of the soul. Ah, it is a great mistake to immolate oneself, for the blood of a single man will not save the world nor even a nation; but it is a still greater mistake not to immolate oneself, for then one lets others be lost, and is oneself lost first of all.

I greet you, therefore, Martyrs of Morocco; you do not regret your madness, I am sure, and if ever some righteous pedant gone astray in the groves of paradise undertakes to demonstrate to you that it would have been better worth while to remain in your own country, and found a worthy family of virtuous laborers, I fancy that Miramolin, there become your best friend, will take the trouble to refute him.

You were mad, but I envy such madness, for you felt that the essential thing in this world is not to serve this ideal or that one, but with all one's soul to serve the ideal which one has chosen.

When, a few months after, the story of their glorious end arrived at Assisi, Francis discerned a feeling of pride among his companions and reproached them in lively terms; he who would so have envied the lot of the martyrs felt himself humbled because God had not judged him worthy to share it. As the story was mingled with some words of eulogy of the founder of the Order, he forbade the further reading of it. [18]

Immediately after the chapter he had himself undertaken a mission of the same kind as he had confided to the Brothers of Morocco, but he had proceeded in it in an entirely different manner: his was not the blind zeal which courts death in a sort of frenzy and forgets all the rest; perhaps he already felt that the persistent effort after the better, the continual immolation of self for truth, is the martyrdom of the strong.

This expedition, which lasted more than a year, is mentioned by the biographers in a few lines. [19] Happily we have a number of other papers regarding it; but their silence suffices to prove the sincerity of the primitive Franciscan authors; if they had wanted to amplify the deeds of their subject, where could they have found an easier opportunity or a more marvellous theme? Francis quitted Portiuncula in the middle of June and went to Ancona, whence the Crusaders were to set sail for Egypt on St. John's Day (June 24th).

Many friars joined him—a fact which was not without its inconveniences for a journey by sea, where they were obliged to depend upon the charity of the owners of the boats, or of their fellow-travellers.

We can understand Francis's embarrassment on arriving at Ancona and finding himself obliged to leave behind a number of those who so earnestly longed to go with him. The Conformities relate here an incident for which we might desire an earlier authority, but which is certainly very like Francis; he led all his friends to the port and explained to them his perplexities. "The people of the boat, " he told them, "refuse to take us all, and I have not the courage to make choice among you; you might think that I do not love you all alike; let us then try to learn the will of God. " And he called a child who was playing close by, and the little one, charmed to take the part of Providence put upon him, pointed out with his finger the eleven friars who were to set sail. [20]

We do not know what itinerary they followed. A single incident of the journey has come down to us: that of the chastisement inflicted in the isle of Cyprus on Brother Barbaro, who had been guilty of the fault which the master detested above all others—evil-speaking. He was implacable with regard to the looseness of language so customary among pious folk, and which often made a hell of religious houses apparently the most peaceful. The offence this time appeared to him the more grave for having been uttered in the presence of a stranger, a knight of that district. The latter was stupefied on hearing Francis command the guilty one to eat a lump of ass's dung which lay there, adding: "The mouth which has distilled the venom of hatred against my brother must eat this excrement. " Such indignation, no less than the obedience of the unhappy offender, filled him with admiration. [21]

It is very probable, as Wadding has supposed, that the missionaries debarked at St. Jean d'Acre. They arrived there about the middle of July. [22] In the environs of this city, doubtless, Brother Elias had been established for one or two years. Francis there told off a few of his companions, whom he sent to preach in divers directions, and a few days afterward he himself set out for Egypt, where all the efforts of the Crusaders were concentrated upon Damietta.

From the first he was heart-broken with the moral condition of the Christian army. Notwithstanding the presence of numerous prelates and of the apostolic legate, it was disorganized for want of discipline. He was so affected by this that when there was talk of battle he felt it his duty to advise against it, predicting that the Christians would infallibly be beaten. No one heeded him, and on August 29th the Crusaders, having attacked the Saracens, were terribly routed. [23]

His predictions won him a marvellous success. It must be owned that the ground was better prepared than any other to receive the new seed; not surely that piety was alive there, but in this mass of men come together from every corner of Europe, the troubled, the seers, the enlightened ones, those who thirsted for righteousness and truth, were elbowed by rascals, adventurers, those who were greedy for gold and plunder, capable of much good or much evil, the sport of fleeting impulses, loosed from the bonds of the family, of property, of the habits which usually twine themselves about man's will, and only by exception permit a complete change in his manner of life; those among them who were sincere and had come there with generous purposes were, so to speak, predestined to enter the peaceful army of the Brothers Minor. Francis was to win in this mission fellow-laborers who would assure the success of his work in the countries of northern Europe.

Jacques de Vitry, in a letter to friends written a few days later, thus describes the impression produced on him by Francis:

> "I announce to you that Master Reynier, Prior of St. Michael, has entered the Order of the Brothers Minor, an Order which is multiplying rapidly on all sides, because it imitates the primitive Church and follows the life of the Apostles in everything. The master of these Brothers is named Brother Francis; he is so lovable that he is venerated by everyone. Having come into our army, he has not been afraid, in his zeal for the faith, to go to that of our enemies. For days together he announced the word of God to the Saracens, but with little success; then the sultan, King of Egypt, asked him in secret to entreat God to reveal to him, by some miracle, which is the best religion. Colin, the Englishman, our clerk, has entered the same Order, as also two others of our companions, Michael and Dom Matthew, to whom I had given the rectorship of the Sainte Chapelle. Cantor and Henry have done the same, and still others whose names I have forgotten. "[24]

The long and enthusiastic chapter which the same author gives to the Brothers Minor in his great work on the Occident is too diffuse to find a place here. It is a living and accurate picture of the early times of the Order; in it Francis's sermon before the sultan is again related. It was written at a period when the friars had still neither monasteries nor churches, and when the chapters were held once or twice a year; this gives us a date anterior to 1223, and probably even before 1221. We have here, therefore, a verification of the narratives of Thomas of Celano and the Three Companions, and they find in it their perfect confirmation.

As to the interviews between Francis and the sultan, it is prudent to keep to the narratives of Jacques de Vitry and William of Tyre. [25]

Although the latter wrote at a comparatively late date (between 1275 and 1295), he followed a truly historic method, and founded his work on authentic documents; we see that he knows no more than Jacques de Vitry of the proposal said to have been made by Francis to pass through a fire if the priests of Mahomet would do as much, intending so to establish the superiority of Christianity.

We know how little such an appeal to signs is characteristic of St. Francis. Perhaps the story, which comes from Bonaventura, is born of a misconception. The sultan, like a new Pharaoh, may have laid it upon the strange preacher to prove his mission by miracles. However this may be, Francis and his companions were treated with great consideration, a fact the more meritorious that hostilities were then at their height.

Returned to the Crusading camp, they remained there until after the taking of Damietta (November 5, 1219). This time the Christians were victorious, but perhaps the heart of the *gospel man* bled more for this victory than for the defeat of August 29th. The shocking condition of the city, which the victors found piled with heaps of dead bodies, the quarrels over the sharing of booty, the sale of the wretched creatures who had not succumbed to the pestilence, [26] all these scenes of terror, cruelty, greed, caused him profound horror. The "human beast" was let loose, the apostle's voice could no more make itself heard in the midst of the savage clamor than that of a life-saver over a raging ocean.

He set out for Syria[27] and the Holy Places. How gladly would we follow him in this pilgrimage, accompany him in thought through Judea and Galilee, to Bethlehem, to Nazareth, to Gethsemane! What was said to him by the stable where the Son of Mary was born, the workshop where he toiled, the olive-tree where he accepted the bitter cup? Alas! the documents here suddenly fail us. Setting out from Damietta very shortly after the siege (November 5, 1219) he may easily have been at Bethlehem by Christmas. But we know nothing, absolutely nothing, except that his sojourn was more prolonged than had been expected.

Some of the Brothers who were present at Portiuncula at the chapter-general of 1220 (Whitsunday, May 17th) had time enough to go to Syria and still find Francis there; [28] they could hardly have arrived much earlier than the end of June. What had he been doing those eight months? Why had he not gone home to preside at the chapter?

Had he been ill? [29] Had he been belated by some mission? Our information is too slight to permit us even to venture upon conjecture.

Angelo Clareno relates that the Sultan of Egypt, touched by his preaching, gave command that he and all his friars should have free access to the Holy Sepulchre without the payment of any tribute. [30]

Bartholomew of Pisa on his part says incidentally that Francis, having gone to preach in Antioch and its environs, the Benedictines of the Abbey of the Black Mountain, [31] eight miles from that city, joined the Order in a body, and gave up all their property to the Patriarch.

These indications are meagre and isolated indeed, and the second is to be accepted only with reserve. On the other hand, we have detailed information of what went on in Italy during Francis's absence. Brother Giordano's chronicle, recently discovered and published, throws all the light that could be desired upon a plot laid against Francis by the very persons whom he had commissioned to take his place at Portiuncula, and this, if not with the connivance of Rome and the cardinal protector, at least without their opposition. These events had indeed been narrated by Angelo Clareno, but the undisguised feeling which breathes through all his writings and their lack of accuracy had sufficed with careful critics to leave them in doubt. How could it be supposed that in the very lifetime of St. Francis the vicars whom he had instituted could take advantage of his absence to overthrow his work? How could it be that the pope, who during this period was sojourning at Rieti, how that Ugolini, who was still nearer, did not impose silence on these agitators? [32]

Now that all the facts come anew to light, not in an oratorical and impassioned account, but brief, precise, cutting, dated, with every appearance of notes taken day by day, we must perforce yield to evidence.

Does this give us reason clamorously to condemn Ugolino and the pope? I do not think so. They played a part which is not to their honor, but their intentions were evidently excellent. If the famous aphorism that the end justifies the means is criminal where one examines his own conduct, it becomes the first duty in judging that of others. Here are the facts:

On July 25th, about one month after Francis's departure for Syria, Ugolini, who was at Perugia, laid upon the Clarisses of Monticelli (Florence), Sienna, Perugia, and Lucca that which his friend had so obstinately refused for the friars, the Benedictine Rule. [33]

At the same time, St. Dominic, returning from Spain full of new ardor after his retreat in the grotto of Segovia, and fully decided to adopt for his Order the rule of poverty, was strongly encouraged in this purpose and overwhelmed with favors. [34] Honorius III. saw in him the providential man of the time, the reformer of the monastic Orders; he showed him unusual attentions, going so far, for example, as to transfer to him a group of monks belonging to other Orders, whom he appointed to act as Dominic's lieutenants on the preaching tours which he believed it to be his duty to undertake, and to serve, under his direction, an apprenticeship in popular preaching. [35]

That Ugolini was the inspiration of all this, the bulls are here to witness. His ruling purpose at that time was so clearly to direct the two new Orders that he chose a domicile with this end in view, and we find him continually either at Perugia—that is to say, within three leagues of Portiuncula—or at Bologna, the stronghold of the Dominicans.

It now becomes manifest that just as the fraternity instituted by Francis was truly the fruit of his body, flesh of his flesh, so does the Order of the Preaching Friars emanate from the papacy, and St. Dominic is only its putative father. This character is expressed in one word by one of the most authoritative of contemporary annalists, Burchard of Ursperg ([Cross] 1226). "The pope, " he says, "*instituted* and confirmed the Order of the Preachers. "[36]

Francis on his journey in the Orient had taken for special companion a friar whom we have not yet met, Pietro di Catana or *dei Cattani*. Was he a native of the town of Catana? There is no precise indication of it. It appears more probable that he belonged to the noble family *dei Cattani*, already known to Francis, and of which Orlando, Count of Chiusi in Casentino, who gave him the Verna, was a member. However that may be, we must not confound him with the Brother Pietro who assumed the habit in 1209, at the same time with Bernardo of Quintavallo, and died shortly afterward. Tradition, in reducing these two men to a single personage, was influenced not merely by the similarity of the names, but also by the very natural desire to increase the prestige of one who in 1220-1221 was to play an important part in the direction of the Order. [37]

At the time of his departure for the East Francis had left two vicars in his place, the Brothers Matteo of Narni and Gregorio of Naples. The former was especially charged to remain at Portiuncula to admit postulants; [38] Gregorio of Naples, on the other hand, was to pass through Italy to console the Brothers. [39]

The two vicars began at once to overturn everything. It is inexplicable how men still under the influence of their first fervor for a Rule which in the plenitude of their liberty they had promised to obey could have dreamed of such innovations if they had not been urged on and upheld by those in high places. To alleviate the vow of poverty and to multiply observances were the two points toward which their efforts were bent.

In appearance it was a trifling matter, in reality it was much, for it was the first movement of the old spirit against the new. It was the effort of men who unconsciously, I am willing to think, made religion an affair of rite and observance, instead of seeing in it, like St. Francis, the conquest of the liberty which makes us free in all things, and leads each soul to obey that divine and mysterious power which the flowers of the fields adore, which the birds of the air bless, which the symphony of the stars praises, and which Jesus of Nazareth called *Abba*, that is to say, Father.

The first Rule was excessively simple in the matter of fasts. The friars were to abstain from meat on Wednesdays and Fridays; they might add Mondays and Saturdays, but only on Francis's special authorization. The vicars and their adherents complicated this rule in a surprising manner. At the chapter-general held in Francis's absence (May 17, 1220), they decided, first, that in times of feasting the friars were not to provide meat, but if it were offered to them spontaneously they were to eat it; second, that all should fast on Mondays as well as Wednesdays and Fridays; third, that on Mondays and Saturdays they should abstain from milk products unless by chance the adherents of the Order brought some to them. [40]

These beginnings bear witness also to an effort to imitate the ancient Orders, not without the vague hope that they would be substituted for them. Brother Giordano has preserved to us only this decision of the chapter of 1220, but the expressions of which he makes use sufficiently prove that it was far from being the only one, and that the malcontents had desired, as in the chapters of Citeaux and Monte Cassino, to put forth veritable constitutions.

These modifications of the Rule did not pass, however, without arousing the indignation of a part of the chapter; a lay brother made himself their eager messenger, and set out for the East to entreat Francis to return without delay, to take the measures called for by the circumstances.

There were also other causes of disquiet. Brother Philip, a Zealot of the Clarisses, had made haste to secure for them from Ugolini the privileges which had already been under consideration. [41]

A certain Brother Giovanni di Conpello[42] had gathered together a great number of lepers of both sexes, and written a Rule, intending to form with them a new Order. He had afterward presented himself before the supreme pontiff with a train of these unfortunates to obtain his approbation.

Many other distressing symptoms, upon which Brother Giordano does not dwell, had manifested themselves. The report of Francis's death had even been spread abroad, so that the whole Order was disturbed, divided, and in the greatest peril. The dark presentiments which Francis seems to have had were exceeded by the reality. [43] The messenger who brought him the sad news found him in Syria, probably at St. Jean d'Acre. He at once embarked with Elias, Pietro di Catana, Cæsar of Speyer, and a few others, and returned to Italy in a vessel bound for Venice, where he might easily arrive toward the end of July.

FOOTNOTES:

[1]   One proof of the obscurity in which Dominic remained so long as Rome did not apotheosize him, is that Jacques de Vitry, who consecrates a whole chapter of his *Historia Occidentalis* to the Preaching Friars (27, p. 333) does not even name the founder. This is the more significant since a few pages farther on, the chapter given to the Brothers Minor is almost entirely filled with the person of St. Francis. This silence about St. Dominic has been remarked and taken up

by Moschus, who finds no way to explain it. Vide *Vitam J. de Vitriaco*, at the head of the Douai edition of 1597.

[2]   Francis, who died in 1226, is canonized in 1228; Anthony of Padua, 1231 and 1233; Elisabeth of Thuringia, 1231 and 1235; Dominic, 1221 and 1234.

[3]   3 Soc., 61.

[4]   Shed abroad, Lord, thy Spirit, and all shall be created, and thou shalt renew the face of the earth.

[5]   2 Cel., 3. 87; *Spec.* , 132b; *Conform.* , 207a, 112a; *Fior.* , 18. The historians of St. Dominic have not received these details kindly, but an incontestable point gained from diplomatic documents is that in 1218 Dominic, at Rome, procured privileges in which the properties of his Order were indicated, and that in 1220 he led his friars to profess poverty.

[6]   2 Cel., 3, 9; *Spec.* , 17a.

[7]   *Spec.* , 49a; *Tribul.* , Laur. MS., 11a-12b; *Spec.* , 183a; *Conform.* , 135b 1.

[8]   The principal sources are indicated in A. SS., Augusti, t. i., pp. 470 ff.

[9]   Giord., 18; 3 Soc., 62.

[10]   Sbaralea, *Bull. fr.* , t. i, p. 2; Potthast, 6081: Wadding, *ann. 1219*, No. 28, indicates the works where the text may be found. Cf. A. SS., p. 839.

[11]   The title sufficiently indicated the contents: *Domenico priori S. Romani tolosani ejusque fratribus, eos in protectionem recipit eorumque Ordinem cum bonis et privilegiis confirmat. Religiosam vitam*: December 22, 1216; Pressuti, t. i., 175, text in Horoy t. ii., col. 141-144.

[12]   Vide A. SS., pp. 608 ff. and 838 ff.

[13] Vide Bull *Multi divinæ* of August 13, 1218. Horoy, t. iii., col. 12; Potthast, 5891.

[14] The contradiction is so striking that the Bollandists have made of it the principal argument for defending the error in their manuscript (1 Cel., 75), and insisting in the face of, and against everything that Francis had taken that journey. A. SS., 607.

[15] He died at Cahors, October 31, 1272. His legend is found in MS. Riccardi, 279, f°. 69a. *Incipit vita f. Christophori quam compilavit fr. Bernardus de Bessa custodiæ Caturcensis: Quasi vas auri solidum.* Cf. Mark of Lisbon, t. ii., pp. 106-113, t. iii., p. 212, and Glassberger, *An. fr.* , t. ii., p. 14.

[16] A. SS., Aprilis, t. iii., p. 224; *Conform.* , 118b, 1; 54a; Mark of Lisbon, t. ii., p. 1—Brother Luke had been sent to Constantinople, in 1219, at latest. Vide *Constitutus* of December 9, 1220. Sbaralea, *Bull. fr.* , t. i., p. 6; Potthast, 6431.

[17] We owe to M. Müller (*Anfänge*, p. 207) the honor of this publication, copied from a manuscript of the Cottoniana.

[18] Giord., 8.

[19] 1 Cel., 57; Bon., 133-138; 154 and 155; 2 Cel., 2, 2; *Conform.* , 113b, 2; 114a, 2; *Spec.* , 55b; *Fior.* , 24.

[20] *Conform.* , 113b, 2; cf. A. SS., p. 611.

[21] 2 Cel., 3, 92; *Spec.* , 30b. Cf. 2 Cel., 3, 115. *Conform.* , 142b, 1. This incident may possibly have taken place on the return.

[22] With the facilities of that period the voyage required from twenty to thirty days. The *diarium* of a similar passage may be found in Huillard-Bréholles, *Hist. Dipl.* , t. i., 898-901. Cf. *Ibid.* , Introd., p. cccxxxi.

[23] 2 Cel., 22; Bon 154, 155; cf. A. SS., p. 612.

[24] Jacques de Vitry speaks only incidentally of Francis here in the midst of salutations; from the critical point of view this

only enhances the value of his words. See the Study of the Sources, p. 428.

[25]   Vide below, the Study of the Sources, p. 430.

[26]   All this is related at length by Jacques de Vitry.

[27]   "Cil hom qui comença l'ordre des Frères Mineurs, si ot nom frère François... vint en l'ost de Damiate, e i fist moult de bien, et demora tant que la ville fut prise. Il vit le mal et le péché qui comença à croistre entre les gens de l'ost, si li desplot, par quoi il s'en parti, e fu une pièce en Surie, et puis s'en rala en son pais. " Historiens des Croisades, ii. *L'Est de Eracles Empereur*, liv. xxxii., chap. xv. Cf. Sanuto; *Secreta fid. cruc.* , lib. iii., p. xi., cap. 8, in Bongars.

[28]   Giord., Chron., 11-14.

[29]   The episode of Brother Leonard's complaints, related below, gives some probability to this hypothesis.

[30]   *Tribul.* , Laur. MS., 9b. Cf. 10b: *Sepulcro Domini visitato festinat ad Christianorum terram.*

[31]   Upon this monastery see a letter *ad familiares* of Jacques de Vitry, written in 1216 and published in 1847 by Baron Jules de St. Genois in t. xiii. of the *Mémoires de l'Académie royale des sciences et des beaux arts de Bruxelles* (1849). *Conform.* , 106b, 2; 114a, 2; *Spec.* , 184.

[32]   A. SS., pp. 619-620, 848, 851, 638.

[33]   Vide Bull *Sacrosancta* of December 9, 1219. Cf. those of September 19, 1222; Sbaralea, i., p. 3, 11 ff. ; Potthast, 6179, 6879a, b, c.

[34]   Vide Potthast, 6155, 6177, 6184, 6199, 6214, 6217, 6218, 6220, 6246. See also *Chartularium Universitatis Par.* , t. i., 487.

[35]   Bull *Quia qui seminant* of May 12, 1220. Ripalli, *Bul. Præd.* , t. i., p. 10 (Potthast, 6249).

[36]   *Mon. Germ. hist. Script.* , t. 23, p. 376. This passage is of
extreme importance because it sums up in a few lines the
ecclesiastical policy of Honorius III. After speaking of the
perils with which the *Humiliati* threatened the Church,
Burchard adds: *Quæ volens corrigere dominus papa ordinem
Predicatorum instituit et confirmavit.*   Now these *Humiliati*
were an approved Order. But Burchard, while classing them
with heretics beside the Poor Men of Lyons, expresses in a
word the sentiments of the papacy toward them; it had for
them an invincible repugnance, and not wishing to strike
them directly it sought a side issue. Similar tactics were
followed with regard to the Brothers Minor, with that
overplus of caution which the prodigious success of the
Order inspired. It all became useless when in 1221 Brother
Elias became Francis's vicar, and especially when, after the
latter's death, he had all the liberty necessary for directing
the Order according to the views of Ugolini, now become
Gregory IX.

[37]   1 Cel., 25; cf. A. SS., p. 581. Pietro di Catana had the title of
doctor of laws, Giord., 11, which entirely disagrees with
what is related of Brother Pietro, 3 Soc., 28 and 29. Cf. Bon.,
28 and 29; *Spec.* , 5b; *Fior.* , 2; *Conform.* , 47; 52b, 2; *Petrus vir
litteratus erat et nobilis*, Giord., 12.

[38]   We know nothing more of him except that after his death he
had the gift of miracles. Giord., 11; *Conform.* , 62a, 1.

[39]   He was not an ordinary man; a remarkable administrator
and orator (Eccl., 6), he was minister in France before 1224
and again in 1240, thanks to the zeal with which he had
adopted the ideas of Brother Elias. He was nephew of
Gregory IX., which throws some light upon the practices
which have just been described. After having been swept
away in Elias's disgrace and condemned to prison for life, he
became in the end Bishop of Bayeux. I note for those who
take an interest in those things that manuscripts of two of his
sermons may be found in the National Library of Paris. The
author of them being indicated simply as *fr. Gr. min.* , it has
only lately become known whose they were. These sermons
were preached in Paris on Holy Thursday and Saturday. MS.
new. acq., Lat., 338 f° 148, 159.

[40]   Giord., 11. Cf. *Spec.* , 34b. *Fior.* , 4; *Conform.* , 184a, 1.

[41]   Giord., 12. Cf. Bull *Sacrosancta* of December 9, 1219.

[42]   Giord., 12. Ought we, perhaps, to read di Campello? Half way between Foligno and Spoleto there is a place of this name. On the other hand, the 3 Soc., 35, indicate the entrance into the Order of a Giovanni di Capella who in the legend became the Franciscan Judas. *Invenit abusum capelle et ab ipsa denominatus est: ab ordine recedens factus leprosus laqueo ut Judas se suspendit. Conform.* , 104a, 1. Cf. *Bernard de Besse*, 96a; *Spec.* , 2; *Fior.* , 1. All this is much mixed up. Perhaps we should believe that Giovanni di Campello died shortly afterward, and that later on, when the stories of this troubled time were forgotten, some ingenious Brother explained the note of infamy attached to his memory by a hypothesis built upon his name itself.

[43]   Giord., 12, 13, and 14.

CHAPTER XIV

THE CRISIS OF THE ORDER[1]

Autumn, 1220

On his arrival in Venice Francis informed himself yet more exactly concerning all that had happened, and convoked the chapter-general at Portiuncula for Michaelmas (September 29, 1220). [2] His first care was doubtless to reassure his sister-friend at St. Damian; a short fragment of a letter which has been preserved to us gives indication of the sad anxieties which filled his mind:

> "I, little Brother Francis, desire to follow the life and the poverty of Jesus Christ, our most high Lord, and of his most holy Mother, persevering therein until the end; and I beg you all and exhort you to persevere always in this most holy life and poverty, and take good care never to depart from it upon the advice or teachings of any one whomsoever. "[3]

A long shout of joy sounded up and down all Italy when the news of his return was heard. Many zealous brethren were already despairing, for persecutions had begun in many provinces; so when they learned that their spiritual father was alive and coming again to visit them their joy was unbounded. From Venice Francis went to Bologna. The journey was marked by an incident which once more shows his acute and wise goodness. Worn out as much by emotion as by fatigue, he one day found himself obliged to give up finishing the journey on foot. Mounted upon an ass, he was going on his way, followed by Brother Leonard of Assisi, when a passing glance showed him what was passing in his companion's mind. "My relatives, " the friar was thinking, "would have been far enough from associating with Bernardone, and yet here am I, obliged to follow his son on foot. "

We may judge of his astonishment when he heard Francis saying, as he hastily dismounted from his beast: "Here, take my place; it is most unseemly that thou shouldst follow me on foot, who art of a noble and powerful lineage. " The unhappy Leonard, much confused, threw himself at Francis's feet, begging for pardon. [4]

Scarcely arrived at Bologna, Francis was obliged to proceed against those who had become backsliders. It will be remembered that the Order was intended to possess nothing, either directly or indirectly. The monasteries given to the friars did not become their property; so soon as the proprietor should desire to take them back or anyone else should wish to take possession of them, they were to be given up without the least resistance; but on drawing near to Bologna he learned that a house was being built, which was already called *The house of the Brothers*. He commanded its immediate evacuation, not even excepting the sick who happened to be there. The Brothers then resorted to Ugolini, who was then in that very city for the consecration of Santa Maria di Rheno. [5] He explained to Francis at length that this house did not belong to the Order; he had declared himself its proprietor by public acts; and he succeeded in convincing him. [6]

Bolognese piety prepared for Francis an enthusiastic reception, the echo of which has come down even to our times:

> "I was studying at Bologna, I, Thomas of Spalato, archdeacon in the cathedral church of that city, when in the year 1220, the day of the Assumption, I saw St. Francis preaching on the piazza of the Lesser Palace, before almost every man in the city. The theme of his discourse was the following: Angels, men, the demons. He spoke on all these subjects with so much wisdom and eloquence that many learned men who were there were filled with admiration at the words of so plain a man. Yet he had not the manner of a preacher, his ways were rather those of conversation; the substance of his discourse bore especially upon the abolition of enmities and the necessity of making peaceful alliances. His apparel was poor, his person in no respect imposing, his face not at all handsome; but God gave such great efficacy to his words that he brought back to peace and harmony many nobles whose savage fury had not even stopped short before the shedding of blood. So great a devotion was felt for him that men and women flocked after him, and he esteemed himself happy who succeeded in touching the hem of his garment. "

Was it at this time that the celebrated Accurso the Glossarist, [7] chief of that famous dynasty of jurisconsults who during the whole thirteenth century shed lustre upon the University of Bologna, welcomed the Brothers Minor to his villa at Ricardina, near the city? [8] We do not know.

It appears that another professor, Nicolas dei Pepoli, also entered the Order. [9] Naturally the pupils did not lag behind, and a certain number asked to receive the habit. Yet all this constituted a danger; this city, which in Italy was as an altar consecrated to the science of law, was destined to exercise upon the evolution of the Order the same influence as Paris; the Brothers Minor could no more hold aloof from it than they could keep aloof from the ambient air.

This time Francis remained here but a very short time. An ancient tradition, of which his biographers have not preserved any trace, but which nevertheless appears to be entirely probable, says that Ugolini took him to pass a month in the Camaldoli, in the retreat formerly inhabited by St. Romuald in the midst of the Casentino forest, one of the noblest in Europe, within a few hours' walk of the Verna, whose summit rises up gigantic, overlooking the whole country.

We know how much Francis needed repose. There is no doubt that he also longed for a period of meditation in order to decide carefully in advance upon his line of conduct, in the midst of the dark conjectures which had called him home. The desire to give him the much-needed rest was only a subordinate purpose with Ugolini. The moment for vigorous action appeared to him to have come. We can easily picture his responses to Francis's complaints. Had he not been seriously advised to profit by the counsels of the past, by the experience of those founders of Orders who have been not only saints but skilful leaders of men? Was not Ugolini himself his best friend, his born defender, and yet had not Francis forced him to lay aside the influence to which his love for the friars, his position in the Church, and his great age gave him such just title? Yes, he had been forced to leave Francis to needlessly expose his disciples to all sorts of danger, to send them on missions as perilous as they had proved to be ineffectual, and all for what? For the most trivial point of honor, because the Brothers Minor were determined not to enjoy the smallest privileges. They were not heretics, but they disturbed the Church as much as the heretics did. How many times had he not been reminded that a great association, in order to exist, must have precise and detailed regulations? It had all been labor lost! Of course Francis's humility was doubted by no one, but why not manifest it, not only in costume and manner of living, but in all his acts? He thought himself obeying God in defending his own inspiration, but does not the Church speak in the name of God? Are not the words of her representatives the words of Jesus forever perpetuated on earth? He desired to be a man of the Gospel, an apostolic man, but was not the best way of becoming such to obey the Roman pontiff, the successor of Peter? With an excess of condescension they had let him go on in his own way, and the result was the saddest of lessons. But the situation was not desperate, there was still time to find a remedy; to do that he had only to throw himself at the feet of the pope, imploring his blessing, his light, and his counsel.

Reproaches such as these, mingled with professions of love and admiration on the part of the prelate, could not but profoundly disturb a sensitive heart like that of Francis. His conscience bore him good witness, but with the modesty of noble minds he was ready enough to think that he might have made many mistakes.

Perhaps this is the place to ask what was the secret of the friendship of these two men, so little known to one another on certain sides. How could it last without a shadow down to the very death of Francis, when we always find Ugolini the very soul of the group who are compromising the Franciscan ideal? No answer to this question is possible. The same problem presents itself with regard to Brother Elias, and we are no better able to find a satisfactory answer. Men of loving hearts seldom have a perfectly clear intelligence. They often become fascinated by men the most different from themselves, in whose breasts they feel none of those feminine weaknesses, those strange dreams, that almost sickly pity for creatures and things, that mysterious thirst for pain which is at once their own happiness and their torment.

The sojourn at Camaldoli was prolonged until the middle of September, and it ended to the cardinal's satisfaction. Francis had decided to go directly to the pope, then at Orvieto, with the request that Ugolini should be given him as official protector intrusted with the direction of the Order.

A dream which he had once had recurred to his memory; he had seen a little black hen which, in spite of her efforts, was not able to spread her wings over her whole brood. The poor hen was himself, the chickens were the friars. This dream was a providential indication commanding him to seek for them a mother under whose wings they could all find a place, and who could defend them against the birds of prey. At least so he thought. [10]

He repaired to Orvieto without taking Assisi in his way, since if he went there he would be obliged to take some measures against the fomentors of disturbance; he now proposed to refer everything directly to the pope.

Does his profound humility, with the feeling of culpability which Ugolini had awakened in him, suffice to explain his attitude with regard to the pope, or must we suppose that he had a vague thought of abdicating? Who knows whether conscience was not already murmuring a reproach, and showing him how trivial were all the sophisms which had been woven around him?

"Not daring to present himself in the apartments of so great a prince, he remained outside before the door, patiently waiting till the pope should come out. When he appeared St. Francis made a reverence and said:

"'Father Pope, may God give you peace. ' 'May God bless you, my son, ' replied he. 'My lord, ' then said St. Francis to him, 'you are great and often absorbed by great affairs; poor friars cannot come and talk with you as often as they need to do; you have given me many popes; give me a single one to whom I may address myself when need occurs, and who will listen in your stead, and discuss my affairs and those of the Order. ' 'Whom do you wish I should give you, my son? ' 'The Bishop of Ostia. ' And he gave him to him. "[11]

Conferences with Ugolini now began again; he immediately accorded Francis some amends; the privilege granted the Clarisses was revoked; Giovanni di Conpello was informed that he had nothing to hope from the *curia*, and last of all leave was given to Francis himself to compose the Rule of his Order. Naturally he was not spared counsel on the subject, but there was one point upon which the curia could not brook delay, and of which it exacted the immediate application—the obligation of a year's novitiate for the postulants.

At the same time a bull was issued not merely for the sake of publishing this ordinance, but especially to mark in a solemn manner the commencement of a new era in the relations of the Church and the Franciscans. The fraternity of the Umbrian Penitents became an Order in the strictest sense of the word.

Honorius, bishop, servant of the servants of God, to Brother Francis and the other priors or custodes of the Brothers Minor, greeting and the apostolic benediction.

In nearly all religious Orders it has been wisely ordained that those who present themselves with the purpose of observing the regular life shall make trial of it for a certain time, during which they also shall be tested, in order to leave neither place nor pretext for inconsiderate steps. For these reasons we command you by these presents to admit no one to make profession until after one year of novitiate; we forbid that after profession any brother shall leave the Order, and that any one shall take back again him who has gone out from it. We also forbid that those wearing your habit shall circulate here and there without obedience, lest the purity of your poverty be corrupted. If any friars have had this audacity, you will inflict upon them ecclesiastical censures until repentance. [12]

It is surely only by a very decided euphemism that such a bull can be considered in the light of a privilege. It was in reality the laying of the strong hand of the papacy upon the Brothers Minor.

From this time, in the very nature of things it became impossible for Francis to remain minister general. He felt it himself. Heart-broken, soul-sick, he would fain, in spite of all, have found in the energy of his love those words, those glances which up to this time had taken the place of rule or constitution, giving to his earliest companions the intuition of what they ought to do and the strength to accomplish it; but an administrator was needed at the head of this family which he suddenly found to be so different from what it had been a few years before, and he sadly acknowledged that he himself was not in the slightest degree such a person. [13]

Ah, in his own conscience he well knew that the old ideal was the true, the right one; but he drove away such thoughts as the temptations of pride. The recent events had not taken place without in some degree weakening his moral personality; from being continually talked to about obedience, submission, humility, a certain obscurity had come over this luminous soul; inspiration no longer came to it with the certainty of other days; the prophet had begun to waver, almost to doubt of himself and of his mission. Anxiously he searched himself to see if in the beginning of his work there had not been some vain self-complacency. He pictured to himself beforehand the chapter which he was about to open, the attack, the criticisms of which it would be the object, and labored to convince himself that if he did not endure them with joy he was not a true Brother Minor. [14] The noblest virtues are subject to scruples, that of perfect humility more than any other, and thus it is that excellent men religiously betray their own convictions to avoid asserting themselves. He resolved then to put the direction of the Order into the hands of Pietro di Catana. It is evident that there was nothing spontaneous in this decision, and the fact that this brother was a doctor of laws and belonged to the nobility squarely argues the transformation of the Franciscan institute.

It is not known whether or not Ugolini was present at the chapter of September 29, 1220, but if he was not there in person he was assuredly represented by some prelate, charged to watch over the debates. [15] The bull which had been issued a week before was communicated to the friars, to whom Francis also announced that he was about to elaborate a new Rule. With reference to this matter there were conferences in which the ministers alone appear to have had a deliberative voice. At these conferences the essential points of the new Rule were settled as to principle, leaving to Francis the care of giving them proper form at his leisure. Nothing better reveals the demoralized state into which he had fallen than the decision which was taken to drop out one of the essential passages of the old Rule, one of his three fundamental precepts, that which began with these words, *"Carry nothing with you. "*[16]

How did they go to work to obtain from Francis this concession which, a little while before, he would have looked upon as a denial of his call, a refusal to accept in its integrity the message which Jesus had addressed to him? It is the secret of history, but we may suppose there was in his life at this time one of those moral tempests which overbear the faculties of the strongest, leaving in their wounded hearts only an unutterable pain.

Something of this pain has passed into the touching narrative of his abdication which the biographers have given us.

"From henceforth, " he said to the friars, "I am dead for you, but here is Brother Pietro di Catana, whom you and I will all obey. " And prostrating himself before him he promised him obedience and submission. The friars could not restrain their tears and lamentations when they saw themselves thus becoming in some sort orphans, but Francis arose, and, clasping his hands, with eyes upraised to heaven: "Lord, " he said, "I return to thee this family which thou hast confided to me. Now, as thou knowest, most sweet Jesus, I have no longer strength nor ability to keep on caring for them; I confide them, therefore, to the ministers. May they be responsible before thee at the day of judgment if any brother, by their negligence or bad example, or by a too severe discipline, should ever wander away. "[17]

The functions of Pietro di Catana were destined to continue but a very short time; he died on March 10, 1221. [18]

Information abounds as to this period of a few months; nothing is more natural, since Francis remained at Portiuncula to complete the task confided to him, living there surrounded with brethren who later on would recall to mind all the incidents of which they were witnesses. Some of them reveal the conflict of which his soul was the arena. Desirous of showing himself submissive, he nevertheless found himself tormented by the desire to shake off his chains and fly away as in former days, to live and breathe in God alone. The following artless record deserves, it seems to me, to be better known. [19]

One day a novice who could read the psalter, though not without difficulty, obtained from the minister general—that is to say, from the vicar of St. Francis—permission to have one. But as he had learned that St. Francis desired the brethren to be covetous neither for learning nor for books, he would not take his psalter without his consent. So, St. Francis having come to the monastery where the novice was, "Father, " said he, "it would be a great consolation to have a psalter; but though the minister-general has authorized me to get it, I would not have it unknown to you. " "Look at the Emperor Charles, " replied St. Francis with fire, "Roland, and Oliver and all the paladins, valorous heroes and gallant knights, who gained their famous victories in fighting infidels, in toiling and laboring even unto death! The holy martyrs, they also have chosen to die in the midst of battle for the faith of Christ! But now there are many of those who aspire to merit honor and glory simply by relating their feats. Yes, among us also there are many who expect to receive glory and honor by reciting and preaching the works of the saints, as if they had done them themselves! "

... A few days after, St. Francis was sitting before the fire, and the novice drew near to speak to him anew about his psalter.

"When you have your psalter, " said Francis to him, "you will want a breviary, and when you have a breviary you will seat yourself in a pulpit like a great prelate and will beckon to your companion, 'Bring me my breviary! '"

St. Francis said this with great vivacity, then taking up some ashes he scattered them over the head of the novice, repeating, "There is the breviary, there is the breviary! "

Several days after, St. Francis being at Portiuncula and walking up and down on the roadside not far from his cell, the same Brother came again to speak to him about his psalter. "Very well, go on, " said Francis to him, "you have only to do what your minister tells you. " At these words the novice went away, but Francis began to reflect on what he had said, and suddenly calling to the friar, he cried, "Wait for me! wait for me! " When he had caught up to him, "Retrace your steps a little way. I beg you, " he said. "Where was I when I told you to do whatever your minister told you as to the psalter? " Then falling upon his knees on the spot pointed out by the friar, he prostrated himself at his feet: "Pardon, my brother, pardon! " he cried, "for he who would be Brother Minor ought to have nothing but his clothing. "

This long story is not merely precious because it shows us, even to the smallest particular, the conflict between the Francis of the early years, looking only to God and his conscience, and the Francis of 1220, become a submissive monk in an Order approved by the Roman Church, but also because it is one of those infrequent narratives where his method shows itself with its artless realism. These allusions to the tales of chivalry, and this freedom of manner which made a part of his success with the masses, were eliminated from the legend with an incredible rapidity. His spiritual sons were perhaps not ashamed of their father in this matter, but they were so bent upon bringing out his other qualities that they forgot a little too much the poet, the troubadour, the *joculator Domini*.

Certain fragments, later than Thomas of Celano by more than a century, which relate some incidents of this kind, bear for that very reason the stamp of authenticity.

It is difficult enough to ascertain precisely what part Francis still took in the direction of the Order. Pietro di Catana and later Brother Elias are sometimes called ministers-general, sometimes vicars; the two terms often occur successively, as in the preceding narrative. It is very probable that this confusion of terms corresponds to a like confusion of facts. Perhaps it was even intentional. After the chapter of September, 1220, the affairs of the Order pass into the hands of him whom Francis had called minister-general, though the friars as well as the papacy gave him only the title of vicar. It was essential for the popularity of the Brothers Minor that Francis should preserve an appearance of authority, but the reality of government had slipped from his hands.

The ideal which he had borne in his body until 1209 and had then given birth to in anguish, was now taking its flight, like those sons of our loins whom we see suddenly leaving us without our being able to help it, since that is life, yet not without a rending of our vitals. *Mater dolorosa!* Ah, no doubt they will come back again, and seat themselves piously beside us at the paternal hearth; perhaps even, in some hour of moral distress, they will feel the need of taking refuge in their mother's arms as in the old days; but these fleeting returns, with their feverish haste, only reopen the wounds of the poor parents, when they see how the children hasten to depart again — they who bear their name but belong to them no longer.

FOOTNOTES:

[1]   Giord., 14; *Tribul.* , f° 10.

[2]   Any other date is impossible, since Francis in open chapter relinquished the direction of the Order in favor of Pietro di Catana, who died March 10, 1221.

[3]   This too short fragment is found in § vi. of the Rule of the Damianites (August 9, 1253): Speculum, Morin, Tract. iii., 226b.

[4]   2 Cel., 2, 3; Bon., 162; cf. *Conform.* , 184b, 2, and 62b, 1.

[5]   Sigonius, *Opera*, t. iii. col. 220; cf. Potthast, 5516, and 6086.

[6]   2 Cel., 3, 4; *Spec.* , 11a; *Tribul.* , 13a; *Conform.* , 169b, 2.

[7]   Died in 1229. Cf. Mazzetti, *Repertorio di tutti i professori di Bologna*, Bologna, 1847, p. 11.

[8]   See *Mon. Germ. hist. Script.* , t. 28, p. 635, and the notes.

[9]   Wadding, *ann. 1220*, no. 9. Cf. A. SS., p. 823.

[10]   2 Cel., 1, 16; *Spec.* , 100a-101b.

[11]   Giord., 14; cf. 2 Cel., 1, 17; *Spec.* , 102; 3 Soc., 56 and 63.

[12]   *Cum secundum.* The original is at Assisi with *Datum apud Urbem Veterem X. Kal. Oct. pont. nostri anno quinto* (September 22, 1220). It is therefore by an error that Sbaralea and Wadding make it date from Viterbo, which is the less explicable that all the bulls of this epoch are dated from Orvieto. Wadding, *ann. 1220*, 57; Sbaralea, vol. i., p. 6; Potthast, 6561.

[13]   2 Cel., 3, 118; Ubertin, *Arbor. V.*, 2; *Spec.* , 26; 50; 130b; *Conform.* , 136a, 2; 143a, 2.

[14]   2 Cel., 3, 83; Bon. 77. One should read this account in the *Conform.* according to the *Antigua Legenda*, 142a, 2; 31a, 1; *Spec.* 43b.

[15]   *Tribul.* Laur. MS., 12b; Magl. MS., 71b.

[16]   Luke, ix., 1-6. *Tribul.* , 12b: *Et fecerunt de regula prima ministri removere....* This must have taken place at the chapter of September 29, 1220, since the suppression is made in the Rule of 1221.

[17]   2 Cel., 3, 81; *Spec.* , 26; *Conform.* , 175b, 1; 53a; Bon., 76; A. SS., p. 620.

[18]   The epitaph on his tomb, which still exists at S. M. dei Angeli bears this date: see *Portiuncula, von P. Barnabas aus dem Elsass*, Rixheim, 1884, p. 11. Cf. A. SS., p. 630.

[19]   *Spec.* , 9b; *Arbor. V.*, 3; *Conform.* , 170a, 1; 2 Cel., 3, 124. Cf. Ubertini, *Archiv.* , iii., pp. 75 and 177.

CHAPTER XV

THE RULE OF 1221[1]

The winter of 1220-1221 was spent by Francis chiefly in fixing his thought by writing. Until now he had been too much the man of action to have been able to give much thought to anything but the *living word*, but from this time his exhausted forces compelled him to satisfy his longing for souls by some other means than evangelizing tours. We have seen that the chapter of September 29, 1220, on one side, and the bull *Cum secundum* on the other, had fixed in advance a certain number of points. For the rest, complete liberty had been given him, not indeed to make a final and unchangeable statement of his ideas, but to set them forth. The substance of legislative power had passed into the hands of the ministers. [2]

That which we call the Rule of 1221 is, then, nothing more than a proposed law, submitted to a representative government at its parliament. The head of authority will one day give it to the world, so thoroughly modified and altered that Francis's name at the head of such a document will give but small promise, and quite indirectly, that it will contain his personal opinion.

Never was man less capable of making a Rule than Francis. In reality, that of 1210 and the one which the pope solemnly approved in November 29, 1223, had little in common except the name. In the former all is alive, free, spontaneous; it is a point of departure, an inspiration; it may be summed up in two phrases: the appeal of Jesus to man, "Come, follow me, " the act of man, "He left all and followed him. " To the call of divine love man replies by the joyful gift of himself, and that quite naturally, by a sort of instinct. At this height of mysticism any regulation is not only useless, it is almost a profanation; at the very least it is the symptom of a doubt. Even in earthly loves, when people truly love each other nothing is asked, nothing promised.

The Rule of 1223, on the other hand, is a reciprocal contract. On the divine side the call has become a command; on the human, the free impulse of love has become an act of submission, by which life eternal will be earned.

At the bottom of it all is the antinome of law and love. Under the reign of law we are the mercenaries of God, bound down to an irksome task, but paid a hundred-fold, and with an indisputable right to our wages.

Under the rule of love we are the sons of God, and coworkers with him; we give ourselves to him without bargaining and without expectation; we follow Jesus, not because this is well, but because we can do no otherwise, because we feel that he has loved us and we love him in our turn. An inward flame draws us irresistibly toward him: *Et Spiritus et Sponsa dicunt: Veni.*

It is necessary to dwell a little on the antithesis between these two Rules. That of 1210 alone is truly Franciscan; that of 1223 is indirectly the work of the Church, endeavoring to assimilate with herself the new movement, which with one touch she transforms and turns wholly from its original purpose.

That of 1221 marks an intermediate stage. It is the clash of two principles, or rather of two spirits; they approach, they touch, but they are not merged in one another; here and there is a mixture, but nowhere combination; we can separate the divers elements without difficulty. Their condition is the exact reflection of what was going on in Francis's soul, and of the rapid evolution of the Order.

To aid him in his work Francis joined to himself Brother Cæsar of Speyer, who would be especially useful to him by his profound acquaintance with the sacred texts.

What strikes us first, on glancing over this Rule of 1221, is its extraordinary length; it covers not less than ten folio pages, while that of 1223 has no more than three. Take away from it the passages which emanate from the papacy and those which were fixed at the previous chapter, you will hardly have shortened it by a column; what remains is not a Rule, but a series of impassioned appeals, in which the father's heart speaks, not to command but to convince, to touch, to awaken in his children the instinct of love.

It is all chaotic and even contradictory, [3] without order, a medley of outbursts of joy and bitter sobs, of hopes and regrets. There are passages in which the passion of the soul speaks in every possible tone, runs over the whole gamut from the softest note to the most masculine, from those which are as joyous and inspiring as the blast of a clarion, to those which are agitated, stifled, like a voice from beyond the tomb.

"By the holy love which is in God, I pray all the friars, ministers as well as others, to put aside every obstacle, every care, every anxiety, that they may be able to consecrate themselves entirely to serve, love, and honor the Lord God, with a pure heart and a sincere purpose, which is what he asks above all things. Let us have always in ourselves a tabernacle and a home for him who is the Lord God most mighty, Father, Son, and Holy Spirit, who says, 'Watch and pray always, that you may be found worthy to escape all the things which will come to pass, and to appear upright before the Son of man.'

"Let us then keep in the true way, the life, the truth, and the holy Gospel of Him who has deigned for our sake to leave his Father that he may manifest his name to us, saying, 'Father, I have manifested thy name to those whom thou hast given me, and the words which thou hast given me I have given also unto them. They have received them, and they have known that I am come from thee, and they believe that thou hast sent me. I pray for them; I pray not for the world, but for those whom thou hast given me, that they may be one as we are one. I have said these things, being still in the world, that they may have joy in themselves. I have given them thy words, and the world hath hated them, because they are not of the world. I pray not that thou shouldst take them out of the world, but that thou wilt keep them from the evil. Sanctify them through the truth; thy word is truth. As thou hast sent me into the world I have also sent them into the world, and for their sake I sanctify myself that they may themselves be sanctified in the truth; and neither pray I for these alone, but for all those who shall believe on me through their words, that we all may be one, and that the world may know that thou hast sent me, and that thou lovest them as thou hast loved me. I have made known unto them thy name, that the love wherewith thou hast loved me may be in them and I in them.'

PRAYER.

"Almighty, most high and sovereign God, holy Father, righteous Lord, King of heaven and earth, we give thee thanks for thine own sake, in that by thy holy will, and by thine only Son and thy Holy Spirit thou hast created all things spiritual and corporeal, and that after having made us in thine image and after thy likeness, thou didst place us in that paradise which we lost by our sin. And we give thee thanks because after having created us by thy Son, by that love which is thine, and which thou hast had for us, thou hast made him to be born very God and very man of the glorious and blessed Mary, ever Virgin, and because by his cross, his blood, and his death thou hast willed to ransom us poor captives. And we give thee thanks that thy Son is to return in his glorious majesty to send to eternal fire the accursed ones, those who have not repented and have not known thee; and to say to those who have known and adored thee and served thee by repentance, 'Come, ye blessed of my Father, inherit the kingdom prepared for you from before the foundation of the world. ' And since we, wretched and sinful, are not worthy to name thee, we humbly ask our Lord Jesus Christ, thy well-beloved Son, in whom thou art well pleased, that he may give thee thanks for everything; and also the Holy Spirit, the Paraclete, as it may please thee and them; for this we supplicate him who has all power with thee, and by whom thou hast done such great things for us. Alleluia.

"And we pray the glorious Mother, the blessed Mary, ever Virgin, St. Michael, Gabriel, Raphael, and all the choir of blessed Spirits, Seraphim, Cherubim, Thrones, Dominions, Principalities and Powers, Virtues and Angels, Archangels, John the Baptist, John the Evangelist, Peter, Paul, and the holy Patriarchs, the Prophets, the Holy Innocents, Apostles, Evangelists, Disciples, Martyrs, Confessors, Virgins, the blessed ones, Elijah and Enoch, and all the saints who have been, shall be, and are, we humbly pray them by thy love to give thee thanks for these things, as it pleases thee, sovereign, true, eternal and living God, and also to thy Son, our most holy Lord Jesus Christ, and to the Holy Spirit, the Comforter, forever and ever. Amen. Alleluia.

"And we supplicate all those who desire to serve the Lord God, in the bosom of the Catholic and Apostolic Church, all priests, deacons, sub-deacons, acolytes and exorcists, readers, porters, all clerks, all monks and nuns, all children and little ones, paupers and exiles, kings, and princes, workmen and laborers, servants and masters, the virgins, the continent and the married, laics, men and women, all children, youths, young men and old men, the sick and the well, the small and the great, the peoples of every tribe and tongue and nation, all men in every part of the world whatsoever, who are or who shall be, we pray and beseech them, all we Brothers Minor, unprofitable servants, that all together, with one accord we persevere in the true faith and in penitence, for outside of these no person can be saved.

"Let us all, with all our heart and all our thought, and all our strength, and all our mind, with all our vigor, with all our effort, with all our affection, with all our inward powers, our desires, and our wills, love the Lord God, who has given to us all his body, all his soul, all his life, and still gives them every day to each one of us. He created us, he saved us by his grace alone; he has been, he still is, full of goodness to us, us wicked and worthless, corrupt and offensive, ungrateful, ignorant, bad. We desire nothing else, we wish for nothing else; may nothing else please us, or have any attraction for us, except the Creator, the Redeemer, the Saviour, sole and true God, who is full of goodness, who is all goodness, who is the true and supreme good, who alone is kind, pious, and merciful, gracious, sweet, and gentle, who alone is holy, righteous, true, upright, who alone has benignity, innocence, and purity; of whom, by whom, and in whom is all the pardon, all the grace, all the glory of all penitents, of all the righteous and all the saints who are rejoicing in heaven.

"Then let nothing again hinder, let nothing again separate, nothing again retard us, and may we all, so long as we live, in every place, at every hour, at every time, every day and unceasingly, truly and humbly believe. Let us have in our hearts, let us love, adore, serve, praise, bless, glorify, exalt, magnify, thank the most high, sovereign, eternal God, Trinity and Unity, Father, Son, and Holy Spirit, Creator of all men, both of those who believe and hope in him and of those who love him. He is without beginning and without end, immutable and invisible, ineffable, incomprehensible, indiscernible, blessed, lauded, glorious, exalted, sublime, most high, sweet, lovely, delectable, and always worthy of being desired above all things, in all the ages of ages. Amen. "

Have not these artless repetitions a mysterious charm which steals deliciously into the very depths of the heart? Is there not in them a sort of sacrament of which the words are only the rude vehicle? Francis is taking refuge in God, as the child throws itself upon its mother's bosom, and in the incoherence of its weakness and its joy stammers out all the words it knows, repeating by them all only the eternal "I am thine" of love and faith.

There is in them also something which recalls, not only by citations, but still more by the very inspiration of the thought, that which we call the sacerdotal prayer of Christ. The apostle of poverty appears here as if suspended between earth and heaven by the very strength of his love, consecrated the priest of a new worship by the inward and irresistible unction of the Spirit. He does not offer sacrifice like the priest of the past time; he sacrifices himself, and carries in his body all the woes of humanity.

The more beautiful are these words from the mystical point of view, the less do they correspond with what is expected in a Rule; they have neither the precision nor the brief and imperative forms of one. The transformations which they were to undergo in order to become the code of 1223 were therefore fatal when we consider the definitive intervention of the Church of Rome to direct the Franciscan movement.

It is probable that this rough draft of a Rule, such as we have it now, is that which was distributed in the chapter of Whitsunday, 1221. The variants, sometimes capital, which are found in the different texts, can be nothing other than outlines of the corrections proposed by the provincial ministers. Once admit the idea of considering this document as a rough draft, we are very soon brought to think that it had already undergone a rapid preliminary revision, a sort of pruning, in which ecclesiastical authority has caused to disappear all that was in flagrant contradiction with its own projects for the Order.

If it is asked, who could have made these curtailments, one name springs at once to our lips—Ugolini. He criticised its exaggerated proportions, its want of unity and precision. Later on it is related that

Francis had seen in a dream a multitude of starving friars, and himself unable to satisfy their wants, because though all around him lay innumerable crumbs of bread, they disappeared between his fingers when he would give them to those about him. Then a voice from heaven said to him: "Francis, make of these crumbs a wafer; with that thou shalt feed these starving ones. "

There is little hazard in assuming that this is the picturesque echo of the conferences which took place at this time between Francis and the cardinal; the latter might have suggested to him by such a comparison the essential defects of his project. All this, no doubt, took place during Francis's stay in Rome, in the beginning of 1221. [4]

Before going there, we must cast a glance over the similarity in inspiration and even in style which allies the Rule of 1221 with another of St. Francis's works, that which is known under the title of The Admonitions. [5] This is a series of *spiritual counsels* with regard to the religious life; it is closely united both in matter and form with the work which we have just examined. The tone of voice is so perfectly the same that one is tempted to see in it parts of the original draft of the Rule, separated from it as too prolix to find place in a Rule.

However it may be with this hypothesis, we find in The Admonitions all the anxieties with which the soul of Francis was assailed in this uncertain and troubled hour. Some of these counsels sound like bits from a private journal. We see him seeking, with the simplicity of perfect humility, for reasons for submitting himself, renouncing his ideas, and not quite succeeding in finding them. He repeats to himself the exhortations that others had given him; we feel the effort to understand and admire the ideal monk whom Ugolini and the Church have proposed to him for an example:

The Lord says in the Gospels: "He who does not give up all that he has cannot be my disciple. And he who would save his life shall lose it. " One gives up all he possesses and loses his life when life gives himself entirely into the hands of his superior, to obey him.... And when the inferior sees things which would be better or more useful to his soul than those which the superior commands him, let him offer to God the sacrifice of his will.

Reading this one might think that Francis was about to join the ranks of those to whom submission to ecclesiastical authority is the very essence of religion. But no; even here his true feeling is not wholly effaced, he mingles his words with parentheses and illustrations, timid, indeed, but revealing his deepest thought; always ending by enthroning the individual conscience as judge of last resort. [6]

All this shows clearly enough that we must picture to ourselves moments when his wounded soul sighs after passive obedience, the formula of which, *perinde ac cadaver*, goes apparently much farther back than the Company of Jesus. These were moments of exhaustion, when inspiration was silent.

> One day he was sitting with his companions, when he began to groan and say: "There is hardly a monk upon earth who perfectly obeys his superior. " His companions, much astonished, said: "Explain to us, father, what is perfect and supreme obedience. " Then, comparing him who obeys to a corpse, he replied: "Take a dead body, and put it where you will, it will make no resistance; when it is in one place it will not murmur, when you take it away from there it will not object; put it in a pulpit, it will not look up but down; wrap it in purple, it will only be doubly pale. "[7]

This longing for corpse-like obedience witnesses to the ravages with which his soul had been laid waste; it corresponds in the moral domain to the cry for annihilation of great physical anguish.

The worst was that he was absolutely alone. Everywhere else the Franciscan obedience is living, active, joyful. [8]

He drank this cup to the very dregs, holding sacred the revolts dictated by conscience. One day in the later years of his life a German friar came to see him, and after having long discussed with him pure obedience:

> "I ask you one favor, " he said to him, "it is that if the Brothers ever come to live no longer according to the Rule you will permit me to separate myself from them, alone or with a few others, to observe it in its completeness. " At these words Francis felt a great joy. "Know, " said he, "that Christ as well as I authorize what you have just been asking; "

and laying hands upon him, "Thou art a priest forever, " he added, "after the order of Melchisedec. "[9]

We have a yet more touching proof of his solicitude to safeguard the spiritual independence of his disciples: it is a note to Brother Leo. [10] The latter, much alarmed by the new spirit which was gaining power in the Order, opened his mind thereupon to his master, and doubtless asked of him pretty much the same permission as the friar from Germany. After an interview in which he replied *viva voce*, Francis, not to leave any sort of doubt or hesitation in the mind of him whom he surnamed his little sheep of God, *pecorella di Dio*, wrote to him again:

> Brother Leo, thy brother Francis wishes thee peace and health.

> I reply *yes*, my son, as a mother to her child. This word sums up all we said while walking, as well as all my counsels. If thou hast need to come to me for counsel, it is my wish that thou shouldst do it. Whatever may be the manner in which thou thinkest thou canst please the Lord God, follow it, and live in poverty. Do this (faites le[11]), God will bless thee and I authorize it. And if it were necessary for thy soul, or for thy consolation that thou shouldst come to see me, or if thou desirest it, my Leo, come.

> Thine in Christ.

Surely we are far enough here from the corpse of a few pages back.

It would be superfluous to pause over the other admonitions. For the most part they are reflections inspired by circumstances. Counsels as to humility recur with a frequency which explains both the personal anxieties of the author, and the necessity of reminding the brothers of the very essence of their profession.

The sojourn of St. Francis at Rome, whither he went in the early months of 1221, to lay his plan before Ugolini, was marked by a new effort of the latter to bring him and St. Dominic together. [12]

The cardinal was at this time at the apogee of his success. Everything had gone well with him. His voice was all powerful not only in affairs of the Church, but also in those of the Empire. Frederic II., who seemed to be groping his way, and in whose mind were germinating dreams of religious reformation, and the desire of placing his power at the service of the truth, treated him as a friend, and spoke of him with unbounded admiration. [13]

In his reflections upon the remedies to be applied to the woes of Christianity, the cardinal came at last to think that one of the most efficacious would be the substitution of bishops taken from the two new Orders, for the feudal episcopate almost always recruited from local families in which ecclesiastical dignities were, so to speak, hereditary. In the eyes of Ugolini such bishops were usually wanting in two essential qualities of a good prelate: religious zeal and zeal for the Church.

He believed that the Preaching and the Minor Friars would not only possess those virtues which were lacking in the others, but that in the hands of the papacy they might become a highly centralized hierarchy, truly catholic, wholly devoted to the interests of the Church at large. The difficulties which might occur on the part of the chapters which should elect the bishops, as well as on the side of the high secular clergy, would be put to flight by the enthusiasm which the people would feel for pastors whose poverty would recall the days of the primitive Church.

At the close of his interviews with Francis and Dominic, he communicated to them some of these thoughts, asking their advice as to the elevation of their friars to prelatures. There was a pious contest between the two saints as to which should answer first. Finally, Dominic said simply that he should prefer to see his companions remain as they were. In his turn, Francis showed that the very name of his institute made the thing impossible. "If my friars have been called *Minores*, " he said, "it is not that they may become *Majores*. If you desire that they become fruitful in the Church of God, leave them alone, and keep them in the estate into which God has called them. I pray you, father, do not so act that their poverty shall become a motive for pride, nor elevate them to prelatures which would move them to insolence toward others. "[14]

The ecclesiastical policy followed by the popes was destined to render this counsel of the two founders wholly useless. [15]

Francis and Dominic parted, never again to meet. The *Master* of the Preaching Friars shortly after set out for Bologna, where he died on

August 6th following, and Francis returned to Portiuncula, where Pietro di Catana had just died (March 10, 1221). He was replaced at the head of the Order by Brother Elias. Ugolini was doubtless not without influence in this choice.

Detained by his functions of legate, he could not be present at the Whitsunday chapter (May 30, 1221). [16] He was represented there by Cardinal Reynerio, [17] who came accompanied by several bishops and by monks of various orders. [18] About three thousand friars were there assembled, but so great was the eagerness of the people of the neighborhood to bring provisions, that after a session of seven days they were obliged to remain two days longer to eat up all that had been brought. The sessions were presided over by Brother Elias, Francis sitting at his feet and pulling at his robe when there was anything that he wished to have put before the Brothers.

Brother Giordani di Giano, who was present, has preserved for us all these details and that of the setting out of a group of friars for Germany. They were placed under the direction of Cæsar of Speyer, whose mission succeeded beyond all expectation. Eighteen months after, when he returned to Italy, consumed with the desire to see St. Francis again, the cities of Wurzburg, Mayence, Worms, Speyer, Strasburg, Cologne, Salzburg, and Ratisbon had become Franciscan centres, from whence the new ideas were radiating into all Southern Germany.

The foundation of the Tertiaries, or Third Order, generally in the oldest documents called Brotherhood of Penitence, is usually fixed as occurring in the year 1221; but we have already seen that this date is much too recent, or rather that it is impossible to fix any date, for what was later called, quite arbitrarily, the Third Order is evidently contemporary with the First. [19]

Francis and his companions desired to be the apostles of their time; but they, no more than the apostles of Jesus, desired to have all men enter their association, which was necessarily somewhat restricted, and which, according to the gospel saying, was meant to be the leaven of the rest of humanity. In consequence, their life was literally the *apostolic life*, but the ideal which they preached was the *evangelical life*, such as Jesus had preached it.

St. Francis no more condemned the family or property than Jesus did; he simply saw in them ties from which the *apostle*, and the apostle alone, needs to be free.

If before long sickly minds fancied that they interpreted his thought in making the union of the sexes an evil, and all that concerns the physical activity of man a fall; if unbalanced spirits borrowed the authority of his name to escape from all duty; if married persons condemned themselves to the senseless martyrdom of virginity, he should certainly not be made responsible. These traces of an unnatural asceticism come from the dualist ideas of the Catharists, and not from the inspired poet who sang nature and her fecundity, who made nests for doves, inviting them to multiply under the watch of God, and who imposed manual labor on his friars as a sacred duty.

The bases of the corporation of the *Brothers and Sisters of Penitence* were very simple. Francis gave no new doctrine to the world; what was new in his message was wholly in his love, in his direct call to the evangelical life, to an ideal of moral vigor, of labor, and of love.

Naturally, there were soon found men who did not understand this true and simple beauty; they fell into observances and devotions, imitated, while living in the world, the life of the cloister to which for one reason or another they were not able to retire; but it would be unjust to picture to ourselves the *Brothers of Penitence* as modelled after them.

Did they receive a Rule from St. Francis? It is impossible to say. The one which was given[20] them in 1289 by Pope Nicholas IV. is simply the recasting and amalgamation of all the rules of lay fraternities which existed at the end of the thirteenth century. To attribute this document to Francis is nothing less than the placing in a new building of certain venerated stones from an ancient edifice. It is a matter of façade and ornamentation, nothing more.

Notwithstanding this absence of any Rule emanating from Francis himself, it is clear enough what, in his estimation, this association ought to be. The Gospel, with its counsels and examples, was to be its true Rule. The great innovation designed by the Third Order was concord; this fraternity was a union of peace, and it brought to astonished Europe a new truce of God. Whether the absolute refusal to carry arms[21] was an idea wholly chimerical and ephemeral, the documents are there to prove, but it is a fine thing to have had the power to bring it about for a few years.

The second essential obligation of the Brothers of Penitence appears to have been that of reducing their wants so far as possible, and while preserving their fortunes to distribute to the poor at proper intervals the free portion of the revenue after contenting themselves with the strictly necessary. [22]

To do with joy the duties of their calling; to give a holy inspiration to the slightest actions; to find in the infinitely littles of existence, things apparently the most commonplace, parts of a divine work; to keep pure from all debasing interest; to use things as not possessing them, like the servants in the parable who would soon have to give account of the talents confided to them; to close their hearts to hatred, to open them wide to the poor, the sick, to all abandoned ones, such were the other essential duties of the Brothers and Sisters of Penitence.

To lead them into this royal road of liberty, love, and responsibility, Francis sometimes appealed to the terrors of hell and the joys of paradise, but interested love was so little a part of his nature that these considerations and others of the same kind occupy an entirely secondary place in those of his writings which remain, as also in his biographies.

For him the gospel life is natural to the soul. Whoever comes to know it will prefer it; it has no more need to be proved than the outer air and the light. It needs only to lead prisoners to it, for them to lose all desire to return to the dungeons of avarice, hatred, or frivolity.

Francis and his true disciples make the painful ascent of the mountain heights, impelled solely, but irresistibly, by the inner voice. The only foreign aid which they accept is the memory of Jesus, going before them upon these heights and mysteriously living again before their eyes in the sacrament of the eucharist.

The letter to all Christians in which these thoughts break forth is a living souvenir of St. Francis's teachings to the Tertiaries.

To represent these latter to ourselves in a perfectly concrete form we may resort to the legend of St. Lucchesio, whom tradition makes the first Brother of Penitence. [23]

A native of a little city of Tuscany he quitted it to avoid its political enmities, and established himself at Poggibonsi, not far from Sienna, where he continued to trade in grain. Already rich, it was not difficult for him to buy up all the wheat, and, selling it in a time of scarcity, realize enormous profits. But soon overcome by Francis's preaching, he took himself to task, distributed all his superfluity to the poor, and kept nothing but his house with a small garden and one ass.

From that time he was to be seen devoting himself to the cultivation of this bit of ground, and making of his house a sort of hostelry whither the poor and the sick came in swarms. He not only welcomed them, but he sought them out, even to the malaria-infected Maremma, often returning with a sick man astride on his back and preceded by his ass bearing a similar burden. The resources of the garden were necessarily very limited; when there was no other way, Lucchesio took a wallet and went from door to door asking alms, but most of the time this was needless, for his poor guests, seeing him so diligent and so good, were better satisfied with a few poor vegetables from the garden shared with him than with the most copious repast. In the presence of their benefactor, so joyful in his destitution, they forgot their own poverty, and the habitual murmurs of these wretches were transformed into outbursts of admiration and gratitude.

Conversion had not killed in him all family ties; Bona Donna, his wife, became his best co-laborer, and when in 1260 he saw her gradually fading away his grief was too deep to be endured. "You know, dear companion, " he said to her when she had received the last sacraments, "how much we have loved one another while we could serve God together; why should we not remain united until we depart to the ineffable joy? Wait for me. I also will receive the sacraments, and go to heaven with you. "

So he spoke, and called back the priest to administer them to him. Then after holding the hands of his dying companion, comforting her with gentle words, when he saw that her soul was gone he made over her the sign of the cross, stretched himself beside her, and calling with love upon Jesus, Mary, and St. Francis, he fell asleep for eternity.

FOOTNOTES:

[1]   Text in *Firmamentum*, 10; *Spec.* , 189; *Spec.* , Morin. Tract., iii., 2b. M. Müller (*Anfänge*) has made a study of the Rule of 1221 which is a masterpiece of *exegetical scent*. Nevertheless if he had more carefully collated the different texts he would have arrived at still more striking results, thanks to the variants which he would have been able to establish. I cite a single example.

> Text *Firm.* —Wadding, adopted by Mr. M.

> *Omnes fratres ubicunque sunt vel vadunt, caveant sibi a malo visu et frequentia mulierum et* nullus *cum eis consilietur solus. Sacerdos honeste loquatur cum eis dando penitentiam vel aliud spirituale consilium.*

> Text of the *Speculum*, 189 ff.

> *Omnes fratres ubicunque sunt et vadunt caveant se a* malo *visu et frequentia* mulierum *et nullus cum eis concilietur aut per viam vadat solus aut ad mensam in una paropside comedat. (!!) Sacerdos honeste loquatur cum eis dando... etc.*

This passage is sufficient to show the superiority of the text of the Speculum, which is to be preferred also in other respects, but this is not the place for entering into these details. It is evident that the phrase in which we see the earliest friars sometimes sharing the repast of the sisters and eating from their porringer is not a later interpolation.

[2]   *Tribul.* , 12b; *Spec.* , 54b; *Arbor.* V., 3; *Spec.* , 8b.

[3]   Cf. *cap.* 17 and 21.

[4]   2 Cel., 3, 136.

[5]   See below, p. 354, text in the *Firmamentum*, 19 ff. ; *Speculum*, Morin, tract. iii., 214a ff. ; cf. *Conform.* , 137 ff.

[6]   *Cum facit (subditus) voluntatem (prælati) dummodo benefacit vera obedientia est. Admon. , iii. ; Conform. , 139a, 2.* —*Si vero prælatus subdito aliquid contra animam præcipiat licet ei non obediat tamen ipsum non dimittat. , Ibid.* —*Nullus tenetur ad obedientiam in eo ubi committitus delictum vel peccatum. Epist. , ii.*

[7]   2 Cel., 3, 89; *Spec. , 29b; Conform. , 176b, 1; Bon., 77.*

[8]   *Per caritatem spiritus voluntarii serviant et obediant invicem. Et hæc est vera et sancta obedientia. Reg. , 1221, v.*

[9]   *Tribul. , Laur. MS., 14b; Spec. , 125a; Conform. , 107b, 1; 184b, 1.*

[10]   Wadding gives it (*Epist.* xvi.), after the autograph preserved in the treasury of the Conventuals of Spoleto. The authenticity of this piece is evident.

[11]   This plural, which perplexed Wadding, shows plainly that Brother Leo had spoken in the name of a group.

[12]   This date for the new communications between them seems incontestable, though it has never been proposed; in fact, we are only concerned to find a time when all three could have met at Rome (2 Cel., 3, 86; *Spec. , 27a*), between December 22, 1216 (the approbation of the Dominicans), and August 6, 1221 (death of Dominic). Only two periods are possible: the early months of 1218 (Potthast, 5739 and 5747) and the winter of 1220-1221. At any other time one of the three was absent from Rome.

On the other hand we know that Ugolini was in Rome in the winter of 1220-1221 (Huillard-Bréholles, *Hist. dipl. ,* ii., pp. 48, 123, 142. Cf. Potthast, 6589). —For Dominic see A. SS., Aug., vol. i., p. 503. The later date is imperative because Ugolini could not offer prelatures to the Brothers Minor before their explicit approbation (June 11, 1219), and this offer had no meaning with regard to the Dominicans until after the definitive establishment of their Order.

[13]   See the imperial letters of February 10, 1221; Huillard-Bréholles, vol. ii., pp. 122-127.

[14]   2 Cel., 3, 86; Bon., 78; *Spec.* , 27b.

[15]   Vide K. Eubel: *Die Bischöfe, Cardinäle und Päpste aus dem Minoritenorden bis* 1305, 8vo, 1889.

[16]   He was in Northern Italy. Vide *Registri: Doc.* , 17-28.

[17]   Reynerius, cardinal-deacon with the title of S. M. in Cosmedin, Bishop of Viterbo (cf. Innocent III., *Opera*, Migne, 1, col. ccxiii), 1 Cel., 125. He had been named rector of the Duchy of Spoleto, August 3, 1220. Potthast, 6319.

[18]   Giord, 16. The presence of Dominic at an earlier chapter had therefore been quite natural.

[19]   This view harmonizes in every particular with the witness of 1 Cel., 36 and 37, which shows the Third Order as having been quite naturally born of the enthusiasm excited by the preaching of Francis immediately after his return from Rome in 1210 (cf. *Auctor vit. sec.* ; A. SS., p. 593b). Nothing in any other document contradicts it; quite the contrary. Vide 3 Soc., 60. Cf. *Anon. Perus.* ; A. SS., p. 600; Bon., 25, 46. Cf. A. SS., pp. 631-634. The first bull which concerns the Brothers of Penitence (without naming them) is of December 16, 1221, *Significatum est*. If it really refers to them, as Sbaralea thinks, with all those who have interested themselves in the question to M. Müller inclusively—but which, it appears, might be contested—it is because in 1221 they had made appeal to the pope against the podestàs of Faenza and the neighboring cities. This evidently supposes an association not recently born. Sbaralea, *Bull. fr.* , 1, p. 8; Horoy, vol. iv., col. 49; Potthast, 6736.

[20]   Bull *Supra montem* of August 17, 1289, Potthast. 23044. M. Müller has made a luminous study of the origin of this bull; it may be considered final in all essential points (*Anfänge*, pp. 117-171). By this bull Nicholas IV. —minister-general of the Brothers Minor before becoming pope—sought to draw into the hands of his Order the direction of all associations of pious laics (Third Order of St. Dominic, the Gaudentes, the Humiliati. etc.). He desired by that to give a greater impulse to those fraternities which depended directly on the court of Rome, and augment their power by unifying them.

[21]   Vide Bull *Significatum est* of December 16, 1221. Cf. *Supra montem*, chap. vii.

[22]   The Rule of the Third Order of the Humiliati, which dates from 1201, contains a similar clause. Tiraboschi, vol. ii., p. 132.

[23]   In the A. SS., Aprilis, vol. ii. p. 600-616. Orlando di Chiusi also received the habit from the hands of Francis. Vide *Instrumentum*, etc., below, p. 400. The Franciscan fraternity, under the influence of the other third orders, rapidly lost its specific character. As to this title, Third Order, it surely had originally a hierarchical sense, upon which little by little a chronological sense has been superposed. All these questions become singularly clearer when they are compared with what is known of the Humiliati.

CHAPTER XVI

THE BROTHERS MINOR AND LEARNING

Autumn, 1221-December, 1223

After the chapter of 1221 the evolution of the Order hurried on with a rapidity which nothing was strong enough to check.

The creation of the ministers was an enormous step in this direction; by the very pressure of things the latter came to establish a residence; those who command must have their subordinates within reach, must know at all times where they are; the Brothers, therefore, could no longer continue to do without convents properly so-called. This change naturally brought about many others; up to this time they had had no churches. Without churches the friars were only itinerant preachers, and their purpose could not but be perfectly disinterested; they were, as Francis had wished, the friendly auxiliaries of the clergy. With churches it was inevitable that they should first fatally aspire to preach in them and attract the crowd to them, then in some sort erect them into counter parishes. [1]

The bull of March 22, 1222, [2] shows us the papacy hastening these transformations with all its power. The pontiff accords to Brother Francis and the other friars the privilege of celebrating the sacred mysteries in their churches in times of interdict, on the natural condition of not ringing the bells, of closing the door, and previously expelling those who were excommunicated.

By an astonishing inadvertence the bull itself bears witness to its uselessness, at least for the time in which it was given: "We accord to you, " it runs, "the permission to celebrate the sacraments in times of interdict in your churches, *if you come to have any.* " This is a new proof that in 1222 the Order as yet had none; but it is not difficult to see in this very document a pressing invitation to change their way of working, and not leave this privilege to be of no avail.

Another document of the same time shows a like purpose, though manifested in another direction. By the bull *Ex parte* of March 29, 1222, Honorius III. laid upon the Preachers and Minors of Lisbon conjointly a singularly delicate mission; he gave them full powers to proceed against the bishop and clergy of that city, who exacted from the faithful that they should leave to them by will one-third of their property, and refused the Church's burial service to those who disobeyed. [3]

The fact that the pope committed to the Brothers the care of choosing what measures they should take proves how anxious they were at Rome to forget the object for which they had been created, and to transform them into deputies of the Holy See. It is, therefore, needless to point out that the mention of Francis's name at the head of the former of these bulls has no significance. We do not picture the Poverello seeking a privilege for circumstances not yet existing! We perceive here the influence of Ugolini, [4] who had found the Brother Minor after his own heart in the person of Elias.

What was Francis doing all this time? We have no knowledge, but the very absence of information, so abundant for the period that precedes as well as for that which follows, shows plainly enough that he has quitted Portiuncula, and gone to live in one of those Umbrian hermitages that had always had so strong an attachment for him. [5] There is hardly a hill in Central Italy that has not preserved some memento of him. It would be hard to walk half a day between Florence and Rome without coming upon some hut on a hillside bearing his name or that of one of his disciples.

There was a time when these huts were inhabited, when in these leafy booths Egidio, Masseo, Bernardo, Silvestro, Ginepro, and many others whose names history has forgotten, received visits from their spiritual father, coming to them for their consolation. [6]

They gave him love for love and consolation for consolation. His poor heart had great need of both, for in his long, sleepless nights it had come to him at times to hear strange voices; weariness and regret were laying hold on him, and looking over the past he was almost driven to doubt of himself, his Lady Poverty, and everything.

Between Chiusi and Radicofani—an hour's walk from the village of Sartiano—a few Brothers had made a shelter which served them by way of hermitage, with a little cabin for Francis in a retired spot. There he passed one of the most agonizing nights of his life. The thought that he had exaggerated the virtue of asceticism and not counted enough upon the mercy of God assailed him, and suddenly he came to regret the use he had made of his life. A picture of what he might have been, of the tranquil and happy home that might have been his, rose up before him in such living colors that he felt himself giving way. In vain he disciplined himself with his hempen girdle until the blood came; the vision would not depart.

It was midwinter; a heavy fall of snow covered the ground; he rushed out without his garment, and gathering up great heaps of snow began to make a row of images. "See, " he said, "here is thy wife, and behind her are two sons and two daughters, with the servant and the maid carrying all the baggage. "

With this child-like representation of the tyranny of material cares which he had escaped, he finally put away the temptation. [7]

There is nothing to show whether or not we should fix at the same epoch another incident which legend gives as taking place at Sartiano. One day a brother of whom he asked, "Whence do you come? " replied, "From your cell. " This simple answer was enough to make the vehement lover of Poverty refuse to occupy it again. "Foxes have holes, " he loved to repeat, "and the birds of the air have nests, but the Son of man had not where to lay his head. When the Lord spent forty days and forty nights praying and fasting in the desert, he built himself neither cell nor house, but made the side of a rock his shelter. "[8]

It would be a mistake to think, as some have done, that as time went on Francis changed his point of view. Certain ecclesiastical writers have assumed that since he desired the multiplication of his Order, he for that very reason consented to its transformation. The suggestion is specious, but in this matter we are not left to conjecture; almost everything which was done in the Order after 1221 was done either without Francis's knowledge or against his will. If one were inclined to doubt this, it would need only to glance over that most solemn and also most adequate manifesto of his thought—his Will. There he is shown freed from all the temptations which had at times made him hesitate in the expression of his ideas, bravely gathering himself up to summon back the primitive ideal, and set it up in opposition to all the concessions which had been wrung from his weakness.

The Will is not an appendix to the Rule of 1223, it is almost its revocation. But it would be a mistake to see in it the first attempt made to return to the early ideal. The last five years of his life were only one incessant effort at protest, both by his example and his words.

In 1222 he addressed to the brethren of Bologna a letter filled with sad forebodings. In that city, where the Dominicans, overwhelmed with attentions, were occupied with making themselves a stronghold in the system of instruction, the Brothers Minor were more than anywhere else tempted to forsake the way of simplicity and poverty. Francis's warnings had put on such dark and threatening colors that after the famous earthquake of December 23, 1222, which spread terror over all northern Italy, there was no hesitation in believing that he had predicted the catastrophe. [9] He had indeed predicted a catastrophe which was none the less horrible for being wholly moral, and the vision of which forced from him the most bitter imprecations:

> "Lord Jesus, thou didst choose thine apostles to the number of twelve, and if one of them did betray thee, the others, remaining united to thee, preached thy holy gospel, filled with one and the same inspiration; and behold now, remembering the former days, thou hast raised up the Religion of the Brothers in order to uphold faith, and that by them the mystery of thy gospel may be accomplished. Who will take their place if, instead of fulfilling their mission and being shining examples for all, they are seen to give themselves up to works of darkness? Oh! may they be accursed by thee, Lord, and by all the court of heaven, and by me, thine unworthy servant, they who by their bad example overturn and destroy all that thou didst do in the beginning and ceasest not to do by the holy Brothers of this Order. "[10]

This passage from Thomas of Celano, the most moderate of the biographers, shows to what a pitch of vehemence and indignation the gentle Francis could be worked up.

In spite of very natural efforts to throw a veil of reserve over the anguish of the founder with regard to the future of his spiritual family, we find traces of it at every step. "The time will come, " he said one day, "when our Order will so have lost all good renown that its members will be ashamed to show themselves by daylight. "[11]

He saw in a dream a statue with the head of pure gold, the breast and arms of silver, the body of crystal, and the legs of iron. He thought it was an omen of the future in store for his institute. [12]

He believed his sons to be attacked with two maladies, unfaithful at once to poverty and humility; but perhaps he dreaded for them the demon of learning more than the temptation of riches.

What were his views on the subject of learning? It is probable that he never examined the question as a whole, but he had no difficulty in seeing that there will always be students enough in the universities, and that if scientific effort is an homage offered to God, there is no risk of worshippers of this class being wanting; but in vain he looked about him on all sides, he saw no one to fulfil the mission of love and humility reserved for his Order, if the friars came to be unfaithful to it.

Therefore there was something more in his anguish than the grief of seeing his hopes confounded. The rout of an army is nothing in comparison with the overthrow of an idea; and in him an idea had been incarnated, the idea of peace and happiness restored to mankind, by the victory of love over the trammels of material things.

By an ineffable mystery he felt himself the Man of his age, him in whose body are borne all the efforts, the desires, the aspirations of men; with him, in him, by him humanity yearns to be renewed, and to use the language of the gospel, born again.

In this lies his true beauty. By this, far more than by a vain conformity, an exterior imitation, he is a Christ.

He also bears the affliction of the world, and if we will look into the very depths of his soul we must give this word affliction the largest possible meaning for him as for Jesus. By their pity they bore the physical sufferings of humanity, but their overwhelming anguish was something far different from this, it was the birth-throes of the divine. They suffer, because in them the Word is made flesh, and at Gethsemane, as under the olive-trees of Greccio, they are in agony "because their own received them not. "

Yes, St. Francis forever felt the travail of the transformation taking place in the womb of humanity, going forward to its divine destiny, and he offered himself, a living oblation, that in him might take place the mysterious palingenesis.

Do we now understand his pain? He was trembling for the mystery of the gospel. There is in him something which reminds us of the tremor of life when it stands face to face with death, something by so much the more painful as we have here to do with moral life.

This explains how the man who would run after ruffians that he might make disciples of them could be pitiless toward his fellow-laborers who by an indiscreet, however well-intentioned, zeal forgot their vocation and would transform their Order into a scientific institute.

Under pretext of putting learning at the service of God and of religion, the Church had fostered the worst of vices, pride. According to some it is her title to glory, but it will be her greatest shame.

Must we renounce the use of this weapon against the enemies of the faith? she asks. But can you imagine Jesus joining the school of the rabbins under the pretext of learning how to reply to them, enfeebling his thought by their dialectic subtleties and fantastic exegesis? He might perhaps have been a great doctor, but would he have become the Saviour of the world? You feel that he would not.

When we hear preachers going into raptures over the marvellous spread of the gospel preached by twelve poor fishermen of Galilee, might we not point out to them that the miracle is at once more and less astounding than they say? More—for among the twelve several returned to the shores of their charming lake, and forgetful of the mystic net, thought of the Crucified One, if they thought of him at all, only to lament him, and not to raise him from the dead by continuing his work in the four quarters of the world; less—for if even now, in these dying days of the nineteenth century, preachers would go forth beside themselves with love, sacrificing themselves for each and all as in the old days their Master did, the miracle would be repeated again.

But no; theology has killed religion. The clergy repeat to satiety that we must not confound the two; but what good does this do if in practice we do not distinguish them?

Never was learning more eagerly coveted than in the thirteenth century. The Empire and the Church were anxiously asking of it the arguments with which they might defend their opposing claims. Innocent III. sends the collection of his Decretals to the University of Bologna and heaps favors upon it. Frederick II. founds that of Naples, and the Patarini themselves send their sons from Tuscany and Lombardy to study at Paris.

We remember the success of Francis's preaching at Bologna, [13] in August, 1220; at the same period he had strongly reprimanded Pietro Staccia, the provincial minister and a doctor of laws, not only for having installed the Brothers in a house which appeared to belong to them, but especially for having organized a sort of college there.

It appears that the minister paid no attention to these reproaches. When Francis became aware of his obstinacy he cursed him with frightful vehemence; his indignation was so great that when, later on, Pietro Staccia was about to die and his numerous friends came to entreat Francis to revoke his malediction, all their efforts were in vain. [14]

In the face of this attitude of the founder it is very difficult to believe in the authenticity of the note purporting to be addressed to Anthony of Padua:

"To my very dear Anthony, brother Francis, greetings in Christ.

"It pleases me that you interpret to the Brothers the sacred writings and theology, in such a way, however (conformably to our Rule), that the spirit of holy prayer be not extinguished either in you or in the others, which I desire earnestly. Greetings. "

Must we see in this a pious fraud to weaken the numberless clear declarations of Francis against learning?

It is difficult to picture to ourselves the rivalry which existed at this time between the Dominicans and Franciscans in the attempt to draw the most illustrious masters into their respective Orders. Petty intrigues were organized, in which the devotees had each his part, to lead such or such a famous doctor to assume the habit. [15] If the object of St. Francis had been scientific, the friars of Bologna, Paris, and Oxford could not have done more. [16]

The current was so strong that the elder Orders were swept away in it whether they would or no; twenty years later the Cistercians also desired to become legists, theologians, decretalists, and the rest.

Perhaps Francis did not in the outset perceive the gravity of the danger, but illusion was no longer possible, and from this time he showed, as we have seen, an implacable firmness. If later on his thought was travestied, the guilty ones—the popes and most of the ministers-general—were obliged to resort to feats of prestidigitation that are not to their credit. "Suppose, " he would say, "that you had subtility and learning enough to know all things, that you were acquainted with all languages, the courses of the stars, and all the rest, what is there in that to be proud of? A single demon knows more on these subjects than all the men in this world put together. [17] But there is one thing that the demon is incapable of, and which is the glory of man: to be faithful to God. "[18]

Definite information with regard to the chapters of 1222 and 1223 is wanting. The proposed modifications of the project of 1221 were discussed by the ministers[19] and afterward definitively settled by Cardinal Ugolini. The latter had long conferences on the subject with Francis, who has himself given us the account of them. [20]

The result of them all was the Rule of 1223. Very soon a swarm of marvellous stories, which it would be tedious to examine in detail, came to be clustered around the origin of this document; all that we need to retain of them is the memory that they keep of the struggles of Francis against the ministers for the preservation of his ideal.

Before going to Rome to ask for the final approbation he had meditated long in the solitude of Monte Colombo, near Rieti. This hill was soon represented as a new Sinai, and the disciples pictured their master on its heights receiving another Decalogue from the hands of Jesus himself. [21]

Angelo Clareno, one of the most complacent narrators of these traditions, takes upon himself to point out their slight value; he shows us Honorious III. modifying an essential passage in the plan at the last moment. [22] I have already so far described this Rule that there is no need to return to the subject here.

It was approved November 25, 1223. [23] Many memories appear to have clustered about the journey of Francis to Rome. One day Cardinal Ugolini, whose hospitality he had accepted, was much surprised, and his guests as well, to find him absent as they were about to sit down at table, but they soon saw him coming, carrying a quantity of pieces of dry bread, which he joyfully distributed to all the noble company. His host, somewhat abashed by the proceeding, having undertaken after the meal to reproach him a little, Francis explained that he had no right to forget, for a sumptuous feast, the bread of charity on which he was fed every day, and that he desired thus to show his brethren that the richest table is not worth so much to the poor in spirit as this table of the Lord. [24]

We have seen that during the earlier years the Brothers Minor had been in the habit of earning their bread by going out as servants. Some of them, a very small number, had continued to do so. Little by little, in this matter also all had been changed. Under color of serving, the friars entered the families of the highest personages of the pontifical court, and became their confidential attendants; instead of submitting themselves to all, as the Rule of 1221 ordained, they were above everyone.

Entirely losing sight of the apostolic life, they became courtiers of a special type; their character, half ecclesiastic and half lay, rendered them capable of carrying out a number of delicate missions and of playing a part in the varied intrigues for which the greater number of Roman prelates have always seemed to live. [25] By way of protest Francis had only one weapon, his example.

One day, the Speculum relates, the Blessed Francis came to Rome to see the Bishop of Ostia (Ugolini), and after having remained some time at his house, he went also to visit Cardinal Leo, who had a great devotion for him.

It was winter; the cold, the wind, the rain made any journey impossible, so the cardinal begged him to pass a few days in his house and to take his food there, like the other poor folk who came there to eat.... "I will give you, " he added, "a good lodging, quite retired, where if you like you may pray and eat. " Then Brother Angelo, one of the twelve first disciples, who lived with the cardinal, said to Francis: "There is, close by here, a great tower standing by itself and very quiet; you will be there as in a hermitage. " Francis went to see it and it pleased him. Then, returning to the cardinal, "Monsignor, " he said, "it is possible that I may pass a few days with you. " The latter was very joyful, and Brother Angelo went to prepare the tower for the Blessed Francis and his companion.

But the very first night, when he would have slept, the demons came and smote him. Calling then to his companion, "Brother, " he said, "the demons have come and smitten me with violence; remain near me, I beg, for I am afraid here alone. "

He was trembling in all his members, like one who has a fever. They passed the night both without sleeping. "The demons are commissioned with the chastisements of God, " said Francis; "as a podestà sends his executioner to punish the criminal, so God sends demons, who in this are his ministers.... Why has he sent them to me? Perhaps this is the reason: The cardinal desired to be kind to me, and I have truly great need of repose, but the Brothers who are out in the world, suffering hunger and a thousand tribulations, and also those others who are in hermitages or in miserable houses, when they hear of my sojourn with a cardinal will be moved to repine. 'We endure all privations, ' they will say, 'while he has all that he can desire; 'but I ought to give them a good example—that is my true mission. " ...

Early next morning, therefore he quitted the tower, and having told the cardinal all, took leave of him and returned to the hermitage of Monte Colombo, near Rieti. "They think me a holy man, " he said, "and see, it needed demons to cast me out of prison. "[26]

This story, notwithstanding its strange coloring, shows plainly how strong was his instinct for independence. To compare the hospitality of a cardinal to an imprisonment! He spoke better than he knew, characterizing in one word the relation of the Church to his Order.

The lark was not dead; in spite of cold and the north wind it gayly took its flight to the vale of Rieti.

It was mid-December. An ardent desire to observe to the life the memories of Christmas had taken possession of Francis. He opened his heart to one of his friends, the knight Giovanni di Greccio, who undertook the necessary preparations.

The imitation of Jesus has in all times been the very centre of Christianity; but one must be singularly spiritual to be satisfied with the imitation of the heart. With most men there is need that this should be preceded and sustained by an external imitation. It is indeed the spirit that gives life, but it is only in the country of the angels that one can say that the flesh profiteth nothing.

In the Middle Ages a religious festival was before all things else a representation, more or less faithful, of the event which it recalled; hence the *santons* of Provence, the processions of the *Palmesel*, the Holy Supper of Maundy Thursday, the Road to the Cross of Good Friday, the drama of the Resurrection of Easter, and the flaming tow of Whitsunday. Francis was too thoroughly Italian not to love these festivals where every visible thing speaks of God and of his love.

The population of Greccio and its environs was, therefore, convoked, as well as the Brothers from the neighboring monasteries. On the evening of the vigil of Christmas one might have seen the faithful hastening to the hermitage by every path with torches in their hands, making the forests ring with their joyful hymns.

Everyone was rejoicing—Francis most of all. The knight had prepared a stable with straw, and brought an ox and an ass, whose breath seemed to give warmth to the poor *bambino*, benumbed with the cold. At the sight the saint felt tears of pity bedew his face; he was no longer in Greccio, his heart was in Bethlehem.

Finally they began to chant matins; then the mass was begun, and Francis, as deacon, read the Gospel. Already hearts were touched by the simple recital of the sacred legend in a voice so gentle and so fervent, but when he preached, his emotion soon overcame the audience; his voice had so unutterable a tenderness that they also forgot everything, and were living over again the feeling of the shepherds of Judea who in those old days went to adore the God made man, born in a stable. [27]

Toward the close of the thirteenth century, the author of the *Stabat Mater dolorosa*, Giacopone dei Todi, that Franciscan of genius who spent a part of his life in dungeons, inspired by the memory of Greccio, composed another Stabat, that of joy, *Stabat Mater speciosa*.

This hymn of Mary beside the manger is not less noble than that of Mary at the foot of the cross. The sentiment is even more tender, and it is hard to explain its neglect except by an unjust caprice of fate.

> Stabat Mater speciosa
> Juxtum foenum gaudiosa
> Dum jacebat parvulus.
>
> Quæ gaudebat et ridebat
> Exsultabat cum videbat
> Nati partum inclyti.
>
> Fac me vere congaudere
> Jesulino cohærere
> Donec ego vixero. [28]

FOOTNOTES:

[1]   All this took place with prodigious rapidity. The dimensions of the Basilica of Assisi, the plans of which were made in 1228, no more permits it to be considered as a conventual chapel than Santa-Croce in Florence, San Francesco in Sienna, or the Basilica San Antonio at Padua, monuments commenced between 1230 and 1240. Already before 1245 one party of the episcopate utters a cry of alarm, in which he speaks of nothing less than of closing the door of the secular churches, which have become useless. He complains with incredible bitterness that the Minor and Preaching Friars have absolutely supplanted the parochial clergy. This letter may be found in Pierre de la Vigne, addressed at once to Frederick II. and the Council of Lyons: *Epistolæ*, Basle, 1740, 2 vols., vol. i., pp. 220-222. It is much to be desired that a critical text should be given. See also the satire against the two new Orders, done in rhyme about 1242 by Pierre de la Vigne, and of which, allowing for possible exaggerations, the greater number of the incidents cannot have been invented: E. du Méril, *Poésies pop. lat.* , pp. 153-177, Paris, 8vo, 1847.

[2]   And not of the 29th, as Sbaralea will have it. *Bull. fr.* , vol. i., n. 10. Horoy, vol. iv., col. 129; the original, still in the archives of Assisi, bears the title: *Datum Anagnie 11 Kalendas Aprilis pontificatus nostri anno sexto.*

[3]   Potthast, 6809; Horoy, iv., col. 129. See also the bull *Ecce Venit Deus* of July 14, 1227; L. Auvray: *Registres de Grégoire IX.* , no. 129; cf. 153; Potthast, 8027 and 8028, 8189.

[4]   He had finished his mission as legate in Lombardy toward the close of September, 1221 (see his register; cf. Böhmer, *Acta imp. sel. doc.* , 951). In the spring of 1222 we find him continually near the pope at Anagni, Veroli, Alatri (Potthast, 6807, 6812, 6849). The Holy See had still at that time a marked predilection for the Preachers; the very trite privilege of power to celebrate the offices in times of interdict had been accorded them March 7, 1222, but instead of the formula usual in such cases, a revised form had been made expressly for them, with a handsome eulogy. Ripolli, *Bull. Præd.* , t. i., p. 15.

[5]   2 Cel., 3, 93: *Subtrahebat se a consortio fratrum.*

[6]   It is needless to say that local traditions, in this case, though as to detail they must be accepted only with great reserve, yet on the whole are surely true. The geography of St. Francis's life is yet to be made.

[7]   2 Cel., 3, 59; Bon., 60; *Conform.* , 122b, 2.

[8]   2 Cel., 3, 5; *Spec.* , 12a; *Conform.* , 169b, 2.

[9]   Eccl., 6. Vide Liebermann's text, *Mon. Germ. hist. Script.* , t. 28, p. 663.

[10]   2 Cel., 3, 93; Bon., 104 and 105; *Conform.* , 101a, 2.

[11]   2 Cel., 3, 93; *Spec.* , 49b; 182a; *Conform.* , 182a, 1; *Tribul.* , f° 5a; 2 Cel., 3, 98; 113; 115; 1 Cel., 28, 50; 96; 103; 104; 108; 111; 118.

[12]   2 Cel., 3, 27; *Spec.* , 38b; *Conform.* , 181b, 1; *Tribul.* , 7b. Cf. *Spec.* , 220b; *Conform.* , 103b.

[13]   Francis's successors were nearly all without exception students of Bologna. Pietro di Catana was doctor of laws, as also Giovanni Parenti (Giord., 51). —Elias had been *scriptor* at Bologna. —Alberto of Pisa had been minister there (Eccl.,

6). —Aymon had been reader there (Eccl., 6). —Crescentius wrote works on jurisprudence (*Conform.* , 121b, 1, etc., etc.).

[14]　This name cannot be warranted; he is called Giovanni di Laschaccia in a passage of the *Conformities* (104a, 1); Pietro Schiaccia in the Italian MS. of the *Tribulations* (f° 75a); Petrus Stacia in the Laurentinian MS. (13b; cf. *Archiv.* , ii., p. 258). *Tribul.* , 13b; *Spec.* , 184b. This story has been much amplified in other places. *Spec.* , 126a; *Conform.* , 104b, 1.

[15]　Vide Eccl., 3: History of the entrance of Adam of Oxford into the Order. Cf., *Chartularium Univ. Par.* , t. i., nos. 47 and 49.

[16]　Eccleston's entire chronicle is a living witness to this.

[17]　*Admonitio*, v.; cf. *Conform.* , 141a.

Compare the *Constitutiones antiquæ* (*Speculum*, Morin, iii., f° 195b-206) with the Rule. From the opening chapters the contradiction is apparent: *Ordinamus quod nullus recipiatur in ordine nostro nisi sit talis clericus qui sit competenter instructus in grammatica vel logica; aut nisi sit talis laicus de cujus ingressu esset valde celebris et edificatio in populo et in clero.* This is surely far from the spirit of him who said: *Et quicumque venerit amicus vel adversarius fur vel latro benigne recipiatur.* Rule of 1221, cap. vii. See also the Exposition of the Rule of Bonaventura. *Speculum*, Morin, iii., f° 21-40.

[18]　Upon Francis's attitude toward learning see *Tribul.* , Laur., 14b; *Spec.* , 184a; 2 Cel., 3, 8; 48; 100; 116; 119; 120-124. Bon., chap. 152, naturally expresses only Bonaventura's views. See especially Rule of 1221, cap. xvii. ; of 1223, cap. x.

[19]　*Spec.* , 7b: *Fecit Franciscus regulam quam papa Honorius confirmavit cum bulla, de qua regula multa fuerunt extracta per ministros contra voluntatem b. Francisci.* Cf. 2 Cel., 3, 136.

[20]　Bull *Quo elongati* of September 28, 1230; Sbaralea, i., p. 56.

[21]　Bon., 55 and 56 [3 Soc., 62]; *Spec.* , 76; 124a; *Tribul.* , Laur., 17b-19b; Ubertini, *Arbor. V.*, 5; *Conform.* , 88a, 2.

[22]　*Tribul.* , Laur., 19a; *Archiv.* , t. iii., p. 601. Cf. A. SS., p. 638e.

[23]   Potthast, 7108. —The work of this bull was completed by that of December 18, 1223. (The original of the *Sacro Convento* bears *Datum Laterani XV. Kal. jan.*) *Fratrem Minorum*: Potthast, 7123.

[24]   2 Cel., 3, 19; Bon., 95; *Spec.* , 18b; *Conform.* , 171a, 1.

[25]   2 Cel., 3, 61 and 62. Cf. Eccl., 6, the account of Rod. de Rosa.

[26]   *Spec.* , 47b ff. ; 2 Cel., 3, 61; Bon., 84 and 85.

[27]   1 Cel., 84-87; Bon., 149.

[28]   This little poem was published entire by M. Ozanam in vol. v. of his works, p. 184.

CHAPTER XVII

THE STIGMATA

1224

The upper valley of the Arno forms in the very centre of Italy a country apart, the Casentino, which through centuries had its own life, somewhat like an island in the midst of the ocean.

The river flows out from it by a narrow defile at the south, and on all other sides the Apennines encircle it with a girdle of inaccessible mountains. [1]

This plain, some ten leagues in diameter, is enlivened with picturesque villages, finely posted on hillocks at the base of which flows the stream; here are Bibbiena, Poppi, the antique Romena sung by Dante, the Camaldoli, and up there on the crest Chiusi, long ago the capital of the country, with the ruins of Count Orlando's castle.

The people are charming and refined; the mountains have sheltered them from wars, and on every side we see the signs of labor, prosperity, a gentle gayety. At any moment we might fancy ourselves transported into some valley of the Vivarais or Provence. The vegetation on the borders of the Arno is thoroughly tropical; the olive and the mulberry marry with the vine. On the lower hill-slopes are wheat fields divided by meadows; then come the chestnuts and the oaks, higher still the pine, the fir, the larch, and above all the bare rock.

Among all the peaks there is one which especially attracts the attention; instead of a rounded and so to say flattened top, it uplifts itself slender, proud, isolated; it is the Verna. [2]

One might think it an immense rock fallen from the sky. It is in fact an erratic block set there, a little like a petrified Noah's ark on the summit of Mount Ararat. The basaltic mass, perpendicular on all sides, is crowned with a plateau planted with pines and gigantic beeches, and accessible only by a footpath. [3]

Such was the solitude which Orlando had given to Francis, and to which Francis had already many a time come for quiet and contemplation.

Seated upon the few stones of the Penna, [4] he heard only the whispering of the wind among the trees, but in the splendor of the sunrise or the sunset he could see nearly all the districts in which he had sown the seed of the gospel: the Romagna and the March of Ancona, losing themselves on the horizon in the waves of the Adriatic; Umbria, and farther away, Tuscany, vanishing in the waters of the Mediterranean.

The impression on this height is not crushing like that which one has in the Alps: a feeling infinitely calm and sweet flows over you; you are high enough to judge of men from above, not high enough to forget their existence.

Besides the wide horizons, Francis found there other objects of delight; in this forest, one of the noblest in Europe, live legions of birds, which never having been hunted are surprisingly tame. [5] Subtile perfumes arise from the ground, and in the midst of borage and lichens frail and exquisite cyclamens blossom in fantastic variety.

He desired to return thither after the chapter of 1224. This meeting, held in the beginning of June, was the last at which he was present. The new Rule was there put into the hands of the ministers, and the mission to England decided upon.

It was in the early days of August that Francis took his way toward Verna. With him were only a few Brothers, Masseo, Angelo, and Leo. The first had been charged to direct the little band, and spare him all duties except that of prayer. [6]

They had been two days on the road when it became necessary to seek for an ass for Francis, who was too much enfeebled to go farther on foot.

The Brothers, in asking for this service, had not concealed the name of their master, and the peasant, to whom they had addressed themselves respectfully, asked leave to guide the beast himself. After going on a certain time, "Is it true, " he said, "that you are Brother Francis of Assisi? " "Very well, " he went on, after the answer in the affirmative, "apply yourself to be as good as folk say you are, that they may not be deceived in their expectation; that is my advice. " Francis immediately got down from his beast and, prostrating himself before the peasant, thanked him warmly. [7]

Meanwhile the warmest hour of the day had come on. The peasant, exhausted with fatigue, little by little forgot his surprise and joy; one does not feel the burning of thirst the less for walking beside a saint. He had begun to regret his kindness, when Francis pointed with his finger to a spring, unknown till then, and which has never since been seen. [8]

At last they arrived at the foot of the last precipice. Before scaling it they paused to rest a little under a great oak, and immediately flocks of birds gathered around them, testifying their joy by songs and flutterings of their wings. Hovering around Francis, they alighted on his head, his shoulders, or his arms. "I see, " he said joyfully to his companions, "that it is pleasing to our Lord Jesus that we live in this solitary mount, since our brothers and sisters the birds have shown such great delight at our coming. "[9]

This mountain was at once his Tabor and his Calvary. We must not wonder, then, that legends have flourished here even more numerously than at any other period of his life; the greater number of them have the exquisite charm of the little flowers, rosy and perfumed, which hide themselves modestly at the feet of the fir-trees of Verna.

The summer nights up there are of unparalleled beauty: nature, stifled by the heat of the sun, seems then to breathe anew. In the trees, behind the rocks, on the turf, a thousand voices rise up, sweetly harmonizing with the murmur of the great woods; but among all these voices there is not one which forces itself upon the attention, it is a melody which you enjoy without listening. You let your eyes wander over the landscape, still for long hours illumined with hieratic tints by the departed star of day, and the peaks of the Apennines, flooded with rainbow hues, drop down into your soul what the Franciscan poet called the nostalgia of the everlasting hills. [10]

More than anyone Francis felt it. The very evening of their arrival, seated upon a mound in the midst of his Brothers, he gave them his directions for their dwelling-place.

The quiet of nature would have sufficed to sow in their hearts some germs of sadness, and the voice of the master harmonized with the emotion of the last gleams of light; he spoke with them of his approaching death, with the regret of the laborer overtaken by the shades of evening before the completion of his task, with the sighs of the father who trembles for the future of his children. [11]

For himself he desired from this time to prepare himself for death by prayer and contemplation; and he begged them to protect him from all intrusion. Orlando, [12] who had already come to bid them welcome and offer his services, had at his request hastily caused a hut of boughs to be made, at the foot of a great beech. It was there that he desired to dwell, at a stone's throw from the cells inhabited by his companions. Brother Leo was charged to bring him each day that which he would need.

He retired to it immediately after this memorable conversation, but several days later, embarrassed no doubt by the pious curiosity of the friars, who watched all his movements, he went farther into the woods, and on Assumption Day he there began the Lent which he desired to observe in honor of the Archangel Michael and the celestial host.

Genius has its modesty as well as love. The poet, the artist, the saint, need to be alone when the Spirit comes to move them. Every effort of thought, of imagination, or of will is a prayer, and one does not pray in public.

Alas for the man who has not in his inmost heart some secret which may not be told, because it cannot be spoken, and because if it were spoken it could not be understood. SECRETUM MEUM MIHI! Jesus felt it deeply: the raptures of Tabor are brief; they may not be told.

Before these soul mysteries materialists and devotees often meet and are of one mind in demanding precision in those things which can the least endure it.

The believer asks in what spot on the Verna Francis received the stigmata; whether the seraph which appeared to him was Jesus or a celestial spirit; what words were spoken as he imprinted them upon him; [13] and he no more understands that hour when Francis swooned with woe and love than the materialist, who asks to see with his eyes and touch with his hands the gaping wound.

Let us try to avoid these extremes. Let us hear what the documents give us, and not seek to do them violence, to wrest from them what they do not tell, what they cannot tell.

They show us Francis distressed for the future of the Order, and with an infinite desire for new spiritual progress.

He was consumed with the fever of saints, that need of immolation which wrung from St. Theresa the passionate cry, "Either to suffer or to die! " He was bitterly reproaching himself with not having been found worthy of martyrdom, not having been able to give himself for Him who gave himself for us.

We touch here upon one of the most powerful and mysterious elements of the Christian life. We may very easily not understand it, but we may not for all that deny it. It is the root of true mysticism. [14] The really new thing that Jesus brought into the world was that, feeling himself in perfect union with the heavenly Father, he called all men to unite themselves to him and through him to God: "I am the vine, and ye are the branches; he who abides in me and I in him brings forth much fruit, for apart from me ye can do nothing. "

The Christ not only preached this union, he made it felt. On the evening of his last day he instituted its sacrament, and there is probably no sect which denies that communion is at once the symbol, the principle, and the end of the religious life. For eighteen centuries Christians who differ on everything else cannot but look with one accord to him who in the upper chamber instituted the rite of the new times.

The night before he died he took the bread and brake it and distributed it to them, saying, "TAKE AND EAT, FOR THIS IS MY BODY. "

Jesus, while presenting union with himself as the very foundation of the new life, [15] took care to point out to his brethren that this union was before all things a sharing in his work, in his struggles, and his sufferings: "Let him that would be my disciple take up his cross and follow me. "

St. Paul entered so perfectly into the Master's thought in this respect that he uttered a few years later this cry of a mysticism that has never been equalled: "I have been crucified with Christ, yet I live...

or rather, it is not I who live, but Christ who liveth in me. " This utterance is not an isolated exclamation with him, it is the very centre of his religious consciousness, and he goes so far as to say, at the risk of scandalizing many a Christian: "I fill up in my body that which is lacking of the sufferings of Christ, for his body's sake, which is the Church. "

Perhaps it has not been useless to enter into these thoughts, to show to what point Francis during the last years of his life, where he renews in his body the passion of Christ, is allied to the apostolic tradition.

In the solitudes of the Verna, as formerly at St. Damian, Jesus presented himself to him under his form of the Crucified One, the man of sorrows. [16]

That this intercourse has been described to us in a poetic and inexact form is nothing surprising. It is the contrary that would be surprising. In the paroxysms of divine love there are *ineffabilia* which, far from being able to relate them or make them understood, we can hardly recall to our own minds.

Francis on the Verna was even more absorbed than usual in his ardent desire to suffer for Jesus and with him. His days went by divided between exercises of piety in the humble sanctuary on the mountain-top and meditation in the depths of the forest. It even happened to him to forget the services, and to remain several days alone in some cave of the rock, going over in his heart the memories of Golgotha. At other times he would remain for long hours at the foot of the altar, reading and re-reading the Gospel, and entreating God to show him the way in which he ought to walk. [17]

The book almost always opened of itself to the story of the Passion, and this simple coincidence, though easy enough to explain, was enough of itself to excite him.

The vision of the Crucified One took the fuller possession of his faculties as the day of the Elevation of the Holy Cross drew near (September 14th), a festival now relegated to the background, but in the thirteenth century celebrated with a fervor and zeal very natural for a solemnity which might be considered the patronal festival of the Crusades.

Francis doubled his fastings and prayers, "quite transformed into Jesus by love and compassion, " says one of the legends. He passed the night before the festival alone in prayer, not far from the hermitage. In the morning he had a vision. In the rays of the rising sun, which after the chill of night came to revive his body, he suddenly perceived a strange form.

A seraph, with outspread wings, flew toward him from the edge of the horizon, and bathed his soul in raptures unutterable. In the centre of the vision appeared a cross, and the seraph was nailed upon it. When the vision disappeared, he felt sharp sufferings mingling with the ecstasy of the first moments. Stirred to the very depths of his being, he was anxiously seeking the meaning of it all, when he perceived upon his body the stigmata of the Crucified. [18]

FOOTNOTES:

[1]   The passes that give access to the Casentino have all about one thousand metres of altitude. Until the most recent years there was no road properly so called.

[2]   In France Mount Aiguille, one of the seven wonders of Dauphiny, presents the same aspect and the same geological formation. St. Odile also recalls the Verna, but is very much smaller.

[3]   The summit has an altitude of 1269 metres. In Italian they call it the *Verna*, in Latin *Alvernus*. The etymology, which has tested the acuteness of the learned, appears to be very simple; the verb *vernare*, used by Dante, signifies make cold, freeze.

[4]   Name of the highest point on the plateau. Hardly three-quarters of an hour from the monastery, and not two hours and a half, as these worthy anchorites believed. This is said for the benefit of tourists... and pilgrims.

[5]   The forest has been preserved as a relic. Alexander IV. fulminated excommunication against whomever should cut down the firs of Verna. As to the birds, it is enough to pass a day at the monastery to be amazed at their number and variety. M. C. Beni has begun at Stia (in Casentino) an

ornithological collection which already includes more than five hundred and fifty varieties.

[6]   1 Cel., 91; Bon., 188; *Fior. i., consid.*

[7]   *Fior. i., consid. ; Conform. ,* 176b, 1.

[8]   Cel., 2, 15; Bon., 100. *Fior. i., consid.*

[9]   Bon., 118. *Fior. i., consid.*

[10]   2 Cel., 100.

[11]   *Fior. ii., consid.*

[12]   The ruins of the castle of Chiusi are three quarters of an hour from Verna.

[13]   *Fior. iv. and v. consid.* These two considerations appear to be the result of a reworking of the primitive document. The latter no doubt included the three former, which the continuer has interpolated and lengthened. Cf. *Conform. ,* 231a, 1; *Spec. ,* 91b, 92a, 97; A. SS., pp. 860 ff.

[14]   In current language we often include under the word mysticism all the tendencies—often far from Christian— which give predominance in the religious life to vague poetic elements, impulses of the heart. The name of mystic ought to be applied only to those Christians to whom *immediate* relations with Jesus form the basis of the religious life. In this sense St. Paul (whose theologico-philosophical system is one of the most powerful efforts of the human mind to explain sin and redemption) is at the same time the prince of mystics.

[15]   He did not desire to institute a religion, for he felt the vanity of observances and dogmas. (The apostles continued to frequent the Jewish temple. Acts, ii., 46; iii., 1; v., 25; xxi., 26.) He desired to inoculate the world with a new life.

[16]   2 Cel., 3, 29; cf. 1 Cel., 115; 3 Soc., 13 and 14; 2 Cel., 1, 6; 2 Cel., 3, 123 and 131; Bon., 57; 124; 203; 204; 224; 225; 309; 310; 311; *Conform. ,* 229b ff.

[17]   1 Cel., 91-94; Bon., 189, 190.

[18]   See the annotations of Brother Leo upon the autograph of St. Francis (Crit. Study, p. 357) and 1 Cel., 94, 95; Bon., 191, 192, 193 (3 Soc., 69, 70); *Fior. iii. consid.* Cf. *Auct. vit. sec.* ; A. SS. p. 649. It is to be noted that Thomas of Celano (1 Cel., 95), as well as all the primitive documents, describe the stigmata as being fleshy excrescences, recalling in form and color the nails with which the limbs of Jesus were pierced. No one speaks of those gaping, sanguineous wounds which were imagined later. Only the mark at the side was a wound, whence at times exuded a little blood. Finally, Thomas of Celano says that after the seraphic vision *began to appear, coeperunt apparere signa clavorum.* Vide Appendix: Study of the Stigmata.

CHAPTER XVIII

THE CANTICLE OF THE SUN

Autumn, 1224-Autumn, 1225

The morning after St. Michael's Day (September 30, 1224) Francis quitted Verna and went to Portiuncula. He was too much exhausted to think of making the journey on foot, and Count Orlando put a horse at his disposal.

We can imagine the emotion with which he bade adieu to the mountain on which had been unfolded the drama of love and pain which had consummated the union of his entire being with the Crucified One.

> Amor, amor, Gesu desideroso,
> Amor voglio morire,
> Te abrazando
> Amor, dolce Gesu, meo sposo,
> Amor, amor, la morte te domando,
> Amor, amor, Gesu si pietoso
> Tu me te dai in te transformato
> Pensa ch'io vo spasmando
> Non so o io me sia
> Gesu speranza mia
> Ormai va, dormi in amore.

So sang Giacopone dei Todi in the raptures of a like love. [1]

If we are to believe a recently published document, [2] Brother Masseo, one of those who remained on the Verna, made a written account of the events of this day.

They set out early in the morning. Francis, after having given his directions to the Brothers, had had a look and a word for everything around; for the rocks, the flowers, the trees, for brother hawk, a privileged character which was authorized to enter his cell at all times, and which came every morning, with the first glimmer of dawn, to remind him of the hour of service. [3]

Then the little band set forth upon the path leading to Monte-Acuto. [4] Arrived at the gap from whence one gets the last sight of the Verna, Francis alighted from his horse, and kneeling upon the earth, his face turned toward the mountain, "Adieu, " he said, "mountain of God, sacred mountain, *mons coagulatus, mons pinguis, mons in quo bene placitum est Deo habitare*; adieu Monte-Verna, may God bless thee, the Father, the Son, and the Holy Spirit; abide in peace; we shall never see one another more. "

Has not this artless scene a delicious and poignant sweetness? He must surely have uttered these words, in which suddenly the Italian does not suffice and Francis is obliged to resort to the mystical language of the breviary to express his feelings.

A few minutes later the rock of the ecstacy had disappeared. The descent into the valley is rapid. The Brothers had decided to spend the night at Monte-Casale, the little hermitage above Borgo San-Sepolcro. All of them, even those who were to remain on the Verna, were still following their master. As for him, absorbed in thought he had become entirely oblivious to what was going on, and did not even perceive the noisy enthusiasm which his passage aroused in the numerous villages along the Tiber.

At Borgo San-Sepolcro he received a real ovation without even then coming to himself; but when they had some time quitted the town, he seemed suddenly to awake, and asked his companion if they ought not soon to arrive there. [5]

The first evening at Monte Casale was marked by a miracle. Francis healed a friar who was possessed. [6] The next morning, having decided to pass several days in this hermitage, he sent the brothers back to the Verna, and with them Count Orlando's horse.

In one of the villages through which they had passed the day before a woman had been lying several days between death and life unable to give birth to her child. Those about her had only learned of the passage of the saint through their village when he was too far distant to be overtaken. We may judge of the joy of these poor people when the rumor was spread that he was about to return. They went to meet him, and were terribly disappointed on finding only the friars. Suddenly an idea occurred to them: taking the bridle of the horse consecrated by the touch of Francis's hands, they carried it to the sufferer, who, having laid it upon her body, gave birth to her child without the slightest pain. [7]

This miracle, established by narratives entirely authentic, shows the degree of enthusiasm felt by the people for the person of Francis. As for him, after a few days at Monte-Casale, he set out with Brother Leo for Città di Castello. He there healed a woman suffering from frightful nervous disorders, and remained an entire month preaching in this city and its environs. When he once more set forth winter had almost closed in. A peasant lent him his ass, but the roads were so bad that they were unable to reach any sort of shelter before nightfall. The unhappy travellers were obliged to pass the night under a rock; the shelter was more than rudimentary, the wind drifted the snow in upon them, and nearly froze the unlucky peasant, who with abominable oaths heaped curses on Francis; but the latter replied with such cheerfulness that he made him at last forget both the cold and his bad humor.

On the morrow the saint reached Portiuncula. He seems to have made only a brief halt there, and to have set forth again almost immediately to evangelize Southern Umbria.

It is impossible to follow him in this mission. Brother Elias accompanied him, but so feeble was he that Elias could not conceal his uneasiness as to his life. [8]

Ever since his return from Syria (August, 1220), he had been growing continually weaker, but his fervor had increased from day to day. Nothing could check him, neither suffering nor the entreaties of the Brothers; seated on an ass he would sometimes go over three or four villages in one day. Such excessive toil brought on an infirmity even more painful than any he had hitherto suffered from: he was threatened with loss of sight. [9]

Meanwhile a sedition had forced Honorius III. to leave Rome (end of April, 1225). After passing a few weeks at Tivoli, he established himself at Rieti, where he remained until the end of 1226. [10]

The pope's arrival had drawn to this city, with the entire pontifical court, several physicians of renown; Cardinal Ugolini, who had come in the pope's train, hearing of Francis's malady, summoned him to Rieti for treatment. But notwithstanding Brother Elias's entreaties Francis hesitated a long time as to accepting the invitation.

[11] It seemed to him that a sick man has but one thing to do; place himself purely and simply in the hands of the heavenly Father. What is pain to a soul that is fixed in God! [12]

Elias, however, at last overcame his objections, and the journey was determined upon, but first Francis desired to go and take leave of Clara, and enjoy a little rest near her.

He remained at St. Damian much longer than he had proposed to do[13] (end of July to beginning of September, 1225). His arrival at this beloved monastery was marked by a terrible aggravation of his malady. For fifteen days he was so completely blind that he could not even distinguish light. The care lavished upon him produced no result, since every day he passed long hours in weeping—tears of penitence, he said, but also of regret. [14] Ah, how different they were from those tears of his moments of inspiration and emotion, which had flowed over a countenance all illumined with joy! They had seen him, in such moments, take up two bits of wood, and, accompanying himself with this rustic violin, improvise French songs in which he would pour out the abundance of his heart. [15]

But the radiance of genius and hope had become dimmed. Rachel weeps for her children, and will not be comforted because they are not. There are in the tears of Francis this same *quia non sunt* for his spiritual sons.

But if there are irremediable pains there are none which may not be at once elevated and softened, when we endure them at the side of those who love us.

In this respect his companions could not be of much help to him. Moral consolations are possible only from our peers, or when two hearts are united by a mystical passion so great that they mingle and understand one another.

"Ah, if the Brothers knew what I suffer, " St. Francis said a few days before the impression of the stigmata, "with what pity and compassion they would be moved! "

But they, seeing him who had laid cheerfulness upon them as a duty becoming more and more sad and keeping aloof from them, imagined that he was tortured with temptations of the devil. [16]

Clara divined that which could not be uttered. At St. Damian her friend was looking back over all the past: what memories lived again in a single glance! Here, the olive-tree to which, a brilliant cavalier, he had fastened his horse; there, the stone bench where his friend, the priest of the poor chapel, used to sit; yonder, the hiding-place in which he had taken refuge from the paternal wrath, and, above all, the sanctuary with the mysterious crucifix of the decisive hour.

In living over these pictures of the radiant past, Francis aggravated his pain; yet they spoke to him of other things than death and regret. Clara was there, as steadfast, as ardent as ever. Long ago transformed by admiration, she was now transfigured by compassion. Seated at the feet of him whom she loved with more than earthly love she felt the soreness of his soul, and the failing of his heart. After that, what did it matter that Francis's tears became more abundant to the point of making him blind for a fortnight? Soothing would come; the sister of consolation would give him peace once more.

And first she kept him near her, and, herself taking part in the labor, she made him a large cell of reeds in the monastery garden, that he might be entirely at liberty as to his movements.

How could he refuse a hospitality so thoroughly Franciscan? It was indeed only too much so: legions of rats and mice infested this retired spot; at night they ran over Francis's bed with an infernal uproar, so that he could find no repose from his sufferings. But he soon forgot all that when near his sister-friend. Once again she gave back to him faith and courage. "A single sunbeam, " he used to say, "is enough to drive away many shadows! "

Little by little the man of the former days began to show himself, and at times the Sisters would hear, mingling with the murmur of the olive trees and pines, the echo of unfamiliar songs, which seemed to come from the cell of reeds.

One day he had seated himself at the monastery table after a long conversation with Clara. The meal had hardly begun when suddenly he seemed to be rapt away in ecstasy.

"Laudato sia lo Signore! " he cried on coming to himself. He had just composed the Canticle of the Sun. [17]

TEXT[18]

INCIPIUNT LAUDES CREATURARUM
QUAS FECIT BEATUS FRANCISCUS AD LAUDEM ET HONOREM
DEI
CUM ESSET INFIRMUS AD SANCTUM DAMIANUM.

ALTISSIMU, onnipotente, bon signore,
tue so le laude la gloria e l'onore et onne benedictione.
Ad te sole, altissimo, se konfano
et nullu homo ene dignu te mentovare.
Laudato sie, mi signore, cum tucte le tue creature
spetialmente messor lo frate sole,
lo quale jorna, et illumini per lui;
Et ellu è bellu e radiante cum grande splendore;
de te, altissimo, porta significatione.
Laudato si, mi signore, per sora luna e le stelle,
in celu l' ài formate clarite et pretiose et belle.
Laudato si, mi signore, per frate vento
et per aere et nubilo et sereno et onne tempo,
per le quale a le tue creature dai sustentamento.
Laudato si, mi signore, per sor acqua,
la quale è multo utile et humele et pretiosa et casta.
Laudato si, mi signore, per frate focu,
per lo quale cnnallumini la nocte,
ed ello è bello et jucundo et robustoso et forte.
Laudato si, mi signore, per sora nostra matre terra,
la quale ne sustenta et governa
et produce diversi fructi con colorite flori et herba.
Laudato si, mi signore, per quilli ke perdonano per lo tuo amore
et sosteugo infirmitate et tribulatione,
beati quilli ke sosterrano in pace,
ka da te, altissimo, sirano incoronati.
Laudato si, mi signore, per sora nostra morte corporale,
de la quale nullu homo vivente po skappare:
guai a quilli ke morrano ne le peccata mortali;
beati quilli ke se trovarà ne le tue sanctissime voluntati,
ka la morte secunda nol farrà male.
Laudate et benedicete mi signore et rengratiate
et serviteli cum grande humilitate.

TRANSLATION. [19]

O most high, almighty, good Lord God, to thee belong praise, glory, honor, and all blessing! {To thee alone, Most High, do they belong, and no mortal lips are worthy to pronounce thy Name. }

Praised be my Lord God with all his creatures, and specially our brother the sun, who brings us the day and who brings us the light; fair is he and shines with a very great splendor: O Lord, he signifies to us thee!

Praised be my Lord for our sister the moon, and for the stars, the which he has set clear and lovely in heaven.

Praised be my Lord for our brother the wind, and for air and cloud, calms and all weather by the which thou upholdest life in all creatures.

Praised be my Lord for our sister water, who is very serviceable unto us and humble and precious and clean.

Praised be my Lord for our brother fire, through whom thou givest us light in the darkness; and he is bright and pleasant and very mighty and strong.

Praised be my Lord for our mother the earth, the which doth sustain us and keep us, and bringeth forth divers fruits and flowers of many colors, and grass.

Praised be my Lord for all those who pardon one another for his love's sake, and who endure weakness and tribulation; blessed are they who peaceably shall endure, for thou, O most Highest, shalt give them a crown.

Praised be my Lord for our sister, the death of the body, from which no man escapeth. Woe to him who dieth in mortal sin! Blessed are they who are found walking by thy most holy will, for the second death shall have no power to do them harm.

Praise ye and bless the Lord, and give thanks unto him and serve him with great humility.

Joy had returned to Francis, joy as deep as ever. For a whole week he forsook his breviary and passed his days in repeating the Canticle of the Sun.

During a night of sleeplessness he had heard a voice saying to him, "If thou hadst faith as a grain of mustard seed, thou wouldst say to this mountain, 'Be thou removed from there, ' and it would move away. " Was not the mountain that of his sufferings, the temptation to murmur and despair? "Be it, Lord, according to thy word, " he had replied with all his heart, and immediately he had felt that he was delivered. [20]

He might have perceived that the mountain had not greatly changed its place, but for several days he had turned his eyes away from it, he had been able to forget its existence.

For a moment he thought of summoning to his side Brother Pacifico, the King of Verse, to retouch his canticle; his idea was to attach to him a certain number of friars, who would go with him from village to village, preaching. After the sermon they would sing the Hymn of the Sun; and they were to close by saying to the crowd gathered around them in the public places, "We are God's jugglers. We desire to be paid for our sermon and our song. Our payment shall be that you persevere in penitence. "[21]

"Is it not in fact true, " he would add, "that the servants of God are really like jugglers, intended to revive the hearts of men and lead them into spiritual joy? "

The Francis of the old raptures had come back, the layman, the poet, the artist.

The Canticle of the Creatures is very noble: it lacks, however, one strophe; if it was not upon Francis's lips, it was surely in his heart:

> Be praised, Lord, for Sister Clara; thou hast made her silent, active, and sagacious, and by her thy light shines in our hearts.

FOOTNOTES:

[1]   Thirty-sixth and last strophe of the song

Amor de caritade Perche m' hai si ferito?
found in the collection of St. Francis's works.

[2]   By the Abbé Amoni, at the close of his edition of the Fioretti, Rome, 1 vol., 12mo, 1889, pp. 390-392. We can but once more regret the silence of the editor as to the manuscript whence he has drawn these charming pages. Certain indications seem unfavorable to the author having written it before the second half of the thirteenth century; on the other hand, the object of a forgery is not evident. An apochryphal piece always betrays itself by some interested purpose, but here the story is of an infantine simplicity.

[3]   2 Cel., 3, 104; Bon., 119; *Fior. ii. consid.*

[4]   *Parti san Francesco per Monte-Acuto prendendo la via di Monte-Arcoppe e del foresto.* This road from the Verna to Borgo San-Sepolero is far from being the shortest or the easiest, for instead of leading directly to the plain it lingers for long hours among the hills. Is not all Francis in this choice?

[5]   2 Cel., 3, 41; Bon., 141; *Fior. iv. consid.*

[6]   1 Cel., 63 and 64; *Fior. iv. consid.*

[7]   1 Cel., 70; *Fior. iv. consid.*

[8]   1 Cel., 109; 69; Bon. 208. Perhaps we must refer to this circuit the visit to Celano. 2 Cel., 3, 30; *Spec.* , 22; Bon., 156 and 157.

[9]   1 Cel., 97 and 98; 2 Cel., 3, 137; Bon., 205 and 206.

[10]   Richard of St. Germano, *ann. 1225.* Cf. Potthast, 7400 ff.

[11]   1 Cel., 98 and 99; 2 Cel., 3, 137; *Fior.* , 19.

[12]   2 Cel., 3, 110; Rule of 1221, *cap.* 10.

[13]   See the reference to the sources after the Canticle of the Sun.

[14]   2 Cel., 3, 138.

[15]   This incident appeared to the authors so peculiar that they emphasized it with an *ut oculis videmus*. 2 Cel., 3, 67; *Spec.* , 119a.

[16]   *Spec.* , 123a; 2 Cel., 3, 58.

[17]   I have combined Celano's narrative with that of the Conformities. The details given in the latter document appear to me entirely worthy of faith. It is easy to see, however, why Celano omitted them, and it would be difficult to explain how they could have been later invented. 2 Cel., 3, 138; *Conform.* , 42b, 2; 119b, 1; 184b, 2; 239a, 2; *Spec.* , 123a ff. ; *Fior.* , 19.

[18]   After the Assisan MS., 338, f° 33a. Vide p. 354. Father Panfilo da Magliano has already published it after this manuscript: *Storia compendiosa di San Francesco*, Rome, 2 vols., 18mo, 1874-1876. The Conformities, 202b, 2-203a 1, give a version of it which differs from this only by insignificant variations. The learned philologue Monaci has established a very remarkable critical text in his *Crestomazia italiana dei primi secoli*. Citta di Castello, fas. i., 1889, 8vo, pp. 29-31. This thoroughly scrupulous work dispenses me from indicating manuscripts and editions more at length.

[19]   Matthew Arnold, Essays in Criticism, First Series. Macmillan & Company, 1883.

[20]   2 Cel., 3, 58; *Spec.* , 123a.

[21]   *Spec.* , 124a. Cf. *Miscellanea* (1889), iv., p. 88.

CHAPTER XIX

THE LAST YEAR

September, 1225-End of September, 1226

What did Ugolini think when they told him that Francis was planning to send his friars, transformed into *Joculatores Domini*, to sing up and down the country the Canticle of Brother Sun? Perhaps he never heard of it. His *protégé* finally decided to accept his invitation and left St. Damian in the course of the month of September.

The landscape which lies before the eyes of the traveller from Assisi, when he suddenly emerges upon the plain of Rieti, is one of the most beautiful in Europe. From Terni the road follows the sinuous course of the Velino, passes not far from the famous cascades, whose clouds of mist are visible, and then plunges into the defiles in whose depths the torrent rushes noisily, choked by a vegetation as luxuriant as that of a virgin forest. On all sides uprise walls of perpendicular rocks, and on their crests, several hundred yards above your head, are feudal fortresses, among others the Castle of Miranda, more giddy, more fantastic than any which Gustave Doré's fancy ever dreamed.

After four hours of walking, the defile opens out and you find yourself without transition in a broad valley, sparkling with light.

Rieti, the only city in this plain of several leagues, appears far away at the other extremity, commanded by hills of a thoroughly tropical aspect, behind which rise the mighty Apennines, almost always covered with snow.

The highway goes directly toward this town, passing between tiny lakes; here and there roads lead off to little villages which you see, on the hillside, between the cultivated fields and the edge of the forests; there are Stroncone, Greccio, Cantalice, Poggio-Buscone, and ten other small towns, which have given more saints to the Church than a whole province of France.

Between the inhabitants of the district and their neighbors of Umbria, properly so called, the difference is extreme. They are all of the striking type of the Sabine peasants, and they remain to this day entire strangers to new customs. One is born a Capuchin there as elsewhere one is born a soldier, and the traveller needs to have his wits about him not to address every man he meets as Reverend Father.

Francis had often gone over this district in every direction. Like its neighbor, the hilly March of Ancona, it was peculiarly prepared to receive the new gospel. In these hermitages, with their almost impossible simplicity, perched near the villages on every side, without the least care for material comfort, but always where there is the widest possible view, was perpetuated a race of Brothers Minor, impassioned, proud, stubborn, almost wild, who did not wholly understand their master, who did not catch his exquisite simplicity, his impossibility of hating, his dreams of social and political renovation, his poetry and delicacy, but who did understand the lover of nature and of poverty. [1] They did more than understand him; they lived his life, and from that Christmas festival observed in the woods of Greccio down to to-day they have remained the simple and popular representatives of the Strict Observance. From them comes to us the Legend of the Three Companions, the most life-like and true of all the portraits of the Poverello, and it was there, in a cell three paces long, that Giovanni di Parma had his apocalyptic visions.

The news of Francis's arrival quickly spread, and long before he reached Rieti the population had come out to meet him.

To avoid this noisy welcome he craved the hospitality of the priest of St. Fabian. This little church, now known under the name of Our Lady of the Forest, is somewhat aside from the road upon a grassy mound about a league from the city. He was heartily welcomed, and desiring to remain there for a little, prelates and devotees began to flock thither in the next few days.

It was the time of the early grapes. It is easy to imagine the disquietude of the priest on perceiving the ravages made by these visitors among his vines, his best source of revenue, but he probably exaggerated the damage. Francis one day heard him giving vent to his bad humor. "Father, " he said, "it is useless for you to disturb yourself for what you cannot hinder; but, tell me, how much wine do you get on an average? "

"Fourteen measures, " replied the priest.

"Very well, if you have less than twenty, I undertake to make up the difference. "

This promise reassured the worthy man, and when at the vintage he received twenty measures, he had no hesitation in believing in a miracle. [2]

Upon Ugolini's entreaties Francis had accepted the hospitality of the bishop's palace in Rieti. Thomas of Celano enlarges with delight upon the marks of devotion lavished on Francis by this prince of the Church. Unhappily all this is written in that pompous and confused style of which diplomats and ecclesiastics appear to have by nature the secret.

Francis entered into the condition of a relic in his lifetime. The mania for amulets displayed itself around him in all its excesses. People quarrelled not only over his clothing, but even over his hair and the parings of his nails. [3]

Did these merely exterior demonstrations disgust him? Did he sometimes think of the contrast between these honors offered to his body, which he picturesquely called Brother Ass, and the subversion of his ideal? We cannot tell. If he had feelings of this kind those who surrounded him were not the men to understand them, and it would be idle to expect any expression of them from his pen.

Soon after he had a relapse, and asked to be removed to Monte-Colombo, [4] a hermitage an hour distant from the city, hidden amidst trees and scattered rocks. He had already retired thither several times, notably when he was preparing the Rule of 1223.

The doctors, having exhausted the therapeutic arsenal of the time, decided to resort to cauterization; it was decided to draw a rod of white-hot iron across his forehead.

When the poor patient saw them bringing in the brazier and the instruments he had a moment of terror; but immediately making the sign of the cross over the glowing iron, "Brother fire, " he said, "you are beautiful above all creatures; be favorable to me in this hour; you know how much I have always loved you; be then courteous to-day. "

Afterward, when his companions, who had not had the courage to remain, came back he said to them, smiling, "Oh, cowardly folk, why did you go away? I felt no pain. Brother doctor, if it is necessary you may do it again. "

This experiment was no more successful than the other remedies. In vain they quickened the wound on the forehead, by applying plasters, salves, and even by making incisions in it; the only result was to increase the pains of the sufferer. [5]

One day, at Rieti, whither he had again been carried, he thought that a little music would relieve his pain. Calling a friar who had formerly been clever at playing the guitar, he begged him to borrow one; but the friar was afraid of the scandal which this might cause, and Francis gave it up.

God took pity upon him; the following night he sent an invisible angel to give him such a concert as is never heard on earth. [6] Francis, hearing it, lost all bodily feeling, say the Fioretti, and at one moment the melody was so sweet and penetrating that if the angel had given one more stroke of the bow, the sick man's soul would have left his body. [7]

It seems that there was some amelioration of his state when the doctors left him; we find him during the months of this winter, 1225-1226, in the most remote hermitages of the district, for as soon as he had a little strength he was determined to begin preaching again.

He went to Poggio-Buscone[8] for the Christmas festival. People flocked thither in crowds from all the country round to see and hear him. "You come here, " he said, "expecting to find a great saint; what will you think when I tell you that I ate meat all through Advent? "[9] At St. Eleutheria, [10] at a time of extreme cold which tried him much, he had sewn some pieces of stuff into his own tunic and that of his companion, so as to make their garments a little warmer. One day his companion came home with a fox-skin, with which in his turn he proposed to line his master's tunic. Francis rejoiced much over it, but would permit this excess of consideration for his body only on condition that the piece of fur should be placed on the outside over his chest.

All these incidents, almost insignificant at a first view, show how he detested hypocrisy even in the smallest things.

We will not follow him to his dear Greccio, [11] nor even to the hermitage of St. Urbano, perched on one of the highest peaks of the Sabine. [12] The accounts which we have of the brief visits he made there at this time tell us nothing new of his character or of the history of his life. They simply show that the imaginations of those who surrounded him were extraordinarily overheated; the least incidents immediately took on a miraculous coloring. [13]

The documents do not say how it came about that he decided to go to Sienna. It appears that there was in that city a physician of great fame as an oculist. The treatment he prescribed was no more successful than that of the others; but with the return of spring Francis made a new effort to return to active life. We find him describing the ideal Franciscan monastery, [14] and another day explaining a passage in the Bible to a Dominican.

Did the latter, a doctor in theology, desire to bring the rival Order into ridicule by showing its founder incapable of explaining a somewhat difficult verse? It appears extremely likely. "My good father, " he said, "how do you understand this saying of the prophet Ezekiel, 'If thou dost not warn the wicked of his wickedness, I will require his soul of thee? ' I am acquainted with many men whom I know to be in a state of mortal sin, and yet I am not always reproaching them for their vices. Am I, then, responsible for their souls? "

At first Francis excused himself, alleging his ignorance, but urged by his interlocutor he said at last: "Yes, the true servant unceasingly rebukes the wicked, but he does it most of all by his conduct, by the truth which shines forth in his words, by the light of his example, by all the radiance of his life. "[15]

He soon suffered so grave a relapse that the Brothers thought his last hour had come. They were especially affrighted by the hemorrhages, which reduced him to a state of extreme prostration. Brother Elias hastened to him. At his arrival the invalid felt in himself such an improvement that they could acquiesce in his desire to be taken back to Umbria. Toward the middle of April they set out, going in the direction of Cortona. It is the easiest route, and the delightful hermitage of that city was one of the best ordered to permit of his taking some repose. He doubtless remained there a very short time: he was in haste to see once more the skies of his native country, Portiuncula, St. Damian, the Carceri, all those paths and hamlets which one sees from the terraces of Assisi and which recalled to him so many sweet memories.

Instead of going by the nearest road, they made a long circuit by Gubbio and Nocera, to avoid Perugia, fearing some attempt of the inhabitants to get possession of the Saint. Such a relic as the body of Francis lacked little of the value of the sacred nail or the sacred lance. [16] Battles were fought for less than that.

They made a short halt near Nocera, at the hermitage of Bagnara, on the slopes of Monte-Pennino. [17] His companions were again very much disturbed. The swelling which had shown itself in the lower limbs was rapidly gaining the upper part of the body. The Assisans learned this, and wishing to be prepared for whatever might happen sent their men-at-arms to protect the Saint and hasten his return.

Bringing Francis back with them they stopped for food at the hamlet of Balciano, [18] but in vain they begged the inhabitants to sell them provisions. As the escort were confiding their discomfiture to the friars, Francis, who knew these good peasants, said: "If you had asked for food without offering to pay, you would have found all you wanted. "

He was right, for, following his advice, they received for nothing all that they desired. [19]

The arrival of the party at Assisi was hailed with frantic joy. This time Francis's fellow-citizens were sure that the Saint was not going to die somewhere else. [20]

Customs in this matter have changed too much for us to be able thoroughly to comprehend the good fortune of possessing the body of a saint. If you are ever so unlucky as to mention St. Andrew before an inhabitant of Amalfi, you will immediately find him beginning to shout *"Evviva San Andrea! Evviva San Andrea! "* Then with extraordinary volubility he will relate to you the legend of the *Grande Protettore*, his miracles past and present, those which he might have done if he had chosen, but which he refrained from doing out of charity because St. Januarius of Naples could not do as much. He gesticulates, throws himself about, hustles you, more enthusiastic over his relic and more exasperated by your coldness than a soldier of the Old Guard before an enemy of the Emperor.

In the thirteenth century all Europe was like that.

We shall find here several incidents which we may be tempted to consider shocking or even ignoble, if we do not make an effort to put them all into their proper surroundings.

Francis was installed in the bishop's palace; he would have preferred to be at Portiuncula, but the Brothers were obliged to obey the injunctions of the populace, and to make assurance doubly sure, guards were placed at all the approaches of the palace.

The abode of the Saint in this place was much longer than had been anticipated. It perhaps lasted several months (July to September). This dying man did not consent to die. He rebelled against death; in this centre of the work his anxieties for the future of the Order, which a little while before had been in the background, now returned, more agonizing and terrible than ever.

"We must begin again, " he thought, "create a new family who will not forget humility, who will go and serve lepers and, as in the old times, put themselves always, not merely in words, but in reality, below all men. "[21]

To feel that implacable work of destruction going on against which the most submissive cannot keep from protesting: "My God, my God, why? why hast thou forsaken me? " To be obliged to look on at the still more dreaded decomposition of his Order; he, the lark, to be spied upon by soldiers watching for his corpse—there was quite enough here to make him mortally sad.

During these last weeks all his sighs were noted. The disappearance of the greater part of the legend of the Three Companions certainly deprives us of some touching stories, but most of the incidents have been preserved for us, notwithstanding, in documents from a second hand.

Four Brothers had been especially charged to lavish care upon him: Leo, Angelo, Rufino, and Masseo. We already know them; they are of those intimate friends of the first days, who had heard in the Franciscan gospel a call to love and liberty. And they too began to complain of everything. [22]

One day one of them said to the sick man: "Father, you are going away to leave us here; point out to us, then, if you know him, the one to whom we might in all security confide the burden of the generalship. "

Alas, Francis did not know the ideal Brother, capable of assuming such a duty; but he took advantage of the question to sketch the portrait of the perfect minister-general. [23]

We have two impressions of this portrait, the one which has been retouched by Celano, and the original proof, much shorter and more vague, but showing us Francis desiring that his successor shall have but a single weapon, an unalterable love.

It was probably this question which suggested to him the thought of leaving for his successors, the generals of the Order, a letter which they should pass on from one to another, and where they should find, not directions for particular cases, but the very inspiration of their activity. [24]

> To the Reverend Father in Christ, N ..., Minister-General of the entire Order of the Brothers Minor. May God bless thee and keep thee in his holy love.
>
> Patience in all things and everywhere, this, my Brother, is what I specially recommend. Even if they oppose thee, if they strike thee, thou shouldst be grateful to them and desire that it should be thus and not otherwise.
>
> In this will be manifest thy love for God and for me, his servant and thine; that there shall not be a single friar in the world who, having sinned as much as one can sin, and coming before thee, shall go away without having received thy pardon. And if he does not ask it, do thou ask it for him, whether he wills or not.
>
> And if he should return again a thousand times before thee, love him more than myself, in order to lead him to well-doing. Have pity always on these Brothers.

These words show plainly enough how in former days Francis had directed the Order; in his dream the ministers-general were to stand in a relation of pure affection, of tender devotion toward those under them; but was this possible for one at the head of a family whose branches extended over the entire world? It would be hazardous to say, for among his successors have not been wanting distinguished minds and noble hearts; but save for Giovanni di Parma and two or three others, this ideal is in sharp contrast with the reality. St. Bonaventura himself will drag his master and friend, this very Giovanni of Parma, before an ecclesiastical tribunal, will cause him to be condemned to perpetual imprisonment, and it will need the intervention of a cardinal outside of the Order to secure the commutation of this sentence. [25]

The agonies of grief endured by the dying Francis over the decadence of the Order would have been less poignant if they had not been mingled with self-reproaches for his own cowardice. Why had he deserted his post, given up the direction of his family, if not from idleness and selfishness? And now it was too late to take back this step; and in hours of frightful anguish he asked himself if God would not hold him responsible for this subversion of his ideal.

"Ah, if I could go once again to the chapter-general, " he would sigh, "I would show them what my will is. "

Shattered as he was by fever, he would suddenly rise up in his bed, crying with a despairing intensity: "Where are they who have ravished my brethren from me? Where are they who have stolen away my family? "

Alas, the real criminals were nearer to him than he thought. The provincial ministers, of whom he appears to have been thinking when he thus spoke, were only instruments in the hands of the clever Brother Elias; and he—what else was he doing but putting his intelligence and address at Cardinal Ugolini's service?

Far from finding any consolation in those around him, Francis was constantly tortured by the confidences of his companions, who, impelled by mistaken zeal, aggravated his pain instead of calming it. [26]

"Forgive me, Father, " said one of them to him one day, "but many people have already thought what I am going to say to you. You know how, in the early days, by God's grace the Order walked in the path of perfection; for all that concerns poverty and love, as well as for all the rest, the Brothers were but one heart and one soul. But for some time past all that is entirely changed: it is true that people often excuse the Brothers by saying that the Order has grown too large to keep up the old observances; they even go so far as to claim that infidelities to the Rule, such as the building of great monasteries, are a means of edification of the people, and so the primitive simplicity and poverty are held for nothing. Evidently all these abuses are displeasing to you; but then, people ask, why do you tolerate them? "

"God forgive you, brother. " replied Francis. "Why do you lay at my door things with which I have nothing to do? So long as I had the direction of the Order, and the Brothers persevered in their vocation I was able, in spite of weakness, to do what was needful. But when I saw that, without caring for my example or my teaching, they walked in the way you have described, I confided them to the Lord and to the ministers. It is true that when I relinquished the direction, alleging my incapacity as the motive, if they had walked in the way of my wishes I should not have desired that before my death they should have had any other minister than myself; though ill, though bedridden, even, I should have found strength to perform the duties of my charge. But this charge is wholly spiritual; I will not become an executioner to strike and punish as political governors must. "[27]

Francis's complaints became so sharp and bitter that, to avoid scandal, the greatest prudence was exercised with regard to those who were permitted to see him. [28]

Disorder was everywhere, and every day brought its contingent of subjects for sorrow. The confusion of ideas as to the practice of the Rule was extreme; occult influences, which had been working for several years, had succeeded in veiling the Franciscan ideal, not only from distant Brothers, or those who had newly joined the Order, but even from those who had lived under the influence of the founder. [29]

Under circumstances such as these, Francis dictated the letter to all the members of the Order, which, as he thought would be read at the opening of chapters and perpetuate his spiritual presence in them. [30]

In this letter he is perfectly true to himself; as in the past, he desires to influence the Brothers, not by reproaches but by fixing their eyes on the perfect holiness.

> To all the revered and well-beloved Brothers Minor, to Brother A ..., [31] minister-general, its Lord, and to the ministers-general who shall be after him, and to all the ministers, custodians, and priests of this fraternity, humble in Christ, and to all the simple and obedient Brothers, the oldest and the most recent, Brother Francis, a mean and perishing man, your little servant, gives greeting!

> Hear, my Lords, you who are my sons and my brothers, give ear to my words. Open your hearts and obey the voice of the Son of God. Keep his commandments with all your hearts, and perfectly observe his counsels. Praise him, for he is good, and glorify him by your works.

> God has sent you through all the world, that by your words and example you may bear witness of him, and that you may teach all men that he alone is all powerful. Persevere in discipline and obedience, and with an honest and firm will keep that which you have promised.

After this opening Francis immediately passes to the essential matter of the letter, that of the love and respect due to the Sacrament of the altar; faith in this mystery of love appeared to him indeed as the salvation of the Order.

Was he wrong? How can a man who truly believes in the real presence of the God-Man between the fingers of him who lifts up the host, not consecrate his life to this God and to holiness? One has some difficulty in imagining.

It is true that legions of devotees profess the most absolute faith in this dogma, and we do not see that they are less bad; but faith with them belongs in the intellectual sphere; it is the abdication of reason, and in sacrificing their intelligence to God they are most happy to offer to him an instrument which they very much prefer not to use.

To Francis the question presented itself quite differently; the thought that there could be any merit in believing could never enter his mind; the fact of the real presence was for him of almost concrete evidence. Therefore his faith in this mystery was an energy of the heart, that the life of God, mysteriously present upon the altar, might become the soul of all his actions.

To the eucharistic transubstantiation, effected by the words of the priest, he added another, that of his own heart.

> God offers himself to us as to his children. This is why I beg you, all of you, my brothers, kissing your feet, and with all the love of which I am capable, to have all possible respect for the body and blood of our Lord Jesus Christ.

Then addressing himself particularly to the priests:

> Hearken, my brothers, if the blessed Virgin Mary is justly honored for having carried Jesus in her womb, if John the Baptist trembled because he dared not touch the Lord's head, if the sepulchre in which for a little time he lay is regarded with such great adoration, oh, how holy, pure, and worthy should be the priest who touches with his hands, who receives into his mouth and into his heart, and who distributes to others the living, glorified Jesus, the sight of whom makes angels rejoice! Understand your dignity, brother priests, and be holy, for he is holy. Oh! what great wretchedness and what a frightful infirmity to have him there present before you and to think of other things. Let each man be struck with amazement, let the whole earth tremble, let the heavens thrill with joy when the Christ, the Son of the living God, descends upon the altar into the hands of the priest. Oh, wonderful profundity! Oh, amazing grace! Oh, triumph of humility! See, the Master of all things, God, and the Son of God, humbles himself for our salvation, even to disguising himself under the appearance of a bit of bread.

> Contemplate, my brothers, this humility of God, and enlarge your hearts before him; humble yourselves as well, that you, even you, may be lifted up by him. Keep nothing for yourselves, that he may receive you without reserve, who has given himself to you without reserve.

We see with what vigor of love Francis's heart had laid hold upon the idea of the communion.

He closes with long counsels to the Brothers, and after having conjured them faithfully to keep their promises, all his mysticism breathes out and is summed up in a prayer of admirable simplicity.

> God Almighty, eternal, righteous, and merciful, give to us poor wretches to do for thy sake all that we know of thy will, and to will always what pleases thee; so that inwardly purified, enlightened, and kindled by the fire of the Holy Spirit, we may follow in the footprints of thy well-beloved Son, our Lord Jesus Christ.

What separates this prayer from the effort to discern duty made by choice spirits apart from all revealed religion? Very little in truth; the words are different, the action is the same.

But Francis's solicitudes reached far beyond the limits of the Order. His longest epistle is addressed to all Christians; its words are so living that you fancy you hear a voice speaking behind you; and this voice, usually as serene as that which from the mountain in Galilee proclaimed the law of the new times, becomes here and there unutterably sweet, like that which sounded in the upper chamber on the night of the first eucharist.

As Jesus forgot the cross that was standing in the shadows, so Francis forgets his sufferings, and, overcome with a divine sadness, thinks of humanity, for each member of which he would give his life; he thinks of his spiritual sons, the Brothers of Penitence, whom he is about to leave without having been able to make them feel, as he would have had them feel, the love for them with which he burns: "Father, I have given them the words which thou hast given me.... For them I pray! "

The whole Franciscan gospel is in these words, but to understand the fascination which it exerted we must have gone through the School of the Middle Ages, and there listened to the interminable tournaments of dialectics by which minds were dried up; we must have seen the Church of the thirteenth century, honeycombed by simony and luxury, and only able, under the pressure of heresy or revolt, to make a few futile efforts to scotch the evil.

> To all Christians, monks, clerics, or laymen, whether men or women, to all who dwell in the whole world, Brother Francis, their most submissive servitor, presents his duty

and wishes the true peace of heaven, and sincere love in the Lord.

Being the servitor of all men, I am bound to serve them and to dispense to them the wholesome words of my Master. This is why, seeing I am too weak and ill to visit each one of you in particular, I have resolved to send you my message by this letter, and to offer you the words of our Lord Jesus Christ, the Word of God, and of the Holy Spirit, which are spirit and life.

It would be puerile to expect here new ideas either in fact or form. Francis's appeals are of value only by the spirit which animates them.

After having briefly recalled the chief features of the gospel, and urgently recommended the communion, Francis addresses himself in particular to certain categories of hearers, with special counsels.

Let the podestàs, governors, and those who are placed in authority, exercise their functions with mercy, as they would be judged with mercy by God....

Monks in particular, who have renounced the world, are bound to do more and better than simple Christians, to renounce all that is not necessary to them, and to have in hatred the vices and sins of the body.... They should love their enemies, do good to them who hate them, observe the precepts and counsels of our Redeemer, renounce themselves, and subdue their bodies. And no monk is bound to obedience, if in obeying he would be obliged to commit a fault or a sin....

Let us not be wise and learned according to the flesh, but simple, humble, and pure.... We should never desire to be above others, but rather to be below, and to obey all men.

He closes by showing the foolishness of those who set their hearts on the possession of earthly goods, and concludes by the very realistic picture of the death of the wicked.

His money, his title, his learning, all that he believed himself to possess, all are taken from him; his relatives and his friends to whom he has given his fortune will come to divide it among themselves, and will end by saying: "Curses on him, for he might have given us more and he has not done it; he might have amassed a larger fortune, and he has done nothing of the kind. " The worms will eat his body and the demons will consume his soul, and thus he will lose both soul and body.

I, Brother Francis, your little servitor, I beg and conjure you by the love that is in God, ready to kiss your feet, to receive with humility and love these and all other words of our Lord Jesus Christ and to conform your conduct to them. And let those who devoutly receive them and understand them pass them on to others. And if they thus persevere unto the end, may they be blessed by the Father, the Son, and the Holy Spirit. Amen. [32]

If Francis ever made a Rule for the Third Order it must have very nearly resembled this epistle, and until this problematical document is found, the letter shows what were originally these associations of Brothers of Penitence. Everything in these long pages looks toward the development of the mystic religious life in the heart of each Christian. But even when Francis dictated them, this high view had become a Utopia, and the Third Order was only one battalion more in the armies of the papacy.

We see that the epistles which we have just examined proceed definitely from a single inspiration. Whether he is leaving instructions for his successors, the ministers-general, whether he is writing to all the present and future members of his Order, to all Christians or even to the clergy, [33] Francis has only one aim, to keep on preaching after his death, and perhaps, too, by putting into writing his message of peace and love, to provide that he shall not be entirely travestied or misunderstood.

Considered in connection with those sorrowful hours which saw their birth, they form a whole whose import and meaning become singularly energetic. If we would find the Franciscan spirit, it is here, in the Rule of 1221, and in the Will that we must seek for it.

Neglect, and especially the storms which later overwhelmed the Order, explain the disappearance of several other documents which would cast a glimmer of poetry and joy over these sad days; [34]

Francis had not forgotten his sister-friend at St. Damian. Hearing that she had been greatly disquieted by knowing him to be so ill, he desired to reassure her: he still deceived himself as to his condition, and wrote to her promising soon to go to see her.

To this assurance he added some affectionate counsels, advising her and her companions not to go to extremes with their macerations. To set her an example of cheerfulness he added to this letter a Laude in the vulgar tongue which he had himself set to music. [35]

In that chamber of the episcopal palace in which he was as it were imprisoned he had achieved a new victory, and it was doubtless that which inspired his joy. The Bishop of Assisi, the irritable Guido, always at war with somebody, was at this time quarrelling with the podestà of the city; nothing more was needed to excite in the little town a profound disquiet. Guido had excommunicated the podestà, and the latter had issued a prohibition against selling and buying or making any contract with ecclesiastics.

The difference grew more bitter, and no one appeared to dream of attempting a reconciliation. We can the better understand Francis's grief over all this by remembering that his very first effort had been to bring peace into his native city, and that he considered the return of Italy to union and concord to be the essential aim of his apostolate.

War in Assisi would be the final dissolution of his dream; the voice of events crying brutally to him, "Thou hast wasted thy life! "

The dregs of this cup were spared him, thanks to an inspiration in which breaks forth anew his natural play of imagination. To the Canticle of the Sun he added a new strophe:

> Be praised, Lord, for those who forgive for love of thee,
> and bear trials and tribulations;
> happy they who persevere in peace,
> by thee, Most high, shall they be crowned.

Then, calling a friar, he charged him to beg the governor to betake himself, with all the notables whom he could assemble, to the paved square before the bishop's palace. The magistrate, to whom legend gives the nobler part in the whole affair, at once yielded to the saint's request.

When he arrived and the bishop had come forth from the palace, two friars came forward and said: "Brother Francis has made to the praise of God a hymn to which he prays you to listen piously, " and immediately they began to sing the Hymn of Brother Sun, with its new strophe.

The governor listened, standing in an attitude of profound attention, copiously weeping, for he dearly loved the blessed Francis.

When the singing was ended, "Know in truth, " said he, "that I desire to forgive the lord bishop, that I wish and ought to look upon him as my lord, for if one had even assassinated my brother I should be ready to pardon the murderer. " With these words he threw himself at the bishop's feet, and said: "I am ready to do whatsoever you would, for the love of our Lord Jesus Christ and his servant Francis. "

Then the bishop, taking him by the hand, lifted him up and said, "With my position it would become me to be humble, but since I am naturally too quick to wrath, thou must pardon me. "[36]

This unexpected reconciliation was immediately looked upon as miraculous, and increased still more the reverence of the Assisans for their fellow-citizen.

The summer was drawing to a close. After a few days of relative improvement Francis's sufferings became greater than ever: incapable of movement, he even thought that he ought to give up his ardent desire to see St. Damian and Portiuncula once more, and gave the brothers all his directions about the latter sanctuary: "Never abandon it, " he would repeat to them, "for that place is truly sacred: it is the house of God. "[37]

It seemed to him that if the Brothers remained attached to that bit of earth, that chapel ten feet long, those thatched huts, they would there find the living reminder of the poverty of the early days, and could never wander far from it.

One evening he grew worse with frightful rapidity; all the following night he had hemorrhages which left not the slightest hope; the

Brothers hastening to him, he dictated a few lines in form of a Will and gave them his blessing: "Adieu, my children; remain all of you in the fear of God, abide always united to Christ; great trials are in store for you, and tribulation draws nigh. Happy are they who persevere as they have begun; for there will be scandals and divisions among you. As for me, I am going to the Lord and my God. Yes, I have the assurance that I am going to him whom I have served. "[38]

During the following days, to the great surprise of those who were about him, he again grew somewhat better; no one could understand the resistance to death offered by this body so long worn out by suffering.

He himself began to hope again. A physician of Arezzo whom he knew well, having come to visit him, "Good friend, " Francis asked him, "how much longer do you think I have to live? "

"Father, " replied the other reassuringly, "this will all pass away, if it pleases God. "

"I am not a cuckoo, "[39] replied Francis smiling, using a popular saying, "to be afraid of death. By the grace of the Holy Spirit I am so intimately united to God that I am equally content to live or to die. "

"In that case, father, from the medical point of view, your disease is incurable, and I do not think that you can last longer than the beginning of autumn. "

At these words the poor invalid stretched out his hands as if to call on God, crying with an indescribable expression of joy, "Welcome, Sister Death! " Then he began to sing, and sent for Brothers Angelo and Leo.

On their arrival they were made, in spite of their emotion, to sing the Canticle of the Sun. They were at the last doxology when Francis, checking them, improvised the greeting to death:

> Be praised, Lord, for our Sister the Death of the body,
> whom no man may escape;
> alas for them who die in a state of mortal sin;
> happy they who are found conformed to thy most holy will,
> for the second death will do to them no harm.

From this day the palace rang unceasingly with his songs. Continually, even through the night, he would sing the Canticle of the Sun or some other of his favorite compositions. Then, when wearied out, he would beg Angelo and Leo to go on.

One day Brother Elias thought it his duty to make a few remarks on the subject. He feared that the nurses and the people of the neighborhood would be scandalized; ought not a saint to be absorbed in meditation in the face of death, to await it with fear and trembling instead of indulging in a gayety that might be misinterpreted? [40] Perhaps Bishop Guido was not entirely a stranger to these reproaches; it seems not improbable that to have his palace crowded with Brothers Minor all these long weeks had finally put him a little out of humor. But Francis would not yield; his union with God was too sweet for him to consent not to sing it.

They decided at last to remove him to Portiuncula. His desire was to be fulfilled; he was to die beside the humble chapel where he had heard God's voice consecrating him apostle.

His companions, bearing their precious burden, took the way through the olive-yards across the plain. From time to time the invalid, unable to distinguish anything, asked where they were. When they were half way there, at the hospital of the Crucigeri, where long ago he had tended the leper, and from whence there was a full view of all the houses of the city, he begged them to set him upon the ground with his face toward Assisi, and raising his hand he bade adieu to his native place and blessed it.

FOOTNOTES:

[1]   The following is the list of monasteries which, according to Rodolfo di Tossignano, accepted the ideas of Angelo Clareno before the end of the thirteenth century: Fermo, Spoleto, Camerino, Ascoli, Rieti, Foligno, Nursia, Aquila, Amelia: *Historiarum seraphicæ religionis, libri tres*, Venice, 1586, 1 vol., f^o, 155a.

[2]   *Spec.* , 129b; *Fior.* , 19. In some of the stories of this period the evidence is clear how certain facts have been, little by little, transformed into miracles. Compare, for example, the miracle of St. Urbano in Bon., 68, and 1 Cel., 61. See also 2 Cel., 2, 10; Bon., 158 and 159.

[3]   1 Cel., 87; 2 Cel., 2, 11; *Conform.* , 148a, 2; Bon., 99. Upon this
        visit see 2 Cel., 2, 10; Bon., 158 and 159; 2 Cel., 2, 11; 2 Cel., 3,
        36.

[4]   The present Italian name of the monastery which has also
        been called *Monte-Rainerio* and *Fonte-Palumbo*.

[5]   1 Cel., 101; 2 Cel., 3, 102; Bon., 67; *Spec.* , 134a.

[6]   2 Cel., 3, 66; Bon., 69.

[7]   *Fior. ii. consid.* Cf. Roger Bacon, Opus tertium (*ap. Mon.*
        Germ. hist. , *Script.* t. 28, p. 577). *B. Franciscus jussit fratri*
        cythariste ut dulcius personaret, quatenus mens excitaretur ad
        harmonias coelestes quas pluries andivit. Mira enim musicæ super
        omnes scientias et spectanda potestas.

[8]   Village three hours' walk northward from Rieti. Francis's
        cell still remains on the mountain, three-quarters of an hour
        from the place.

[9]   2 Cel., 3, 71; cf. *Spec.* , 43a.

[10]   Chapel still standing, a few minutes' walk from Rieti. 2 Cel.,
        3, 70; *Spec.* , 15a, 43a.

[11]   2 Cel., 2, 14; Bon., 167; 2 Cel., 3, 10; Bon., 58; *Spec.* , 122b.

[12]   Wadding, *ann. 1213*, n. 14, rightly places St. Urbano in the
        county of Narni. *L'Eremo di S. Urbano* is about half an hour
        from the village of the same name, on Mount San Pancrazio
        (1026 m.), three leagues south of Narni. The panorama is
        one of the finest in Central Italy. The Bollandists allowed
        themselves to be led into error by an interested assertion
        when they placed San Urbano near to Jesi (pp. 623f and
        624a). 1 Cel., 61; Bon., 68. (Vide Bull *Cum aliqua* of May 15,
        1218, where mention is made of San Urbano.)

[13]   As much may be said of the apparition of the three virgins
        between Campilia and San Quirico. 2 Cel., 3, 37; Bon., 93.

[14]   *Spec.* , 12b; *Conform.* , 169a, 1.

[15]   2 Cel., 3, 46; Bon., 153; *Spec.* , 31b; Ezek., xxxiii., 9.

[16]   Two years after, the King of France and all his court kissed and revered the pillow which Francis had used during his illness. 1 Cel., 120.

[17]   Bagnara is near the sources of the Topino, about an hour east of Nocera. These two localities were then dependents of Assisi.

[18]   And not Sartiano. Balciano still exists, about half way between Nocera and Assisi.

[19]   2 Cel., 3, 23; Bon., 98; *Spec.* , 17b; *Conform.* , 239a, 2f.

[20]   2 Cel., 3, 33; 1 Cel., 105, is still more explicit: "The multitude hoped that he would die very soon, and that was the subject of their joy. "

[21]   1 Cel., 103 and 104.

[22]   1 Cel., 102; *Spec.* , 83b.

[23]   2 Cel., 3, 116; *Spec.* , 67a; *Conform.* , 143b, 1, and 225b, 2; 2 Cel., 3, 117; *Spec.* , 130a.

[24]   For the text vide *Conform.* , 136b, 2; 138b, 2; 142 b, 1.

[25]   *Tribul., Archiv.* , ii., pp. 285 ff.

[26]   2 Cel., 3, 118.

[27]   These words are borrowed from a long fragment cited by Ubertini di Casali, as coming from Brother Leo: *Arbor vit. cruc., lib.* v., *cap.* 3. It is surely a bit of the Legend of the Three Companions; it may be found textually in the Tribulations, Laur., f° 16b, with a few more sentences at the end. Cf. *Conform.* , 136a, 2; 143a, 2; *Spec.* , 8b; 26b; 50a; 130b; 2 Cel., 3, 118.

[28]   *Tribul.* , Laur., 17b.

[29]   See, for example, Brother Richer's question as to the books:
         Ubertini, *Loc. cit.* Cf. *Archiv.* , iii., pp. 75 and 177; *Spec.* , 8a;
         Conform. , 71b, 2. See also: Ubertini, *Archiv.* , iii., pp. 75 and
         177; *Tribul.* , 13a; *Spec.* , 9a; *Conform.* , 170a, 1. It is curious to
         compare the account as it found in the documents with the
         version of it given in 2 Cel., 3, 8.

[30]   Assisi MS., 338, f° 28a-31a, with the rubric: *De lictera et
         ammonitione beatissimi patris nostri Francisci quam misit
         fratribus ad capitulum quando erat infirmus.* This letter was
         wrongly divided into three by Rodolfo di Tossignano (f^o
         237), who was followed by Wadding (Epistolæ x., xi., xii.).
         The text is found without this senseless division in the
         manuscript cited and in *Firmamentum*, f° 21; *Spec.* , Morin,
         iii., 217a; Ubertini, *Arbor vit. cruc.* , v., 7.

[31]   This initial (given only by the Assisi MS.) has not failed to
         excite surprise. It appears that there ought to have been
         simply an N... This letter then would have been replaced by
         the copyist, who would have used the initial of the minister
         general in charge at the time of his writing. If this hypothesis
         has any weight it will aid to fix the exact date of the
         manuscript. (Alberto of Pisa minister from 1239-1240; Aimon
         of Faversham, 1240-1244.)

[32]   This epistle also was unskilfully divided into two distinct
         letters by Rodolfo di Tossignano, f° 174a, who was
         followed by Wadding. See Assisi MS., 338, 23a-28a; *Conform.*
         , 137a, 1 ff.

[33]   The letter to the clergy only repeats the thoughts already
         expressed upon the worship of the holy sacrament. We
         remember Francis sweeping out the churches and imploring
         the priests to keep them clean; this epistle has the same
         object: it is found in the Assisi MS., 338, f° 31b-32b, with the
         rubric: *De reverentia Corporis Domini et de munditia altaris ad
         omnes clericos.* Incipit: *Attendamus omnes.* Explicit: *fecerint
         exemplari.* This, therefore, is the letter given by Wadding xiii.,
         but without address or salutation.

[34]   We need not despair of finding them. The archives of the
         monasteries of Clarisses are usually rudimentary enough,
         but they are preserved with pious care.

[35]   Spec. , *117b;* Conform., 185a 1; 135b, 1. Cf. *Test. B. Claræ,* A.
         SS., Aug., ii., p. 747.

[36]   This story is given in the *Spec.* , 128b, as from eye-witnesses.
         Cf. *Conform.* , 184b, 1; 203a, 1.

[37]   1 Cel., 106. These recommendations as to Portiuncula were
         amplified by the Zelanti, when, under the generalship of
         Crescentius (Bull *Is qui ecclesiam,* March 6, 1245), the Basilica
         of Assisi was substituted for Santa Maria degli Angeli as
         mater et caput of the Order. Vide *Spec.* , 32b, 69b-71a; *Conform.*
         , 144a, 2; 218a, 1; 3 Soc., 56; 2 Cel., 1, 12 and 13; Bon., 24, 25;
         see the Appendix, the Study of the Indulgence of August 2.

[38]   2 Cel., 108. As will be seen (below, p. 367) the remainder of
         Celano's narrative seems to require to be taken with some
         reserve. Cf. *Spec.* , 115b; *Conform.* , 225a, 2; Bon., 211.

[39]   *Non sum cuculus,* in Italian *cuculo.*

[40]   *Spec.* , 136b; *Fior. iv. consid.* It is to be noted that Guido,
         instead of waiting at Assisi for the certainly impending
         death of Francis, went away to Mont Gargano. 2 Cel., 3, 142.

CHAPTER XX

FRANCIS'S WILL AND DEATH

End of September-October 3, 1226

The last days of Francis's life are of radiant beauty. He went to meet death, singing, [1] says Thomas of Celano, summing up the impression of those who saw him then.

To be once more at Portiuncula after so long a detention at the bishop's palace was not only a real joy to his heart, but the pure air of the forest must have been much to his physical well-being; does not the Canticle of the Creatures seem to have been made expressly to be sung in the evening of one of those autumn days of Umbria, so soft and luminous, when all nature seems to retire into herself to sing her own hymn of love to Brother Sun?

We see that Francis has come to that almost entire cessation of pain, that renewing of life, which so often precedes the approach of the last catastrophe.

He took advantage of it to dictate his Will. [2]

It is to these pages that we must go to find the true note for a sketch of the life of its author, and an idea of the Order as it was in his dreams.

In this record, which is of an incontestable authenticity, the most solemn manifestation of his thought, the Poverello reveals himself absolutely, with a virginal candor.

His humility is here of a sincerity which strikes one with awe; it is absolute, though no one could dream that it was exaggerated. And yet, wherever his mission is concerned, he speaks with tranquil and serene assurance. Is he not an ambassador of God? Does he not hold his message from Christ himself? The genesis of his thought here shows itself to be at once wholly divine and entirely personal. The individual conscience here proclaims its sovereign authority. "No one showed me what I ought to do, but the Most High himself revealed to me that I ought to live conformably to his holy gospel. "

When a man has once spoken thus, submission to the Church has been singularly encroached upon. We may love her, hearken to her, venerate her, but we feel ourselves, perhaps without daring to avow it, superior to her. Let a critical hour come, and one finds himself heretic without knowing it or wishing it.

"Ah, yes, " cries Angelo Clareno, "St. Francis promised to obey the pope and his successors, but they cannot and must not command anything contrary to the conscience or to the Rule. "[3]

For him, as for all the spiritual Franciscans, when there is conflict between what the inward voice of God ordains and what the Church wills, he has only to obey the former. [4]

If you tell him that the Church and the Order are there to define the true signification of the Rule, he appeals to common sense, and to that interior certitude which is given by a clear view of truth.

The Rule, as also the gospel, of which it is a summary, is above all ecclesiastical power, and no one has the right to say the last word in their interpretation. [5]

The Will was not slow to gain a moral authority superior even to that of the Rule. Giovanni of Parma, to explain the predilection of the Joachimites for this document, points out that after the impression of the stigmata the Holy Spirit was in Francis with still greater plenitude than before. [6]

Did the innumerable sects which disturbed the Church in the thirteenth century perceive that these two writings—the Rule and the Testament—the one apparently made to follow and support the other, substantially identical as it was said, proceeded from two opposite inspirations? Very confusedly, no doubt, but guided by a very sure instinct, they saw in these pages the banner of liberty.

They were not mistaken. Even to-day, thinkers, moralists, mystics may arrive at solutions very different from those of the Umbrian prophet, but the method which they employ is his, and they may not refuse to acknowledge in him the precursor of religious subjectivism.

The Church, too, was not mistaken. She immediately understood the spirit that animated these pages.

Four years later, perhaps to the very day, September 28, 1230, Ugolini, then Gregory IX., solemnly interpreted the Rule, in spite of the precautions of Francis, who had forbidden all gloss or commentary on the Rule or the Will, and declared that the Brothers were not bound to the observation of the Will. [7]

What shall we say of the bull in which the pope alleges his familiar relations with the Saint to justify his commentary, and in which the clearest passages are so distorted as to change their sense completely. "One is stupefied, " cries Ubertini of Casali, "that a text so clear should have need of a commentary, for it suffices to have common sense and to know grammar in order to understand it. " And this strange monk dares to add: "There is one miracle which God himself cannot do; it is to make two contradictory things true. "[8]

Certainly the Church should be mistress in her own house; it would have been nothing wrong had Gregory IX. created an Order conformed to his views and ideas, but when we go through Sbaralea's folios and the thousands of bulls accorded to the spiritual sons of him who in the clearest and most solemn manner had forbidden them to ask any privilege of the court of Rome, we cannot but feel a bitter sadness.

Thus upheld by the papacy, the Brothers of the Common Observance made the Zelanti sharply expiate their attachment to Francis's last requests. Cæsar of Speyer died of violence from the Brother placed in charge of him; [9] the first disciple, Bernardo di Quintavalle, hunted like a wild beast, passed two years in the forests of Monte-Sefro, hidden by a wood-cutter; [10] the other first companions who did not succeed in flight had to undergo the severest usage. In the March of Ancona, the home of the Spirituals, the victorious party used a terrible violence. The Will was confiscated and destroyed; they went so far as to burn it over the head of a friar who persisted in desiring to observe it. [11]

WILL (LITERAL TRANSLATION).

See in what manner God gave it to me, to me, Brother Francis, to begin to do penitence; when I lived in sin, it was very painful to me to see lepers, but God himself led me into their midst, and I remained here a little while. [12] When I left them, that which had seemed to me bitter had become sweet and easy.

A little while after I quitted the world, and God gave me such a faith in his churches that I would kneel down with simplicity and I would say: "We adore thee, Lord Jesus Christ, here and in all thy churches which are in the world, and we bless thee that by thy holy cross thou hast ransomed the world. "

Besides, the Lord gave me and still gives me so great a faith in priests who live according to the form of the holy Roman Church, because of their sacerdotal character, that even if they persecuted me I would have recourse to them. And even though I had all the wisdom of Solomon, if I should find poor secular priests, I would not preach in their parishes without their consent. I desire to respect them like all the others, to love them and honor them as my lords. I will not consider their sins, for in them I see the Son of God and they are my lords. I do this because here below I see nothing, I perceive nothing corporally of the most high Son of God, if not his most holy Body and Blood, which they receive and they alone distribute to others. I desire above all things to honor and venerate all these most holy mysteries and to keep them precious. Whenever I find the sacred names of Jesus or his words in indecent places, I desire to take them away, and I pray that others take them away and put them in some decent place. We ought to honor and revere all the theologians and those who preach the most holy word of God, as dispensing to us spirit and life.

When the Lord gave me some brothers no one showed me what I ought to do, but the Most High himself revealed to me that I ought to live according to the model of the holy gospel. I caused a short and simple formula to be written, and the lord pope confirmed it for me.

Those who presented themselves to observe this kind of life distributed all that they might have to the poor. They contented themselves with a tunic, patched within and without, with the cord and breeches, and we desired to have nothing more.

The clerks said the office like other clerks, and the laymen *Pater noster*.

We loved to live in poor and abandoned churches, and we were ignorant and submissive to all. I worked with my hands and would continue to do, and I will also that all other friars work at some honorable trade. Let those who have none learn one, not for the purpose of receiving the price of their toil, but for their good example and to flee idleness. And when they do not give us the price of the work, let us resort to the table of the Lord, begging our bread from door to door. The Lord revealed to me the salutation which we ought to give: "God give you peace! "

Let the Brothers take great care not to receive churches, habitations, and all that men build for them, except as all is in accordance with the holy poverty which we have vowed in the Rule, and let them not receive hospitality in them except as strangers and pilgrims.

I absolutely interdict all the brothers, in whatever place they may be found, from asking any bull from the court of Rome, whether directly or indirectly, under pretext of church or convent or under pretext of preachings, nor even for their personal protection. If they are not received anywhere let them go elsewhere, thus doing penance with the benediction of God.

I desire to obey the minister-general of this fraternity, and the guardian whom he may please to give me. I desire to put myself entirely into his hands, to go nowhere and do nothing against his will, for he is my lord.

Though I be simple and ill, I would, however, have always a clerk who will perform the office, as it is said in the Rule; let all the other brothers also be careful to obey their guardians and to do the office according to the Rule. If it come to pass that there are any who do not the office according to the Rule, and who desire to make any other change, or if they are not Catholics, let all the Brothers, wherever they may be, be bound by obedience to present them to the nearest custode. Let the custodes be bound by obedience to keep him well guarded like a man who is in bonds night and day, so that he may not escape from their hands until they personally place him in the minister's hands. And let the minister be bound by obedience to send him by brothers who will guard him as a prisoner day and night until they shall have placed him in the hands of the Lord Bishop of Ostia, who is the lord, the protector, and the correcter of all the Fraternity. [13]

And let the Brothers not say: "This is a new Rule; " for this is a reminder, a warning, an exhortation; it is my Will, that I, little Brother Francis, make for you, my blessed Brothers, in order that we may observe in a more catholic way the Rule which we promised the Lord to keep.

Let the ministers-general, all the other ministers and the custodes be held by obedience to add nothing to and take nothing from these words. Let them always keep this writing near them, beside the Rule; and in all the chapters which shall be held, when the Rule is read let these words be read also.

I interdict absolutely, by obedience, all the Brothers, clerics and layman, to introduce glosses in the Rule, or in this Will, under pretext of explaining it. But since the Lord has given me to speak and to write the Rule and these words in a clear and simple manner, without commentary, understand them in the same way, and put them in practice until the end.

And may whoever shall have observed these things be crowned in heaven with the blessings of the heavenly Father, and on earth with those of his well-beloved Son and of the Holy Spirit the consoler, with the assistance of all the heavenly virtues and all the saints.

And I, little Brother Francis, your servitor, confirm to you so far as I am able this most holy benediction. Amen.

After thinking of his Brothers Francis thought of his dear Sisters at St. Damian and made a will for them.

It has not come down to us, and we need not wonder; the Spiritual Brothers might flee away, and protest from the depths of their retreats, but the Sisters were completely unarmed against the machinations of the Common Observance. [14]

In the last words that he addressed to the Clarisses, after calling upon them to persevere in poverty and union, he gave them his benediction. [15] Then he recommended them to the Brothers, supplicating the latter never to forget that they were members of one and the same religious family. [16] After having done all that he could for those whom he was about to leave, he thought for a moment of himself.

He had become acquainted in Rome with a pious lady named Giacomina di Settisoli. Though rich, she was simple and good, entirely devoted to the new ideas; even the somewhat singular characteristics of Francis pleased her. He had given her a lamb which had become her inseparable companion. [17]

Unfortunately all that concerns her has suffered much from later retouchings of the legend. The perfectly natural conduct of the Saint with women has much embarrassed his biographers; hence heavy and distorted commentaries tacked on to episodes of a delicious simplicity.

Before dying Francis desired to see again this friend, whom he smilingly called Brother Giacomina. He caused a letter to be written her to come to Portiuncula; we can imagine the dismay of the narrators at this far from monastic invitation.

But the good lady had anticipated his appeal: at the moment when the messenger with the letter was about to leave for Rome, she arrived at Portiuncula and remained there until the last sigh of the Saint. [18] For one moment she thought of sending away her suite; the invalid was so calm and joyful that she could not believe him dying, but he himself advised her to keep her people with her. This time he felt with no possible doubt that his captivity was about to be ended.

He was ready, he had finished his work.

Did he think then of the day when, cursed by his father, he had renounced all earthly goods and cried to God with an ineffable confidence, "Our Father who art in heaven! " We cannot say; but he desired to finish his life by a symbolic act which very closely recalls the scene in the bishop's palace.

He caused himself to be stripped of his clothing and laid upon the ground, for he wished to die in the arms of his Lady Poverty. With one glance he embraced the twenty years that had glided by since their union: "I have done my duty, " he said to the Brothers, "may the Christ now teach you yours! "[19]

This was Thursday, October 1. [20]

They laid him back upon his bed, and, conforming to his wishes, they again sang to him the Canticle of the Sun.

At times he added his voice to those of his Brothers, [21] and came back with preference to Psalm 142, *Voce mea ad Dominum clamavi*. [22]

> With my voice I cry unto the Lord,
> With my voice I implore the Lord,
> I pour out my complaint before him,
> I tell him all my distress.
> When my spirit is cast down within me,
> Thou knowest my path.
> Upon the way where I walk
> They have laid a snare for me,
> Cast thine eyes to the right and look!
> No one recognizes me;
> All refuge is lost for me,
> No one takes thought for my soul.
> Lord, unto thee I cry;
> I say: Thou art my refuge,
> My portion in the land of the living.
> Be attentive to my cries!
> For I am very unhappy.
> Deliver me from those who pursue me!
> For they are stronger than I.
> Bring my soul out of its prison
> That I may praise thy name.
> The righteous shall compass me about
> When thou hast done good unto me!

The visits of death are always solemn, but the end of the just is the most moving *sursum corda* that we can hear on earth. The hours flowed by and the Brothers would not leave him. "Alas, good Father, " said one of them to him, unable longer to contain himself, "your children are going to lose you, and be deprived of the true light which lightened them: think of the orphans you are leaving and forgive all their faults, give to them all, present and absent, the joy of your holy benediction. "

"See, " replied the dying man, "God is calling me. I forgive all my Brothers, present and absent, their offences and faults, and absolve them according to my power. Tell them so, and bless them all in my name. "[23]

Then crossing his arms he laid his hands upon those who surrounded him. He did this with peculiar emotion to Bernard of Quintavalle: "I desire, " he said, "and with all my power I urge whomsoever shall be minister-general of the Order, to love and honor him as myself; let the provincials and all the Brothers act toward him as toward me. "[24]

He thought not only of the absent Brothers but of the future ones; love so abounded in him that it wrung from him a groan of regret for not seeing all those who should enter the Order down to the end of time, that he might lay his hand upon their brows, and make them feel those things that may only be spoken by the eyes of him who loves in God. [25]

He had lost the notion of time; believing that it was still Thursday he desired to take a last meal with his disciples. Some bread was brought, he broke it and gave it to them, and there in the poor cabin of Portiuncula, without altar and without a priest, was celebrated the Lord's Supper. [26]

A Brother read the Gospel for Holy Thursday, *Ante diem festum Paschæ*: "Before the feast of the Passover, Jesus knowing that his hour was come to go from this world to the Father, having loved his own who were in the world he loved them unto the end. "

The sun was gilding the crests of the mountains with his last rays, there was silence around the dying one. All was ready. The angel of death might come.

Saturday, October 3, 1226, at nightfall, without pain, without struggle, he breathed the last sigh.

The Brothers were still gazing on his face, hoping yet to catch some sign of life, when innumerable larks alighted, singing, on the thatch of his cell, [27] as if to salute the soul which had just taken flight and give the Little Poor Man the canonization of which he was most worthy, the only one, doubtless, which he would ever have coveted.

On the morrow, at dawn, the Assisans came down to take possession of his body and give it a triumphant funeral.

By a pious inspiration, instead of going straight to the city they went around by St. Damian, and thus was realized the promise made by Francis to the Sisters a few weeks before, to come once more to see them.

Their grief was heart-rending.

These women's hearts revolted against the absurdity of death; [28] but there were tears on that day at St. Damian only. The Brothers forgot their sadness on seeing the stigmata, and the inhabitants of Assisi manifested an indescribable joy on having their relic at last. They deposited it in the Church St. George. [29]

Less than two years after, Sunday, July 26, 1228, Gregory IX. came to Assisi to preside in person over the ceremonies of canonization, and to lay, on the morrow, the first stone of the new church dedicated to the Stigmatized.

Built under the inspiration of Gregory IX. and the direction of Brother Elias, this marvellous basilica is also one of the documents of this history, and perhaps I have been wrong in neglecting it.

Go and look upon it, proud, rich, powerful, then go down to Portiuncula, pass over to St. Damian, hasten to the Carceri, and you will understand the abyss that separates the ideal of Francis from that of the pontiff who canonized him.

FOOTNOTES:

[1]   *Mortem cantando suscepit.* 2 Cel., 3, 139.

[2]   The text here taken as a basis is that of the Assisi MS., 338 (f° 16a-18a). It is also to be found in *Firmamentum,* f° 19, col. 4; *Speculum,* Morin, *tract.* iii., 8a; Wadding, *ann. 1226,* 35; A. SS., p. 663; Amoni, *Legenda Trium Sociorum;* Appendix, p. 110. Everything in this document proclaims its authenticity,

but we are not reduced to internal proof. It is expressly cited in 1 Cel., 17 (before 1230); by the Three Companions (1246), 3 Soc., 11; 26; 29; by 2 Cel., 3, 99 (1247). These proofs would be more than sufficient, but there is another of even greater value: the bull *Quo elongati* of September 28, 1230, where Gregory IX. cites it textually and declares that the friars are not bound to observe it.

[3] *Promittet Franciscus obedientiam... papæ... et successoribus... qui non possunt nec debent eis præcipere aliquid quod sit contra animam et regulam. Archiv. , i, p. 563.*

[4] *Quod si quando a quocumque... pontifice aliquid... mandaretur quod esset contra fidem... et caritatem et fructus ejus tunc obediet Deo magis quam hominibus. Ib., p. 561.*

[5] *Est [Regula] et stat et intelligitur super eos... Cum spei fiducia pace fruemur cum conscientiæ et Christi spiritus testimonio certo.* Ib., pp. 563 and 565.

[6] *Archiv. , ii., p. 274.*

[7] *Ad mandatum illud vos dicimus non teneri: quod sine consensu Fratrum maxime ministrorum, quos universos tangebat obligare nequivit nec successorem suum quomodolibet obligavit; cum non habeat imperium par in parem.* The sophism is barely specious; Francis was not on a par with his successors; he did not act as minister-general, but as founder.

[8] *Arbor vit. cruc. , lib. v., cap.* 3 and 5. See above, p. 185.

[9] *Tribul. ,* Laur., 25b; *Archiv. ,* i., p. 532.

[10] At the summit of the Apennines, about half way between Camerino and Nocera (Umbria). *Tribul. ,* Laur., 26b; Magl., 135b.

[11] *Declaratio Ubertini, Archiv. ,* iii., p. 168. This fact is not to be questioned, since it is alleged in a piece addressed to the pope, in response to the liberal friars, to whom it was to be communicated.

[12]   *Feci moram cum illis.* , MS., 338. Most of the printed texts give *miseracordiam*, which gives a less satisfactory meaning. Cf. Miscellanea iii. (1888), p. 70; 1 Cel., 17; 3 Soc., 11.

[13]   It is evident that heresy is not here in question. The Brothers who were infected with it were to be delivered to the Church.

[14]   Urban IV. published, October 18, 1263, Potthast (18680), a Rule for the Clarisses which completely changed the character of this Order. Its author was the cardinal protector Giovanni degli Ursini (the future Nicholas III.), who by way of precaution forbade the Brothers Minor under the severest penalties to dissuade the Sisters from accepting it. "It differs as much from the first Rule, " said Ubertini di Casali "as black and white, the savory and the insipid. " *Arbor. vit. cruc. lib.* v., *cap.* vi.

[15]   V. *Test. B. Claræ; Conform.* , 185a 1; Spec., 117b.

[16]   2 Cel., 3, 132.

[17]   Bon., 112.

[18]   The Bollandists deny this whole story, which they find in opposition to the prescriptions of Francis himself. A. SS., p. 664 ff. But it is difficult to see for what object authors who take great pains to explain it could have had for inventing it. *Spec.* , 133a; *Fior.* iv. ; *consid.* ; *Conform.* , 240a. I have borrowed the whole account from Bernard of Besse: *De Laudibus*, f° 113b. It appears that Giacomina settled for the rest of her life at Assisi, that she might gain edification from the first companions of Francis. *Spec.* , 107b. (What a lovely scene, and with what a Franciscan fragrance!) The exact date of her death is not known. She was buried in the lower church of the basilica of Assisi, and on her tomb was engraved: *Hic jacit Jacoba sancta nobilisque romana.* Vide Fratini: *Storia della basilica*, p. 48. Cf. Jacobilli: *Vite dei Santi e Beati dell' Umbria*, Foligno, 3 vols., 4to, 1647; i., p. 214.

[19]   2 Cel., 3, 139; Bon., 209, 210; *Conform.* , 171b, 2.

[20]   2 Cel., 3, 139: *Cum me videritis... sicut me nudius tertius nudum vidistis.*

[21]   1 Cel., 109; 2 Cel., 3, 139.

[22]   1 Cel., 109; Bon., 212.

[23]   1 Cel., 109. Cf. *Epist. Eliæ.*

[24]   *Tribul.* Laur., 22b. Nothing better shows the historic value of the chronicle of the Tribulations than to compare its story of these moments with that of the following documents: *Conform.* , 48b, 1; 185a, 2; *Fior.* , 6. ; *Spec.* , 86a.

[25]   2 Cel., 3, 139; *Spec.* , 116b; *Conform.* , 224b, 1.

[26]   2 Cel., 3, 139. A simple comparison between this story in the *Speculum* (116b) and that in the *Conformities* (224b, 1) is enough to show how in certain of its parts the *Speculum* represents a state of the legend anterior to 1385.

[27]   Bon., 214. This cell has been transformed into a chapel and may be found a few yards from the little church of Portiuncula. Church and chapel are now sheltered under the great Basilica of Santa Maria degli Angeli. See the picture and plan, A. SS., p. 814, or better still in *P. Barnabas aus dem Elsass, Portiuncula oder Geschichte U. L. F. v. den Engeln.* Rixheim, 1884, 1 vol., 8vo, pp. 311 and 312.

[28]   1 Cel., 116 and 117; Bon., 219; *Conform.* 185a, 1.

[29]   To-day in the *cl'ture* of the convent St. Clara. Vide Miscellanea 1, pp. 44-48, a very interesting study by Prof. Carattoli upon the coffin of St. Francis.

CRITICAL STUDY OF THE SOURCES

* * * * *

SUMMARY

I.   ST. FRANCIS'S WORKS.

II.   BIOGRAPHIES PROPERLY SO CALLED.

1.   Preliminary Note.

2.   First Life by Thomas of Celano.

3.   Review of the History of the Order 1230-1244.

4.   Legend of the Three Companions.

5.   Fragments of the Suppressed Portion of the Legend.

6.   Second Life by Thomas of Celano. First Part.

7.   Second Life by Thomas of Celano. Second Part.

8.   Documents of Secondary Importance:

Biography for Use of the Choir.
Life in Verse.
Biography by Giovanni di Ceperano. Life by
Brother Julian.

9.   Legend of St. Bonaventura.

10. De Laudibus of Bernard of Besse.

III. DIPLOMATIC DOCUMENTS.

1.   Donation of the Verna.

2.   Registers of Cardinal Ugolini.

3.   Bulls.

IV.   CHRONICLERS OF THE ORDER.

      1.   Chronicle of Brother Giordano di Giano.

      2.   Eccleston: Arrival of the Friars in England.

      3.   Chronicle of Fra Salimbeni.

      4.   Chronicle of the Tribulations.

      5.   The Fioretti and their Appendices.

      6.   Chronicle of the XXIV. Generals.

      7.   The Conformities of Bartolommeo di Pisa.

      8.   Glassberger's Chronicle.

      9.   Chronicle of Mark of Lisbon.

V.   CHRONICLERS NOT OF THE ORDER.

      1.   Jacques de Vitry.

      2.   Thomas of Spalato.

      3.   Divers Chroniclers.

CRITICAL STUDY OF THE SOURCES

There are few lives in history so abundantly provided with documents as that of St. Francis. This will perhaps surprise the reader, but to convince himself he has only to run over the preceding list, which, however, has been made as succinct as possible.

It is admitted in learned circles that the essential elements of this biography have disappeared or have been entirely altered. The exaggeration of certain religious writers, who accept everything, and among several accounts of the same fact always choose the longest and most marvellous, has led to a like exaggeration in the contrary sense.

If it were necessary to point out the results of these two excesses as they affect each event, this volume would need to be twice and even four times as large as it is. Those who are interested in these questions will find in the notes brief indications of the original documents on which each narrative is based. [1]

To close the subject of the errors which are current in the Franciscan documents, and to show in a few lines their extreme importance, I shall take two examples. Among our own contemporaries no one has so well spoken on the subject of St. Francis as M. Renan; he comes back to him with affecting piety, and he was in a better condition than any one to know the sources of this history. And yet he does not hesitate to say in his study of the Canticle of the Sun, Francis's best known work: "The authenticity of this piece appears certain, but we must observe that we have not the Italian original. The Italian text which we possess is a translation of a Portuguese version, which was itself translated from the Spanish. "[2]

And yet the primitive Italian exists[3] not only in numerous manuscripts in Italy and France, particularly in the Mazarine Library, [4] but also in the well-known book of the *Conformities*. [5]

An error, grave from quite another point of view, is made by the same author when he denies the authenticity of St. Francis's Will; this piece is not only the noblest expression of its author's religious feeling, it constitutes also a sort of autobiography, and contains the solemn and scarcely disguised revocation of all the concessions which had been wrung from him. We have already seen that its authenticity is not to be challenged. [6] This double example will, I hope, suffice to show the necessity of beginning this study by a conscientious examination of the sources.

If the eminent historian to whom I have alluded were still living, he would have for this page his large and benevolent smile, that simple, *Oui, oui*, which once made his pupils in the little hall of the Collège de France to tremble with emotion.

I do not know what he would think of this book, but I well know that he would love the spirit in which it was undertaken, and would easily pardon me for having chosen him for scape-goat of my wrath against the learned men and biographers.

The documents to be examined have been divided into five categories.

The first includes *St. Francis's works.*

The second, *biographies properly so called.*

The third, *diplomatic documents.*

The fourth, *chronicles of the Order.*

The fifth, *chronicles of authors not of the Order.*

FOOTNOTES:

[1]   If any student finds himself embarrassed by the extreme rarity of certain works cited, I shall make it my duty and pleasure to send them to him, as well as a copy of the Italian manuscripts.

[2]   E. Renan: *Nouvelles études d'histoire religieuse*, Paris, 1884, 8vo, p. 331.

[3]   See above, pp. 304 ff.

[4]   Mazarine Library, MS. 8531: *Speculum perfectionis S. Francisci*; the Canticle is found at fo. 51. Cf. MS., 1350 (date of 1459). That text was published by Boehmer in the *Romanische Studien*, Halle, 1871. pp. 118-122. *Der Sonnengesang v. Fr. d'A.*

[5]   *Conform.* (Milan, 1510), 202b, 2s. For that matter it is correct that Diola, in the *Croniche degli ordini instituti da S. Francisco* (Venice, 1606, 3 vols. 4to), translated after the Castilian version of the work composed in Portuguese by Mark of Lisbon, was foolish enough to render into Italian this translation of a translation.

[6]   See pages 333 ff.

I

ST. FRANCIS'S WORKS

The writings of St. Francis[1] are assuredly the best source of acquaintance with him; we can only be surprised to find them so neglected by most of his biographers. It is true that they give little information as to his life, and furnish neither dates nor facts, [2] but they do better, they mark the stages of his thought and of his spiritual development. The legends give us Francis as he appeared, and by that very fact suffer in some degree the compulsion of circumstances; they are obliged to bend to the exigencies of his position as general of an Order approved by the Church, as miracle-worker, and as saint. His works, on the contrary, show us his very soul; each phrase has not only been thought, but lived; they bring us the Poverello's emotions, still alive and palpitating.

So, when in the writings of the Franciscans we find any utterance of their master, it unconsciously betrays itself, sounding out suddenly in a sweet, pure tone which penetrates to your very heart, awakening with a thrill a sprite that was sleeping there.

This bloom of love enduing St. Francis's words would be an admirable criterion of the authenticity of those opuscules which tradition attributes to him; but the work of testing is neither long nor difficult. If after his time injudicious attempts were here and there made to honor him with miracles which he did not perform, which he would not even have wished to perform, no attempt was ever made to burden his literary efforts with false or supposititious pieces. [3] The best proof of this is that it is not until Wadding—that is to say, until the seventeenth century—that we find the first and only serious attempt to collect these precious memorials. Several of them have been lost, [4] but those which remain are enough to give us in some sort the refutation of the legends.

In these pages Francis gives himself to his readers, as long ago he gave himself to his companions; in each one of them a feeling, a cry of the heart, or an aspiration toward the Invisible is prolonged down to our own time.

Wadding thought it his duty to give a place in his collection to several suspicious pieces; more than this, instead of following the oldest manuscripts that he had before him, he often permitted himself to be led astray by sixteenth-century writers whose smallest concern was to be critical and accurate. To avoid the tedious and entirely negative task to which it would be necessary to proceed if I took him for my starting-point I shall confine myself to a positive study of this question.

All the pieces which will be enumerated are found in his collection. They are sometimes cut up in a singular way; but in proportion as each document is studied we shall find sufficient indications to enable us to make the necessary rectifications.

The archives of Sacro Convento of Assisi[5] possess a manuscript whose importance is not to be overestimated. It has already been many times studied, [6] and bears the number 338.

It appears, however, that a very important detail of form has been overlooked. It is this: that No. 338 is not *one* manuscript, but *a collection* of manuscripts of very different periods, which were put together because they were of very nearly the same size, and have been foliated in a peculiar manner.

This artificial character of the collection shows that each of the pieces which compose it needs to be examined by itself, and that it is impossible to say of it as a whole that it is of the thirteenth or the fourteenth century.

The part that interests us is perfectly homogeneous, is formed of three parchment books (fol. 12a-44b) and contains a part of Francis's works.

1. The Rule, definitively approved by Honorius III., November 20, 1223[7] (fol. 12a-16a).

2. St. Francis's Will[8] (fol. 16a-18a).

3. The Admonitions[9] (fol. 18a-23b).

4. The Letter to all Christians[10] (fol. 23b-28a).

5. The letter to all the members of the Order assembled in Chapter-general[11] (fol. 28a-31a).

6. Counsel to all clerics on the respect to be paid to the Eucharist[12] (fol., 31b-32b).

7. A very short piece preceded by the rubric: "Of the virtues which adorn the Virgin Mary and which ought to adorn the holy soul"[13] (fol. 32b).

8. The *Laudes Creaturarum*, or Canticle of the Sun[14] (fol. 33a).

9. A paraphrase of the *Pater* introduced by the rubric: *Incipiunt laudes quas* ordinavit. *B. pater noster Franciscus et dicebat ipsas ad omnes horas diei et noctis et ante officium B. V. Mariæ sic incipiens: Sanctissime Pater*[15] (fol. 34a).

10. The office of the Passion (34b-43a). This office, where the psalms are replaced by several series of biblical verses, are designed to make him who repeats them follow, hour by hour, the emotions of the Crucified One from the evening of Holy Thursday. [16]

11. A rule for friars in retreat in hermitages[17] (fol. 43a-43b).

A glance over this list is enough to show that the works of Francis here collected are addressed to all the Brothers, or are a sort of encyclicals, which they are charged to pass on to those for whom they are destined.

The very order of these pieces shows us that we have in this manuscript the primitive library of the Brothers Minor, the collection of which each minister was to carry with him a copy. It was truly their viaticum.

Matthew Paris tells us of his amazement at the sight of these foreign monks, clothed in patched tunics, and carrying their books in a sort of case suspended from their necks. [18]

The Assisi manuscript was without doubt destined to this service; if it is silent on the subject of the journeys it has made, and of the Brothers to whom it has been a guide and an inspiration, it at least brings us, more than all the legends, into intimacy with Francis, makes us thrill in unison with that heart which never admitted a separation between joy, love, and poetry. As to the date of this manuscript, one must needs be a paleographer to determine. We have already found a hypothesis which, if well grounded, would carry it back to the neighborhood of 1240. [19]

Its contents seem to countenance this early date. In fact, it contains several pieces of which the *Manual of the Brother Minor* very early rid itself.

Very soon they were content to have only the Rule to keep company with the breviary; sometimes they added the Will. But the other writings, if they did not fall entirely into neglect, ceased at least to be of daily usage.

Those of St. Francis's writings which are not of general interest or do not concern the Brothers naturally find no place in this collection. In this new category we must range the following documents:

1. The Rule of 1221. [20]

2. The Rule of the Clarisses, which we no longer possess in its original form. [21]

3. A sort of special instruction for ministers-general. [22]

4. A letter to St. Clara. [23]

5. Another letter to the same. [24]

6. A letter to Brother Leo. [25]

7. A few prayers. [26]

8. The benediction of Brother Leo. The original autograph, which is preserved in the treasury of Sacro Convento, has been very well reproduced by heliograph. [27]

As to the two famous hymns *Amor de caritade*[28] and *In foco l'amor mi mise*, [29] they cannot be attributed to St. Francis, at least in their present form.

It belongs to M. Monaci and his numerous and learned emulators to throw light upon these delicate questions by publishing in a scientific manner the earliest monuments of Italian poetry.

I have already spoken of several tracts of which assured traces have been found, though they themselves are lost. They are much more numerous than would at first be supposed. In the missionary zeal of the early years the Brothers would not concern themselves with collecting documents. We do not write our memoirs in the fulness of our youth.

We must also remember that Portiuncula had neither archives nor library. It was a chapel ten paces long, with a few huts gathered around it. The Order was ten years old before it had seen any other than a single book: a New Testament. The Brothers did not even keep this one. Francis, having nothing else, gave it to a poor woman who asked for alms, and when Pietro di Catania, his vicar, expressed his surprise at this prodigality: "Has she not given her two sons to the Order? " replied the master[30] quickly.

FOOTNOTES:

[1]   Collected first by Wadding (Antwerp, 1623, 4to), they have been published many times since then, particularly by De la Haye (Paris, 1641, f^o). These two editions having become scarce, were republished—in a very unsatisfactory manner— by the Abbé Horoy: *S. Francisci Assisiatis opera omnia* (Paris, 1880, 4to). For want of a more exact edition, that of Father Bernardo da Flvizzaiio is the most useful· *Opuscoli di S. Francesco d'Assisi*, 1 vol., 12mo, pp. 564, Florence, 1880. The Latin text is accompanied by an Italian translation.

[2]   *"Die Briefe, die unter seinem Namen gehen, mögen theilweise ächt sein. Aber sie tragen kaum etwas zur näheren Kenntniss bei und können daher fast ganz ausser Acht bleiben. "* Müller, *Die Anfänge des Minoritenordens*, Freiburg, 1 vol., 8vo, 1885, p. 3.

[3]   Pieces have been often attributed to St. Francis which do not belong to him; but those are unintentional errors and made without purpose. The desire for literary exactness is relatively of recent date, and it was easier for those who were ignorant of the author of certain Franciscan writings to attribute them to St. Francis than to admit their ignorance or to make deep researches.

[4]   For example, the first Rule; probably also a few canticles; a letter to the Brothers in France, Eccl., 6; another to the

Brothers in Bologna: *"Prædixerat per litteram in qua fuit plurimum latinum, "* Eccl., ib. ; a letter to Antony of Padua, other than the one we have, since on the witness of Celano it was addressed: *Fratri Antonio episcopo meo* (2 Cel., 3, 99); certain letters to St. Clara: *"Scripsit Claræ et sororibus ad consolationem litteram in quâ dabat benedictionem suam et absolvebat, "* etc. *Conform.* , f°. 185a, 1; cf. *Test. B. Claræ.* A. SS., Augusti, t. ii., p. 767: *"Plura scripta tradidit nobis, ne post mortem suam declinaremus a paupertate; "* certain letters to Cardinal Ugolini, 3 Soc., 67.

It is not to negligence alone that we must attribute the loss of many of the epistles: *"Quod nephas est cogitare, in provincia Marchie et in pluribus aliis* locis *testamentum beati Francisci mandaverunt (prelati ordinis) districte per obedientiam ab omnibus auferi et comburi. Et uni fratri devoto et sancto, cujus nomen est N. de Rocanato combuxerunt dicum testamentum super caput suum. Et toto conatu fuerunt solliciti, annulare scripta beati patris nostri Francisci, in quibus sua intentio de observantia regule declaratur. "* Ubertino di Casali, *apud Archiv.* , iii., pp. 168-169.

[5]   Italy is too obliging to artists, archæologists, and scholars not to do them the favor of disposing in a more practical manner this trust, the most precious of all Umbria. Even with the indefatigable kindness of the curator, M. Alessandro, and of the municipality of Assisi, it is very difficult to profit by these treasures heaped up in a dark room without a table to write upon.

[6]   In particular by Ehrle: *Die historischen Handschriften von S. Francesco in Assisi. Archiv.* , t. i., p. 484.

[7]   See pages 252 ff... and 283.

[8]   See pages 333 ff.

[9]   See pages 259 ff.

[10]   See page 325 ff.

[11]   See pages 322 ff.

[12]   See page 327.

[13]   I give it entire: "*Regina sapientia, Dominus te salvet, cum tua sorore sancta pura simplicitate. —Domina sancta paupertas, Domimus te salvet, cum tua sorore sancta humilitate. —Domina sancta caritas, Dominus te salvet, cum tua sorrore sancta obedientia. Sanctissimæ virtutes omnes, vos salvet Dominus, a quo venitis et proceditis.* " Its authenticity is guaranteed by a citation by Celano: 2 Cel., 3, 119. Cf. 126b and 127a.

[14]   See pages 304 f.

[15]   I shall not recur to this: the text is in the Conformities 138a 2.

[16]   The authenticity of this service, to which there is not a single allusion in the biographies of St. Francis, is rendered certain by the l ife of St. Clara: "*Officium crucis, prout crucis amator Franciscus instituerat (Clara) didicit et affectu simili frequentavit.* " A. SS., Augusti, t. ii., p. 761a.

[17]   It begins: *Illi qui volunt stare in heremis.* This text is also found in the Conformities, 143a, 1. Cf. 2 Cel., 3, 43; see p. 97.

[18]   *Nudis pedibus incedentes, funiculis cincti, tunicis griseis et talaribus peciatis, insuto capucio utentes... nihil sibi ultra noctem reservantes... libros continue suos... in forulis a collo dependentes bajulantes.* Historia Anglorum, Pertz: *Script.* , t. 28, p. 397. Cf. 2 Cel., 3, 135; *Fior.* , 5; *Spec.* , 45b.

[19]   See page 322 n.

[20]   See page 252.

[21]   See page 157.

[22]   See pages 318 ff.

[23]   See page 239.

[24]   See page 327.

[25]   See page 262.

[26] *a.* *Sanctus Dominus Deus noster.* Cf. *Spec.* , 126a; *Firmamentum,* 18b, 2; *Conform.* , 202b, 1.

   b. Ave Domina sancta. Cf. *Spec.* , 127a; *Conform.* , 138a, 2.

   c. Sancta Maria virgo. Cf. *Spec.* , 126b; *Conform.* , 202b, 2.

[27] Vide S. François, in 4to, Paris. 1885 (Plon), p. 233. The authenticity of this benediction appears to be well established, since it was already jealously guarded during the life of Thomas of Celano. No one has ever dreamed of requiring historical proof of this writing. Is this perhaps a mistake? The middle of the sheet is taken up with the benediction which was dictated to Brother Leo: *Benedicat tibi Dominus et custodiat te, ostendat faciem suam tibi et misereatur tui convertat vultum suum ad te et det tibi pacem.* At the bottom, Francis added the letter *tau.* ~[Greek: Tau]~, which was, so to speak, his signature (Bon., 51; 308), and the words: *Frater Leo Dominus benedicat te.*

   Then when this memorial became a part of the relics of the Saint, Brother Leo, to authenticate it in a measure, added the following notes: toward the middle: *Beatus Franciscus scripsit manu sua istam benedictionem mihi fratri Leoni;* toward the close: *Simili modo fecit istud signum thau cum capite manu sua.* But the most valuable annotation is found at the top of the sheet: *Beatus Franciscus duobus annis ante mortem suam fecit quadragesimam in loco Alvernæ ad honorem Beatæ Virginia Mariæ matris Dei et beati Michael archangeli a festo assumptionis sanctæ Mariæ Virginis usque ad festum sancti Michael septembris et facta est super eum manus Domini per visionem et allucotionem seraphym et impressionem stigmatum in corpore suo. Fecit has laudes ex alio latere catule scriptas et manu, sua scripsit gratias agens Domino de beneficio sibi collato.* Vide 2 Cel., 2, 18.

[28] Wadding gives the text according to St. Bernardino da Siena. *Opera,* t. iv., *sermo 16, extraord. et sermo feriæ sextæ Parasceves.* Amoni: *Legenda trium sociorum,* p. 166.

[29] Wadding has drawn the text from St. Bernardino, *loc. cit.* , *sermo iv., extraord.* It was also reproduced by Amoni, *loc. cit.* , p. 165. Two very curious versions may be found in the Miscellanea, 1888, pp. 96 and 190.

[30]   2 Cel., 3, 35. This took place under the vicariat of Pietro di Catania; consequently between September 29, 1220, and March 10, 1221.

II
BIOGRAPHIES PROPERLY SO CALLED

1. PRELIMINARY NOTE

To form a somewhat exact notion of the documents which are to occupy us, we must put them back into the midst of the circumstances in which they appeared, study them in detail, and determine the special value of each one.

Here, more than anywhere else, we must beware of facile theories and hasty generalizations. The same life described by two equally truthful contemporaries may take on a very different coloring. This is especially the case if the man concerned has aroused enthusiasm and wrath, if his inmost thought, his works, have been the subject of discussion, if the very men who were commissioned to realize his ideals and carry on his work are divided, and at odds with one another.

This was the case with St. Francis. In his lifetime and before his own eyes divergences manifested themselves, at first secretly, then in the light of day.

In a rapture of love he went from cottage to cottage, from castle to castle, preaching absolute poverty; but that buoyant enthusiasm, that unbounded idealism, could not last long. The Order of the Brothers Minor in process of growth was open not only to a few choice spirits aflame with mystic fervor, but to all men who aspired after a religious reformation; pious laymen, monks undeceived as to the virtues of the ancient Orders, priests shocked at the vices of the secular clergy, all brought with them—unintentionally no doubt and even unconsciously—too much of their old man not by degrees to transform the institution.

Francis perceived the peril several years before his death, and made every effort to avert it. Even in his dying hour we see him summoning all his powers to declare his Will once again, and as clearly as possible, and to conjure his Brothers never to touch the Rule, even under pretext of commenting upon or explaining it. Alas! four years had not rolled away when Gregory IX., at the prayer of the Brothers themselves, became the first one of a long series of pontiffs who have explained the Rule. [1]

Poverty, as Francis understood it, soon became only a memory. The unexampled success of the Order brought to it not merely new recruits, but money. How refuse it when there were so many works to found? Many of the friars discovered that their master had exaggerated many things, that shades of meaning were to be observed in the Rule, for example, between counsels and precepts. The door once opened to interpretations, it became impossible to close it. The Franciscan family began to be divided into opposing parties often difficult to distinguish.

At first there were a few restless, undisciplined men who grouped themselves around the older friars. The latter, in their character of first companions of the Saint, found a moral authority often greater than the official authority of the ministers and guardians. The people turned to them by instinct as to the true continuers of St. Francis's work. They were not far from right.

They had the vigor, the vehemence of absolute convictions; they could not have temporized had they desired to do so. When they emerged from their hermitages in the Apennines, their eyes shining with the fever of their ideas, absorbed in contemplation, their whole being spoke of the radiant visions they enjoyed; and the amazed and subdued multitude would kneel to kiss the prints of their feet with hearts mysteriously stirred.

A larger group was that of those Brothers who condemned these methods without being any the less saints. Born far away from Umbria, in countries where nature seems to be a step-mother, where adoration, far from being the instinctive act of a happy soul soaring upward to bless the heavenly Father, is, on the contrary, the despairing cry of an atom lost in immensity, they desired above all things a religious reformation, rational and profound. They dreamed of bringing the Church back to the purity of the ancient days, and saw in the vow of poverty, understood in its largest sense, the best means of struggling against the vices of the clergy; but they forgot the freshness, the Italian gayety, the sunny poetry that there had been in Francis's mission.

Full of admiration for him, they yet desired to enlarge the foundations of his work, and for that they would neglect no means of influence, certainly not learning.

This tendency was the dominant one in France, Germany, and England. In Italy it was represented by a very powerful party, powerful if not in the number, at least in the authority, of its representatives. This was the party favored by the papacy. It was the party of Brother Elias and all the ministers-general of the Order in the thirteenth century, if we except Giovanni di Parma (1247-1257) and Raimondo Gaufridi (1289-1295).

In Italy a third group, the liberals, was much more numerous; men of mediocrity to whom monastic life appeared the most facile existence, vagrant monks happy to secure an aftermath of success by displaying the new Rule, formed in this country the greater part of the Franciscan family.

We can understand without difficulty that documents emanating from such different quarters must bear the impress of their origin. The men who are to bring us their testimony are combatants in the struggle over the question of poverty, a struggle which for two centuries agitated the Church, aroused all consciences, and which had its monsters and its martyrs.

To determine the value of these witnesses we must first of all discover their origin. It is evident that the narratives of the no-compromise party of the right or the left can have but slender value where controverted points are concerned; whence the conclusion that the authority of a narrator may vary from page to page, or even from line to line.

These considerations, so simple that one almost needs to beg pardon for uttering them, have not, however, guided those who have studied St. Francis's life. The most learned, like Wadding and Papini, have brought together the narratives of different biographers, here and there pruning those that are too contradictory; but they have done this at random, with neither rule nor method, guided by the impression of the moment.

The long work of the Bollandist Suysken is vitiated by an analogous fault; fixed in his principle that the oldest documents are always the best, [2] he takes his stand upon the first Life of Thomas of Celano as upon an impregnable rock, and judges all other legends by that one. [3]

When we connect the documents with the disturbed circumstances which brought them into being, some of them lose a little of their authority, others which have been neglected, as being in contradiction with witnesses who have become so to say official, suddenly recover credit, and in fact all gain a new life which doubles their interest.

This altered point of view in the valuation of the sources, this criticism which I am inclined to call reciprocal and organic, brings about profound alterations in the biography of St. Francis. By a phenomenon which may appear strange we end by sketching a portrait of him much more like that which exists in the popular imagination of Italy than that made by the learned historians above mentioned.

When Francis died (1226) the parties which divided the Order had already entered into conflict. That event precipitated the crisis: Brother Elias had been for five years exercising the functions of minister-general with the title of vicar. He displayed an amazing activity. Intrenched in the confidence of Gregory IX. he removed the *Zelanti* from their charges, strengthened the discipline even in the most remote provinces, obtained numerous privileges from the curia, and with incredible rapidity prepared for the building of the double basilica, destined for the repose of the ashes of the Stigmatized Saint; but notwithstanding all his efforts, the chapter of 1227 set him aside and chose Giovanni Parenti as minister-general.

Furious at this check, he immediately set all influences to work to be chosen at the following chapter. It even seems as if he paid no attention to the nomination of Giovanni Parenti, and continued to go on as if he had been minister. [4]

Very popular among the Assisans, who were dazzled by the magnificence of the monument which was springing up on the *Hill of Hell*, now become the *Hill of Paradise*, sure of being supported by a considerable party in the Order and by the pope, he pushed forward the work on the basilica with a decision and success perhaps unique in the annals of architecture. [5]

All this could not be done without arousing the indignation of the Zealots of poverty. When they saw a monumental poor-box, designed to receive the alms of the faithful, upon the tomb of him who had forbidden his disciples the mere contact of money, it seemed to them that Francis's prophecy of the apostasy of a part of the Order was about to be fulfilled. A tempest of revolt swept over the hermitages of Umbria. Must they not, by any means, prevent this abomination in the holy place?

They knew that Elias was terrible in his severities, but his opponents felt in themselves courage to go to the last extremity, and suffer everything to defend their convictions. One day the poor-box was found shattered by Brother Leo and his friends. [6]

To this degree of intensity the struggle had arrived. At this crisis the first legend appeared.

2. First Life by Thomas of Celano[7]

Thomas of Celano, in writing this legend, to which he was later to return for its completion, obeyed an express order of Pope Gregory IX. [8]

Why did he not apply to one of the Brothers of the Saint's immediate circle? The talent of this author might explain this choice, but besides the fact that literary considerations would in this case hold a secondary place, Brother Leo and several others proved later that they also knew how to handle the pen.

If Celano was put in trust with the official biography, it is because, being equally in sympathy with Gregory IX. and Brother Elias, his absence had kept him out of the conflicts which had marked the last years of Francis's life. Of an irenic temper, he belonged to the category of those souls who easily persuade themselves that obedience is the first of virtues, that every superior is a saint; and if unluckily he is not, that we should none the less act as though he were.

We have some knowledge of his life. A native of Celano in the Abruzzi, he discreetly observes that his family was noble, even adding, with a touch of artless simplicity, that the master had a peculiar regard for noble and educated Brothers. He entered the Order about 1215, [9] on the return of Francis from Spain.

At the chapter of 1221 Cæsar of Speyer, charged with the mission to Germany, took him among those who were to accompany him. [10] In 1223 he was named custode of Mayence, Worms, Cologne, and Speyer. In April of the same year, when Cæsar returned to Italy, devoured with the longing to see St. Francis again, he commissioned

Celano to execute his functions until the arrival of the new provincial. [11]

We have no information as to where he was after the chapter-general held at Speyer September 8, 1223. He must have been in Assisi in 1228, for his account of the canonization is that of an eye-witness. He was there again in 1230, and doubtless clothed with an important office, since he could commit to Brother Giordano the relics of St. Francis. [12]

Written in a pleasing style, very often poetic, his work breathes an affecting admiration for his hero; his testimony at once makes itself felt as sincere and true: when he is partial it is without intention and even without his knowledge. The weak point in this biography is the picture which it outlines of the relations between Brother Elias and the founder of the Order: from the chapters devoted to the last two years we receive a very clear impression that Elias was named by Francis to succeed him. [13]

Now if we reflect that at the time when Celano wrote, Giovanni Parenti was minister-general, we at once perceive the bearing of these indications. [14] Every opportunity is seized to give a preponderating importance to Elias. [15] It is a true manifesto in his favor.

Have we reason to blame Celano? I think not. We must simply remember that his work might with justice be called the legend of Gregory IX. Elias was the pope's man, and the biography is worked up from the information he gave. He could not avoid dwelling with peculiar satisfaction upon his intimacy with Francis.

On the other hand, we cannot expect to find here such details as might have sustained the pretension of the adversaries of Elias, those unruly Zealots who were already proudly adorning themselves with the title of *Companions of the Saint* and endeavoring to constitute a sort of spiritual aristocracy in the Order. Among them were four who during the last two years had not, so to say, quitted Francis. We can imagine how difficult it was not to speak of them. Celano carefully omits to mention their names under pretext of sparing their modesty; [16] but by the praises lavished upon Gregory IX., Brother Elias, [17] St. Clara, [18] and even upon very secondary persons, he shows that his discretion is far from being always so alert.

All this is very serious, but we must not exaggerate it. There is an evident partiality, but it would be unjust to go farther and believe, as men did later, that the last part of Francis's life was an active struggle against the very person of Elias. A struggle there surely was, but it was against tendencies whose spring Francis did not perceive. He carried with him to his tomb his delusion as to his co-laborer.

For that matter this defect is after all secondary so far as the physiognomy of Francis himself is concerned. In Celano's Life, as in the Three Companions or the Fioretti, he appears with a smile for all joys, and floods of tears for all woes; we feel everywhere the restrained emotion of the writer; his heart is subjected by the moral beauty of his hero.

3. SURVEY OF THE HISTORY OF THE ORDER FROM 1230-1244

When Thomas of Celano closed his legend he perceived more than anyone the deficiencies of his work, for which he had been able to collect but insufficient material.

Elias and the other Assisan brothers had told him of Francis's youth and his activity in Umbria; but besides that he would have preferred, whether from prudence or from love of peace, to keep silence upon certain events, [19] there were long periods upon which he had not received a single item of information. [20]

He therefore seems to indicate his intention of resuming and completing his work. [21]

This is not the place to write the history of the Order, but a few facts are necessary to put the documents into their proper surroundings.

Elected minister-general in 1232, Brother Elias took advantage of the fact to labor with indomitable energy toward the realization of his own ideas. In all the provinces new collections were organized for the Basilica of Assisi, the work upon which was pushed with an activity which however injured neither the strength of the edifice nor the beauty of its details, which are as finished and perfect as those of any monument in Europe.

We may conceive of the enormous sums which it had been necessary to raise in order to complete such an enterprise in so short a time.

More than that, Brother Elias exacted absolute obedience from all his subordinates; naming and removing the provincial ministers according to his personal views, he neglected to convoke the chapter-general, and sent his emissaries under the name of visitors into all the provinces to secure the execution of his orders.

The moderate party in Germany, France, and England very soon found his yoke insupportable. It was hard for them to be directed by an Italian minister resident at Assisi, a small town quite aside from the highways of civilization, entirely a stranger to the scientific movement concentred in the universities of Oxford, Paris, and Bologna.

In the indignation of the *Zelanti* against Elias and his contempt for the Rule, they found a decisive support. Very soon the minister had for his defence nothing but his own energy, and the favor of the pope and of the few Italian moderates. By a great increase of vigilance and severity he repressed several attempts at revolt.

His adversaries, however, succeeded in establishing secret intelligence at the court of Rome; even the pope's confessor was gained; yet in spite of all these circumstances, the success of the conspiracy was still uncertain when the chapter of 1239 opened.

Gregory IX., still favorable to Elias, [22] presided. Fear gave sudden courage to the conspirators; they threw their accusations in their enemy's face.

Thomas of Eccleston gives a highly colored narrative of what took place. Elias was proud, violent, even threatening. There were cries and vociferations from both sides; they were about to come to blows when a few words from the pope restored silence. He had made up his mind to abandon his *protégé*. He asked for his resignation. Elias indignantly refused.

Gregory IX. then explained that in keeping him in charge he had thought himself acting in accordance with the wishes of the majority: that he had no intention to dominate the Order, and, since the Brothers no longer desired Elias, he declared him deposed from the generalate.

The joy of the victors, says Eccleston, was immense and ineffable. They chose Alberto di Pisa, provincial of England, to succeed him, and from that time bent all their efforts to represent Elias as a creature of Frederick II. [23] The former minister wrote indeed to the pope to explain his conduct, but the letter did not reach its destination. It must have reached the hands of his successor, and not been sent forward; when Alberto of Pisa died it was found in his tunic. [24]

All the fury of the aged pontiff was unchained against Elias. One must read the documents to see to what a height his anger could rise. The friar retorted with a virulence which though less wordy was far more overpowering. [25]

These events gained an indescribable notoriety[26] all over Europe and threw the Order into profound disturbance. Many of the partisans of Elias became convinced that they had been deceived by an impostor, and they drew toward the group of Zealots, who never ceased to demand the observance pure and simple of the Rule and the Will.

Thomas of Celano was of this number. [27] With profound sadness he saw the innumerable influences that were secretly undermining the Franciscan institute and menacing it with ruin. Already a refrain was going the rounds of the convents, singing the victory of Paris over Assisi, that is, of learning over poverty.

The Zealots gained new courage. Unaccustomed to the subtleties of ecclesiastical politics, they did not perceive that the pope, while condemning Brother Elias, had in nowise modified the general course which he had marked out for the Order. The ministers-general, Alberto di Pisa, 1239-1240, Aymon of Faversham, 1240-1244, Crescentius de Jesi, 1244-1247, were all, with different shades of meaning, representatives of the moderate party.

Thomas of Celano's first legend had become impossible. The prominence there given to Elias was almost a scandal. The necessity of working it over and completing it became clearly evident at the chapter of Genoa (1244).

All the Brothers who had anything to tell about Francis's life were invited to commit it to writing and send it to the minister Crescentius de Jesi. [28] The latter immediately caused a tract to be drawn up in the form of a dialogue, commencing with the words: *"Venerabilium gesta Patrum. "* So soon after as the time of Bernard de Besse, only fragments of this were left. [29]

But happily several of the works which saw the light in consequence of the decision of this chapter have been preserved to us. It is to this that we owe the Legend of the Three Companions and the Second Life by Thomas of Celano.

4. LEGEND OF THE THREE COMPANIONS[30]

The life of St. Francis which has come down to us under the name of the Legend of the Three Companions was finished on August 11, 1246, in a little convent in the vale of Rieti, which appears often in the course of this history, that of Greccio. This hermitage had been Francis's favorite abode, especially in the latter part of his life. He had thus made it doubly dear to the hearts of his disciples. [31] It naturally became, from the earliest days of the Order, the headquarters of the Observants, [32] and it remains through all the centuries one of the purest centres of Franciscan piety.

The authors of this legend were men worthy to tell St. Francis's story, and perhaps the most capable of doing it: the friars Leo, Angelo, and Rufino. All three had lived in intimacy with him, and had been his companions through the most important years. More than this, they took the trouble to go to others for further information, particularly to Filippo, the visitor of the Clarisses, to Illuminato di Rieti, Masseo di Marignano, John, the confidant of Egidio, and Bernardo di Quintavalle.

Such names as these promise much, and happily we are not disappointed in our expectation. As it has come down to us, this document is the only one worthy from the point of view of history to be placed beside the First Life by Celano.

The names of the authors and the date of the composition indicate before examination the tendency with which it is likely to be in harmony. It is the first manifesto of the Brothers who remained faithful to the spirit and letter of the Rule. This is confirmed by an attentive reading; it is at least as much a panegyric of Poverty as a history of St. Francis.

We naturally expect to see the Three Companions relating to us with a very particular delight the innumerable features of the legends of which Greccio was the theatre; we turn to the end of the volume, expecting to find the story of the last years of which they were witnesses, and are lost in surprise to find nothing of the kind.

While the first half of the work describes Francis's youth, filling out here and there Celano's First Life, the second[33] is devoted to a picture of the early days of the Order, a picture of incomparable freshness and intensity of life; but strangely enough, after having told us so much at length of Francis's youth and then of the first days of the Order, the story abruptly leaps over from the year 1220 to the death and the canonization, to which after all only a few pages are given. [34]

This is too extraordinary to be the result of chance. What has happened? It is evident that the Legend of the Three Companions as we have it to-day is only a fragment of the original, which was no doubt revised, corrected, and considerably cut down by the authorities of the Order before they would permit it to be circulated. [35] If the authors had been interrupted in their work, and obliged to cut short the end, as might have been the case, they would have said so in their letter of envoy, but there are still other arguments in favor of our hypothesis.

Brother Leo having had the first and principal part in the production of the work of the Three Companions, it is often called Brother Leo's Legend; now Brother Leo's Legend is several times cited by Ubertini di Casali, arraigned before the court of Avignon by the party of the Common Observance. Evidently Ubertini would have taken good care not to appeal to an apocryphal document; a false citation would have been enough to bring him to confusion, and his enemies would not have failed to make the most of his imprudence. We have at hand all the documents of the trial, [36] attacks, replies, counter replies, and nowhere do we see the Liberals accuse their adversary of falsehood. For that matter, the latter makes his citations with a precision that admits of no cavil. [37] He appeals to writings to be found in a press in the convent of Assisi, of which he gives sometimes a copy, sometimes an original. [38] We are then authorized to conclude that we have here fragments which have survived the suppression of the last and most important part of the Legend of the Three Companions.

It is not surprising that the work of Francis's dearest friends should have been so seriously mutilated. It was the manifesto of a party that Crescentius was hunting down with all his power.

After the fleeting reaction of the generalate of Giovanni di Parma we shall see a man of worth like St. Bonaventura moving for the suppression of all the primitive legends that his own compilation may be substituted for them.

It is truly singular that no one has perceived the fragmentary state of the work of the Three Companions. The prologue alone might have suggested this idea. Why should it take three to write a few pages? Why this solemn enumeration of Brothers whose testimony and collaboration are asked for? There would be a surprising disproportion between the effort and the result.

More than all, the authors say that they shall not stop at relating the miracles, but they desire above all to exhibit the ideas of Francis and his life with the Brothers, but we search in vain for any account of miracles in what we now have. [39]

An Italian translation of this legend, published by Father Stanislaus Melchiorri, [40] has suddenly given me an indirect confirmation of this point of view. This monk is only its publisher, and has simply been able to discover that in 1577 it was taken from a very ancient manuscript by a certain Muzio Achillei di San Severino. [41]

This Italian translation contained only the last chapters of the legend, those which tell of the death, the stigmata, and the translation of the remains. [42] It was, then, made at a time when the suppressed portion had not been replaced by a short summary of the other legends.

From all this two conclusions emerge for the critics: 1. This final summary has not the same authority as the rest of the work, since the time when it was added is unknown. 2. Fragments of a legend by Brother Leo or by the Three Companions scattered through later compilations may be perfectly authentic.

In its present condition this legend of the Three Companions is the finest piece of Franciscan literature, and one of the most delightful productions of the Middle Ages. There is something indescribably sweet, confiding, chaste, in these pages, an energy of virile youth which the Fioretti suggest but never attain to. At more than six hundred years of distance the purest dream that ever thrilled the Christian Church seems to live again.

These friars of Greccio, who, scattered over the mountain, under the shade of the olive-trees, passed their days in singing the Hymn of the Sun, are the true models of the primitive Umbrian Masters. They are all alike; they are awkwardly posed; everything in and around them sins against the most elementary rules of art, and yet their memory pursues you, and when you have long forgotten the works of impeccable modern artists you recall without effort these creations of those unknown painters; for love calls for love, and these vapid personages have very true and pure hearts, a more than human love shines forth from their whole being, they speak to you and make you better.

Such is this book, the first utterance of the Spiritual Franciscans, in which we already see the coming to life of some of those bold doctrines that not only divided the Franciscan family into two hostile branches, but which were to bring some of their defenders to the heretic's stake. [43]

5. FRAGMENTS OF THE SUPPRESSED PART OF THE LEGEND OF THE THREE COMPANIONS

We may now take a step forward and try to group the fragments of the Legend of the Three Companions, or of Brother Leo, which are to be found in later writings.

We must here be more than ever on our guard against absolute theories; one of the most fruitful principles of historic criticism is to prefer contemporary documents, or at least those which are nearest them; but even with these it is necessary to use a little discretion.

It seems impossible to attack the reasoning of the Bollandists, who refuse to know anything of legends written after that of St. Bonaventura (1260), under pretext that, coming after several other authorized biographies, he was better situated than anyone for getting information and completing the work of his predecessors. [44] In reality this is absurd, for it assumes that Bonaventura undertook to write as a historian. This is to forget that he wrote not only for the purpose of edification, but also as minister-general of the Minor Brothers. From this fact his first duty was to keep silent on many facts, and those not the least interesting. What shall we say of a biography where Francis's Will is not even mentioned?

It is easy to turn away from a writing of the fourteenth century, on the ground that the author did not see what was going on a hundred years before; still we must not forget that many books of the end of the Middle Ages resemble those old mansions at which four or five generators have toiled. An inscription on their front often only shows the touch of the last restorer or the last destroyer, and the names which are set forth with the greatest complacency are not always those of the real workmen.

Such have been many Franciscan books; to attribute them to any one author would be impracticable; very different hands have worked upon them, and such an amalgam has its own charm and interest.

Turning them over—I had almost said associating with them—we come to see clearly into this tangled web, for every work of man bears the trace of the hand that made it: this trace may perhaps be of an almost imperceptible delicacy; it exists none the less, ready to reveal itself to practised eyes. What is more impersonal than the photograph of a landscape or of a painting, and yet among several hundreds of proofs the amateur will go straight to the work of the operator he prefers.

These reflections were suggested by the careful study of a curious book printed many times since the sixteenth century, the *Speculum Vitæ S. Francisci et sociorum ejus.* [45] A complete study of this work, its sources, its printed editions, the numerous differences in the manuscripts, would by itself require a volume and an epitome of the history of the Order. I can give here only a few notes, taking for base the oldest edition, that of 1504.

The confusion which reigns here is frightful. Incidents in the life of Francis and his companions are brought together with no plan; several of them are repeated after the interval of a few pages in a quite different manner; [46] certain chapters are so awkwardly introduced that the compiler has forgotten to remove the number that they bore in the work from which he borrowed them; [47] finally, to our great surprise, we find several *Incipit.* [48]

However, with a little perseverance we soon perceive a few openings in the labyrinth. In the first place, here are several chapters of the legend of Bonaventura which seem to have been put in the van as if to protect the rest of the book. If we abstract them and the whole series of chapters from the Fioretti, we shall have diminished the work by nearly three-quarters.

If we take away two more chapters taken from St. Bernard of Clairvaux and those containing Franciscan prayers, or various attestations concerning the indulgence of Portiuncula, we finally arrive at a sort of residue, if the expression may be forgiven, of a remarkable homogeneity.

Here the style is very different from that in the surrounding pages, closely recalling that of the Three Companions; a single thought inspires these pages, that the corner-stone of the Order is the love of poverty.

Why should we not have here some fragments of the original legend of the Three Companions? We find here nothing which does not fit in with what we know, nothing which suggests the embellishments of a late tradition.

To confirm this hypothesis come different passages which we find cited by Ubertini di Casali and by Angelo Clareno as being by Brother Leo, and an attentive comparison of the text shows that these authors can neither have drawn them from the Speculum nor the Speculum from them.

There is, besides, one phrase which, apart from the inspiration and style, will suffice at the first glance to mark the common origin of most of these pieces. [49] *Nos qui cum ipso fuimus.* "We who have been with him. " These words, which recur in almost every incident, [49] are in many cases only a grateful tribute to their spiritual father, but sometimes, too, they have a touch of bitterness. These hermits of Greccio suddenly recall to mind their rights. Are we not the only, the true interpreters of the Saint's instructions—we who lived continually with him; we who, hour after hour, have meditated upon his words, his sighs, and his hymns?

We can understand that such pretensions were not to the taste of the Common Observance, and that Crescentius, with an incontestable authority, has suppressed nearly all this legend. [51]

As for the fragments that have been preserved to us, though they furnish many details about the last years of St. Francis's life, they still are not those whose loss is so much to be regretted. The authors who reproduce them were defending a cause. We owe them little more than the incidents which in one way or another concern the question of poverty. They had nothing to do with the other accounts, as they were not writing a biography. But even within these narrow limits these fragments are in the first order of importance; and I have not hesitated to use them largely. It is needless to say that while ascribing their origin to the Three Companions, and in particular to Brother Leo, we must not suppose that we have the very letter in the texts which have come down to us. The pieces given by Ubertini di Casali and Angelo Clareno are actual citations, and deserve full confidence as such. As for those which are preserved to us in the Speculum, they may often have been abridged, explanatory notes may have slipped into the text, but nowhere do we find interpolations in the bad sense of the word. [52]

Finally, if we compare the fragments with the corresponding accounts in the Second Life of Celano, we see that the latter has often borrowed verbatim from Brother Leo, but generally he has considerably abridged the passages, adding reflections here and there, especially retouching the style to make it more elegant.

Such a comparison soon proves that Brother Leo's narratives are the original and that it is impossible to see in them a later amplification of those of Thomas of Celano, as we might at first be tempted to think them. [53]

6. SECOND LIFE BY THOMAS OF CELANO[54]

First Part

In consequence of the decision of the chapter of 1244 search was begun in all quarters for memorials of the early times of the Order. In view of the ardor of this inquiry, in which zeal for the glory of the Franciscan institute certainly cast the interests of history into the background, the minister-general, Crescentius, was obliged to take certain precautions.

Many of the pieces that he received were doing double duty; others might contradict one another; many of them, under color of telling the life of the Saint, had no other object than to oppose the present to the past.

It soon became imperative to constitute a sort of commission charged to study and coördinate all this matter. [55] What more natural than to put Thomas of Celano at its head? Ever since the approbation of the first legend by Gregory IX. he had appeared to be in a sense the official historiographer of the Order. [56]

This view accords perfectly with the contents of the seventeen chapters which contain the first part of the second legend. It offers itself at the outset as a compilation. Celano is surrounded with companions who help him. [57] A more attentive examination shows that its principal source is the Legend of the Three Companions, which the compilers worked over, sometimes filling out certain details, more often making large excisions.

Everything that does not concern St. Francis is ruthlessly proscribed; we feel the well-defined purpose to leave in the background the disciples who so complacently placed themselves in the foreground. [58]

The work of the Three Companions had been finished August 11, 1246. On July 13, 1247, the chapter of Lyons put an end to the powers of Crescentius. It is, therefore, between these two dates that we must place the composition of the first part of Thomas of Celano's Second Life. [59]

7. SECOND LIFE BY THOMAS OF CELANO[59]

Second Part

The election of Giovanni di Parma (1247-1257) as successor of Crescentius was a victory for the Zealots. This man, in whose work-table the birds came to make their nests, [61] was to astonish the world by his virtues. No one saw more deeply into St. Francis's heart, no one was more worthy to take up and continue his work.

He soon asked Celano to resume his work. [62] The latter was perhaps alone at first, but little by little a group of collaborators formed itself anew about him. [63] Thenceforth nothing prevented his doing with that portion of the work of the Three Companions which Crescentius had suppressed what he had already done with the part he had approved.

The Legend of Brother Leo has thus come down to us, entirely worked over by Thomas of Celano, abridged and with all its freshness gone, but still of capital importance in the absence of the major part of the original.

The events of which we possess two accounts permit us to measure the extent of our loss. We find, in fact, in Celano's compilation all that we expected to find in the Three Companions: the incidents belong especially to the last two years of Francis's life, and the scene of many of them is either Greccio or one of the hermitages of the vale of Rieti; [64] according to tradition, Brother Leo was the hero of a great number of the incidents here related[65] and all the citations that Ubertini di Casali makes from Brother Leo's book find their correspondents here. [66]

This second part of the Second Life perfectly reflects the new circumstances to which it owes its existence. The question of Poverty dominates everything; [67] the struggle between the two parties in the Order reveals itself on every page; the collaborators are determined that each event narrated shall be an indirect lesson to the Liberals, to whom they oppose the Spirituals; the popes had commented on the Rule in the large sense; they, on their side, undertook to comment on it in a sense at once literal and spiritual, by the actions and words of its author himself.

History has hardly any part here except as the vehicle of a thesis, a fact which diminishes nothing of the historic value of the information given in the course of these pages. But while in Celano's First Life and in the Legend of the Three Companions the facts succeed one another organically, here they are placed side by side. Therefore when we come to read this work we are sensible of a fall; even from the literary point of view the inferiority makes itself cruelly felt. Instead of a poem we have before us a catalogue, very cleverly made, it is true, but with no power to move us.

8. NOTES ON A FEW SECONDARY DOCUMENTS

a. *Celano's Life of St. Francis for Use in the Choir.*

Thomas of Celano made also a short legend for use in the choir. It is divided into nine lessons and served for the Franciscan breviaries up to the time when St. Bonaventura made his *Legenda Minor*.

That of Celano may be found in part (the first three lessons) in the Assisi MS. 338, fol. 52a-53b; it is preceded by a letter of envoy: *"Rogasti me frater Benedicte, ut de legenda B. P. N. F. quædam exciperem et in novem lectionum seriem ordinarem... etc. B. Franciscus de civitate Assisii ortus a puerilibus annis nutritus extitit insolenter. "*

This work has no historic importance.

b. *Life of St. Francis in Verse.*

In the list of biographers has sometimes been counted a poem in hexameter verse[68] the text of which was edited in 1882 by the lamented Cristofani. [69]

This work does not furnish a single new historic note. It is the Life by Celano in verse and nothing more; the author's desire was to figure as a poet. It is superfluous, therefore, to concern ourselves with it. [69]

c. *Biography of St. Francis by Giovanni di Ceperano.*

One of the biographies which disappeared, no doubt in consequence of the decision of the chapter of 1266, [71] is that of Giovanni di Ceperano. The resemblance of his name to that of Thomas of Celano has occasioned much confusion. [72] The most precious information which we have respecting him is given by Bernard of Besse in the opening of his *De laudibus St. Francisci*: *"Plenam virtutibus B. Francisci vitam scripsit in Italia exquisitæ vir eloquentiæ fr. Thomas jubente Domino Gregorio papa IX. et eam quæ incipit: Quasi stella matutina vir venerabilis Dominus et fertur Joannes, Apostolicæ sedis notarius. "*[73]

In the face of so precise a text all doubt as to the existence of the work of Giovanni di Ceperano is impossible. The Reverend Father Denifle has been able to throw new light upon this question. In a manuscript containing the liturgy of the Brothers Minor and finished in 1256 he found the nine lessons for the festival of St. Francis preceded by the title: *Ex gestis ejus abbreviatis quæ sic incipiunt: Quasi stella* (*Zeitschrift für kath. Theol.* , vii., p. 710. Cf. *Archiv.* , i., p. 148). This summary of Ceperano's work gives, as we should expect, no new information; but perhaps we need not despair of finding the very work of this author.

d. *Life of St. Francis by Brother Julian.*

It was doubtless about 1230 that Brother Julian, the Teuton, who had been chapel-master at the court of the King of France, was commissioned to put the finishing touches to the Office of St. Francis. [74] Evidently such a work would contain nothing original, and its loss is little felt.

9. LEGEND OF ST. BONAVENTURA

Under the generalate of Giovanni di Parma (1247-1257) the Franciscan parties underwent modifications, in consequence of which their opposition became still more striking than before.

The Zelanti, with the minister-general at their head, enthusiastically adopted the views of Gioacchino di Fiore. The predictions of the Calabrian abbot corresponded too well with their inmost convictions for any other course to be possible: they seemed to see Francis, as a new Christ, inaugurating the third era of the world.

For a few years these dreams moved all Europe; the faith of the Joachimites was so ardent that it made its way by its own force; sceptics like Salimbeni told themselves that on the whole it was surely wiser not to be taken unawares by the great catastrophe of 1260, and hastened in crowds to the cell of Hyères to be initiated by Hugues de Digne in the mysteries of the new times: as to the people, they waited, trembling, divided between hope and terror. Nevertheless their adversaries did not consider themselves beaten, and the Liberal party still remained the most numerous. Of an angelic purity, Giovanni di Parma believed in the omnipotence of example: events showed how mistaken he was; at the close of his term of office scandals were not less flagrant than ten years earlier. [75]

Between these two extreme parties, against which he was to proceed with equal rigor, stood that of the Moderates, to which belonged St. Bonaventura. [76]

A mystic, but of a formal and orthodox mysticism, he saw the revolution toward which the Church was hastening if the party of the eternal Gospel was to triumph; its victory would not be that of this or that heresy in detail, it would be, with brief delay, the ruin of the entire ecclesiastical edifice; he was too perspicacious not to see that in the last analysis the struggle then going on was that of the individual conscience against authority. This explains, and up to a certain point gains him pardon for, his severities against his opponents; he was supported by the court of Rome and by all those who desired to make the Order a school at once of piety and of learning.

No sooner was he elected general than, with a purpose that never knew hesitation, and a will whose firmness made itself everywhere felt, he took his steps to forward this double aim. On the very morrow of his nomination he sketched the programme of reforms against the Liberal party, and at the same time secured the summons of the Joachimite Brothers before an ecclesiastical tribunal at Città-della-Pieve. This tribunal condemned them to perpetual imprisonment, and it needed the personal intervention of Cardinal Ottobonus, the future Adrian V., for Giovanni di Parma to be left free to retire to the Convent of Greccio.

The first chapter held under the presidence of Bonaventura, in the extended decisions of which we find everywhere tokens of his influence, assembled at Narbonne in 1260. He was then commissioned to compose a new life of St. Francis. [77]

We easily understand the anxieties to which this decision of the Brothers was an answer. The number of legends had greatly increased, for besides those which we have first studied or noted there were others in existence which have completely disappeared, and it had become equally difficult for the Brothers who went forth on missions either to make a choice between them or to carry them all.

The course of the new historian was therefore clearly marked out: he must do the work of compiler and peacemaker. He failed in neither. His book is a true sheaf, or rather it is a millstone under which the indefatigable author has pressed, somewhat at hazard, the sheaves of his predecessors. Most of the time he inserts them just as they are, confining himself to the work of harvesting them and weeding out the tares.

Therefore, when we reach the end of this voluminous work we have a very vague impression of St. Francis. We see that he was a saint, a very great saint, since he performed an innumerable quantity of miracles, great and small; but we feel very much as if we had been going through a shop of objects of piety. All these statues, whether they are called St. Anthony the Abbot, St. Dominic, St. Theresa, or St. Vincent de Paul, have the same expression of mincing humility, of a somewhat shallow ecstasy. These are saints, if you please, miracle-workers; they are not men; he who made them made them by rule, by process; he has put nothing of his heart in these ever-bowed foreheads, these lips with their wan smile.

God forbid that I should say or think that St. Bonaventura was not worthy to write a life of St. Francis, but the circumstances controlled his work, and it is no injustice to him to say that it is fortunate for Francis, and especially for us, that we have another biography of the Poverello than that of the Seraphic Doctor.

Three years after, in 1263, he brought his completed work to the chapter-general convoked under his presidence at Pisa. It was there solemnly approved. [78]

It is impossible to say whether they thought that the presence of the new legend would suffice to put the old ones out of mind, but it seems that at this time nothing was said about the latter.

It was not so at the following chapter. This one, held at Paris, came to a decision destined to have disastrous results for the primitive Franciscan documents. This decree, emanating from an assembly presided over by Bonaventura in person, is too important not to be quoted textually: "Item, the Chapter-general ordains on obedience that all the legends of the Blessed Francis formerly made shall be destroyed. The Brothers who shall find any without the Order must try to make away with them since the legend made by the General is compiled from accounts of three who almost always accompanied the Blessed Francis; all that they could certainly know and all that is proven has been carefully inserted therein. "[79] It would have been difficult to be more precise. We see the perseverance with which Bonaventura carried on his struggle against the extreme parties. This decree explains the almost complete disappearance of the manuscripts of Celano and the Three Companions, since in certain collections even those of Bonaventura's legend are hardly to be found.

As we have seen, Bonaventura aimed to write a sort of official or canonical biography; he succeeded only too well. Most of the accounts that we already know have gone into his collection, but not without at times suffering profound mutilations. We are not surprised to find him passing over Francis's youth with more discretion than Celano in the First Life, but we regret to find him ornamenting and materializing some of the loveliest incidents of the earlier legends.

It is not enough for him that Francis hears the crucifix of St. Daraian speak; he pauses to lay stress on the assertion that he heard it *corporeis auribus* and that no one was in the chapel at that moment! Brother Monaldo at the chapter of Arles sees St. Francis appear *corporeis oculis*. He often abridges his predecessors, but this is not his invariable rule. When he reaches the account of the stigmata he devotes long pages to it, [79] relates a sort of consultation held by St. Francis as to whether he could conceal them, and adds several miracles due to these sacred wounds; further on he returns to the subject to show a certain Girolamo, Knight of Assisi, desiring to touch with his hands the miraculous nails. [81] On the other hand, he uses a significant discretion wherever the companions of the Saint are in question. He names only three of the first eleven disciples, [82] and no more mentions Brothers Leo, Angelo, Rufino, Masseo, than their adversary, Brother Elias.

As to the incidents which we find for the first time in this collection, they hardly make us regret the unknown sources which must have been at the service of the famous Doctor; it would appear that the healing of Morico, restored to health by a few pellets of bread soaked in the oil of the lamp which burned before the altar of the Virgin, [83] has little more importance for the life of St. Francis than the story of the sheep given to Giacomina di Settesoli which awakened its mistress to summon her to go to mass. [84] What shall we think of that other sheep, of Portiuncula, which hastened to the choir whenever it heard the psalmody of the friars, and kneeled devoutly for the elevation of the Holy Sacrament? [85]

All these incidents, the list of which might be enlarged, [86] betrays the working-over of the legend. St. Francis becomes a great thaumaturgist, but his physiognomy loses its originality.

The greatest fault of this work is, in fact, the vagueness of the figure of the Saint. While in Celano there are the large lines of a soul-history, a sketch of the affecting drama of a man who attains to the conquest of himself, with Bonaventura all this interior action disappears before divine interventions; his heart is, so to speak, the geometrical locality of a certain number of visitants; he is a passive instrument in the hands of God, and we really cannot see why he should have been chosen rather than another.

And yet Bonaventura was an Italian; he had seen Umbria; he must have knelt and celebrated the sacred mysteries in Portiuncula, that cradle of the noblest of religious reformations; he had conversed with Brother Egidio, and must have heard from his lips an echo of the first Franciscan fervor; but, alas! nothing of that rapture passed into his book, and if the truth must be told, I find it quite inferior to much later documents, to the Fioretti, for example; for they understood, at least in part, the soul of Francis; they felt the throbbing of that heart, with all its sensitiveness, admiration, indulgence, love, independence, and absence of carefulness.

10. DE LAUDIBUS OF BERNARD OF BESSE[87]

Bonaventura's work did not discourage the biographers. The historic value of their labor is almost nothing, and we shall not even attempt to catalogue them.

Bernard of Besse, a native probably of the south of France[88] and secretary of Bonaventura, [89] made a summary of the earlier legends. This work, which brings us no authentic historic indication, is interesting only for the care with which the author has noted the places where repose the Brothers who died in odor of sanctity, and relates a mass of visions all tending to prove the excellence of the Order. [89]

Still the publication of this document will perform the valuable office of throwing a little light upon the difficult question of the sources. Several passages of the *De laudibus* appear again textually in the Speculum, [91] and as a single glance is enough to show that the Speculum did not copy the *De laudibus*, it must be that Bernard of

Besse had before him a copy, if not of the Speculum at least of a document of the same kind.

FOOTNOTES:

[1]   Bull *Quo elongati* of September 28, 1230. See p. 336.

[2]   It is needless to say that I have no desire to put myself in opposition to that principle, one of the most fruitful of criticism, but still it should not be employed alone.

[3]   The learned works that have appeared in Germany in late years err in the same way. They will be found cited in the body of the work.

[4]   Eccl., 13. *Voluerunt ipsi, quos ad capitulam concesserat venire frater Helias; nam* omnes *concessit, etc. An. fr., t. i.* , p. 241. Cf. *Mon. Germ. hist. Script.* , t., 28, p. 564.

[5]   The death of Francis occurred on October 3, 1226. On March 29, 1228, Elias acquired the site for the basilica. The *Instrumentum donationis* is still preserved at Assisi: Piece No. 1 of the twelfth package of *Instrumenta diversa pertinentia ad Sacrum Conventum*. It has been published by Thode: *Franz von Assisi*, p. 359.

On July 17th of the same year, the day after the canonization, Gregory IX. solemnly laid the first stone. Less than two years afterward the Lower church was finished, and on May 25, 1230, the body of the Saint was carried there. In 1236 the Upper church was finished. It was already decorated with a first series of frescos, and Giunta Pisano painted Elias, life size, kneeling at the foot of the crucifix over the entrance to the choir. In 1239 everything was finished, and the campanile received the famous bells whose chimes still delight all the valley of Umbria. Thus, then, three months and a half before the canonization, Elias received the site of the basilica. The act of canonization commenced at the end of May, 1228 (1 Cel., 123 and 124. Cf. Potthast, 8194ff).

[6]   *Spec.* , 167a. Cf. *An. fr.* , ii., p. 45 and note.

[7]   The Bollandists followed the text (A. SS., Octobris, t. ii., pp. 683-723) of a manuscript of the Cistercian abbey of Longpont in the diocese of Soissons. It has since been published in Rome in 1806, without the name of the editor (in reality by the Convent Father Rinaldi), under the title: *Seraphici viri S. Francisci Assisiatis vitæ dual auctore B. Thoma de Celano*, according to a manuscript (of Fallerone, in the March of Ancona) which was stolen in the vicinity of Terni by brigands from the Brother charged with bringing it back. The second text was reproduced at Rome in 1880 by Canon Amoni: *Vita prima S. Francisci, auctore B. Thoma de Celano. Roma, tipografia della pace*, 1880, in 8vo, 42 pp. The citations will follow the divisions made by the Bollandists, but in many important passages the Rinaldi-Amoni text gives better readings than that of the Bollandists. The latter has been here and there retouched and filled out. See, for example, 1 Cel., 24 and 31. As for the manuscripts, Father Denifle thinks that the oldest of those which are known is that at Barcelona: *Archivo de la corona de Aragon*, Ripoll, n. 41 (*Archiv.* , t. i., p. 148). There is one in the National Library of Paris, Latin alcove, No. 3817, which includes a curious note: *"Apud Perusium felix domnus papa Gregorius nonus gloriosi secundo pontificus sui anno, quinto kal. martii (February 25, 1229) legendam hanc recepit, confirmavit et censuit fore tenendam. "* Another manuscript, which merits attention, both because of its age, thirteenth century, and because of the correction in the text, and which appears to have escaped the researches of the students of the Franciscans, is the one owned by the École de Médicine at Montpellier, No. 30, in vellum folio: *Passionale vetus ecclesiæ S. Benigni divionensis*. The story of Celano occupies in it the fos. 257a-271b. The text ends abruptly in the middle of paragraph 112 with *supiriis ostendebant*. Except for this final break it is complete. Cf. Archives Pertz, t. vii., pp. 195 and 196. Vide General catalogue of the manuscripts of the public libraries of the departments, t. i., p. 295.

[8]   Vide 1 Cel., Prol. *Jubente domino et glorioso Papa Gregorio*. Celano wrote it after the canonization (July 16, 1228) and before February 25, 1229, for the date indicated above raises no difficulty.

[9]   1 Cel., 56. Perhaps he was the son of that Thomas, Count of
        Celano, to whom Ryccardi di S. Germano so often made
        allusion in his chronicle: 1219-1223. See also two letters of
        Frederick II. to Honorius III., on April 24 and 25, 1223,
        published in Winckelmann: *Acta imperii inedita*, t. i., p. 232.

[10]   Giord., 19.

[11]   Giord., 30 and 31.

[12]   Giord., 59. Cf. Glassberger, ann. 1230. The question whether
        he is the author of the *Dies iræ* would be out of place here.

[13]   This is so true that the majority of historians have been
        brought to believe in two generalates of Elias, one in 1227-
        1230, the other in 1236-1239. The letter *Non ex odio* of
        Frederick II. (1239) gives the same idea: Revera *papa iste
        quemdam religiosum et timoratum fratrem Helyam, ministrum
        ordinis fratrum minorum ab ipso beato Francisco patre ordinis
        migrationis suæ tempore constitutum... in odium nostrum...
        deposuit.* Huillard-Breholles: *Hist. dipl. Fred. II.* , t. v., p. 346.

[14]   He is named only once, 1 Cel., 48.

[15]   1 Cel., 95, 98, 105, 109. The account of the Benediction is
        especially significant. *Super quem inquit (Franciscus) tenes
        dexteram meam? Super* fratrem *Heliam, inquiunt. Et ego sic volo,
        sit....* 1 Cel., 108. Those last words obviously disclose the
        intention. Cf. 2 Cel., 3, 139.

[16]   1 Cel., 102; cf. 91 and 109. Brother Leo is not even named in
        the whole work. Nor Angelo, Illuminato, Masseo either!

[17]   1 Cel., Prol., 73-75; 99-101; 121-126. Next to St. Francis,
        Gregory IX. and Brother Elias (1 Cel., 69; 95; 98; 105; 108; 109)
        are in the foreground.

[18]   1 Cel., 18 and 19; 116 and 117.

[19]   Those which occurred during the absence of Francis (1220-
        1221). He overlooks the difficulties met at Rome in seeking
        the approbation of the first Rule; he mentions those
        connected neither with the second nor the third, and makes

no allusion to the circumstances which provoked them. He recognized them, however, having lived in intimacy with Cæsar of Speyer, the collaborator of the second (1221).

[20]   For example, Francis's journey to Spain.

[21]   1 Cel., 1, 88. *Et sola quæ necessaria magis occurrunt* ad præsens *intendimus* adnotare. It is to be observed that in the prologue he speaks in the singular.

[22]   In 1238 he had sent Elias to Cremona, charged with a mission for Frederick II. Salembeni, ann. 1229. See also the reception given by Gregory IX. to the appellants against the General. Giord., 63.

[23]   See the letter of Frederick II. to Elias upon the translation of St. Elizabeth, May, 1236. Winkelmann, *Acta* i., p. 299. Cf. Huillard-Bréholles, *Hist. dipl.* Intr. p. cc.

[24]   The authorities for this story are: *Catalogus ministrorum* of Bernard of Besse, *ap* Ehrle, *Zeitschrift*, vol. 7 (1883), p. 339; *Speculum*, 207b, and especially 167a-170a; Eccl., 13; Giord., 61-63; *Speculum*, Morin., tract i., fo. 60b.

[25]   *Asserabat etiam ipse prædictus frater Helyas... papam... fraudem facere de* pecunia *collecta ad succursum Terræ Sanctæ, scripta etiam ad beneplacitum suum in camera sua bullare clam et sine fratrum assensu et etiam cedulas vacuas, sed bullatas, multas nunciis suis traderet... et alia multa enormia imposuit domino papæ ponens os suum in celo.* Matth. Paris, *Chron. Maj.* , ann. 1239, *ap Mon. Ger. hist. Script.* , t. 28, p. 182. Cf. Ficker, n. 2685.

[26]   Vide Ryccardi di S. Germano, *Chron.* , *ap Mon. Ger. hist. Script.* , t. 19, p. 380, ann. 1239. The letter of Frederick complaining of the deposition of Elias (1239): Huillard-Bréholles, *Hist. Dipl.* , v., pp. 346-349. Cf. the Bull, *Attendite ad petram*, at the end of February, 1240, ibid., pp. 777-779; Potthast, 10849.

[27]   He was without doubt one of the bitterest adversaries of the emperor. His village had been burnt in 1224, by order of Frederick II., and the inhabitants transported to Sicily,

afterward to Malta. Ryccardi di S. Germano, *loc. cit.* , *ann.* 1223 and 1224.

[28]   Vide the prologue to 2 Cel. and to the 3 Soc. Cf. Glassberger, ann. 1244, *An. fr.* , ii., p. 68. *Speculum*, Morin, tract. i., 61b.

[29]   *Catalogus ministrorum*, edited by Ehrle: *Zeitschrift*, t. 7 (1883). no. 5. Cf. *Spec.* , 208a. Mark of Lisbon speaks of it a little more at length, but he gives the honor of it to Giovanni of Parma, ed. Diola, t. ii., p. 38. On the other hand, in manuscript 691 of the archives of the Sacro-Convento at Assisi (a catalogue of the library of the convent made in 1381) is found, fo. 45a, a note of that work: *"Dyalogus sanctorum fratrum cum postibus cujus principium est: Venerabilia gesta patrum dignosque memoria, finis vero; non indigne feram me quoque reperisse consortem. In quo libro omnes quaterni sunt xiii. "*

[30]   The text was published for the first time by the Bollandists (A. SS., Octobris, t. ii., pp. 723-742), after a manuscript of the convent of the Brothers Minor of Louvain. It is from this edition that we make our citations. The editions published in Italy in the course of this century, cannot be found, except the last, due to Abbé Amoni. This one, unfortunately, is too faulty to serve as the basis of a scientific study. It appeared in Rome in 1880 (8vo, pp. 184) under the title: *Legenda S. Francisci Assisiensis quæ dicitur Legenda trium sociorum ex cod. membr. Biblioth. Vatic. num. 7339.*

[31]   2 Cel., 2, 5; 3, 7; 1 Cel., 60; Bon., 113; 1 Cel., 84; Bon., 149; 2 Cel., 2, 14; 3, 10.

[32]   Giovanni di Parma retired thither in 1276 and lived there almost entirely until his death (1288). *Tribul.* , *Archiv.* , vol. ii. (1886), p. 286.

[33]   3 Soc., 25-67.

[34]   3 Soc., 68-73.

[35]   The minister-general Crescentius of Jesi was an avowed adversary of the Zealots of the Rule. The contrary idea has been held by M. Müller (*Anfänge*, p. 180); but that learned scholar is not, it appears, acquainted with the recitals of the

Chronicle of the Tribulations, which leave not a single doubt as to the persecutions which he directed against the Zealots (*Archiv.* , t. ii., pp. 257-260). Anyone who attempts to dispute the historical worth of this proof will find a confirmation in the bulls of August 5, 1244, and of February 7, 1246 (Potthast, 11450 and 12007). It was Crescentius, also, who obtained a bull stating that the Basilica of Assisi was *Caput et Mater ordinis*, while for the Zealots this rank pertained to the Portiuncula (1 Cel., 106; 3 Soc., 56; Bon., 23; 2 Cel., 1, 12; *Conform.* , 217 ff). (See also on Crescentius, Glassberger, ann. 1244, *An. fr.* , p. 69; Sbaralea, *Bull. fr.* , i., p. 502 ff; *Conform.* , 121b. 1.) M. Müller has been led into error through a blunder of Eccleston, 9 (*An. fr.* , i., p. 235). It is evident that the chapter of Genoa (1244) could not have pronounced against the *Declaratio Regulæ* published November 14, 1245. On the contrary, it is Crescentius who called forth this *Declaratio*, against which, not without regret, the Zealots found a majority of the chapter of Metz (1249) presided over by Giovanni of Parma, a decided enemy of any *Declaratio* (*Archiv.* , ii., p. 276). This view is found to be confirmed by a passage of the Speculum Morin (Rouen, 1509), f° 62a: *In hoc capitulo (Narbonnæ) fuit ordinatum quod declaratio D. Innocentii, p. iv., maneat suspensa sicut in Capitulo* METENSI. *Et præceptum est omnibus ne quis utatur ea in iis in quibus expositioni D. Gregorii IX. contradicit.*

[36]   Published with all necessary scientific apparatus by F. Ehrle, S. J., in his studies *Zur Vorgeschichte des Concils von Vienne.* *Archiv.* , ii., pp. 353-416; iii., pp. 1-195.

[37]   See, for example, *Archiv.* , iii., p. 53 ff. Cf. 76. *Adduxi verba et facta b. Francisci sicut est aliquando in legenda et sicut a sociis sancti patris audivi et in cedulis* sanctæ *memoriæ fratris Leonis legi manu sua conscriptis, sicut ab ore beati Francisci audivit.* Ib., p. 85.

[38]   *Hæc omnia patent per sua [B. Francisci] verba expressa per sanctum fratrem virum Leonem ejus socium tam de mandato sancti patris quam etiam de devotione* prædicti *fratris fuerunt solemniter conscripta, in libro qui habetur in armario fratrum de Assisio et in rotulis ejus, quos apud me habeo, manu ejusdem fratris Leonis conscriptis. Archiv.* , iii., p. 168. Cf. p. 178.

[39]   3 Soc., Prol. *Non* contenti *narrare solum miracula... conversationis insignia et pii beneplaciti voluntatem.*

[40]   *Leggenda di S. Francesco, tipografia Morici et Badaloni*, Recanati, 1856, 1 vol., 8vo.

[41]   See Father Stanislaus's preface.

[42]   3 Soc., 68-73.

[43]   The book lacks little of representing St. Francis as taking up the work of Jesus, interrupted (by the fault of the secular clergy) since the time of the apostles. The *viri evangelici* consider the members of the clergy *filios extraneos.* 3 Soc., 48 and 51. Cf. 3 Soc., 48. *Inveni virum... per quem, credo Dominus velit in toto mundo fedem sanctæ Ecclesiæ reformare.* Cf. 2 Cel., 3, 141. *Videbatur revera fratri et omnium comitatium turbæ quod Christi et b. Francisci una persona foret.*

[44]   A. SS. p. 552.

[45]   *Venetiis, expensis domini Jordani de Dinslaken per Simonem de Luere,* 30 januarii, 1504. *Impressum Metis per Jasparem Hochffeder,* Anno Domini 1509. These two editions are identical, small 12mos, of 240 folios badly numbered. Edited under the same title by Spoelberch, Antwerp, 1620, 2 tomes in one volume, 8vo, 208 and 192 pages, with a mass of alterations. The most important manuscript resembles that of the Vatican 4354. There are two at the Mazarin Library, 904 and 1350, dated 1459 and 1460, one at Berlin (MS. theol. lat., 4to, no. 196 sæc. 14). Vide Ehrle, *Zeitschrift.* t. vii. (1883), p. 392f; *Analecta fr.* , t. i., p. xi. ; *Miscellanea,* 1888, pp. 119. 164. Cf. A. SS., pp. 550-552.

The chapters are numbered in the first 72 folios only, but these numbers teem with errors; fo. 38b. caput lix., 40b, lix., 41b, lxi. ibid., lxii., 42a, lx., 43a, lxi. Besides at fos. 46b and 47b there are two chapters lxvi. There are two lxxi., two lxxii., two lxxiii., etc.

[46]   For example, the history of the brigands of Monte-Casale, fos. 46b, and 58b. The remarks of Brother Elias to Francis, who is continually singing, 136b and 137a. The visit of

Giacomina di Settesoli, 133a and 138a. The autograph benediction given to Brother Leo, 87a; 188a.

[47] At fo. 20b we read: *Tertium capitulam de charitate et compassione et condescensione ad proximum. Capitulum* xxvi. Cf. 26a, 83a, 117b, 119a, 122a, 128b, 133b, 136b, where there are similar indications.

[48] Fo. 5b: *Incipit* Speculum *vitæ b. Francesci et sociorum ejus.* Fo. 7b; *Incipit Speculum perfectionis.*

[49] We should search for it in vain in the other pieces of the Speculum, and it reappears in the fragments of Brother Leo cited by Ubertini di Casali and Angelo Clareno.

[50] Fo. 8b, 11a, 12a, 15a, 18b, 21b, 23b, 26a, 29a, 33b, 43b, 41a, 48b, 118a, 129a, 130a, 134a, 135a, 136a.

[51] Does not Thomas de Celano say in the prologue of the Second Life: *"Oramus ergo, benignissime pater, ut laboris hujus non contemnenda munuscula... vestra benedictione consecrare velitis, corrigendo errata et superflua resecantes. "*

[52] The legend of 3 Soc. was preserved in the Convent of Assisi: *"Omnia... fuerunt* conscripta... *per Leonem,... in libro qui habetur in armario fratrum de Assisio. "* Ubertini, *Archiv. ,* iii., p. 168. Later, Brother Leo seems to have gone more into detail as to certain facts; he confided these new manuscripts to the Clarisses: *"In rotulis ejus quos apud me habeo, manu ejusdem fratres Leonis conscriptis, "* ibid. Cf. p. 178. *"Quod sequitur a sancto fratre Conrado predicto et viva voce audivit a sancto fratre Leone qui presens erat et regulam scripsit. Et hoc ipsum in quibusdam rotulis manu sua conscriptis quos commendavit in monasterio S. Claræ custodiendos.... In illis multa scripsit... quæ industria fr. Bonaventura omisit et noluit in legenda publice scribere, maxime quia aliqua erant ibi in quibus ex tunc deviatio regulæ publice monstrabatur et nolebat fratres ante tempus in famare. "* Arbor. , lib. v., cap 5. Cf. *Antiquitates,* p. 146. Cf. *Speculum,* 50b. *"Infra scripta verba, frater Leo socius et Confessor B. Francisci, Conrado de Offida, dicebat se habuisse ex ore Beati Patris nostri Francisci, quæ idem Frater Conradus retulit, apud Sanctum Damianum prope Assisium. "* Conrad di Offidia copied, then, both the book of Brother Leo and his *rotuli*; he

added to it certain oral information (*Arbor, vit. cruc.* , lib. v., cap. 3), and so perhaps composed the collection so often cited by the Conformists under the title of *Legenda Antiqua* and reproduced in part in the Speculum. The numbering of the chapters, which the Speculum has awkwardly inserted without noting that they were not in accord with his own division, were vestiges of the division adopted by Conrad di Offida.

It may well be that, after the interdiction of his book and its confiscation at the Sacro Convento, Brother Leo repeated in his *rotuli* a large part of the facts already made, so that the same incident, while coming solely from Brother Leo, could be presented under two different forms, according as it would be copied from the book or the *rotuli*.

[53]   Compare, for example, 2 Cel., 120: Vocation of John the Simple, and Speculum, f° 37a. From the account of Thomas de Celano, one does not understand what drew John to St. Francis; in the Speculum everything is explained, but Celano has not dared to depict Francis going about preaching with a broom upon his shoulder to sweep the dirty churches.

[54]   It was published for the first time at Rome, in 1806, by Father Rinaldi, following upon the First Life (vide above, p. 365, note 2), and restored in 1880 by Abbé Amoni: *Vita secunda S. Francisci Assisiensis auctore B. Thomade Celano ejus discipulo. Romæ, tipografia della pace*, 1880, 8vo, 152 pp. The citations are from this last edition, which I collated at Assisi with the most important of the rare manuscripts at present known: Archives of Sacro Convento, MS. 686, on parchment of the end of the thirteenth century, if I do not mistake, 130 millim. by 142; 102 numbered pages. Except for the fact that the book is divided into two parts instead of three, the last two forming only one, I have not found that it noticeably differs from the text published by Amoni; the chapters are divided only by a paragraph and a red letter, but they have in the table which occupies the first seven pages of the volume the same titles as in the edition Amoni.

This Second Life escaped the researches of the Bollandists. It is impossible to explain how these students ignored the worth of the manuscript which Father Theobaldi, keeper of the records of Assisi, mentioned to them, and of which he offered them a copy (A. SS., *Oct.* , t. ii., p. 546f). Father Suysken was thus thrown into inextricable difficulties, and exposed to a failure to understand the lists of biographies of St. Francis arranged by the annalists of the Order; he was at the same time deprived of one of the most fruitful sources of information upon the acts and works of the Saint. Professor Müller (*Die Anfänge,* pp. 175-184) was the first to make a critical study of this legend. His conclusions appear to me narrow and extreme. Cf. *Analecta* fr., t. ii., pp. xvii. -xx. Father Ehrle mentions two manuscripts, one in the British Museum, Harl., 47; the other at Oxford, Christ College, cod. 202. *Zeitschrift,* 1883, p. 390.

[55] The Three Companions foresee the possibility of their legend being incorporated with other documents: *quibus (legendis) hæc pauca quæ scribimus poleritis facere inseri, si vestra discretio viderit esse justum.* 3 Soc., Prol.

[56] One phrase of the Prologue (2 Cel.) shows that the author received an entirely special commission: *Placuit... robis... parvitati nostræ injungere,* while on the contrary the 3 Soc. shows that the decision of the chapter only remotely considered them: *Cum de mandato proeteriti capituli fratres teneantur... visum est nobis... pauca de multis... sanctitati vestræ intimare.* 3 Soc., Prol.

[57] Compare the Prologue of 2 Cel. with that of 1 Cel.

[58] *Longum esset de singulis persequi, qualiter bravium supernæ vocationis attigerit.* 2 Cel., 1, 10.

[59] This first part corresponds exactly to that portion of the legend of the 3 Soc., which Crescentius had authorized.

[60] Observe that the Assisi MS. 686 divides the Second Life into two parts only by joining the last two.

[61] Salimbeni, ann. 1248.

[62] Glassberger, ann. 1253. *An. fr.* t. ii., p. 73. *Frater Johannes de Parma minister generalis, multiplicatis litteris præcipit fr. Thomæ de Celano (cod. Ceperano), ut vitam beati Francisci quæ antiqua Legenda dicitur perficeret, quia solum de ejus conversatione et*

verbis in primo tractatu, de mandato, Fr. Crescentii olim generalis compilato, ommissis miraculis fecerat mentionem, et sic secundum tractatum de miraculis sancti Patris compilavit, quem cum epistola quæ incipit: Religiosa vestra sollicitudo eidem generali misit.

This treatise on the miracles is lost, for one cannot identify it, as M. Müller suggests (*Anfänge*, p. 177), with the second part (counting three with the Amoni edition) of the Second Life: 1°, epistle *Religiosa vestra sollicitudo* does not have it; 2°, this second part is not a collection of *miracles*, using this word in the sense of miraculous cures which it had in the thirteenth century. The twenty-two chapters of this second part have a marked unity; they might be entitled *Francis a prophet*, but not *Francis a thaumaturgus*.

[63]   In the Prologue (2 Cel., 2, Prol.) Insignia patrum the author speaks in the singular, while the Epilogue is written in the name of a group of disciples.

[64]   Greccio, 2 Cel., 2, 5; 14; 3, 7; 10; 103. —Rieti, 2 Cel., 2, 10; 11; 12; 13; 3, 36; 37; 66; 103.

[65]   St. Francis gives him an autograph, 2 Cel., 2, 18. Cf. *Fior.* ii. *consid.* ; his tunic, 2 Cel., 2, 19; he predicts to him a famine, 2 Cel., 2, 21; cf. *Conform.* , 49b. Fr. Leo ill at Bologna, 2 Cel., 3, 5.

[66]   The text of Ubertini di Casali may be found in the *Archiv.* , t. iii., pp. 53, 75, 76, 85, 168, 178, where Father Ehrle points out the corresponding passages of 2 Cel.

[67]   It is the subject of thirty-seven narratives (1, 2 Cel., 3, 1-37), then come examples on the spirit of prayer (2 Cel., 3, 38-44), the temptations (2 Cel., 3, 58-64), true happiness (2 Cel., 3, 64-79), humility (2 Cel., 3, 79-87), submission (2 Cel., 3, 88, 91), etc.

[68]   Le Monnier, t. i., p. xi. ; F. Barnabé, *Portiuncula*, p. 15. Cf. *Analecta fr.* , t. ii., p. xxi. *Zeitschrift für kath. Theol.* , vii. (1883), p. 397.

[69]   *Il piu antico poema della vita di S. Francisco d'Assisi scritto inanzi all' anno 1230 ora per la prima volta pubblicato et tradotto da Antonio Cristofani*, Prato, 1882, 1 vol., 8vo. 288 pp.

[70]   Note, however, two articles of the Miscellanea, one on the manuscript of this biography which is found in the library at Versailles, t. iv. (1889), p. 34 ff. ; the other on the author of the poem, t. v. (1890), pp. 2-4 and 74 ff.

[71]   See below, p. 410.

[72]   Vide Glassberger, ann. 1244; *Analecta*, t. ii., p. 68. Cf. A. SS., p. 545 ff.

[73]   Manuscript in the Library of Turin, J. vi., 33, f° 95a.

[74]   *Plenam virtutibus S. Francisci vitam scripsit in Italia... frater Thomas... in Francia vero frater Julianus scientia et sanctitate conspicuus qui etiam nocturnali sancti officium in littera et cantu possuit præter hymnos et aliquas antiphonas quae summus ipse Pontifex et aliqui de Cardinalibus in sancti præconium ediderunt.* Opening of the *De laudibus* of Bernard of Besse. See below, p. 413. Laur. MS., f° 95a. Cf. Giord., 53; *Conform.* , 75b.

[75]   In proof of this is the circular letter, *Licet insufficentiam nostram*, addressed by Bonaventura, April 23, 1257, immediately after his election, to the provincials and custodes upon the reformation of the Order. Text: *Speculum*, Morin, tract. iii., f° 213a.

[76]   Salimbeni, ann. 1248, p. 131. The *Chronica tribulationum* gives a long and dramatic account of these events: *Archiv.* , t. ii., pp. 283 ff. *"Tunc enim sapientia et sanctitas fratris Bonaventuræ eclipsata paluit et obscurata est et ejus manswetudo (sic) ab agitante spiritu in furorum et iram defecit. "* Ib., p. 283.

[77]   Bon., 3. 1. At the same chapter were collected the constitutions of the Order according to edicts of the preceding chapters; new ones were added to them and all were arranged. In the first of the twelve rubrics the chapter prescribed that, upon the publication of the account, all the old constitutions should be destroyed. The text was published in the *Firmamentum trium ordinum*, f° 7b, and

restored lately by Father Ehrle: *Archiv.* , t. vi. (1891), in his beautiful work *Die ältesten Redactionen der General-constitutionen des Franziskanerordens*. Cf. *Speculum* Morin, fo. 195b of tract. iii.

[78]   The *Legenda Minor* of Bonaventura was also approved at this time; it is simply an abridgment of the *Legenda Major* arranged for use of the choir on the festival of St. Francis and its octave.

[79]   *"Item præcipit Generale capitulum per obedientiam quod omnes legenæ de B. Francisco olim factæ deleantur et ubi inveniri poterant extra ordinem ipsas fratres studeant amovere, cum illa legenda quæ facta est per Generalem sit compilata prout ipse habuit ab ore illorum qui cum B. Francisco quasi semper fuerunt et cuncta certitudinaliter sciverint et probata ibi sint posita diligenter. "* This precious text has been found and published by Father Rinaldi in his preface to the text of Celano: *Seraphici viri Francisci vitæ duæ*, p. xi. Wadding seems to have known of it, at least indirectly, for he says: *"Utramque Historiam, longiorem et breviorem, obtulit (Bonaventura) triennio post in comitiis Pisanis patribus Ordinis, quas reverentur cum gratiarum actione,* SUPRESSIS ALIIS QUIBUSQUE LEGENDIS, ADMISERUNT. " Ad ann., 1260, no. 18. Cf. Ehrle, *Zeitschrift für kath. Theol.* , t. vii. (1883), p. 386. — *"Communicaverat sanctus Franciscus plurima sociis suis et fratribus antiquis, que oblivioni tradita sunt, tum quia que scripta erant in legenda prima, nova edita a fratre. Bonaventura deleta et destructa sunt,* IPSOJUBENTE *tum quia... "* Chronica tribul. , *Archiv.* , t. ii., p. 256.

[80]   Bon., 188-204.

[81]   Bon., 218.

[82]   Bernardo (Bon., 28), Egidio (Bon., 29), and Silvestro (Bon., 30).

[83]   Bon., 49.

[84]   Bon., 112.

[85]   Bon., 111.

[86]   Vide Bon., 115; 99, etc. M. Thode has enumerated the stories relating especially to Bonaventura: (*Franz von Assisi*, p. 535).

[87]   Manuscript I, iv., 33, of the library of the University of Turin. It is a 4to upon parchment of the close of the fourteenth century, 124 ff. It comprises first the biography of St. Francis by St. Bonaventura and a legend of St. Clara, afterwards at f° 95 the *De laudibus*. The text will soon be published in the *Analecta franciscana* of the Franciscans of Quaracchi, near Florence.

[88]   In reading it we quickly discover that he was specially well acquainted with the convents of the Province of Aquitania, and noted with care everything that concerned them.

[89]   Wadding, ann. 1230, no. 7. Many passages prove at least that he accompanied Bonaventura in his travels: "*Hoc enim* (the special aid of Brother Egidio) *in iis quæ ad bonum animæ pertinent devotus Generalis et Cardinalis predictus... nos docuit.*" F^o 96a. *Jamdudum ego per Theutoniæ partes et Flandriæ cum Ministro transiens Generali.* Ibid., f° 106a.

[90]   Bernard de Besse is the author of many other writings, notably an important *Calalogus Ministrorum generalium* published after the Turin manuscript by Father Ehrle (*Zeitschrift für kath. Theol.* , t. vii., pp. 338-352), with a very remarkable critical introduction (ib., pp. 323-337). Cf. *Archiv für Litt. u. Kirchg.* , i., p. 145. —Bartolommeo di Pisa, when writing his *Conformities,* had before him a part of his works, f° 148b, 2; 126a, 1; but he calls the author sometimes *Bernardus de Blesa,* then again *Johannes de Blesa.* See also Mark of Lisbon, t. ii., p. 212, and Hauréau, *Notices et extraits,* t. vi., p. 153.

[91]   "*Denique primos Francisci xii. discipulos... omnes sanctos fuisse audirimus preter unum qui Ordinem exiens leprosus factus laqueo vel alter Judas interiit, ne Francisco cum Christo vel in discipulis similitudo deficeret,* " f° 96a.

III

DIPLOMATIC DOCUMENTS

In this category we place all the acts having a character of public authenticity, particularly those which were drawn up by the pontifical cabinet.

This source of information, where each document has its date, is precisely the one which has been most neglected up to this time.

1. DONATION OF THE VERNA

The *Instrumentum donationis Montis Alvernæ*, a notarial document preserved in the archives of Borgo San Sepolcro, [1] not only gives the name of the generous friend of Francis, and many picturesque details, but it fixes with precision a date all the more important because it occurs in the most obscure period of the Saint's life. It was on May 8, 1213, that *Orlando dei Catani*, Count of Chiusi in Casentino, gave the Verna to Brother Francis.

2. REGISTERS OF CARDINAL UGOLINI

The documents of the pontifical chancellery addressed to Cardinal Ugolini, the future Gregory IX., and those which emanate from the hand of the latter during his long journeys as apostolic legate, [2] are of first rate importance.

It would be too long to give even a simple enumeration of them. Those which mark important facts have been carefully indicated in the course of this work. It will suffice to say that by bringing together these two series of documents, and interposing the dates of the papal bulls countersigned by Ugolini, we are able to follow almost day by day this man, who was, perhaps without even excepting St. Francis, the one whose will most profoundly fashioned the Franciscan institute. We see also the pre-eminent part which the Order had from the beginning in the interest of the future pontiff, and we arrive at perfect accuracy as to the dates of his meetings with St. Francis.

3. BULLS

The pontifical bulls concerning the Franciscans were collected and published in the last century by the monk Sbaralea. [3] But from these we gain little help for the history of the origins of the Order. [4]

The following is a compendious list; the details have been given in the course of the work:

No. 1. August 18, 1218. —Bull *Literæ tuæ* addressed to Ugolini. The pope permits him to accept donations of landed property in behalf of women fleeing the world (Clarisses) and to declare that these monasteries are holden by the Apostolic See.

No. 2. June 11, 1219. —*Cum delecti filii.* This bull, addressed in a general way to all prelates, is a sort of safe conduct for the Brothers Minor.

No. 3. December 19, 1219. —*Sacrosancta romana.* Privileges conceded to the Sisters (Clarisses) of Monticelli, near Florence.

No. 4. May 29, 1220. —*Pro dilectis.* The pope prays the prelates of France to give a kindly reception to the Brothers Minor.

No. 5. September 22, 1220. —*Cum secundum.* Honorius III. prescribes a year of noviciate before the entry into the Order.

No. 6. December 9, 1220. —*Constitutus in præsentia.* This bull concerns a priest of Constantinople who had made a vow to enter the Order. As there is question here of *frater Lucas Magister fratrum Minorem de partibus Romaniæ* we have here indirect testimony, all the more precious for that reason, as to the period of the establishment of the Order in the Orient.

No. 7. February 13, 1221. —New bull for the same priest.

No. 8. December 16, 1221. —*Significatum est nobis.* Honorius III. recommends to the Bishop of Rimini to protect the Brothers of Penitence (Third Order).

No. 9. March 22, 1222. [5]—*Devotionis vestræ.* Concession to the Franciscans, under certain conditions, to celebrate the offices in times of interdict.

No. 10. March 29, 1222. —*Ex parte Universitatis.* Mission given to the Dominicans, Franciscans, and Brothers of the Troops of San Iago in Lisbon.

Nos. 11, 12, and 13. —September 19, 1222. —*Sacrosancta Romana.* Privileges for the monasteries (Clarisses) of Lucca, Sienna, and Perugia.

No. 14. November 29, 1223. —*Solet annuere.* Solemn approbation of the Rule, which is inserted in the bull.

No. 15. December 18, 1223. —*Fratrum Minorum.* Concerns apostates from the Order.

No. 16. December 1, 1224. —*Cum illorum.* Authorization given to the Brothers of Penitence to take part in the offices in times of interdict, etc.

No. 17. December 3, 1224. —*Quia populares tumultus.* Concession of the portable altar.

No. 18. August 28, 1225. —*In hiis.* Honorius explains to the Bishop of Paris and the Archbishop of Rheims the true meaning of the privileges accorded to the Brothers Minor.

No. 19. October 7, 1225. —*Vineae Domini.* This bull contains divers authorizations in favor of the Brothers who are going to evangelize Morocco.

This list includes only those of Sbaralea's bulls which may directly or indirectly throw some light upon the life of St. Francis and his institute. Sbaralea's nomenclature is surely incomplete and should be revised when the Registers of Honorius III. shall have been published in full. [6]

FOOTNOTES:

[1]   It was published by Sbaralea, Bull., t. iv., p. 156, note h. This act was drawn up July 9, 1274, at a time when the son of Orlando as well as the Brothers Minor desired to authenticate the donation, which until then had been verbal.

[2]   See *Registri dei Cardinali Ugolino d'Ostia e Ottaviano degli Ubaldini pubblicati a cura di Guido Levi dall'Istituto storico italiano.* —*Fonti per la storia d'Italia*, Roma, 1890, 1 vol., 4to, xxviii. and 250 pp. This edition follows the manuscript of the National Library, Paris: Ancien fonds Colbert lat., 5152A. We must draw attention to a very beautiful work due also to Mr. G. Levi: *Documenti ad illustrazione del Registro del Card. Ugolino*, in the *Archivio della societa Romana di storia patria*, t. xii. (1889), pp. 241-326.

[3]   *Bullarium franciscanum seu Rom. Pontificum constitutiones epistolæ diplomata ordinibus Minorum, Clarissarum et Poenitentium concessa, edidit Joh. Hyac. Sbaralea ord. min. conv. ,* 4 vols., fol., Rome, t. i. (1759), t. ii. (1761), t. iii. (1763), t iv., (1768)—*Supplementum ab Annibale de Latera ord. min. obs. Romæ*, 1780. —Sbaralea had a comparatively easy task, because of the number of collections made before his. I shall mention only one of those which I have before me. It is, comparatively, very well done, and appears to have escaped the researches of the Franciscan bibliographers: *Singularissimum eximiumque opus universis mortalibus sacratissimi ordinis seraphici patris nostri Francisci a Domino Jesu mirabili modo approbati necnon a quampluribus nostri Redemptoris sanctissimis vicariis romanis pontificabus multipharie declarati notitiam habere cupientibus profecto per necessarium. Speculum Minorum... per Martinum Morin... Rouen*, 1509. It is 8vo, with numbered folios, printed with remarkable care. It contains besides the bulls the principal dissertations upon the Rule, elaborated in the thirteenth century, and a *Memoriale ordinis* (first part, f° 60-82), a kind of catalogue of the ministers-general, which would have prevented many of the errors of the historians, if it had been known.

[4]   The Bollandists themselves have entirely overlooked those sources of information, thinking, upon the authority of a single badly interpreted passage, that the Order had not obtained a single bull before the solemn approval of Honorius III., November 29, 1223.

[5]   And not March 29, as Sbaralea has it. The original, which I have had under my eyes in the archives of Assisi, bears in

fact: *Datum Anagnie XI. Kal. aprilis pontificatus nostri anno sexto.*

[6]   The Abbé Horoy has indeed published in five volumes what he entitles the *Opera omnia* of Honorius III., but he omits, without a word of explanation, a great number of letters, certain of which are brought forward in the well-known collection of Potthast. The Abbé Pietro Pressuti has undertaken to publish a compendium of all the bulls of this pope according to the original Registers of the Vatican. *I regesti del Pontifice Onorio III.* Roma, t. i., 1884. Volume i. only has as yet appeared.

IV

CHRONICLERS OF THE ORDER

1. CHRONICLE OF BROTHER GIORDANO DI GIANO[1]

Born at Giano, in Umbria, in the mountainous district which closes the southern horizon of Assisi, Brother Giordano was in 1221 one of the twenty-six friars who, under the conduct of Cæsar of Speyer, set out for Germany. He seems to have remained attached to this province until his death, even when most of the friars, especially those who held cures, had been transferred, often to a distance of several months' journey, from one end of Europe to the other. It is not, then, surprising that he was often prayed to commit his memories to writing. He dictated them to Brother Baldwin of Brandenburg in the spring of 1262. He must have done it with joy, having long before prepared himself for the task. He relates with artless simplicity how in 1221, at the chapter-general of Portiuncula, he went from group to group questioning as to their names and country the Brothers who were going to set out on distant missions, that he might be able to say later, especially if they came to suffer martyrdom: "I knew them myself! "[2]

His chronicle bears the imprint of this tendency. What he desires to describe is the introduction of the Order into Germany and its early developments there, and he does it by enumerating, with a complacency which has its own coquetry, the names of a multitude of friars[3] and by carefully dating the events. These details, tedious for the ordinary reader, are precious to the historian; he sees there the diverse conditions from which the friars were recruited, and the rapidity with which a handful of missionaries thrown into an unknown country were able to branch out, found new stations, and in five years cover with a network of monasteries, the Tyrol, Saxony, Bavaria, Alsace, and the neighboring provinces.

It is needless to say that it is worth while to test Giordano's chronology, for he begins by praying the reader to forgive the errors which may have escaped him on this head; but a man who thus marks in his memory what he desires later to tell or to write is not an ordinary witness.

Reading his chronicle, it seems as if we were listening to the recollections of an old soldier, who grasps certain worthless details and presents them with an extraordinary power of relief, who knows not how to resist the temptation to bring himself forward, at the risk sometimes of slightly embellishing the dry reality. [4]

In fact this chronicle swarms with anecdotes somewhat personal, but very artless and welcome, and which on the whole carry in themselves the testimony to their authenticity. The perfume of the Fioretti already exhales from these pages so full of candor and manliness; we can follow the missionaries stage by stage, then when they are settled, open the door of the monastery and read in the very hearts of these men, many of whom are as brave as heroes and harmless as doves.

It is true that this chronicle deals especially with Germany, but the first chapters have an importance for Francis's history that exceeds even that of the biographers. Thanks to Giordano of Giano, we are from this time forward informed upon the crises which the institute of Francis passed through after 1219; he furnishes us the solidly historical base which seems to be lacking in the documents emanating from the Spirituals, and corroborates their testimony.

2. ECCLESTON: ARRIVAL OF THE FRIARS IN ENGLAND[5]

Our knowledge of Thomas of Eccleston is very slight, for he has left no more trace of himself in the history of the Order than of Simon of Esseby, to whom he dedicates his work. A native no doubt of Yorkshire, he seems never to have quitted England. He was twenty-five years gathering the materials of his work, which embraces the course of events from 1224 almost to 1260. The last facts that he relates belong to years very near to this date.

Of almost double the length of that of Giordano, Eccleston's work is far from furnishing as interesting reading. The former had seen nearly everything that he described, and thence resulted a vigor in his story that we cannot find in an author who writes on the testimony of others. More than this, while Giordano follows a chronological order, Eccleston has divided his incidents under fifteen rubrics, in which the same people continually reappear in a confusion which at length becomes very wearisome. Finally, his document is amazingly partial: the author is not content with merely proving that the English friars are saints; he desires to show that the province of England surpasses all others[6] by its fidelity to the Rule and its courage against the upholders of new ways, Brother Elias in particular.

But these few faults ought not to make us lose sight of the true value of this document. It embraces what we may call the heroic period of the Franciscan movement in England, and describes it with extreme simplicity.

Aside from all question of history, we have here enough to interest all those who are charmed by the spectacle of moral conquest. On Monday, September 10th, the Brothers Minor landed at Dover. They were nine in number: a priest, a deacon, two who had only the lesser Orders, and five laymen. They visited Canterbury, London, Oxford, Cambridge, Lincoln, and less than ten months later all who have made their mark in the history of science or of sanctity had joined them; it may suffice to name Adam of Marisco, Richard of Cornwall, Bishop Robert Grossetête, one of the proudest and purest figures of the Middle Ages, and Roger Bacon, that persecuted monk who several centuries before his time grappled with and answered in his lonely cell the problems of authority and method, with a firmness and power which the sixteenth century would find it hard to surpass.

It is impossible that in such a movement human weaknesses and passions should not here and there reveal themselves, but we owe our chronicler thanks for not hiding them. Thanks to him, we can for a moment forget the present hour, call to life again that first Cambridge chapel—so slight that it took a carpenter only one day to build it—listen to three Brothers chanting matins that same night, and that with so much ardor that one of them—so rickety that his two companions were obliged to carry him—wept for joy: in England as in Italy the Franciscan gospel was a gospel of peace and joy. Moral ugliness inspired them with a pity which we no longer know. There are few historic incidents finer than that of Brother Geoffrey of Salisbury confessing Alexander of Bissingburn; the noble penitent was performing this duty without attention, as if he were telling some sort of a story; suddenly his confessor melted into tears, making him blush with shame and forcing tears also from him, working in him so complete a revolution that he begged to be taken into the Order.

The most interesting parts are those where Thomas gives us an intimate view of the friars: here drinking their beer, there hastening, in spite of the Rule, to buy some on credit for two comrades who have been maltreated, or again clustering about Brother Solomon, who had just come in nearly frozen with cold, and whom they could not succeed in warming—*sicut porcis mos est cum comprimendo foverunt*, says the pious narrator. [7] All this is mingled with dreams, visions, numberless apparitions, [8] which once more show us how different were the ideas most familiar to the religious minds of the thirteenth century from those which haunt the brains and hearts of to-day.

The information given by Eccleston bears only indirectly on this book, but if he speaks little of Francis he speaks much at length of some of the men who have been most closely mingled with his life.

3. CHRONICLE OF FRA SALIMBENI[9]

As celebrated as it is little known, this chronicle is of quite secondary value in all that concerns the life of St. Francis. Its author, born October 9, 1221, entered the Order in 1238, and wrote his memoirs in 1282-1287; it is therefore especially for the middle years of the thirteenth century that his importance is capital. Notwithstanding this, it is surprising how small a place the radiant figure of the master holds in these long pages, and this very fact shows, better than long arguments could do, how profound was the fall of the Franciscan idea.

4. THE CHRONICLE OF THE TRIBULATIONS BY ANGELO CARENO[10]

This chronicle was written about 1330; we might therefore be surprised to see it appear among the sources to be consulted for the life of St. Francis, dead more than a century before; but the picture which Clareno gives us of the early days of the Order gains its importance from the fact that in sketching it he made constant appeal to eye-witnesses, and precisely to those whose works have disappeared.

Angelo Clareno, earlier called Pietro da Fossombrone[11] from the name of his native town, and sometimes da Cingoli, doubtless from the little convent where he made profession, belonged to the Zelanti of the March of Ancona as early as 1265. Hunted and persecuted by his adversaries during his whole life, he died in the odor of sanctity June 15, 1339, in the little hermitage of Santa Maria d' Aspro in the diocese of Marsico in Basilicata.

Thanks to published documents, we may now, so to speak, follow day by day not only the external circumstances of his life, but the inner workings of his soul. With him we see the true Franciscan live again, one of those men who, while desiring to remain the obedient son of the Church, cannot reconcile themselves to permit the domain of the dream to slip away from them, the ideal which they have hailed. Often they are on the borders of heresy; in these utterances against bad priests and unworthy pontiffs there is a bitterness which the sectaries of the sixteenth century will not exceed. [12] Often, too, they seem to renounce all authority and make final appeal to the inward witness of the Holy Spirit; [13] and yet Protestantism would be mistaken in seeking its ancestors among them. No, they desired to die as they had lived, in the communion of that Church which was as a stepmother to them and which they yet loved with that heroic passion which some of the ci-devant nobles brought in '93 to the love of France, governed though she was by Jacobins, and poured out their blood for her.

Clareno and his friends not only believed that Francis had been a great Saint, but to this conviction, which was also that of the Brothers of the Common Observance, they added the persuasion that the work of the Stigmatized could only be continued by men who should attain to his moral stature, to which men might arrive through the power of faith and love. They were of the violent who take the kingdom of heaven by force; so when, after the frivolous and senile interests of every day we come face to face with them, we feel ourselves both humbled and exalted, for we suddenly find unhoped-for powers, an unrecognized lyre in the human heart.

There is one of Jesus's apostles of whom it is difficult not to think while reading the chronicle of the Tribulations and Angelo Clareno's correspondence: St. John. Between the apostle's words about love and those of the Franciscan there is a similarity of style all the more striking because they were written in different languages. In both of these the soul is that of the aged man, where all is only love, pardon, desire for holiness, and yet it sometimes wakes with a sudden thrill—like that which stirred the soul of the seer of Patmos—of indignation, wrath, pity, terror, and joy, when the future unveils itself and gives a glimpse of the close of the great tribulation.

Clareno's works, then, are in the strictest sense of the word partisan; the question is whether the author has designedly falsified the facts or mutilated the texts. To this question we may boldly answer, No. He commits errors, [14] especially in his earlier pages, but they are not such as to diminish our confidence.

Like a good Joachimite, he believed that the Order would have to traverse seven tribulations before its final triumph. The pontificate of John XXII. marked, he thought, the commencement of the seventh; he set himself, then, to write, at the request of a friend, the history of the first six. [15]

His account of the first is naturally preceded by an introduction, the purpose of which is to exhibit to the reader, taking the life of St. Francis as a framework, the intention of the latter in composing the Rule and dictating the Will.

Born between 1240 and 1250, Clareno had at his service the testimony of several of the first disciples; [16] he found himself in relations with Angelo di Rieti, [17] Egidio, [18] and with that Brother Giovanni, companion of Egidio, mentioned in the prologue of the Legend of the Three Companions. [19]

His chronicle, therefore, forms as it were the continuation of that legend. The members of the little circle of Greccio are they who recommend it to us; it has also their inspiration.
But writing long years after the death of these Brothers, Clareno feels the need of supporting himself also on written testimony; he repeatedly refers to the four legends from which he borrows a part of his narrative; they are those of Giovanni di Ceperano, Thomas of Celano, Bonaventura, and Brother Leo. [20] Bonaventura's work is mentioned only by way of reference; Clareno borrows nothing from him, while he cites long passages from Giovanni di Ceperano, [21] Thomas of Celano[22] and Brother Leo. [23]

Clareno takes from these writers narratives containing several new and extremely curious facts. [24]

I have dwelt particularly upon this document because its value appears to me not yet to have been properly appreciated. It is indeed partisan; the documents of which we must be most wary are not those whose tendency is manifest, but those where it is skilfully concealed.

The life of St. Francis and a great part of the religious history of the thirteenth century will surely appear to us in an entirely different light when we are able to fill out the documents of the victorious party by those of the party of the vanquished. Just as Thomas of Celano's first legend is dominated by the desire to associate closely St. Francis, Gregory IX., and Brother Elias, so the Chronicle of the Tribulations is inspired from beginning to end with the thought that the troubles of the Order—to say the word, the apostasy—began so early as 1219. This contention finds a striking confirmation in the Chronicle of Giordano di Giano.

5. THE FIORETTI[25]

With the Fioretti we enter definitively the domain of legend. This literary gem relates the life of Francis, his companions and disciples, as it appeared to the popular imagination at the beginning of the fourteenth century. We have not to discuss the literary value of this document, one of the most exquisite religious works of the Middle Ages, but it may well be said that from the historic point of view it does not deserve the neglect to which it has been left.

Most authors have failed in courage to revise the sentence lightly uttered against it by the successors of Bollandus. Why make anything of a book which Father Suysken did not even deign to read! [26]

Yet that which gives these stories an inestimable worth is what for want of a better term we may call their atmosphere. They are legendary, worked over, exaggerated, false even, if you please, but they give us with a vivacity and intensity of coloring something that we shall search for in vain elsewhere—the surroundings in which St. Francis lived. More than any other biography the Fioretti transport us to Umbria, to the mountains of the March of Ancona; they make us visit the hermitages, and mingle with the life, half childish, half angelic, which was that of their inhabitants.

It is difficult to pronounce upon the name of the author. His work was only that of gathering the flowers of his bouquet from written and oral tradition. The question whether he wrote in Latin or Italian has been much discussed and appears to be not yet settled; what is certain is that though this work may be anterior to the Conformities, [27] it is a little later than the Chronicle of the Tribulations, for it would be strange that it made no mention of Angelo Clareno, if it was written after his death.

This book is in fact an essentially local[28] chronicle; the author has in mind to erect a monument to the glory of the Brothers Minor of the March of Ancona. This province, which is evidently his own, "does it not resemble the sky blazing with stars? The holy Brothers who dwelt in it, like the stars in the sky, have illuminated and adorned the Order of St. Francis, filling the world with their examples and teaching. " He is acquainted with the smallest villages, [29] each having at a short distance its monastery, well apart, usually near a torrent, in the edge of a wood, and above, near the hilltop, a few almost inaccessible cells, the asylums of Brothers even more than the others in love with contemplation and retirement. [30]

The chapters that concern St. Francis and the Umbrian Brothers are only a sort of introduction; Egidio, Masseo, Leo on one side, St. Clara on the other, are witnesses that the ideal at Portiuncula and St. Damian was indeed the same to which in later days Giachimo di Massa, Pietro di Monticulo, Conrad di Offida, Giovanni di Penna, and Giovanni della Verna endeavored to attain.

While most of the other legends give us the Franciscan tradition of the great convents, the Fioretti are almost the only document which shows it as it was perpetuated in the hermitages and among the people. In default of accuracy of detail, the incidents which are related here contain a higher truth—their tone is true. Here are words that were never uttered, acts that never took place, but the soul and the heart of the early Franciscans were surely what they are depicted here.

The Fioretti have the living truth that the pencil gives. Something is wanting in the physiognomy of the Poverello when we forget his conversation with Brother Leo on the perfect joy, his journey to Sienna with Masseo, or even the conversion of the wolf of Gubbio.

We must not, however, exaggerate the legendary side of the Fioretti: there are not more that two or three of these stories of which the kernel is not historic and easy to find. The famous episode of the wolf of Gubbio, which is unquestionably the most marvellous of all the series, is only, to speak the engraver's language, the third state of the story of the robbers of Monte Casale[31] mingled with a legend of the Verna.

The stories crowd one another in this book like flocks of memories that come upon us pell-mell, and in which insignificant details occupy a larger place than the most important events; our memory is, in fact, an overgrown child, and what it retains of a man is generally a feature, a word, a gesture. Scientific history is trying to react, to mark the relative value of facts, to bring forward the important ones, to cast into shade that which is secondary. Is it not a mistake? Is there such a thing as the important and the secondary? How is it going to be marked?

The popular imagination is right: what we need to retain of a man is the expression of countenance in which lives his whole being, a heart-cry, a gesture that expresses his personality. Do we not find all of Jesus in the words of the Last Supper? And all of St. Francis in his address to brother wolf and his sermon to the birds?

Let us beware of despising these documents in which the first Franciscans are described as they saw themselves to be. Unfolding under the Umbrian sky at the foot of the olives of St. Damian, or the firs of the March of Ancona, these wild flowers have a perfume and an originality which we look for in vain in the carefully cultivated flowers of a learned gardener.

APPENDICES OF THE FIORETTI

In the first of these appendices the compiler has divided into five chapters all the information on the stigmata which he was able to gather. It is easy to understand the success of the Fioretti. The people fell in love with these stories, in which St. Francis and his companions appear both more human and more divine than in the other legends; and they began very soon to feel the need of so completing them as to form a veritable biography. [32]

The second, entitled Life of Brother Ginepro, is only indirectly connected with St. Francis; yet it deserves to be studied, for it offers the same kind of interest as the principal collection, to which it is doubtless posterior. In these fourteen chapters we find the principal features of the life of this Brother, whose mad and saintly freaks still furnish material for conversation in Umbrian monasteries. These unpretending pages discover to us one aspect of the Franciscan heart. The official historians have thought it their duty to keep silence upon this Brother, who to them appeared to be a supremely indiscreet personage, very much in the way of the good name of the

Order in the eyes of the laics. They were right from their point of view, but we owe a debt of gratitude to the Fioretti for having preserved for us this personality, so blithe, so modest, and with so arch a good nature. Certainly St. Francis was more like Ginepro than like Brother Elias or St. Bonaventura. [33]

The third, Life of Brother Egidio, appears to be on the whole the most ancient document on the life of the famous Ecstatic that we possess. It is very possible that these stories might be traced to Brother Giovanni, to whom the Three Companions appeal in their prologue.

In the defective texts given us in the existing editions we perceive the hand of an annotator whose notes have slipped into the text, [34] but in spite of that this life is one of the most important of the secondary texts. This always itinerant brother, one of whose principal preoccupations is to live by his labor, is one of the most original and agreeable figures in Francis's surroundings, and it is in lives of this sort that we must seek the true meaning of some of the passages of the Rule, and precisely in those that have had the most to suffer from the enterprise of exegetes.

The fourth includes the favorite maxims of Brother Egidio; they have no other importance than to show the tendencies of the primitive Franciscan teaching. They are short, precise, practical counsels, saturated with mysticism, and yet in them good sense never loses its rights. The collection, just as it is in the Fioretti, is no doubt posterior to Egidio, for in 1385 Bartolommeo of Pisa furnished a much longer one. [35]

6. CHRONICLE OF THE XXIV. GENERALS[36]

We find here at the end of the life of Francis that of most of his companions, and the events that occurred under the first twenty-four generals.

It is a very ordinary work of compilation. The authors have sought to include in it all the pieces which they had succeeded in collecting, and the result presents a very disproportioned whole. A thorough study of it might be interesting and useful, but it would be possible only after its publication. This cannot be long delayed: twice (at intervals of fifteen months) when I have desired to study the Assisi manuscript it was found to be with the Franciscans of Quaracchi, who were preparing to print it.

It is difficult not to bring the epoch in which this collection was closed near to that when Bartolommeo of Pisa wrote his famous work. Perhaps the two are quite closely related.

This chronicle was one of Glassberger's favorite sources.

7. THE CONFORMITIES OF BARTOLOMMEO OF PISA[37]

The Book of the Conformities, to which Brother Bartolommeo of Pisa devoted more than fifteen years of his life, [38] appears to have been read very inattentively by most of the authors who have spoken of it. [39] In justice to them we must add that it would be hard to find a work more difficult to read; the same facts reappear from ten to fifteen times, and end by wearying the least delicate nerves.

It is to this no doubt that we must attribute the neglect to which it has been left. I do not hesitate, however, to see in it the most important work which has been made on the life of St. Francis. Of course the author does not undertake historical criticism as we understand it to-day, but if we must not expect to find him a historian, we can boldly place him in the front rank of compilers. [40]

If the Bollandists had more thoroughly studied him they would have seen more clearly into the difficult question of the sources, and the authors who have come after them would have been spared numberless errors and interminable researches.

Starting with the thought that Francis's life had been a perfect imitation of that of Jesus, Bartolommeo attempted to collect, without losing a single one, all the instances of the life of the Poverello scattered through the diverse legends still known at that time.

He regretted that Bonaventura, while borrowing the narratives of his predecessors, had often abridged them, [41] and himself desired to preserve them in their original bloom. Better situated than any one for such a work, since he had at his disposal the archives of the Sacro Convento of Assisi, it may be said that he has omitted nothing of importance and that he has brought into his work considerable pieces from nearly all the legends which appeared in the thirteenth and fourteenth centuries; they are there only in fragments, it is true, but with perfect accuracy. [42]

When his researches were unsuccessful he avows it simply, without attempting to fill out the written testimonies with his own conjectures. [43] He goes farther, and submits the documents he has before him to a real testing, laying aside those he considers uncertain. [44] Finally he takes pains to point out the passages in which his only authority is oral testimony. [45]

As he is almost continually citing the legends of Celano, the Three Companions, and Bonaventura, and as the citations prove on verification to be literally accurate, as well as those of the Will, the divers Rules, or the pontifical bulls, it seems natural to conclude that he was equally accurate with the citations which we cannot verify, and in which we find long extracts from works that have disappeared. [46]

The citations which he makes from Celano present no difficulty; they are all accurate, corresponding sometimes with the First sometimes with the Second Legend. [47]

Those from the Legend of the Three Companions are accurate, but it appears that Bartolommeo drew them from a text somewhat different from that which we have. [48]

With the citations from the *Legenda Antiqua* the question is complicated and becomes a nice one. Was there a work of this name? Certain authors, and among them the Bollandist Suysken, seem to incline toward the negative, and believe that to cite the *Legenda Antiqua* is about the same as to refer vaguely to tradition. Others among contemporaries have thought that after the approbation and definitive adoption of Bonaventura's *Legenda Major* by the Order the Legends anterior to that, and especially that of Celano, were called *Legenda Antiqua*. The Conformities permit us to look a little closer into the question. We find, in fact, passages from the *Legenda Antiqua* which reproduce Celano's First Life. [49] Others present points of contact with the Second, sometimes a literary exactitude, [50] but often these are the same stories told in too different a way for us to consider them borrowed. [51]

Finally there are many of these extracts from the *Legenda Antiqua* of which we find no source in any of the documents already discussed.

[52] This would suffice to show that the two are not to be confounded. It has absorbed them and brought about certain changes while completing them with others. [53]

The study of the fragments which Bartolommeo has preserved to us shows immediately that this collection belonged to the party of the Zealots of Poverty; we might be tempted to see in it the work of Brother Leo.

Most fortunately there is a passage where Bartolommeo di Pisa cites as being by Conrad di Offida a fragment which he had already cited before as borrowed from the *Legenda Antiqua*. [54] I would not exaggerate the value of an isolated instance, but it seems an altogether plausible hypothesis to make Conrad di Offida the author of this compilation. All that we know of him, of his tendencies, his struggle for the strict observance, accords with what the known fragments of the *Legenda Antiqua* permit us to infer as to its author. [55]

However this may be, it appears that in this collection the stories have been given us (the principal source being the Legend of Brother Leo or the Three Companions before its mutilation) in a much less abridged form than in the Second Life of Celano. This work is hardly more than a second edition of that of Brother Leo, here and there completed with a few new incidents, and especially with exhortations to perseverance addressed to the persecuted Zealots. [56]

8. CHRONICLE OF GLASSBERGER[57]

Evidently this work, written about 1508, cannot be classed among the sources properly so called; but it presents in a convenient form the general history of the Order, and thanks to its citations permits us to verify certain passages in the primitive legends of which Glassberger had the MS. before his eyes. It is thus in particular with the chronicle of Brother Giordano di Giano, which he has inserted almost bodily in his own work.

9. CHRONICLE OF MARK OF LISBON[58]

This work is of the same character as that of Glassberger; it can only be used by way of addition. There is, however, a series of facts in which it has a special value; it is when the Franciscan missions in

Spain or Morocco are in question. The author had documents on this subject which did not reach the friars in distant countries.

FOOTNOTES:

[1]   *Chronica fratris Jordani a Giano.* The text was published for the first time in 1870 by Dr. G. Voigt under the title: "*Die Denkwürdigkeiten des Minoriten Jordanus von Giano* in the *Abhandlungen der philolog. histor. Cl. der Königl. sächsischen Gesellschaft der Wissenschaften,* " pp. 421-545, Leipsic, by Hirzel, 1870. Only one manuscript is known; it is in the royal library at Berlin (Manuscript. theolog. lat., 4to, n. 196, sæc. xiv., foliorum 141). It has served as the base of the second edition: *Analecta franciscana sive Chronica aliaque documenta ad historiam minorum spectantia. Ad Claras Aquas (Quaracchi) ex typographia collegii S. Bonaventuræ,* 1885, t. i., pp. 1-19. Except where otherwise noted, I cite entirely this edition, in which is preserved the division into sixty-three paragraphs introduced by Dr. Voigt.

[2]   Giord., 81.

[3]   He names more than twenty four persons.

[4]   It does not seem to me that we can look upon the account of the interview between Gregory IX. and Brother Giordano as rigorously accurate. Giord., 63.

[5]   *Liber de adventu Minorum in Angliam,* published under the title of *Monumenta Franciscana* (in the series of *Rerum Britannicarum medii Ævi scriptores, Roll series*) in two volumes, 8vo; the first through the care of J. S. Brewer (1858), the second through that of R. Howlett (1882). This text is reproduced without the scientific dress of the *Analecta franciscana,* t. i., pp. 217-257. Cf. English Historical Review, v. (1890), 754. He has published an excellent critical edition of it, but unfortunately partial, in vol. xxviii., *Scriptorum,* of the *Monumenta Germaniæ Historica* by Mr. Liebermann, Hanover, 1888, folio, pp. 560-569.

[6]   Eccl., 11; 13; 14; 15. Cf. Eccl., 14, where the author takes pains to say that Alberto of Pisa died at Rome, surrounded by English Brothers "*inter Anglicos.* "

[7]   Eccl., 4; 12.

[8]   Eccl., 4; 5; 6; 7; 10; 12; 13; 14; 15.

[9]   It was published, but with many suppressions, in 1857, at Parma. The Franciscans of Quaracchi prepared a new edition of it, which appeared in the *Analecta Franciscana*. This work is in manuscript in the Vatican under no. 7260. Vide Ehrle. *Zeitschrift für kath. Theol.* (1883), t. vii., pp. 767 and 768. The work of Mr. Clédat will be read with interest: *De fratre Salembene et de ejus chronicæ auctoritate*, Paris, 4to, 1877, with fac simile.

[10]   Father Ehrle has published it, but unfortunately not entire, in the *Archiv.* , t. ii., pp. 125-155, text of the close of the fifth and of the sixth tribulation; pp. 256-327 text of the third, of the fourth, and of the commencement of the fifth. He has added to it introductions and critical notes. For the parts not published I will cite the text of the Laurentian manuscript (Plut. 20, cod. 7), completed where possible with the Italian version in the National Library at Florence (Magliabecchina, xxxvii. -28). See also an article of Professor Tocco in the *Archivio storico italiano*, t. xvii. (1886), pp. 12-36 and 243-61, and one of Mr. Richard's: Library of the École des chartes, 1884, 5th livr. p. 525. Cf. Tocco, the *Eresia nel medio Evo*, p. 419 ff. As to the text published by Döllinger in his *Beiträge zur Sektengeschichte des Mittelalters*, Münich, 1890, 2 vols., 8vo, II. *Theil Dokumente*, pp. 417-427, it is of no use. It can only beget errors, as it abounds with gross mistakes. Whole pages are wanting.

[11]   *Archiv.* , t. iii., pp. 406-409.

[12]   Vide *Archiv.* , i., p. 557... "*Et hoc totum ex rapacitate et malignitate luporum pastorum qui voluerunt esse pastores, sed operibus negaverunt deum,* " et seq. Cf., p. 562: "*Avaritia et symoniaca heresis absque pallio regnat et fere totum invasit ecclesie corpus.* "

[13]   "*Qui excommunicat et hereticat altissimam evangelii paupertatem, excommunicatus est a Deo et hereticus coram Christo, qui est eterna et in commutabilis veritas.* " Arch. , i., p. 509. "*Non est potestas contra christum Dominum et contra evangelium.* " Ib. p.

560. He closes one of his letters with a sentence of a mysticism full of serenity, and which lets us see to the bottom of the hearts of the Spiritual Brothers. "*Totum igitur studium esse debet quod unum inseparabiliter simus per Franciscum in Christo.* " Ib., p. 564.

[14] For example in the list of the first six generals of the Order.

[15] The first (1219-1226) extends from the departure of St. Francis for Egypt up to his death; the second includes the generalate of Brother Elias (1232-1239); the third that of Crescentius (1244-1248); the fourth, that of Bonaventura (1257-1274); the fifth commences with the epoch of the council of Lyon (1274) and extends up to the death of the inquisitor, Thomas d'Aversa (1204). And the sixth goes from 1308 to 1323.

[16] "*Supererant adhuc multi de sociis b. Francisci... et alii non pauci de quibus ego vidi et ab ipsis audivi quæ narro.* " Laur. Ms., cod. 7, pl. xx., f° 24a: "*Qui passi sunt eam (tribulationem tertiam) socii fundatoris fratres Aegdius et Angelus, qui supererant me audiente referibant.* " Laur. Ms., f° 27b. Cf., Italian Ms., xxxvii., 28, Magliab., f° 138b.

[17] The date of his death is unknown; on August 11, 1253, he was present at the death-bed of St. Clara.

[18] Died April 23, 1261.

[19] "*Quem (fratrem Jacobum de Massa) dirigente me fratre Johanne socio fratris prefati Egidii videre laboravi. Hic enim frater Johannes... dixit mihi....* " Arch. , ii., p. 279.

[20] "*... Tribulationes preteritas memoravi, ut audivi ab illis qui sustinuerunt eas et aliqua commemoravi de hiis que didici in quatuor legendis quas vidi et legi.* " Arch. , ii., p. 135. —"*Vitam pauperis et humilis viri Dei Francisci trium ordinum fundatoris quatuor solemnes personæ scripserunt, fratres videlicet scientia et sanctitate præclari, Johannes et Thomas de Celano, frater Bonaventura unus post Beatum Franciscum Generalis Minister et vir miræ simplicitatis et sanctitatis frater Leo, ejusdem sancti Francisci socius. Has quatuor descriptiones seu historias qui legerit....* " Laurent. MS., pl. xx., c. 7, f° 1a. Did the Italian

translator think there was an error in this quotation? I do not know, but he suppressed it. At f° 12a of manuscript xxxvii., 28, of the Magliabecchina, we read: "*Incominciano alcune croniche del ordine franciscano, come la vita del povero e humile servo di Dio Francesco fondatore del minorico ordine fu scripta da San Bonaventura e da quatro altri frati. Queste poche scripture ovveramente hystorie quello il quale diligentemente le leggiera, expeditamente potra cognoscere... la vocatione la santita di San Francisco.* "

[21] Laur. MS., f° 4b ff. On the other hand we read in a letter of Clareno: "*Ad hanc (paupertatem) perfecte servandam Christus Franciscum vocavit et elegit in hac hora novissima et precepit ei evangelicam assumere regulam, et a papa Innocentio fuit omnibus annuntiatum in concilio generali, quod de sua auctoritate et obedientia sanctus Franciscus evangelicam vitam et regulam assumpserat et Christo inspirante servare promiserat, sicut sanctus vir fr. Leo scribit et fr. Johannes de Celano.* " Archiv. , i., p. 559.

[22] "*Audiens enim semel quorundam fratrum enormes excessus, ut fr. Thomas de Celano scribit, et malum exemplum per eos secularibus datum.* " Laur. MS., f° 13b. The passage which follows evidently refers to 2 Cel., 3, 93 and 112.

[23] "*Et fecerunt de regula prima ministri removeri capitulum istud de prohibitionibus sancti evangelii, sicut frater Leo scribit.* " Laur. Ms. f° 12b. Cf. *Spec.* , 9a, see p. 248. "*Nam cum rediisset de partibus ultramarinis, minister quidam loquebatur cum eo, ut frater Leo refert, de capitulo paupertatis,* " f° 13a, cf. *Spec.* , 9a, "*S. Franciscus, teste fr. Leone, frequenter et cum multo studio recitabat fabulam... quod oportebat finaliter ordinem humiliari et ad sue humilitatis principia confitenda et tenenda reduci.* " Archiv. , ii., p. 129.

There is only one point of contact between the Legend of the Three Companions, such as it is to-day, and these passages; but we find on the contrary revised accounts in the *Speculum* and in the other collections, where they are cited as coming from Brother Leo.

[24] Clareno, for example, holds that the Cardinal Ugolini had sustained St. Francis without approving of the first Rule, in

concert with Cardinal Giovanni di San Paolo. This is possible, since Ugolini was created cardinal in 1198 (Vide Cardella: *Memorie storiche de' Cardinali*, 9 vols., 8vo, Rome, 1792-1793, t. i., pt. 2, p. 190). Besides this would better explain the zeal with which he protected the divers Orders founded by St. Francis, from 1217. The chapter where Clareno tells how St. Francis wrote the Rule shows the working over of the legend, but it is very possible that he has borrowed it in its present form from Brother Leo. It is to be noted that we do not find in this document a single allusion to the Indulgences of Portiuncula.

[25]   The manuscripts and editions are well-nigh innumerable. M. Luigi Manzoni has studied them with a carefulness that makes it much to be desired that he continue this difficult work. *Studi sui Fioretti*: Miscelenea, 1888, pp. 116-119, 150-152, 162-168; 1889, 9-15, 78-84, 132-135. When shall we find some one who can and will undertake to make a scientific edition of them? Those which have appeared during our time in the various cities of Italy are insignificant from a critical point of view. See Mazzoni Guido, *Capitoli inediti dei Fioretti di S. Francesco*, in the *Propugnatore*, Bologna, 1888, vol. xxi., pp. 396-411.

[26]   Vide A. SS., p. 865: *"Floretum non legi, nec curandum putavi. "* Cf. 553f: *"Floretum ad manum non habeo. "*

[27]   Bartolommeo di Pisa compiled it in 1385; then certain manuscripts of the Fioretti are earlier. Besides, in the stories that the Conformities borrow from the Fioretti, we perceive Bartolommeo's work of abbreviation.

[28]   I am speaking here only of the fifty-three chapters which form the true collection of the Fioretti.

[29]   The province of the March of Ancona counted seven custodias: 1, Ascoli; 2, Camerino; 3, Ancona; 4, Jesi; 5, Fermo; 6, Fano; 7, Felestro. The Fioretti mention at least six of the monasteries of the custodia of Fermo: Moliano, 51, 53; Fallerone, 32, 51; Bruforte and Soffiano, 46, 47; Massa, 51; Penna, 45; Fermo, 41, 49, 51.

[30]   At each page we are reminded of those groves which were originally the indispensable appendage of the Franciscan monasteries: *La selva ch' era allora allato a S. M. degli Angeli*, 3, 10, 15, 16, etc. *La selva d' un luogo deserto del val di Spoleto* (Carceri?), 4; *selva di Forano*, 42. *di Massa*, 51, etc.

[31]   The *Speculum*, 46b, 58b, 158a, gives us three states. Cf. *Fior.* , 26 and 21; *Conform.* , 119b, 2.

[32]   This desire was so natural that the manuscript of the Angelica Library includes many additional chapters, concerning the gift of Portiuncula, the indulgence of August 2d, the birth of St. Francis, etc. (Vide Amoni, Fioretti, Roma, 1889, pp. 266, 378-386.) It would be an interesting study to seek the origin of these documents and to establish their relationship with the Speculum and the Conformities. Vide *Conform.* , 231a, 1; 121b; *Spec.* , 92-96.

[33]   Ginepro was received into the Order by St. Francis. In 1253 he was present at St. Clara's death. A. SS., *Aug.* , t. ii., p. 764d. The Conformities speak of him in detail, f° 62b.

[34]   The first seven chapters form a whole. The three which follow are doubtless a first attempt at completing them.

[35]   Conformities, f° 55b, 1-60a, 1.

[36]   See *Archiv.* , t. i., p. 145, an article of Father Denifle: *Zur Quellenkunde der Franziskaner Geschichte,* where he mentions at least eight manuscripts of this work. Cf. Ehrle: *Zeitschrift*, 1883, p. 324, note 3. I have studied only the two manuscripts of Florence: Riccardi, 279, paper, 243 fos. of two cols. recently numbered. The Codex of the Laurentian Gaddian. rel., 53, is less careful. It is also on paper, 20 x 27, and counts 254 fos. of 1 column. F^o 1 was formerly numbered 88. The order of the chapters is not the same as in the preceding.

[37]   The citations are always made from the edition of Milan, 1510, 4to of 256 folios of two columns. The best known of the subsequent editions are those of Milan, 1513, and Bologna, 1590.

[38] He began it in 1385 (f° 1), and it was authorized by the chapter general August 2, 1399 (f° 256a, 1). Besides, on f° 150a, 1, he set down the date when he was writing. It was in 1390.

[39] I am not here concerned with the foolish attacks of certain Protestant authors upon this life. That is a quarrel of the theologians which in no way concerns history. Nowhere does Bartolommeo of Pisa make St. Francis the equal of Jesus, and he was able even to forestall criticism in this respect. The Bollandists are equally severe: *"Cum Pisanus fuerit scriptor magis pius et credulus quam crisi severa usus.... "* A. SS., p. 551e.

[40] He has avoided the mistakes so unfortunately committed by Wadding in his list of ministers general. Vide 66a. 2, 104a, 1, 118b, 2. He was lecturer on theology at Bologna, Padua, Pisa, Sienna, and Florence. He preached for many years and with great success in the principal villages of the Peninsula and could thus take advantage of his travels by collecting useful notes. Mark of Lisbon has preserved for us a notice of his life. Vide *Croniche dei fratri Minori*, t. iii., p. 6 ff. of the Diola edition. He died December 10, 1401. For further details see Wadding, ann. 1399, vii., viii., and above all Sbaralea, *Supplementum*, p. 109. He is the author of an exposition of the Rule little known which can be found in the Speculum Morin, Rouen, 1509, f° 66b-83a, of part three.

[41] This opinion is expressed in a guarded manner. For example, f° 207a, 1, Bartolommeo relates the miracle of the Chapter of the Mats, first following St. Bonaventura, then adding: *"Et quia non aliter tangit dicta pars (legendæ majoris) hoc insigne miraculum: antiqua legenda hoc refertur in hunc modum. "* Cf. 225a, 2m. *"Et quia fr. Bonaventura succincte multa tangit et in brevi: pro evidentia prefatorum notandum est... ut dicit antiqua legenda. "*

[42] However, it is necessary to note that not only are there considerable differences between the editions published, but also that the first (that of Milan, 1510) has been completed and revised by its editor. The judgments passed upon Raymond Ganfridi, 104a, 1, and Boniface VIII., 103b, 1, show traces of later corrections. (Cf. 125a, 1. At f° 72a, 2m, is

indicated the date of the death of St. Bernardin, which was in 1444, etc.) Besides, we are surprised to find beside the pages where the sources are indicated with clearness others where stories follow one another coming one knows not from whence.

[43] F^o 70a, 1: "*Cujus nomen non reperi.* " 1a, 2: "*Multaque non ex industria sed quia ea noscere non valui omittendo.* "

[44] F^o 78a, 1: *Informationes quas non scribo quia imperfectas reperi.* Cf. 229b, 2: "*De aliis multis apparitionibus non reperi scripturam, quare hic non pono.* "

[45] F^o 69a, 1: "*Hec ut audivi posui quia ejus legendam non vidi.* " Cf. 68b, 2m: *Fr. Henricus generalis minister mihi magistro Bartholomeo dixit ipse oretenus.*

[46] The citations from Bonaventura are decidedly more frequent. We should not be surprised, since this story is the official biography of St. Francis; the chapter from which Bartolommeo takes his quotations is almost always indicated, and, naturally, follows the old division in five parts. Opening the book at hazard at folio 136a I find no less than six references to the *Legenda Major* in the first column. To give an idea of the style of Bartolommeo of Pisa I shall give in substance the contents of a page of his book. See, for example, f° 111a (lib. i., conform. x., pars. ii., Franciscus predicator). In the third line he cites Bonaventura: "*Fr. Bonaventura in quarta parte majoris legende dicit quod b. Franciscus videbatur intuentibus homo alterius seculi.* " Textual citation of Bonaventure, 45. Three lines further on: "*Verum qualis esset b. F. quoad personam sic habetur in legenda antiqua... homo facundissimus, facie hilaris,* etc. " The literal citation of the sketch of Francis follows as 1 Celano, 83, gives it as far as: "*inter peccatores quasi unus ex illis,* " and to mark the end of the quotation Bartolommeo adds: "*Hec legenda antiqua.* " In the next column paragraph 4 commences with the words: *B. Francisci predicationem reddebat mirabilem et gloriosam ipsius sancti loquutio: etenim legenda trium Sociorum dicit et Legenda major parte tertia: B. Francisei eloquia erant non inania, neo risu digna,* etc., which corresponds literally with 3 Soc., 25, and Bon., 28. Then come two chapters of Bonaventura almost entire, beginning with: *In duodecima parte legende majoris dicit*

Fr. Bonaventura: Erat enim verbum ejus, etc. Textual quotation of Bon., 178 and 179. The page ends with another quotation from Bonaventura: *Sic dicebat prout recitat Bonaventura in octava parte Legende majoris: Hac officium patri misericordiarum.* Vide Bonav., 102 end and 103 entire. This suffices without doubt to show with what precision the authorities have been quoted in this work, with what attention and confidence ought to be examined those portions of documents lost or mislaid which he has here preserved for us.

[47] F^o 31b, 2: *ut dicit fr. Thomas in sua legenda*, cf. 2 Cel., 3, 60. — 140a, 2: *Fr. in leg. fr. Thome*, cf. 2 Cel., 3, 60. —140a 1, cf. 2 Cel., 3 16. —142b, 1: *Fr. in leg. Thome capitulo de charitate*, cf. 2 Cel., 3, 115. —144b, 1: *Fr. in leg. fr. Thome capitulo de oratione*, cf. 2 Cel., 3, 40. —144b, 1, cf. 2 Cel., 3, 65. —144b, 2, cf. 2 Cel., 3, 78. —176b, 2, cf. 2 Cel., 3, 79. —182b, 2, cf. 2 Cel., 2, 1. — 241b, 1, cf. 2 Cel., 3, 141. —181a, 2, cf. 1 Cel., 27. It is needless to say that these lists of quotations do not pretend to be complete.

[48] F^o 36b, 2. *Ut enim habetur in leg.* 3 Soc., cf. 3 Soc., 10. —46b, 1, cf. 3 Soc., 25-28. —38b 2, cf. 3 Soc. 3. —111a, 2, cf. 3 Soc., 25. —134a, 2, cf. 3 Soc., 4. —142b, 2, cf. 3 Soc., 57 and 58. —167b, 2, cf. 3 Soc., 3 and 8. —168a, 1, cf. 3 Soc., 10. —170b, 1, cf. 3 Soc., 39, 4. —175b, 2, cf. 3 Soc., 59. —180b, 2, cf. 3 Soc., 4. — 181a, 1, cf. 3 Soc., 5, 7, 24, 33, and 67. —181a. 2, cf. 3 Soc., 36. —229b, 2, cf. 3 Soc., 14. etc. The reading of 3 Soc. which Bartolommeo had before his eyes was pretty much the same we have to day, for he says, 181a, 2. referring to 3 Soc., 67: "*Ut habetur quasi in fine leg.* 3 Soc. "

[49] F^o 111a, 1, *Sic habetur in leg. ant.* , corresponds literally with 1 Cel., 83. —144a, 2. *Franciscus in leg. ant. cap. v. de zelo ad religionem*, to 1 Cel. 106.

[50] F^o 111b, 1. *De predicantibus loqueus sic dicebat in ant. leg.* Cf. 2 Cel., 3, 99 and 106. 140b, 1. Cf. 2 Cel., 3, 84. —144b, 1, cf. 2 Cel., 3, 45—144a, 1, cf. 2 Cel., 3, 95 and 15. —225b, 2, cf. 2 Cel., 3, 116.

[51] F^o 31a, 1. Vide 2 Cel., 3, 83. —143a, 2. Vide 2 Cel., 3, 65 and 116. —144a, 1. Vide 2 Cel., 3, 94. —170b. 1. Vide 2 Cel., 3, 11.

[52]   F^o 14a, 2. −32a. 1. −101a, 2. −169b, 1. −144b, 2. −142a, 2.
         −143b, 2. −168b, 1. −144b, 1.

[53]   Chapters 18 (chapter of the mats) and 25 (lepers cured) of the
         Fioretti are found in Latin in the Conf. as borrowed from the
         Leg. Ant. Vide 174b, 1, and 207a. 1.

         Finally, according to f° 168b, 2, it is also from the Leg. Ant.
         that the description of the coat, such as we find at the end of
         the *Chronique des Tribulations,* was borrowed. See *Archiv.* , t.
         ii., p. 153.

[54]   F^o 182a, 2; cf. 51b, 1; 144a, 1.

[55]   He died December 12, 1306, at Bastia, near Assisi. See upon
         him *Chron. Tribul. Archiv.* , ii. ; 311 and 312; *Conform.* , 60, 119,
         and 153.

[56]   Although the history of the Indulgence of Portiuncula was of
         all subjects the one most largely treated in the Conformities,
         151b, 2−157a, 2, not once does Bartolommeo of Pisa refer to
         it in the *Legenda Antiqua*. It seems, then, that this collection
         also was silent as to this celebrated pardon.

[57]   Published with extreme care by the Franciscan Fathers of the
         Observance in t. ii. of the *Analecta Franciscana, ad Claræ Aquas*
         (Quaracchi, near Florence), 1888, 1 vol., crown 8vo, of xxxvi.
         -612 pp. This edition, as much from the critical point of view
         of the text, its correctness, its various readings and notes, as
         from the material point of view, is perfect and makes the
         more desirable a publication of the chronicles of the xxiv.
         generals and of Salimbeni by the same editors. The
         beginning up to the year 1262 has been published already by
         Dr. Karl Evers under the title *Analecta ad Fratrum Minorum
         historiam*, Leipsic, 1882, 4to of 89 pp.

[58]   I have been able only to procure the Italian edition published
         by Horatio Diola under the title *Croniche degli Ordini instituti
         dal P. S. Francesco*, 3 vols., 8vo, Venice, 1606.

V

CHRONICLES OUTSIDE OF THE ORDER

1. JACQUES DE VITRY

The following documents, which we can only briefly indicate, are of inestimable value; they emanate from men particularly well situated to give us the impression which the Umbrian prophet produced on his generation.

Jacques de Vitry[1] has left extended writings on St. Francis. Like a prudent man who has already seen many religious madmen, he is at first reserved; but soon this sentiment disappears, and we find in him only a humble and active admiration for the *Apostolic Man*.

He speaks of him in a letter which he wrote immediately after the taking of Damietta (November, 1219), to his friends in Lorraine, to describe it to them. [2] A few lines suffice to describe St. Francis and point out his irresistible influence. There is not a single passage in the Franciscan biographers which gives a more living idea of the apostolate of the Poverello.

He returns to him more at length in his *Historia Occidentalis*, devoting to him the thirty-second chapter of this curious work. [3] These pages, vibrating with enthusiasm, were written during Francis's lifetime, [4] at the time when the most enlightened members of the Church, who had believed themselves to be living in the evening of the world, *in vespere mundi tendentis ad occasum*, suddenly saw in the direction of Umbria the light of a new day.

2. THOMAS OF SPALATO

An archdeacon of the Cathedral of Spalato, who in 1220 was studying at Bologna, has left us a very living portrait of St. Francis and the memory of the impression which his preachings produced in that learned town. [5]

Something of his enthusiasm has passed into his story; we feel that that day, August 15, 1220, when he met the Poverello of Assisi, was one of the best of his life. [6]

3. DIVERS CHRONICLES

The continuation of William of Tyre[7] brings us a new account of Francis's attempt to conquer the Soudan. This narrative, the longest of all three we have on this subject, contains no feature essentially new, but it gives one more witness to the historic value of the Franciscan legends.

Finally, there are two chronicles written during Francis's life, which, without giving anything new, speak with accuracy of his foundation, and prove how rapidly that religious renovation which started in Umbria was being propagated to the very ends of Europe. The anonymous chronicler of Monte Sereno[8] in fact wrote about 1225, and tells us, not without regret, of the brilliant conquests of the Franciscans.

Burchard, [9] Abbot Prémontré d'Ursberg (died in 1226), who was in Rome in 1211, leaves us a very curious criticism of the Order.

The Brothers Minor appeared to him a little like an orthodox branch of the Poor Men of Lyons. He even desires that the pope, while approving the Franciscans, should do so with a view to satisfy, in the measure of the possible, the aspirations manifested by that heresy and that of the Humiliati.

It is impossible to attribute any value whatever to the long pages given to St. Francis by Matthew Paris. [10] His information is correct wherever the activities of the friars are concerned, and he could examine the work around him. [11] They are absolutely fantastic when he comes to the life of St. Francis, and we can only feel surprised to find M. Hase[12] adopting the English monk's account of the stigmata.

The notice which he gives of Francis contains as many errors as sentences; he makes him born of a family illustrious by its nobility, makes him study theology from his infancy (*hoc didicerat in litteris et theologicis disciplinis quibus ab ætate tenera incubuerat, usque ad notitiam perfectam*), etc. [13]

It would be useless to enlarge this list and mention those chroniclers who simply noticed the foundation of the Order, its approbation, and the death of St. Francis, [14] or those which spoke of him at length, but simply by copying a Franciscan legend. [15]

It suffices to point out by way of memory the long chapter consecrated to St. Francis in the Golden Legend. Giachimo di Voraggio ([Cross] 1298) there sums up with accuracy but without order the essential features of the first legends and in particular the Second Life by Celano. [16]

As for the inscription of Santa Maria del Vescovado at Assisi it is too unformed to be anything but a simple object of curiosity. [17]

* * * * *

I have given up preparing a complete bibliography of works concerning St. Francis, that task having been very well done by the Abbé Ulysse Chevalier in his *Répertoire des sources historiques du moyen age*, Bio-Bibliographie, cols. 765-767 and 2588-2590, Paris, 1 vol., 4to, 1876-1888. To it I refer my readers.

FOOTNOTES:

[1]   He was born at Vitry sur Seine, became Curé of Argenteuil, near Paris; Canon of Oignies, in the diocese of Namur, preached the crusade against the Albigenses, and accompanied the Crusaders to Palestine; having been made Bishop of Acre, he was present in 1219 at the siege and at the capture of Damietta and returned to Europe in 1225; created Cardinal-bishop of Frascati in 1229, he died in 1244, leaving a number of writings. For his life, see the preface of his *Historiæ*, edition of Douai, 1597.

[2]   This letter may be found in (Bongars) *Gesta Dei per Francio*, pp. 1146-1149.

[3]   *Jacobi de Vitriaco Libri duo quorum prior Orientalis, alter* Occidentalis *Historiæ nomine inscribitur studio Fr. Moschi Duaci ex officina Balthazaris Belleri*, 1597, 16mo, 480 pp. Chapter xxxii. fills pages 349-353, and is entitled *De ordine et prædicatione fratrum Minorum*. See above, p. 229.

[4]   This appears from the passage: *Videmus primus ordinis fundatorem magestrum cui tanquam summo Priori suo omnes alii obediunt*. *Loc. cit.* , p. 352.

[5] It is inserted in the treatise of Sigonius on the bishops of Bologna: *Caroli Sigonii de episcopis Bononiensibus libri quinque cum notis L. C. Rabbii*, a work which occupies cols. 353-590 of t. iii. of his *Opera omnia*, Milan, 1732-1737, 6 vols., f^o. We find our fragment in col. 432.

[6] This passage will be found above, p. 241.

[7] Guillelmi *Tyrensis arch. Continuala belli sacri historia* in Martène: *Amplissima Collectio*, t. v. pp. 584-572. The piece concerning Francis is cols. 689-690.

[8] *Chronicon Montis Sereni* (at present Petersberg, near Halle), edited by Ehrenfeuchter in the *Mon. Germ. hist. Script.* , t. 23, pp. 130-226, 229.

[9] *Burchardi et Cuonradi Urspergensium chronicon* ed., A. Otto Abel and L. Weiland, *apud Mon. Germ, hist.* , t. 23, pp. 333-383. The monastery of Ursperg was half-way between Ulm and Augsburg. Vide p. 376.

[10] *Matthæi Parisiensis monachie Albanensis, Historia major*, edition Watts, London, 1640. The Brothers Minor are first mentioned in the year 1207, p. ???, then 1227, pp. 339-342.

[11] See the article, *Minores*, in the table of contents of the *Mon. Germ. hist.* Script. , t. xxviii.

[12] *Franz von Assisi*, p. 168 ff.

[13] See above, p. 97, his story of the audience with Innocent III.

[14] For example, *Chronica Albrici trium fontium* in Pertz: *Script.* , t. 23, *ad ann.* 1207, 1226, 1228. Vide Fragment of the chron. of Philippe Mousket ([Cross] before 1245). *Recueil des historiens*, t. xxii., p. 71, lines 30347-30360. The number of annalists in this century is appalling, and there is not one in ten who has omitted to note the foundation of the Minor Brothers.

[15] For example, Vincent de Beauvais ([Cross] 1264) gives in his *Speculum historiale*, lib. 29, cap. 97-99, lib. 30, cap. 99-111, nearly every story given by the Bollandists under the title of *Secunda legenda* in their *Commentarium prævium*.

[16]   *Legenda aurea*, Graesse, Breslau, 1890, pp. 662-674.

[17]   A good reproduction of it will be found in the *Miscellanea francescana*, t. ii., pp. 33-37, accompanied by a learned dissertation by M. Faloci Pulignani.

APPENDIX

CRITICAL STUDY OF THE STIGMATA AND THE INDULGENCE
OF AUGUST 2

I. THE STIGMATA

A dissertation upon the possibility of miracles would be out of place
here; a historic sketch is not a treatise on philosophy or dogmatics.

Still, I owe the reader a few explanations, to enable him with
thorough understanding to judge of my manner of viewing the
subject.

If by miracle we understand either the suspension or subversion of
the laws of nature, or the intervention of the first cause in certain
particular cases, I could not concede it. In this negation physical and
logical reasons are secondary; the true reason—let no one be
surprised—is entirely religious; the miracle is immoral. The equality
of all before God is one of the postulates of the religious
consciousness, and the miracle, that good pleasure of God, only
degrades him to the level of the capricious tyrants of the earth.

The existing churches, making, as nearly all of them do, this notion
of miracle the very essence of religion and the basis of all positive
faith, involuntarily render themselves guilty of that emasculation of
manliness and morality of which they so passionately complain. If
God intervenes thus irregularly in the affairs of men, the latter can
hardly do otherwise than seek to become courtiers who expect all
things of the sovereign's *favor*.

The question changes its aspect, if we call miracle, as we most
generally do, all that goes beyond ordinary experience.

Many apologists delight in showing that the unheard of, the
inexplicable, are met with all through life. They are right and I agree
with them, on condition that they do not at the close of their
explanation replace this new notion of the supernatural by the
former one.

It is thus that I have come to conclude the reality of the stigmata.
They may have been a unique fact without being more miraculous

than other phenomena; for example, the mathematical powers or the musical ability of an infant prodigy.

There are in the human creature almost indefinite powers, marvellous energies; in the great majority of men these lie in torpid slumber, but awaking to life in a few, they make of them prophets, men of genius, and saints who show humanity its true nature.

We have caught but fleeting glimpses into the domain of mental pathology, so vast is it and unexplored; the learned men of the future will perhaps make, in the realms of psychology and physiology, such discoveries as will bring about a complete revolution in our laws and customs.

It remains to examine the stigmata from the point of view of history. And though in this field there is no lack of difficulties, small and great, the testimony appears to me to be at once too abundant and too precise not to command conviction.

We may at the outset set aside the system of those who hold that Brother Elias helped on their appearance by a pious fraud. Such a claim might indeed be defended if these marks had been gaping wounds, as they are now or in most cases have been represented to be; but all the testimony agrees in describing them, with the exception of the mark on the side, as blackish, fleshy excrescences, like the heads of nails, and in the palms of the hands like the points of nails clinched by a hammer. There was no bloody exudation except at the side.

On the other hand, any deception on the part of Elias would oblige us to hold that his accomplices were actually the heads of the party opposed to him, Leo, Angelo, and Rufino. Such want of wit would be surprising indeed in a man so circumspect.

Finally the psychological agreement between the external circumstances and the event is so close that an invention of this character would be as inexplicable as the fact itself. That which indeed almost always betrays invented or unnatural incidents is that they do not fit into the framework of the facts. They are extraneous events, purely decorative elements whose place might be changed at will.

Nothing of the sort is the case here: Thomas of Celano is so veracious and so exact, that though holding the stigmata to be miraculous, he gives us all the elements necessary for explaining them in a diametrically opposite manner.

1. The preponderating place of the passion of Jesus in Francis's conscience ever since his conversion (1 Cel., 115; 2 Cel., 1, 6; 3, 29; 49; 52).

2. His sojourn in the Verna coincides with a great increase of mystical fervor.

3. He there observes a Lent in honor of the archangel St. Michael.

4. The festival of the exaltation of the cross comes on, and in the vision of the crucified seraph is blended the two ideas which have taken possession of him, the angels and the crucifix (1 Cel., 91-96, 112-115).

This perfect congruity between the circumstances and the prodigy itself forms a moral proof whose value cannot be exaggerated.

It is time to pass the principal witnesses in review.

1. Brother Elias, 1226. On the very day after the death of Francis, Brother Elias, in his capacity of vicar, sent letters to the entire Order announcing the event and prescribing prayers. [1]

After having expressed his sorrow and imparted to the Brothers the blessing with which the dying Francis had charged him for them, he adds: "I announce to you a great joy and a new miracle. Never has the world seen such a sign, except on the Son of God who is the Christ God. For a long time before his death our Brother and Father appeared as crucified, having in his body five wounds which are truly the stigmata of Christ, for his hands and his feet bore marks as of nails without and within, forming a sort of scars; while at the side he was as if pierced with a lance, and often a little blood oozed from it. "

2. Brother Leo. We find that it is the very adversary of Elias who is the natural witness, not only of the stigmata, but of the circumstances of their imprinting. This fact adds a peculiar value to his account.

We learned above (Critical Study, p. 377) the untoward fate of a part of the Legend of Brothers Leo, Angelo, and Rufino. The chapters with which it now closes (68-73) and in which the narrative of the miracle occurs, were not originally a part of it. They are a summary added at a later time to complete this document. This appendix, therefore, has no historic value, and we neither depend on it with the ecclesiastical authors to affirm the miracle, nor with M. Hase to call it in question.

Happily the testimony of Brother Leo has come down to us in spite of that. We are not left even to seek for it in the Speculum, the Fioretti, the Conformities, where fragments of his work are to be found; we find it in several other documents of incontestable authority.

The authenticity of the autograph of St. Francis preserved at Assisi appears to be thoroughly established (see Critical Study, p. 357); it contains the following note by Brother Leo's hand: "The Blessed Francis two years before his death kept on the Verna in honor of the B. V. Mary mother of God, and St. Michael Archangel, a Lent from the festival of the Assumption of the B. V. M. to the festival of St. Michael in September, and the hand of God was upon him by the vision and the address of the seraph and the impression of the stigmata upon his body. He made the laudes that are on the other side,... etc. "

Again, Eccleston (13) shows us Brother Leo complaining to Brother Peter of Tewkesbury, minister in England, that the legend is too brief concerning the events on the Verna, and relating to him the greater number of the incidents which form the nucleus of the Fioretti on the stigmata. These memorials are all the more certain that they were immediately committed to writing by Peter of Tewkesbury's companion, Brother Garin von Sedenfeld.

Finally Salembeni, in his chronicle (ad ann. 1224) in speaking of Ezzelino da Romano is led to oppose him to Francis. He suddenly remembers the stigmata and says, "Never man on earth, but he, has had the five wounds of Christ. His companion, Brother Leo, who was present when they washed the body before the burial, told me that he looked precisely like a crucified man taken down from the cross. "

3. Thomas of Celano, before 1230. He describes them more at length than Brother Elias (1 Cel., 94, 95, 112).

The details are too precise not to suggest a lesson learned by heart. The author nowhere assumes to be an eye-witness, yet he has the tone of a legal deposition.

These objections are not without weight, but the very novelty of the miracle might have induced the Franciscans to fix it in a sort of canonical and so to say, stereotyped narrative.

4. The portrait of Francis, by Berlinghieri, dated 1236, [2] preserved at Pescia (province of Lucca) shows the stigmata as they are described in the preceding documents.

5. Gregory IX. in 1237. Bull of March 31; *Confessor Domini* (Potthast, 10307. Cf. 10315). A movement of opinion against the stigmata had been produced in certain countries. The pope asks all the faithful to believe in them. Two other bulls of the same day, one addressed to the Bishop of Olmütz, the other to the Dominicans, energetically condemns them for calling the stigmata in question (Potthast, 10308 and 10309).

6. Alexander IV., in his bull *Benigna operatio* of October 29, 1255 (Potthast, 16077), states that having formerly been the domestic prelate of Cardinal Ugolini, he knew St. Francis familiarly, and supports his description of the stigmata by these relations.

To this pontiff are due several bulls declaring excommunicate all those who deny them. These contribute nothing new to the question.

7. Bonaventura (1260) repeats in his legend Thomas of Celano's description (Bon., 193; cf. 1 Cel. 94 and 95), not without adding some new factors (Bon., 194-200 and 215-218), often so coarse and clumsy that they inevitably awaken doubt (see for example, 201).

8. Matthew Paris ([Cross] 1259). His discordant witness barely deserves being cited by way of memoir (see Critical Study, p. 431). To be able to forgive the fanciful character of his long disquisitions on St. Francis, we are forced to recall to mind that he owed his information to the verbal account of some pilgrim. He makes the stigmata appear a fortnight before the Saint's death, shows them continually emitting blood, the wound on the side so wide open that

the heart could be seen. The people gather in crowds to see the sight, the cardinals come also, and all together listen to Francis's strange declarations. (*Historia major*, Watts's edition London, 1 vol. fol., 1640, pp. 339-342.)

This list might be greatly lengthened by the addition of a passage from Luke bishop of Tuy (Lucas Tudensis) written in 1231; [3] based especially on the Life by Thomas of Celano, and oral witnesses.

The statement of Brother Boniface, an eye-witness, at the chapter of Genoa (1254). (Eccl. 13.)

Finally and especially, we should study the strophes relating to the stigmata in the proses, hymns, and sequences composed in 1228 by the pope and several cardinals for the Office of St. Francis; but such a work, to be done with accuracy, would carry us very far, and the authorities already cited doubtless suffice without bringing in others. [4]

The objections which have been opposed to these witnesses may be reduced, I think, to the following: [5]

a. Francis's funeral took place with surprising precipitation. Dead on Saturday evening, he was buried Sunday morning.

b. His body was enclosed in a coffin, which is contrary to Italian habits.

c. At the time of the removal, the body, wrested from the multitude, is so carefully hidden in the basilica that for centuries its precise place has been unknown.

d. The bull of canonization makes no mention of the stigmata.

e. They were not admitted without a contest, and among those who denied them were some bishops.

None of these arguments appears to me decisive.

a. In the Middle Ages funerals almost always took place immediately after death (Innocent III. dying at Perugia July 16, 1216, is interred the 17th; Honorius III. dies March 18, 1227, and is interred the next day).

b. It is more difficult than many suppose to know what were the habits concerning funerals in Umbria in the thirteenth century. However that may be, it was certainly necessary to put Francis's body into a coffin. He being already canonized by popular sentiment, his corpse was from that moment a relic for which a reliquary was necessary; nay more, a strong box such as the secondary scenes in Berlinghieri's picture shows it to have been. Without such a precaution the sacred body would have been reduced to fragments in a few moments. Call to mind the wild enthusiasm that led the devotees to cut off the ears and even the breasts of St. Elizabeth of Hungary. [*Quædam aures illius truncabant, etiam summitatem mamillarum ejus quidam praecidebant et pro reliquiis sibi servabant.* —*Liber de dictis iv. ancillarum*, Mencken, vol. ii., p. 2032.]

c. The ceremony of translation brought an innumerable multitude to Assisi. If Brother Elias concealed the body, [6] he may have been led to do so by the fear of some organized surprise of the Perugians to gain possession of the precious relic. With the customs of those days, such a theft would have been in nowise extraordinary. These very Perugians a few years later stole away from Bastia, a village dependent on Assisi, the body of Conrad of Offida, which was performing innumerable miracles there. (*Conform.* , 60b, 1; cf. Giord., 50.) Similar affrays took place at Padua over the relics of St. Anthony. (Hilaire, *Saint Antoine de Padoue, sa légende primitive*, Montreuil-sur-Mer, 1 vol., 8vo, 1890, pp. 30-40.)

d. The bull of canonization, with the greater number of such documents, for that matter, makes no historic claim. In its wordy rhetoric we shall sooner learn the history of the Philistines, of Samson, or even of Jacob, than of St. Francis. Canonization here is only a pretext which the old pontiff seizes for recurring to his favorite figures.

This silence signifies nothing after the very explicit testimony of other bulls by the same pontiff in 1227, and after the part given to the stigmata in the liturgical songs which in 1228 he composed for the office of St. Francis.

e. These attacks by certain bishops are in nowise surprising; they are episodes in the struggle of the secular clergy against the mendicant orders.

At the time when these negations were brought forward (1237) the narrative of Thomas of Celano was official and everywhere known; nothing therefore would have been easier, half a score of years after the events, than to bring witnesses to expose the fraud if there had been any; but the Bishop of Olmütz and the others base their objections always and only upon dogmatic grounds.

As to the attacks of the Dominicans, it is needless to recall the rivalry between the two Orders; [7] is it not then singular to find these protestations coming from Silesia (!) and never from Central Italy, where, among other eye-witnesses, Brother Leo was yet living ([Cross] 1271)?

Thus the witnesses appear to me to maintain their integrity. We might have preferred them more simple and shorter, we could wish that they had reached us without details which awake all sorts of suspicions, [8] but it is very seldom that a witness does not try to prove his affirmations and to prop them up by arguments which, though detestable, are appropriate to the vulgar audience to which he is speaking.

II. THE PARDON OF AUGUST 2D, CALLED INDULGENCE OF PORTIUNCULA[9]

This question might be set aside; on the whole it has no direct connection with the history of St. Francis.

Yet it occupies too large a place in modern biographies not to require a few words: it is related that Francis was in prayer one night at Portiuncula when Jesus and the Virgin appeared to him with a retinue of angels. He made bold to ask an unheard-of privilege, that of plenary indulgence of all sins for all those who, having confessed and being contrite, should visit this chapel. Jesus granted this at his mother's request, on the sole condition that his vicar the pope would ratify it.

The next day Francis set out for Perugia, accompanied by Masseo, and obtained from Honorius the desired indulgence, but only for the day of August 2d.

Such, in a few lines, is the summary of this legend, which is surrounded with a crowd of marvellous incidents.

The question of the nature and value of indulgences is not here concerned. The only one which is here put is this: Did Francis ask this indulgence and did Honorius III. grant it?

Merely to reduce it to these simple proportions is to be brought to answer it with a categorical No.

It would be tedious to refer even briefly to the difficulties, contradictions, impossibilities of this story, many a time pointed out by orthodox writers. In spite of all they have come to the affirmative conclusion: *Roma locuta est.*

Those whom this subject may interest will find in the note above detailed bibliographical indications of the principal elements of this now quieted discussion. I shall confine myself to pointing out the impossibilities with which tradition comes into collision; they are both psychological and historical. The Bollandists long since pointed out the silence of Francis's early biographers upon this question. Now that the published documents are much more numerous, this silence is still more overwhelming. Neither the First nor the Second Life by Thomas of Celano, nor the anonymous author of the second life given in the Acta Sanctorum, nor even the anonymous writer of Perugia, nor the Three Companions, nor Bonaventura say a single word on the subject. No more do very much later works mention it, which sin only by excessive critical scruples: Bernard of Besse, Giordano di Giano, Thomas Eccleston, the Chronicle of the Tribulations, the Fioretti, and even the Golden Legend.

This conspiracy of silence of all the writers of the thirteenth century would be the greatest miracle of history if it were not absurd.

By way of explanation, it has been said that these writers refrained from speaking of this indulgence for fear of injuring that of the Crusade; but in that case, why did the pope command seven bishops to go to Portiuncula to proclaim it in his name?

The legend takes upon itself to explain that Francis refused a bull or any written attestation of this privilege; but, admitting this, it would still be necessary to explain why no hint of this matter has been preserved in the papers of Honorius III. And how is it that the bulls sent to the seven bishops have left not the slightest trace upon this pontiff's register?

Again, how does it happen, if seven bishops officially promulgated this indulgence in 1217, that St. Francis, after having related to Brother Leo his interview with the pope, said to him: "*Teneas secretum hoc usque circa mortem tuam; quia non habet locum adhuc. Quia hæc indulgentia occultabitur ad tempus; sed Dominus trahet eam extra et manifestabitur.* " *Conform.* , 153b, 2. Such an avowal is not wanting in simplicity. It abundantly proves that before the death of Brother Leo (1271) no one had spoken of this famous pardon.

After this it is needless to insist upon secondary difficulties; how is it that the chapters-general were not fixed for August 2d, to allow the Brothers to secure the indulgence?

How explain that Francis, after having received in 1216 a privilege unique in the annals of the Church, should be a stranger to the pope in 1219!

There is, however, one more proof whose value exceeds all the others—Francis's Will:

"I forbid absolutely all the Brothers by their obedience, in whatever place they may be, to ask any bull of the court of Rome, whether directly or indirectly, nor under pretext of church or convent, nor under pretext of preaching, nor even for their personal protection. "

Before closing it remains for us to glance at the growth of this legend.

It was definitively constituted about 1330-1340, but it was in the air long before. With the patience of four Benedictines (of the best days) we should doubtless be able to find our way in the medley of documents, more or less corrupted, from which it comes to us, and little by little we might find the starting-point of this dream in a friar who sees blinded humanity kneeling around Portiuncula to recover sight. [10]

It is not difficult to see in general what led to the materialization of this graceful fancy: people remembered Francis's attachment to the chapel where he had heard the decisive words of the gospel, and where St. Clara in her turn had entered upon a new life.

When the great Basilica of Assisi was built, drawing to itself pilgrims and privileges, an opposition of principles and of inspiration came to be added to the petty rivalry between it and Portiuncula.

The zealots of poverty said aloud that though the Saint's body rested in the basilica his heart was at Portiuncula. [11] By dint of repeating and exaggerating what Francis had said about the little sanctuary, they came to give a precise and so to say doctrinal sense to utterances purely mystical.

The violences and persecutions of the party of the Large Observance under the generalship of Crescentius[12] (1244-1247) aroused a vast increase of fervor among their adversaries. To the bull of Innocent IV. declaring the basilica thenceforth *Caput et Mater* of the Order[13] the Zealots replied by the narratives of Celano's Second Life and the legends of that period. [14] They went so far as to quote a promise of Francis to make it in perpetuity the *Mater et Caput* of his institute. [15]

In this way the two parties came to group themselves around these two buildings. Even to-day it is the same. The Franciscans of the Strict Observance occupy Portiuncula, while the Basilica of Assisi is in the hands of the Conventuals (Large Observance), who have adopted all the interpretations and mitigations of the Rules; they are worthy folk, who live upon their dividends. By a phenomenon, unique, I think, in the annals of the Church, they have pushed the freedom of their infidelity to the point of casting off the habit, the popular brown cassock. Dressed all in black, shod and hatted, nothing distinguishes them from the secular clergy except a modest little cord.

Poor Francis! That he may have the joy of feeling his tomb brushed by a coarse gown, some daring friar must overcome his very natural repugnances, and come to kneel there. The indulgence of August 2d is then the reply of the Zealots to the persecutions of their brothers.

An attentive study will perhaps show it emerging little by little under the generalship of Raimondo Gaufridi (1289-1295); Conrad di Offida ([Cross] 1306) seems to have had some effect upon it, but only with the next generation do we find the legend completed and avowed in open day.

Begun in a misapprehension it ends by imposing itself upon the Church, which to-day guarantees it with its infallible authority, and yet in its origin it was a veritable cry of revolt against the decisions of Rome.

FOOTNOTES:

[1]   The text was published in 1620 by Spoelberch (in his *Speculum vitæ B. Francisci*, Antwerp, 2 vols., 12mo, ii., pp. 103-106), after the copy addressed to Brother Gregory, minister in France, and then preserved in the convent of the Recollects in Valenciennes. It was reproduced by Wadding (Ann. 1226, no. 44) and the Bollandists (pp. 668 and 669).

So late an appearance of a capital document might have left room for doubts; there is no longer reason for any, since the publication of the chronicle of Giordano di Giano, who relates the sending of this letter (Giord., 50). The Abbé Amoni has also published this text (at the close of his *Legenda trium Sociorum*, Rome, 1880, pp. 105-109), but according to his deplorable habit, he neglects to tell whence he has drawn it. This is the more to be regretted since he gives a variant of the first order: *Nam diu ante mortem* instead of *Non diu*, as Spoelberch's text has it. The reading *Nam diu* appears preferable from a philological point of view.

[2]   Engraved in Saint François d'Assise, Paris, 4to, 1885, p. 277.

[3]   *Bibliotheca Patrum.* Lyons, 1677, xxv., *adv. Albigenses*, lib. ii., cap. 11., cf. iii., 14 and 15. Reproduced in the A. SS., p. 652.

[4]   The curious may consult the following sources: Salimbeni, ann. 1250—*Conform.* , 171b 2, 235a 2; Bon., 200; Wadding, *ann. 1228*, no. 78; A. SS., p. 800. Manuscript 340 of the *Sacro Convento* contains (fo. 55b-56b) four of these hymns. Cf. *Archiv.* i., p. 485.

[5]   See in particular Hase: *Franz v. Assisi*. Leipsic, 1 vol., 8vo., 1856. The learned professor devotes no less than sixty closely printed pages to the study of the stigmata, 142-202.

[6]   The more I think about it, the more incapable I become of attributing any sort of weight to this argument from the

disappearance of the body; for in fact, if there had been any pious fraud on Elias's part, he would on the contrary have displayed the corpse.

[7]   See, for example, 2 Cel., 3, 86, as well as the encyclical of Giovanni di Parma and Umberto di Romano, in 1225.

[8]   The following among many others: Francis had particularly high breeches made for him, to hide the wound in the side (Bon., 201). At the moment of the apparition, which took place during the night, so great a light flooded the whole country, that merchants lodging in the inns of Casentino saddled their beasts and set out on their way. *Fior., iii. consid.*

        Hase, in his study, is continually under the weight of the bad impression made upon him by Bonaventura's deplorable arguments; he sees the other witness only through him. I think that if he had read simply Thomas of Celano's first Life, he would have arrived at very different conclusions.

[9]   The most important document is manuscript 344 of the archives of Sacro Convento at Assisi. *Liber indulgentiæ S. Mariæ de Angelis sive de Portiuncula in quo libra ego fr. Franciscus Bartholi de Assisio posui quidquid potui sollicite invenire in legendis antiquis et novis b. Francisci et in aliis dictis sociorum ejus de loco eodem et commendatione ipsius loci et quidquid veritatis et certitudinis potui invenire de sacra indulgentia prefati loci, quomodo scilicet fuit impetrata et data b. Francisco de miraculis ipsius indulgentiæ quæ ipsam declarant certam et veram.* Bartholi lived in the first half of the fourteenth century. His work is still unpublished, but Father Leo Patrem M. O. is preparing it for publication. The name of this learned monk gives every guaranty for the accuracy of this difficult work; meanwhile a detailed description and long extracts may be found in the Miscellanea (ii., 1887). *La storia del perdono di Francesco de Bartholi*, by Don Michele Faloci Pulignani, pp. 149-153 (cf. *Archiv.* , i., p. 486). See also in the Miscellanea (i., 1886, p. 15) a bibliographical note containing a detailed list of fifty-eight works (cf. ibid., pp. 48, 145). The legend itself is found in the *Speculum*, 69b-83a, and in the *Conformities*, 151b-157a. In these two collections it is still found laboriously worked in and is not an integral part of the rest of the work. In the latter, Bartolemmeo di Pisa has

carried accuracy so far as to copy from end to end all the documents that he had before him, and as they belong to different periods he thus gives us several phases of the development of the tradition. The most complete work is that of the Recollect Father Grouwel: *Historia critica S. Indulgentiæ B. Mariæ Angelorum vulgo de Portiuncula... contra Libellos aliquos anonymo ac famosos nuper editos*, Antwerp, 1726, 1 vol., 8vo. pp. 510. The Bollandist Suysken also makes a long study of it (A. SS., pp. 879-910), as also the Recollect Father Candide Chalippe, *Vie de saint François d'Assise*, 3 vols., 8vo, Paris, 1874 (the first edition is of 1720), vol. iii., pp. 190-327.

In each of these works we find what has been said in all the others. The numerous writings against the Indulgence are either a collection of vulgarities or dogmatic treatises; I refrain from burdening these pages with them. The principal ones are indicated by Grouwel and Chalippe.

Among contemporaries Father Barnabas of Alsace: *Portiuncula oder Geschichte Unserer lieben Frau von den Engeln* (Rixheim, 1 vol., 8vo. 1884), represents the tradition of the Order, and the Abbé Le Monnier (*Histoire de Saint François*, 2 vols., 8vo, Paris, 1889), moderate Catholic opinion in non-Franciscan circles.

The best summary is that of Father Panfilo da Magliano in his *Storia compendiosa*. It has been completed and amended in the German translation: *Geschichte des h. Franciscus und der Franziskaner übersetzt und* bearbeitet von Fr. Quintianus Müller, vol. i., Munich, 1883, pp. 233-259.

[10]   2 Cel., 1, 13; 3 Soc., 56; Bon., 24.

[11]   *Conform.* , 239b, 2.

[12]   See in particular *Archiv.* , ii., p. 259, and the bull of February 7, 1246. Potthast, 12007; Glassberger, *ann. 1244* (*An. fr.* t. ii., p. 69).

[13]   *Is qui ecclesiam*, March. 6, 1245, Potthast, 11576.

[14] 2 Cel., 1, 12 (cf. *Conform.* , 218a, 1); 3 Soc., 56; *Spec.* , 32b ff. ; 49b ff. ; *Conform.* , 144a, 2.

[15] *Conform.* , 169a; 2, 217b. 1 ff. Cf. *Fior.* , Amoni's ed. (Appendix to the Codex of the Bib. Angelica), p. 378.

Lightning Source UK Ltd.
Milton Keynes UK
UKHW010812311220
376198UK00001B/20